Foreign Direct Investment in China

This book provides an insightful exploration of whether foreign direct investment (FDI) can promote the productivity of domestic enterprises. The book is based on a series of dedicated research conducted in the context of the Chinese economy, which has been the largest FDI host among the developing economies since 1993.

The main themes of this book: (a) are based on the latest literature and first-hand research, outlining possible mechanisms through which foreign direct investment could promote the productivity of domestic enterprises; (b) develop a comprehensive research framework to quantify the spillover effects with cutting-edge methodology; (c) construct a decision support system for evaluating FDI policy reforms with advanced computer simulation techniques; and (d) evaluate the broader impact of FDI spillovers on banking system and trade pattern.

The book examines topical economic issues in the contemporary world economy from innovative perspectives, namely, how the presence of multinational enterprises has been one of the most important microeconomic drivers for the Chinese economy; how foreign banks have helped to enable the Chinese banking system survive the global financial crisis; and how the domestic enterprises have learned to export from multinational affiliates and have changed the landscape of US-Asian trade. The book incorporates the latest development of economic theory as well as a computational economics model.

Ziliang Deng is Assistant Professor at the School of Business, Renmin University of China. He possesses BA and MA degrees from Renmin University of China, a Postgraduate Research Certificate from Nanyang Technological University (Singapore), and a PhD degree from the University of Nottingham (UK). Dr Deng has taken various consultancy activities for the Ministry of Commerce (China), and has teaching experiences at Nanyang Technological University, the University of Nottingham, the University of Manchester (UK), and Keele University (UK). This research conducted for this monograph is sponsored by UK–China Scholarships for Excellence, jointly funded by the Ministry of Education (China) and the Department for Business, Innovation and Skills (UK).

Routledge studies in the modern world economy

1 **Interest Rates and Budget Deficits**
A study of the advanced economies
Kanhaya L. Gupta and Bakhtiar Moazzami

2 **World Trade after the Uruguay Round**
Prospects and policy options for the twenty-first century
Edited by Harald Sander and András Inotai

3 **The Flow Analysis of Labour Markets**
Edited by Ronald Schettkat

4 **Inflation and Unemployment**
Contributions to a new macroeconomic approach
Edited by Alvaro Cencini and Mauro Baranzini

5 **Macroeconomic Dimensions of Public Finance**
Essays in honour of Vito Tanzi
Edited by Mario I. Blejer and Teresa M. Ter-Minassian

6 **Fiscal Policy and Economic Reforms**
Essays in honour of Vito Tanzi
Edited by Mario I. Blejer and Teresa M. Ter-Minassian

7 **Competition Policy in the Global Economy**
Modalities for co-operation
Edited by Leonard Waverman, William S. Comanor and Akira Goto

8 **Working in the Macro Economy**
A study of the US labor market
Martin F. J. Prachowny

9 **How Does Privatization Work?**
Edited by Anthony Bennett

10 **The Economics and Politics of International Trade**
Freedom and trade: volume II
Edited by Gary Cook

11 **The Legal and Moral Aspects of International Trade**
Freedom and trade: volume III
Edited by Asif Qureshi, Hillel Steiner and Geraint Parry

12 **Capital Markets and Corporate Governance in Japan, Germany and the United States**
Organizational response to market inefficiencies
Helmut M. Dietl

13 **Competition and Trade Policies**
Coherence or conflict
Edited by Einar Hope

14 **Rice**
The primary commodity
A. J. H. Latham

15 **Trade, Theory and Econometrics**
Essays in honour of John S. Chipman
Edited by James C. Moore, Raymond Riezman and James R. Melvin

16 **Who benefits from Privatisation?**
Edited by Moazzem Hossain and Justin Malbon

17 **Towards a Fair Global Labour Market**
Avoiding the new slave trade
Ozay Mehmet, Errol Mendes and Robert Sinding

18 **Models of Futures Markets**
Edited by Barry Goss

19 **Venture Capital Investment**
An agency analysis of UK practice
Gavin C. Reid

20 **Macroeconomic Forecasting**
A sociological appraisal
Robert Evans

21 **Multimedia and Regional Economic Restructuring**
Edited by Hans-Joachim Braczyk, Gerhard Fuchs and Hans-Georg Wolf

22 **The New Industrial Geography**
Regions, regulation and institutions
Edited by Trevor J. Barnes and Meric S. Gertler

23 **The Employment Impact of Innovation**
Evidence and policy
Edited by Marco Vivarelli and Mario Pianta

24 **International Health Care Reform**
A legal, economic and political analysis
Colleen Flood

25 **Competition Policy Analysis**
Edited by Einar Hope

26 **Culture and Enterprise**
The development, representation and morality of business
Don Lavoie and Emily Chamlee-Wright

27 **Global Financial Crises and Reforms**
Cases and caveats
B. N. Ghosh

28 **Geography of Production and Economic Integration**
Miroslav N. Jovanović

29 **Technology, Trade and Growth in OECD Countries**
Does specialisation matter?
Valentina Meliciani

30 **Post-Industrial Labour Markets**
Profiles of North America and Scandinavia
Edited by Thomas P. Boje and Bengt Furaker

31 **Capital Flows without Crisis**
Reconciling capital mobility and economic stability
Edited by Dipak Dasgupta, Marc Uzan and Dominic Wilson

32 **International Trade and National Welfare**
Murray C. Kemp

33 **Global Trading Systems at Crossroads**
A post-seattle perspective
Dilip K. Das

34 **The Economics and Management of Technological Diversification**
Edited by John Cantwell, Alfonso Gambardella and Ove Granstrand

35 **Before and Beyond EMU**
Historical lessons and future prospects
Edited by Patrick Crowley

36 **Fiscal Decentralization**
Ehtisham Ahmad and Vito Tanzi

37 **Regionalisation of Globalised Innovation**
Locations for advanced industrial development and disparities in participation
Edited by Ulrich Hilpert

38 **Gold and the Modern World Economy**
Edited by MoonJoong Tcha

39 **Global Economic Institutions**
Willem Molle

40 **Global Governance and Financial Crises**
Edited by Meghnad Desai and Yahia Said

41 **Linking Local and Global Economies**
The ties that bind
Edited by Carlo Pietrobelli and Arni Sverrisson

42 **Tax Systems and Tax Reforms in Europe**
Edited by Luigi Bernardi and Paola Profeta

43 **Trade Liberalization and APEC**
Edited by Jiro Okamoto

44 **Fiscal Deficits in the Pacific Region**
Edited by Akira Kohsaka

45 **Financial Globalization and the Emerging Market Economies**
Dilip K. Das

46 **International Labor Mobility**
Unemployment and increasing returns to scale
Bharati Basu

47 **Good Governance in the Era of Global Neoliberalism**
Conflict and depolitization in Latin America, Eastern Europe, Asia and Africa
Edited by Jolle Demmers, Alex E. Fernández Jilberto and Barbara Hogenboom

48 **The International Trade System**
Alice Landau

49 **International Perspectives on Temporary Work and Workers**
Edited by John Burgess and Julia Connell

50 **Working Time and Workers' Preferences in Industrialized Countries**
Finding the balance
Edited by Jon C. Messenger

51 **Tax Systems and Tax Reforms in New EU Members**
Edited by Luigi Bernardi, Mark Chandler and Luca Gandullia

52 Globalization and the Nation State
The impact of the IMF and the World Bank
Edited by Gustav Ranis, James Vreeland and Stephen Kosak

53 Macroeconomic Policies and Poverty Reduction
Edited by Ashoka Mody and Catherine Pattillo

54 Regional Monetary Policy
Carlos J. Rodríguez-Fuentez

55 Trade and Migration in the Modern World
Carl Mosk

56 Globalisation and the Labour Market
Trade, technology and less-skilled workers in Europe and the United States
Edited by Robert Anderton, Paul Brenton and John Whalley

57 Financial Crises
Socio-economic causes and institutional context
Brenda Spotton Visano

58 Globalization and Self Determination
Is the nation-state under siege?
Edited by David R. Cameron, Gustav Ranis and Annalisa Zinn

59 Developing Countries and the Doha Development Round of the WTO
Edited by Pitou van Dijck and Gerrit Faber

60 Immigrant Enterprise in Europe and the USA
Prodromos Panayiotopoulos

61 Solving the Riddle of Globalization and Development
Edited by Manuel Agosín, David Bloom, George Chapelier and Jagdish Saigal

62 Foreign Direct Investment and the World Economy
Ashoka Mody

63 The World Economy
A global analysis
Horst Siebert

64 Production Organizations in Japanese Economic Development
Edited by Tetsuji Okazaki

65 The Economics of Language
International analyses
Edited by Barry R. Chiswick and Paul W. Miller

66 Street Entrepreneurs
People, place and politics in local and global perspective
Edited by John Cross and Alfonso Morales

67 Global Challenges and Local Responses
The east Asian experience
Edited by Jang-Sup Shin

68 Globalization and Regional Integration
The origins, development and impact of the single European aviation market
Alan Dobson

69 Russia Moves into the Global Economy
Breaking out
John M. Letiche

70 **The European Economy in an American Mirror**
Barry Eichengreen, Michael Landesmann and Dieter Stiefel

71 **Working Time Around the World**
Trends in working hours, laws, and policies in a global comparative perspective
Jon C. Messenger, Sangheon Lee and Deidre McCann

72 **International Water Treaties**
Negotiation and cooperation along transboundary rivers
Shlomi Dinar

73 **Economic Integration in the Americas**
Edited by Joseph A. McKinney and H. Stephen Gardner

74 **Expanding Frontiers of Global Trade Rules**
The political economy dynamics of the international trading system
Nitya Nanda

75 **The Macroeconomics of Global Imbalances**
European and Asian perspectives
Edited by Marc Uzan

76 **China and Asia**
Economic and financial interactions
Edited by Yin-Wong Cheung and Kar-Yiu Wong

77 **Regional Inequality in China**
Trends, explanations and policy responses
Edited by Shenggen Fan, Ravi Kanbur and Xiaobo Zhang

78 **Governing Rapid Growth in China**
Equity and institutions
Edited by Ravi Kanbur and Xiaobo Zhang

79 **The Indonesian Labour Market**
Shafiq Dhanani, Iyanatul Islam and Anis Chowdhury

80 **Cost-Benefit Analysis in Multi-level Government in Europe and the USA**
The case of EU cohesion policy and of US federal investment policies
Alessandro Ferrara

81 **The Economic Geography of Air Transportation**
Space, time, and the freedom of the sky
John Bowen

82 **Cartelization, Antitrust and Globalization in the US and Europe**
Mark LeClair

83 **The Political Economy of Integration**
Jeffrey Cason

84 **Critical Issues in Air Transport Economics and Business**
Rosario Macario and Eddy Van de Voorde

85 **Financial Liberalisation and Economic Performance**
Luiz Fernando de Paula

86 **A General Theory of Institutional Change**
Shiping Tang

87 **The Dynamics of Asian Financial Integration**
Edited by Michael Devereux, Philip Lane, Park Cyn-Young and Wei Shang-Jin

88 **Innovative Fiscal Policy and Economic Development in Transition Economies**
Aleksandr Gevorkyan

89 **Foreign Direct Investments in Asia**
Edited by Chalongphob Sussangkarn, Yung Chul Park and Sung Jin Kang

90 **Time Zones, Communications Networks, and International Trade**
Toru Kikuchi

91 **Miraculous Growth and Stagnation in Post-War Japan**
Edited by Koichi Hamada, Keijiro Otsuka, Gustav Ranis, and Ken Togo

92 **Multilateralism and Regionalism in Global Economic Governance**
Trade, investment and finance
Edited by Junji Nakagawa

93 **Economic Growth and Income Inequality in China, India and Singapore**
Trends and policy implications
Pundarik Mukhopadhaya, G. Shantakumar and Bhanoji Rao

94 **Foreign Direct Investment in China**
Spillover effects on domestic enterprises
Ziliang Deng

Foreign Direct Investment in China

Spillover effects on domestic enterprises

Ziliang Deng

Routledge
Taylor & Francis Group
LONDON AND NEW YORK

First published 2011
by Routledge
2 Park Square, Milton Park, Abingdon, Oxon, OX14 4RN

Simultaneously published in the USA and Canada
by Routledge
711 Third Avenue, New York, NY 10017

Routledge is an imprint of the Taylor & Francis Group, an informa business

British Library Cataloguing in Publication Data
A catalogue record for this book is available from the British Library

Library of Congress Cataloging-in-Publication Data
Deng, Ziliang.
Foreign direct investment in China: spillover effects on domestic enterprises/Ziliang Deng.
p. cm. – (Routledge studies in the modern world economy; 94)
Includes bibliographical references and index.
1. Investments, Foreign–China. 2. Industrial productivity–China.
3. China–Economic conditions.
I. Title.
HG5782.D47 2011
332.67'30951–dc22 2011001990

ISBN: 978-0-415-59142-3 (hbk)
ISBN: 978-0-203-80902-0 (ebk)

Typeset in Times New Roman by Sunrise Setting Ltd, Torquay, UK

MIX
Paper from responsible sources
FSC
www.fsc.org
FSC® C004839

Printed and bound in Great Britain by the MPG Books Group

The wisdom of "productivity spillovers"

"When I walk along with two others, they may serve me as my teachers. I will select their good qualities and follow them, their bad qualities and avoid them."

The Analects, Confucius (551–479 BC)

Contents

List of figures

List of tables

List of abbreviations

BL	backward linkages
CES	constant elasticity of substitution
CET	constant elasticity of transformation
CGE	computable general equilibrium
CIESY	China Industrial Economy Statistical Yearbook
CSY	China Statistical Yearbook
EXCO	export concentration of foreign-invested enterprises
FDI	foreign direct investment
FIEs	foreign-invested enterprises
FL	forward linkages
GAMS	General Algebraic Modeling System
GE	general equilibrium
HMT	Hong Kong, Macau and Taiwan
HZDS	horizontal demonstration by foreign-invested enterprises
I/O	Input–output Table of China
MMU	mining, manufacturing and utilities sectors
MNEs	multinational enterprises
MOFCOM	Ministry of Commerce of China
MPSGE	Mathematical Programming System for General Equilibrium Analysis
NBS	National Bureau of Statistics of China
PE	partial equilibrium
Private	all domestic enterprises except SOEs
RMB	Renminbi, the currency of the People's Republic of China
SAM	social accounting matrix
SHEs	state-holding enterprises
SOEs	state-owned enterprises
TFP	total factor productivity
TNCs	trans-national corporations
UNCTAD	United Nations Conference on Trade and Development

Foreword

The topic of this volume lies at the conjunction of two of the major developments in the international economy over the last two decades – the integration of China into the world economy and the growth of foreign direct investment. The author's objective is to assess the economic impact of productivity-enhancing spillovers generated by foreign direct investment in China.

Productivity improvements are now recognised as the primary source of long-run growth in income per capita, and innovation, broadly defined to include both organisational and technological advances, as the source of productivity growth. But these advances largely originate in enterprises located in a few developed countries, and their transfer to enterprises in other countries relies on a variety of formal and informal channels. The formal channels, such as foreign direct investment, technology licensing and the use of imported equipment embodying advanced technologies, are relatively well understood. But the informal channels, typically referred to as 'technology spillovers', are less well understood. Domestic enterprises can acquire productivity improvements through upstream and downstream linkages with foreign enterprises in both domestic and export markets, competing with foreign enterprises in the domestic market and through hiring skilled workers and managers previously employed by foreign enterprises.

The fact that spillovers are intrinsically very difficult to quantify and their effects are correspondingly difficult to measure makes this an ambitious project. But its importance is highlighted by the widespread belief that spillovers are facilitated by the presence of high-tech enterprises in the domestic market; a belief that has provided a rationale for policies encouraging foreign direct investment. How foreign investors view these spillovers is likely to depend on their relationship to the beneficiaries. While they may benefit from spillovers that make their suppliers and buyers more efficient, spillovers that make their domestic competitors more efficient will be less attractive to them. The task of the policy-maker is to design inward foreign investment incentives that encourage both investment and spillovers. Success in this task relies on knowledge of the relative importance of the spillover channels and their effects, and this work is an important step in providing that information.

Prior analyses of productivity spillovers have tended to focus on establishing their presence in a few of the possible channels. This work is much more ambitious, first checking their existence and then going on to analyse their effects on firms, industries and the aggregate economy. Given the range of channels through which spillovers may occur, an understanding of their full effects requires a general equilibrium framework, and the author employs a computable general equilibrium model. Importantly, this model is sufficiently flexible to allow for consideration of different market structures including recent developments involving heterogeneous firms.

China is a natural case for a study of foreign productivity spillovers. Technology transfer is essential for China's development and productivity spillovers can be an important part of that process. China is an important foreign direct investment host, reflecting its economic size, rapid growth and significance in the global economy, as well as its strategy of 'trading market access for productivity spillovers'. Further, the effects of spillovers depend on local conditions and here China's mix of state-owned and privately-owned enterprises provides an interesting study of the importance of ownership type in determining an enterprise's ability to take advantage of productivity spillovers. The role of productivity spillovers in the Chinese economy is examined in a range of contexts, including tax reform, the global financial crisis and US–China trade disputes. In this research monograph the study of productivity spillovers is taken to a new level, making it important reading for academics, practitioners and policy-makers involved in the study of foreign direct investment, both in China and elsewhere.

Professor Rodney Falvey

Rodney Falvey is Professor of Economics at Bond University, Australia. He was Leverhulme Professor of International Economics at the University of Nottingham, UK, Reader of Economics and Head of Department at National University of Australia. He has published papers extensively in top economics journals including *American Economic Review*, *Quarterly Journal of Economics*, *Journal of Political Economy*, *Economic Journal*, *International Economic Review*, *Journal of International Economics* and *Journal of Development Economics*. He was an Associate Editor of the *Review of International Economics* and *Economic Bulletin*, and is a member of the Advisory Board of *The World Economy*.

21 February 2011

Acknowledgements

This book was developed from my PhD thesis, which I wrote at the University of Nottingham from 2005 to 2009. First of all, I would like to express my deep gratitude to my PhD supervisors, Professor Rod Falvey (now at Bond University) and Professor Adam Blake (now at Bournemouth University). Without their invaluable guidance and encouragement, I would not have been able to complete this work. I would also like to thank them for allowing me to publish some of our joint research output in this book.

My PhD research was generously supported by the UK–China Scholarships for Excellence (2005–2009) co-sponsored by the Department for Business, Innovation and Skills (UK) and the Ministry of Education (China). The research was also supported by postgraduate research conference funding from Nottingham School of Economics, University of Nottingham.

Earlier versions of the model and related research findings were presented at the nineteenth Chinese Economics Association Annual Conference (Cambridge) and the seventh GEP Postgraduate Conference (Nottingham) in April 2008, the eleventh Annual Global Economic Conference (Helsinki) in June 2008, the University of Oxford China Centre for Economic Research Conference (Oxford) in September 2008, the Inaugural Conference of the International Forum for Contemporary Chinese Studies (Nottingham) in November 2008, and two internal seminars at Keele University (Keele) in December 2008 and March 2009. I sincerely thank the participants of the above events.

This research has particularly benefited from the comments and suggestions of Professor Sourafel Girma, Dr Richard Kneller, Dr Chengqi Wang, Professor Shujie Yao, and Dr Zhihong Yu at the University of Nottingham; Dr Edward Balistreri at Colorado School of Mines; Dr Yundan Gong at Aston University; Professor Aoife Hanley at Christian Albrechts University of Kiel; Dr Beata Javorcik at the University of Oxford; Professor Shantong Li at Development Research Centre of State Council (China); Professor Thomas Rutherford at Swiss Federal Institute of Technology Zurich (ETH); Dr David Tarr at the World Bank; Dr Fan Zhai at China Investment Corporation; and Dr Xiaobo Zhang at the International Food Policy Research Institute.

I am very grateful to Professor Chris Milner at the University of Nottingham and Dr Jeffery Round at the University of Warwick, who were the internal and external examiners of my PhD viva voce examination respectively, for their constructive comments and suggestions for refining the thesis.

I am deeply indebted to my parents, my brother and sister-in-law for allowing me to be fully committed to this research, especially in the end of July 2008 when my father was critically ill. I owe them so much. My wife Guilan, herself doing PhD research at the University of Manchester, sacrificed much time and energy and took care of our daughter, Langqing.

Special thanks go to Dr Honglin Guo at Renmin University of China, and Professor Yongnian Zheng who is now at the National University of Singapore and was at the University of Nottingham at the same time as I was pursuing my PhD studies in Nottingham.

Finally, I sincerely thank Mr Robert Langham, the Routledge Senior Editor for Economics and Finance, who warmly invited and encouraged me to kick-start the proposal of this book in the end of 2008. Excellent and timely editorial services have been provided by Miss Lam Yongling (Associate Editor), Ms Lisa Salonen (Production Editor) and their colleagues.

Part I
Stylised facts and literature review

1 Stylised facts on foreign direct investment inflow to China and its spillovers

Stylised facts on FDI in China

Foreign direct investment (FDI) is the movement of capital across borders in a manner that grants the investors control over the acquired assets. FDI is different from portfolio investment in that the latter does not offer such control. There are two forms of FDI – greenfield investment which initiates direct investment in new assets; and mergers and acquisitions in which a foreign firm acquires part (or all) of the assets of an existing host firm. Firms that conduct FDI activities are called multinationals enterprises (MNEs) or transnational corporations (TNCs). FDI plays an increasingly significant role in the global economy.

In the late 1970s China ended its isolation from the outside world and began to implement a "reform and opening-up" strategy. With its enormous labour supply and low labour cost (Ceglowski and Golub 2007), stable political and economic environment, and pro-FDI policies, China has become an attractive FDI destination. As a result, FDI inflows[1] to China increased dramatically from US$0.9 billion in 1983 to $90.0 billion in 2009, as shown in Figure 1.1.

Since 1993, China has been the largest FDI recipient among the developing countries, and in 2003 it was the largest FDI recipient in the world. In 2009, China was still the world's second largest destination for FDI, the United States being the largest. Since the majority of FDI flows into developed countries (see Figure 1.2), it is amazing that China, as a relatively backward country, holds such a strong attraction for foreign capital.

More than 95 per cent of the FDI in China falls into one of the following three entry modes (see Table 1.1):

(1) Solely foreign-owned enterprises that are exclusively invested in and owned by foreign companies, enterprises, and other economic organizations or individuals;
(2) Joint ventures that are joint investments by foreign companies, enterprises, and other economic organizations or individuals and Chinese companies, enterprises, and other economic organizations. The latest Law on Chinese-Foreign Joint Ventures (2001) states in Article 4 that "the proportion of the investment contributed by the foreign partner(s) should not be less than 25 per cent of the registered capital of a joint venture";

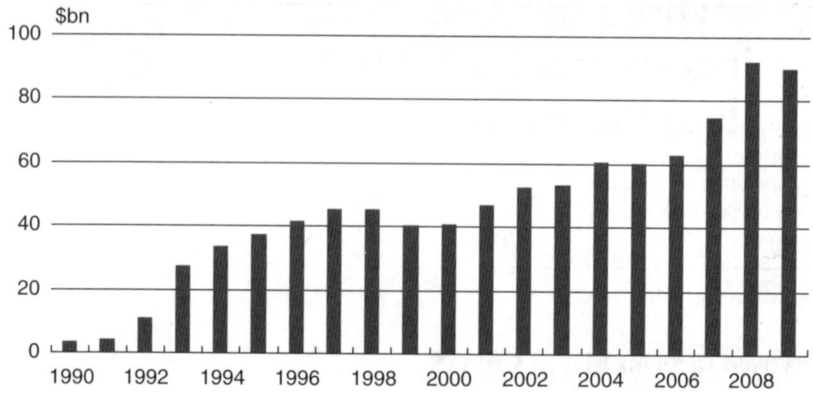

Figure 1.1 FDI inflow to China, 1990–2009 (US$ billion).

Note: Here and throughout this book, current prices are quoted unless otherwise stated.

Source: China Economic Information Network (http://www.cei.gov.cn/).

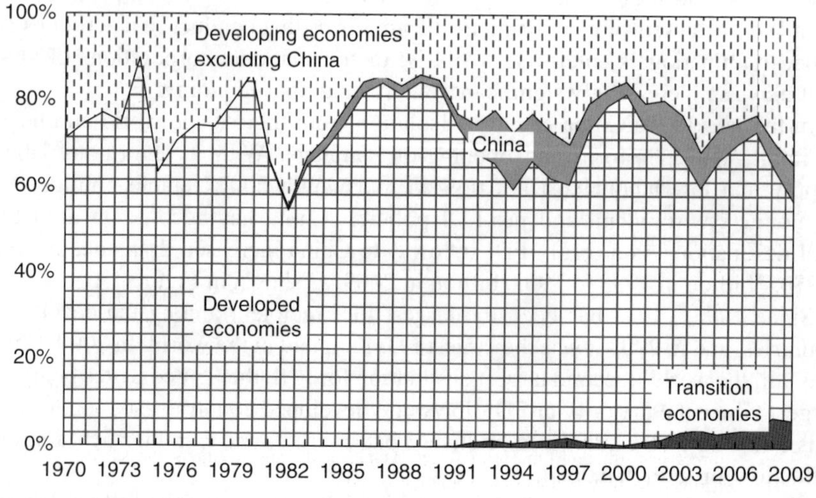

Figure 1.2 FDI inflows, global and by group of economies, 1970–2009.

Source: UNCTAD Database (http://unctadstat.unctad.org/).

(3) Cooperative enterprises that are established based on cooperative terms and conditions agreed upon by foreign companies, enterprises, and other economic organizations or individuals and their Chinese counterparts.

As for the sources of FDI, East Asia and Southeast Asia have contributed more than 60 per cent as of 2009, as shown in Table 1.2. However, the FDI stock from East Asia and Southeast Asia only accounted for 12 per cent of world total outward FDI stock as at the end of 2009, while the outward FDI from Europe and

Table 1.1 FDI entry modes, 1978–2009

	Signed contracts		*Actual FDI*	
	Number	*Per cent*	*Amount ($bn)*	*Per cent*
Solely foreign-owned	335,908	49.2	526.8	54.8
Joint ventures	287,184	42.0	301.6	31.4
Cooperative enterprises	59,556	8.7	98.9	10.3
Other types	557	0.1	34.0	3.5
Total	683,265	100.0	961.2	100.0

Source: as Figure 1.1.

Table 1.2 Top 10 sources of FDI in China, 1978–2009

	Actual FDI	
	Amount ($bn)	*Per cent*
Hong Kong	394.6	41.1
Virgin Islands	101.0	10.5
Japan	69.3	7.2
United States	62.1	6.5
Taiwan	49.5	5.1
South Korea	44.5	4.6
Singapore	41.2	4.3
Cayman Islands	19.1	2.0
United Kingdom	16.3	1.7
Germany	16.3	1.7
Others	147.6	15.4
Total	961.2	100.0

Source: Investment in China, Ministry of Commerce of China (http://www.fdi.gov.cn/); China Economic Information (http://www.cei.gov.cn/).

Note: Throughout this book, "China" refers to the People's Republic of China, i.e. mainland China, unless stated otherwise. In mainland China, direct investment from Hong Kong, Macau and Taiwan enjoys the same favourable treatment as FDI from other sources.

North America accounted for 80 per cent of world total outward FDI stock (see Figure 1.2).

There are many factors leading to the unusually large-scale Asian FDI in China. "Chinese connections" constitute the first factor, including ethnic Chinese networks, similar languages and culture, and geographic proximity (Zhang 2005). Second is the perfect match between the relocations of export-oriented manufacturing sectors from Asia's newly industrial economies (due to their rising labour cost) and China's national strategy of export orientation. By transferring manufacturing centres to China, the resource-seeking FDI helps multinationals maintain their cost advantage in the international market (Deng *et al.* 2007).

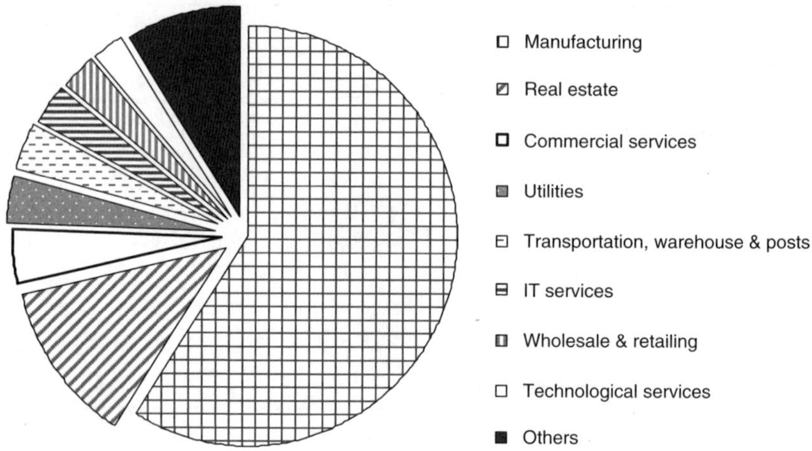

Figure 1.3 Industry distribution of contract FDI inflow in China, 2004–2009.
Source: as Figure 1.1.

In terms of industry distribution, 58 per cent of accumulated FDI flows to the manufacturing sectors in China (see Figure 1.3). This ratio is much higher than the proportion of manufacturing in China's total gross domestic product (GDP), which has remained within a relatively narrow band between 37 per cent and 44 per cent since 1978. By transferring manufacturing and assembly centres to China, FDI is viewed to have brought significant technology spillover to these sectors (Buckley *et al.* 2002, 2004, 2007a; Girma and Gong 2008a; Liu 2008).

Productivity spillover of FDI

One of the most important aspects of FDI is that it embodies advanced technologies and business practices which can be transferred to the host economies. Domestic firms can improve their productivity through their connections with MNEs. This externality is referred to as FDI "productivity spillover" or "technology diffusion" in the recent economic literature (Blomström and Kokko 1998; Görg and Strobl 2001; Görg and Greenaway 2004; Keller 2004). Productivity spillovers do not include contract-based transfer or illegal acquisition of intellectual property rights, know-how, or any kind of technology. Productivity spillovers are a relatively intangible and intractable phonomenon and can take place through four channels, namely, labour mobility, vertical linkages, export of MNE affiliates, and horizontal effects.

(1) Labour mobility. Employees trained by MNE affiliates will benefit from the production knowledge and management expertise they have acquired after they return to domestic firms or establish their own enterprises (Fosfuri *et al.* 2001; Görg and Strobl 2005; Markusen and Trofimenko 2009).

(2) Vertical linkages. MNE affiliates help upstream and downstream domestic firms to set up production facilities, providing them with technical assistance and management and organization training. Besides, the presence of MNEs may also trigger competition among upstream and downstream firms (Markusen and Venables 1999; Javorcik 2004; Girma and Gong 2008a; Girma *et al.* 2008).
(3) Exports of MNE affiliates. MNEs transfer and relocate their manufacturing centres to export-oriented economies which are relatively labour-abundant, e.g. China and Vietnam, and export assembled product to third markets. This can help domestic firms gain access to international markets and promote their productivity (Aitken *et al.* 1997; Clerides *et al.* 1998; Greenaway *et al.* 2004; Greenaway and Kneller 2008).
(4) Demonstration and competition. MNEs usually possess an advantage in technology (Dunning 1977, 1981; Markusen 2002b) and exert a strong demonstration effect on the domestic firms in host countries. In observing the market activities of MNE affiliates and competing with MNE affiliates, local firms can imitate MNE technology and make corresponding innovations (Koizumi and Kopecky 1977; Findlay 1978; Wang and Blomström 1992).

Productivity spillovers are not only beneficial to domestic firms in the host countries, but may also benefit the multinational affiliates by fostering a more productive economic environment in the host market.

Factors governing productivity spillovers of FDI in China

The potential for the foreign capital inflow attracted by preferential FDI policies, low labour cost, and improved infrastructure to bring positive productivity spillovers to Chinese indigenous enterprises has been strengthened by the following factors:

(1) Freer labour market. During the process of marketisation, the Chinese government abandoned the life-long employment system, lowered the barriers between rural and urban areas, and gradually constructed a freer labour market (Knight and Yueh 2004). A variety of "new" ownerships emerged, such as foreign-invested enterprises (FIEs) and private firms, which ended the dominance of state-owned enterprises. Employees are free to leave FIEs and set up their own private firms using the management techniques they have acquired during their work experience.
(2) Stronger linkages with FIEs. Upstream domestic enterprises have developed quickly in the past three decades and their product quality has improved. So FIEs in China are more willing to source locally from those qualified domestic firms, creating the opportunity for productivity spillovers via input–output linkages (Farrell *et al.* 2004; Long 2005).
(3) Learning to export by observation. The striking export performance of FIEs has provided examples for domestic firms to learn to enter overseas markets.

They have also familiarised the world with Chinese exports. Both can effectively lower the entry cost of domestic firms' exportation (Kneller and Pisu 2007).

(4) Increased but moderate competition. The competition caused by the increased foreign presence has stimulated domestic firms to improve their productivity and performance. At the same time, the competition in most industries is not so fierce as to force a mass exit of domestic firms. The Chinese domestic market is growing sufficently fast that domestic firms have the opportunity to find their own niche (Long 2005).

However, FDI productivity spillovers are neither free nor automatic. In fact, there have been debates over whether spillovers really occur, and if so, their magnitude. The following factors influence the size of spillovers:

(1) Low absorptive capacity. For domestic enterprises with low absorptive capacity due to a lack of research and development (R&D) activity or the absence of employee skills, the foreign presence could lead to no spillovers at all (Buckley *et al.* 2002; Girma and Gong 2008a, b). Many less qualified domestic firms are forced to exit before even starting to absorb spillover benefits.
(2) Limited scope of spillovers. Evidence shows that firms in Chinese cities take advantage of FDI spillovers not only from local FDI inflows, but also from FDI inflows to adjacent cities (Madariaga and Poncet 2007). However, due to the inter-regional trade barriers imposed by local governments, the inter-regional linkages are restricted (Young 2000). Given that, by the end of 2006, 85 per cent of the accumulated FDI flowed to 11 eastern and costal provinces, little inter-regional spillover from FDI will be received by the other 20 technologically backward inland provinces which are home to 61 per cent of China's population and contribute 40 per cent of total GDP (Girma and Gong 2008b).
(3) Different FIE technology intensity. FDI in China can be largely differentiated by technology intensity, with less technology-intensive FDI from Hong Kong, Macau and Taiwan (HMT), and more technology-intensive FDI from the rest of world, especially from Europe and North America (Buckley *et al.* 2007a). These two types of FDI generate different productivity spillover effects. The enterprises invested by FDI from HMT tend to engage in labour-intensive manufacturing with standardised rather than state-of-the-art technologies. Empirical studies show that the spillover of HMT FDI falls beyond a certain critical point of foreign presence due to the competition with domestic enterprises for limited resources (Buckley *et al.* 2007a).
(4) Short-term learning costs. Facilitating spillovers is not free for numerous reasons. First, domestic firms need to pay a higher salary to attract employees with experience in FIEs. Second, domestic enterprises need to make additional investments to improve their product standards in order to become qualified candidate suppliers of FIEs (Wang and Blomström 1992). Third, after observing the success of FIE exports, domestic firms also need to undertake costly overseas market investigation in preparing for exportation. Given these costs,

the perceived effect of spillovers over a short time span is often negative, although we observe a positive effect on long-term productivity growth (Liu 2008).

(5) Labour turnover and "reverse spillover". To survive in an emerging market like China, FIEs have to recruit local employees who are familiar with the cultural and political environment, and the idiosyncratic business practices in China. With a competitive salary package and attractive work environment, FIEs can easily "cherry-pick" experienced managers and salesmen from state-owned enterprises (SOEs) and other domestic firms. Evidence shows that SOEs with little care for the human capital development of their employees (i.e. no labour training expenditure) face a high possibility of losing talent and incurring negative spillovers (Girma and Gong 2008a).

(6) Suppressed indigenous technological capability. Technological transfer through FDI may substitute for domestic technologies in production (Fan and Hu 2007) and thus discourage indigenous R&D activities (Long 2005). For example, when Volkswagen established a joint venture with Shanghai Automobile in 1985, it introduced an outdated model Santana into the Chinese automobile market, and this model continued to be produced with little improvement for 20 years. At the same time the cars produced based on indigenous intellectual property struggled for a small market share (22 per cent in 2007).

In brief, the roles of spillover channels are heavily dependent on a range of factors, and when investigating how FDI productivity spillovers occur, it is important to take these factors into consideration where possible.

Research questions

Although the productivity spillovers of FDI are appreciated in the literature and favourable FDI policies have been common policy practice worldwide (United Nations Conference on Trade and Development 2006, pp. 23–24), there is still debate on how to quantitatively measure productivity spillover and whether favourable FDI policies are necessary for host countries to pursue this benefit.

This book aims to answer the following research questions which concern the nature of FDI productivity spillover, the theory and methodology to address FDI productivity spillover, the costs and benefits of preferential FDI policies, and broader impacts of FDI spillovers:

(a) Can we examine the effects of FDI productivity spillovers in China at the macro as well as micro level by using sector and national variables, e.g. sector output, value added and GDP?

(b) In the economics literature, there have been alternative market structure assumptions, e.g. perfect competition, monopolistic competition with homogeneous firms, and monopolistic competition with heterogeneous firms. These assumptions form distinct market environments in which FDI productivity spillovers may take place. How do different market structure assumptions affect the ways in which FDI productivity spills over to domestic enterprises and the magnitude of such spillovers?

(c) In 2008, the Chinese government abolished its preferential corporate tax treatments for FIEs in China. How has this tax harmonisation impacted on the FDI productivity spillover effects?
(d) Have FDI spillovers improved the performance of Chinese domestic banks?
(e) Have FDI spillovers contributed to the phenomenal US–China trade imbalance?

This study constructs a static computable general equilibrium (CGE) model to quantify the productivity spillover from FDI. This research is conducted in the context of the Chinese economy in that China has been the largest FDI host country as a developing economy since 1993, and FDI productivity spillovers in China as a technologically backward country are potentially important.

This book makes five contributions to the literature. First, the productivity improvement in manufacturing sectors caused by productivity spillover is captured as an endogenous phenomenon by linking the spillover effects to spillover channels in a CGE model. Second, it compares the FDI productivity spillover effects in three different market structures, namely perfect competition, monopolistic competition with homogeneous firms (Dixit and Stiglitz 1977) and monopolistic competition with firm heterogeneity (Melitz 2003). Third, it assesses how China's 2008 corporate income tax reform has affected the FDI productivity spillover effects. Fourth, it is the first work to explore the FDI productivity spillover in the banking sector. Finally, the broader impact of FDI spillover effects is examined in terms of its role in the US–China trade imbalance.

Book structure

This chapter has discussed the stylised facts on FDI inflow to China. FDI in China has been increasing dramatically, which has potentially important productivity spillover effects on domestic enterprises via labour market mobility, industrial linkages, export of FIEs, demonstration and competition. However, there also exist various factors which constrain FDI productivity spillovers, such as absorptive capacity, geographic scope of spillovers, technology intensity of FIEs, short-term learning cost, cherry-picking effects in the labour market, and potentially oppressed indigenous technology advancement ability. These factors influence the sign of the overall spillover effects.

Chapter 2 reviews the literature on the origin and channels of FDI productivity spillover, factors governing FDI productivity spillover effects, and empirical methodologies to address FDI productivity spillovers.

The theories constructed in the "ownership, location, internalisation" paradigm assume that firms engaging in FDI activities are homogeneous and more productive than their domestic rivals in a host economy so that they can overcome the cost disadvantages of overseas business operations. The latest theories built on the assumption of "firms with heterogeneous productivity" find that firms engaging in FDI are more productive than firms which only export, while the latter are more productive than firms which serve the domestic market only. The above two generations of FDI theories both imply that multinational enterprises are the most productive in a host economy, implying the possibility of FDI productivity spillovers.

The review also shows that possible channels of FDI productivity spillovers include labour mobility and vertical input–output linkages between multinational affiliates and domestic enterprises, export of MNEs, demonstration, increased competition, and resource reallocation.

Various factors determine the effects of FDI productivity spillovers. These include FDI intensity, technology intensity, geographic proximity to multinational affiliates, absorptive capacity of domestic enterprises, legal environment with respect to intellectual property rights in host countries, and learning cost.

Available empirical methodologies include econometric and CGE models. The former are more widely adopted for firm-level and industry-level analysis, while the latter are more suitable for economy-wide analysis.

Chapter 3 uses a firm-level dataset for Chinese manufacturing, to estimate productivity spillovers from FDI to local firms. There have been some firm-level studies on FDI productivity spillovers in the Chinese economy. However, none of these studies has integrated all four spillover channels into a single empirical model. Given the extraordinarily high export propensity of FIEs in China, their exports are potentially an important source of spillovers, yet this channel has generally been underestimated in the literature. Similarly, a lack of data availability means inter-ownership labour turnover has not been investigated.

We will use a dataset derived from a sample of 998 Chinese firms in five manufacturing industries. This dataset has the advantage of including information on whether workers had previously been employed in foreign-owned firms, which allows us to investigate all four spillover channels in a single regression equation. It is particularly interesting to examine how labour transfer between FIEs and local firms affects the productivity of local firms which employ foreign-trained workers.

The results indicate that the absorptive capacity of local firms is important in determining the extent to which spillovers are effective in raising their productivity. Exports by MNE affiliates have positive spillovers for all local firms that export. Labour transfers and foreign firm presence in an industry (horizontal effects) also generate spillovers, but only to SOEs. Backward and forward linkages do not appear to generate spillovers.

Chapter 4 analyses the productivity spillovers from an industrial perspective. It is found that there exists a significant relationship between the productivity of domestic enterprises and the presence of FDI. Both SOEs and private domestic firms benefit from FIEs in upstream and horizontal sectors, and the coefficients for private enterprises are larger and more statistically significant. But neither SOEs nor private enterprises benefit from the contacts with the FIEs in downstream sectors. The exports of MNE affiliates has no effect on improving the productivity of SOEs. Private enterprises are even negatively affected by the MNE exports.

Chapter 5 introduces the theoretical foundation and construction of a typical CGE model. CGE modelling involves designing a large-scale general equilibrium model across all the industries and implementing computer-based simulations of counterfactual scenarios.

CGE models are a class of models that explore the overall economic impact of policy, technology or other external "shocks". The microeconomic foundation for CGE models is Walrasian general equilibrium theory. A CGE model consists of (1) a series of equations of production, consumption, utility and so on, which cover the whole economy, including the activities of all industries, governments, and households; and (2) a detailed database consistent with the model equations.

As a general equilibrium model, a CGE model is inappropriate for the analysis of small-scale, sector-specific changes, but is well tailored to the investigation of broadly based policy innovations where inter-region and inter-industry feedbacks and interdependences are important. Most of the applications of CGE fall into the categories of tax and trade policy research and, more recently, resource and environment research.

The simulation work in a CGE model is based on a social accounting matrix (SAM) or input–output table in a base year. A SAM expands a cross-industry input–output table by incorporating non-production sectors (e.g. households and government) in a more comprehensive way. A SAM or input–output table statistically represents flows of all economic transactions that take place within an economy.

The GAMS (General Algebraic Modeling System) software provides a tailored and powerful higher-level coding platform for CGE modellers. MPSGE (Mathematical Programming System for General Equilibrium Analysis), as a subsystem of GAMS, is specially designed for a mix of complementarity problems that are most frequently met in general equilibrium models. CGE modelling provides a convincing structural research framework for FDI productivity spillovers and the associated FDI policy assessment. A CGE model can decompose FDI spillovers effects into benefit obtained through different channels, namely vertical linkages, export of MNEs and horizontal demonstration. However, due to the data constraint and the only option of a single year as the benchmark year, the reliability of CGE modelling is subject to sensitivity tests.

Chapter 6 provides the data sources used in this research and discusses the data compilations. Data employed are mainly from the China Statistical Yearbook 2003, the China Industry Economy Statistical Yearbook 2003 and the China Input–Output Table 2002. The transformation of the original input–output table involves a complex data manipulation process, which mainly involves three types of work: (1) aggregating the original 122 × 122 input–output table into a 39 × 39 one; (2) disaggregating the 39 × 39 table into a 101 × 101 one with information on different ownerships, which enables the CGE model constructed on this input–output table to address issues regarding ownership (i.e. spillovers from FIEs to domestic enterprises); (3) data balancing and consistency check.

Chapter 7 constructs a CGE model tailored for this research on FDI productivity spillover in China. Theoretical models for three market structures are also discussed, namely perfect competition, monopolistic competition and firm heterogeneity.

A benchmark CGE model for the Chinese economy will be presented with the original forms and "calibrated duality forms" of constant elasticity of substitution (CES) functions. The model contains blocks of value-added production, output production, constant elasticity of transformation (CET) into export and domestic consumption, labour and capital disaggregation, Armington aggregation, export and import, representative domestic agent, representative agent for multinational enterprises, and government. Equations for equilibria of factor marks, Armington markets, aggregate export and import will also be presented.

This model will then be extended to incorporate FDI productivity spillovers under perfect competition. The coefficients of four spillover channels estimated in Chapter 4 will be carried forward into the CGE modelling.

FDI productivity spillovers will be modelled in an alternative market structure, namely monopolistic competition with homogeneous firms. In this scenario, the mark-up rate of a representative firm of each sector is derived, which is essential to extending a CGE model to incorporate monopolistic competition. A CGE model to study FDI spillovers under monopolistic competition can also reflect the changes of product varieties and quantities caused by the spillovers.

Finally, FDI productivity spillovers will be modelled in another alternative market structure – monopolistic competition with heterogeneous firms. This market structure has only recently been explored in the literature, and is potentially important in explaining the productivity change of domestic firms. A CGE model under firm heterogeneity is composed of a general equilibrium module and a partial equilibrium module. The former is a model with FDI spillovers under perfect competition. The latter deals with firm heterogeneity, assuming a virtual "quasi-representative" firm and "summarising" the distribution of firm productivity in each sector. The CGE model in this scenario can provide an alternative perspective on the effects of spillovers by examining productivity improvement under FDI productivity spillovers in a more direct way.

Chapter 8 discusses how an FDI shock to the benchmark economy, together with productivity spillovers, affects economic performance. Simulations are conducted under three different market structures, namely, perfect competition, monopolistic competition and firm heterogeneity.

Results show that (1) in terms of national aggregate indicators, an FDI shock is beneficial to the economy, and FDI productivity spillovers are followed by positive spillover premiums under the three market structures; (2) for domestic enterprises (including SOEs and private enterprises), FDI productivity spillovers promote their performance and always outweigh the negative impact of an FDI shock; (3) for FIEs, FDI productivity spillovers cause resources to be attracted away by their rivals that are more productive thanks to the FDI spillovers, thus making the increase in FIEs' total output lower than otherwise (this finding also applies to all the three market structures); (4) product variety and production scale per variety can both be improved by an FDI shock, and FDI productivity spillovers can exert positive "spillover premiums" under certain conditions; and (5) the experiments under monopolistic competition assumption show that FDI productivity spillovers are more prominent in an industry with a lower initial degree of competition.

Chapter 9 simulates the impact of corporate income tax reform in 2008 on the FDI productivity spillover effect in China. It introduces the major tax incentives to attract FDI in China, and discusses the cost and benefit of such preferential FDI treatment. The results of the tax reform simulations show that the original dual corporate income tax system was indeed good for FDI productivity spillovers in that it helped strengthen the foreign presence which is vital for FDI productivity spillovers.

A higher corporate income tax levied on FIEs alone distorts the economy's structure and lowers total output, welfare and GDP. However, an integrated tax reform formula can do a better job by increasing the output level of domestic enterprises and by promoting national welfare. Under firm heterogeneity, the spillover benefit of integrated reform is even more prominent, because the reform can increase the average productivity of all existing enterprises, and raise the possibility of productivity spillovers and the absorptive capacity of domestic enterprises. This is more beneficial to the productivity spillovers from FIEs to domestic enterprises.

Neither single-sided reform nor integrated reform can increase the proportion of productivity spilt over from foreign firms to domestic firms in the total productivity of domestic enterprises. Taking into consideration the changing pattern of productivity under firm heterogeneity, the tax reform will only temporarily lower the FDI productivity spillover effects. However, it may promote the speed and magnitude of spillovers later.

Chapter 10 employs stochastic frontier analysis to analyse the efficiency of the Chinese banking sector in 2001–2007 using data from 126 banks. First, it outlines five micro channels via which FDI efficiency spillovers took place in the banking system in China: (a) an increased degree of competition in the banking system stimulated the domestic banks to expedite their reforms; (b) foreign banks exerted a very strong demonstration effect in high-end businesses (e.g. personal banking, credit card and financial product innovation); (c) expert turnovers from foreign banks to domestic banks helped domestic banks to improve their efficiency; (d) collaborations with strategic investors have improved the corporate governance of domestic banks; (e) foreign banking shareholders applied their financial innovation techniques to Chinese banks.

Second, stochastic frontier analysis is employed to analyse the efficiency of the Chinese banking sector during 2001 and 2007. The logarithm of profit before tax and the logarithm of bank loans are employed as dependent variables. Foreign presence is measured in three alternative ways: (a) the market share of total assets and liabilities of foreign banks in non-financial institutions and households; (b) the share of total assets of foreign banks in the whole Chinese banking system; (c) the share of number of foreign banks with legal person status in the whole banking system.

The results of the empirical study suggest that the presence of foreign banks has indeed exerted prominent efficiency spillover – it has helped improve the overall profitability of the Chinese banking sector, and has also effectively constrained the scale of loans. The state shares of domestic banks do not significantly contribute to their efficiency improvement. More importantly, the results of this chapter highlight the importance of efficiency spillovers which can be introduced by cautious financial liberalization to a transition economy.

Chapter 11 tries to identify the causal link between FDI productivity spillovers and the dramtically high US–China trade imbalance. Over the last three decades, industry transfer from East Asia has, via FDI, transformed China from an autarchy into an integral player in the East Asian production chain. As a last-stage assembler in this value-added chain, China is maintaining an increasingly high trade surplus with the United States. The worsening US–China trade disputes are addressed in such a politicised way that "fair" trade has become the central issue of bilateral trade consultation. However, due to its enormous labour force and impressive macroeconomic prospects, China will continue to play its current role as a world assembly centre. An 11-economy, 25-year panel dataset is developed and analysed, and the results indicate that the productivity spillover through exports of multinational affiliates in China has indeed helped to increase Chinese firms' productivity and export capability. This phenomenon, together with the massive East Asian industry transfer, has a strong export transfer effect, and directly contributes to the expanding US–China trade imbalance and long-lasting trade disputes. Therefore, it is unlikely that the US–China trade imbalance will be greatly alleviated in the next five to ten years. Trade disputes between Beijing and Washington will continue to be a big headache and both sides need to tackle the problem through more dialogue and negotiation.

Chapter 12 summarises the methodologies, contributions and main findings of the book and discusses possible directions for future research.

2 A review of foreign direct investment and productivity spillovers

Theories of FDI

Theories of MNEs in Dunning's paradigm

Multinational affiliates can compete with local firms in host countries due to their advantage in productivity. Without productivity advantage, multinational affiliates can never survive in competition with local firms as the former face extra cost in doing business in overseas markets, including communication cost, higher pay for stationing employees overseas, and barriers of language and culture (Hymer 1976).

Dunning (1977; 1981) conceptualises this productivity advantage and attributes it to three factors of a multinational firm which outweigh the cost disadvantages of producing in a host country:

(1) ownership advantages, in the form of both tangible (e.g. special equipment) and intangible assets (e.g. know-how, patents, trade marks), neither of which is easily replicable to host firms;
(2) location advantages, which include the benefitd which a multinational can get by circumventing tariffs and transportation costs incurred in trade, and by getting closer access to consumers in local markets;
(3) internalisation advantages, meaning that profitable production processes can be fully exploited by multinationals in setting up overseas subsidiaries rather than licensing them out.

Markusen (2002b) proposes the concept of "knowledge capital" which refers to the firm-level R&D activities shared by headquarters and subsidiaries. Markusen argues that knowledge capital offers foundations for Dunning's (1977; 1981) ownership, location and internationalization advantages of multinational enterprises. He constructed a "knowledge capital model", which attributes the origin of vertical and horizontal FDI to the knowledge capital of multinationals. The theoretical hypotheses drawn from this model fit well with the results of econometric studies.

Theories of MNEs with heterogeneous productivity

The implicit assumption of the above theories is that all firms in a country have identical productivities and every firm is productive enough to go abroad and engage in more costly and risky overseas production. However, this assumption contradicts the prevailing evidence that multinationals are typically more productive than those national firms that only engage in domestic business (e.g. Girma *et al.* 2005; Tomiura 2007; Yasar and Paul 2007). This contradiction has largely been solved by the latest developments in FDI theories, namely the theory of firm heterogeneity (Helpman *et al.* 2004) and the theory of incomplete contracts (Antràs and Helpman 2004). Both theories have predicted that only the most productive firms can engage in FDI, implying the possibility of FDI productivity spillover in host countries.

Firm heterogeneity model

Helpman *et al.* (2004) emphasise the role of productivity differences across firms in determining the sales of MNEs relative to the exports of national enterprises. They find that only the most productive firms can afford the high fixed costs of setting up foreign subsidiaries, whereas less productive firms remain as national enterprises and may serve foreign markets by exporting. The least productive firms can only serve the domestic market.

The model of Helpman *et al.* (2004) is supported by many empirical studies. Using firm-level data from UK manufacturing sectors, Girma *et al.* (2005) find that the cumulative productivity distribution of British MNEs lies to the right of that of non-MNEs – that is, the productivity of MNEs is generally higher than non-MNEs. Similarly, the productivity distribution of exporters lies to the right of that of non-exporters.

With firm-level panel data from Japanese industries, Kimura and Kiyota (2006) also find evidence supporting the prediction of Helpman *et al.* (2004) – productivity is indeed an important factor explaining the decision to engage in FDI as well as export. They also find that the highest-productivity firms export as well as engage in FDI. This does not contradict Helpman *et al.* (2004), as for a multi-product firm operating in a several countries different in size and wages, it is possible that the firm will adopt both exports and FDI as complementary rather than substitute strategies, as discussed by Girma *et al.* (2005).

In their model with heterogeneous multinational firms, Falvey *et al.* (2007b) assume that the unit cost of a multinational subsidiary is jointly determined by the parent firm's cost in its home country and a random cost drawn from a distribution that is common to all indigenous entrants in the host country. They find that a subsidiary is less likely to shut down when its parent firm's productivity is higher and the counterpart domestic firm's productivity is relatively lower.

Nocke and Yeaple (2007) further differentiate FDI activities into cross-border mergers and acquisitions (M&A) and greenfield FDI, and find that for R&D-intensive industries where the heterogeneous productivity at firm level mainly originates from firms' technological know-how, firms engaging in either M&A or greenfield FDI are more productive than firms engaging in exporting only.

The technological superiority of greenfield FDI is supported by an empirical study of US multinational firms (Nocke and Yeaple 2008). It is found that US parent firms that choose greenfield FDI are systematically more productive than those firms that choose M&A. This stylised fact has been generalised as a theoretical proposition in a general equilibrium model of the world economy (Nocke and Yeaple 2008).

Incomplete contract model

Antràs and Helpman (2004) model how a firm sources abroad either through foreign outsourcing or FDI with the notion of the "incomplete contract". An incomplete contract denotes a contract of an intermediate product between its supplier and user, which, however, cannot specify the legal consequences of every possible state of the intermediate product the supplier sells to the user. In their model, the high-productivity firms source overseas by engaging in FDI; the low-productivity firms acquire intermediates only within the home country; and the firms with medium productivity choose foreign sourcing.

Tomiura (2007) finds evidence supporting the theoretical propositions of Antràs and Helpman (2004) and Helpman *et al.* (2004). With a firm-level dataset of 118,300 Japanese firms, Tomiura documents how productivity varies as firms engage in different internationalisation modes. Foreign outsourcers and exporters tend to be more productive than domestic firms, but less productive than firms active in FDI or in multiple globalization modes. This productivity hierarchy is robust to the inclusion of control variables such as firm size and factor intensity.

In brief, the section above has reviewed the theories of FDI. The theories constructed in Dunning's "ownership, location, internalisation" paradigm assume that firms engaging in FDI activities are homogeneous and more productive than their domestic rivals so that they can overcome the cost disadvantages of overseas business operations. The latest theories built on the assumption of "firms with heterogeneous productivity" find that firms engaging in FDI are more productive than firms which only export, while the latter are more productive than firms which serve the domestic market only. The above two generations of FDI theories both imply that multinational enterprises are the most productive, giving rise to the possibility of FDI productivity spillovers.

Channels of FDI productivity spillovers

Labour mobility

Productivity spillovers may take place when workers or managers in foreign-invested firms move to domestic firms or set up their own enterprises. In this process, the workers or managers will apply their knowledge, legally acquired while working for multinationals, in their new domestic firm and exert a positive impact on its productivity. Fosfuri *et al.* (2001) construct a two-period model where a multinational trains a local worker to run its subsidiary in the first period, then in the second period the multinational and a local firm compete to employ the trained worker. Only if the MNE pays a higher wage can it stop the worker from moving to the local firm. Regardless of whether the worker moves to the local firm, the domestic economy can always benefit from the FDI presence. When the informed worker is hired by the local firm, a technological spillover takes place, while if the informed worker is retained by the multinational subsidiary at a higher wage, then a pecuniary benefit arises. These technological spillover and pecuniary benefits are echoed by Glass and Saggi (2002) who construct a model with multiple host and source firms.

Markusen and Trofimenko (2009) situate the issue of FDI productivity spillover via labour mobility in a general equilibrium (rather than partial equilibrium) framework. When the analysis is applied to Colombian firm-level data, the authors confirm that the inter-ownership mobility of workers with skills acquired from contacts with foreign experts has substantial and persistent positive effects (though not always immediate) on the value added per worker of domestic firms.

Görg and Strobl (2005) investigate FDI spillovers through the channel of labour mobility using detailed firm-level data for a sample of manufacturing firms in Ghana. Specifically, the authors have data on whether the entrepreneurs of the domestic firms in the sample have worked for a foreign multinational or have taken professional training in an MNE before they joined or established their current companies. They control for the underlying ability of entrepreneurs, using years of schooling and previous experience in the same industry. This avoids a potential ambiguity in the causality between the productivity of the firms and the labour mobility: firstly, foreign firms might hire or provide training to more skilled workers as they already demonstrate stronger ability, possibly through higher education; secondly, better domestic firms may attract better workers and managers. The econometric analysis shows that the FDI spillovers via labour mobility are significant and industry-specific.

Vertical input–output linkages

MNE affiliates may help upstream and downstream domestic firms to set up production facilities, and provide them with technical assistance and training in management and organization. (Markusen and Venables 1999; Javorcik 2004; Girma and Gong 2008a; Girma *et al.* 2008.) Vertical input–output linkages include backward and forward linkages, as illustrated in Figure 2.1.

Backward linkages result in backward feedback from multinational affiliates in downstream sectors to upstream indigenous firms. Sourcing locally can effectively reduce the production cost of multinational affiliates and thus is a natural choice for them. This can trigger competition among upstream domestic firms. Moreover, multinationals usually set high technical standards for their intermediate inputs, and it is likely that downstream foreign firms need to transfer necessary techniques to the upstream domestic firms (Javorcik 2004), improving technological capacity of the latter in the process. Thus the competition effect and high standards, together with the knowledge transfer, all as a result of backward linkages, act as a channel of FDI productivity spillover.

Forward linkages promote the forward transfer of knowledge from multinational affiliates in upstream sectors to downstream indigenous firms. Domestic

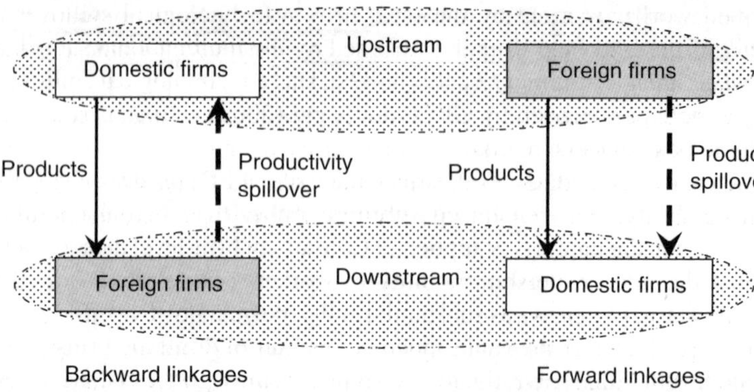

Figure 2.1 Backward and forward linkages as spillover channels.

firms can improve their productivity via forward linkages in two ways. The first is by purchasing high-quality intermediate products from multinational firms. Similar spillover effects via forward linkages in international trade have been widely acknowledged in the literature (Falvey *et al.* 2004; Keller 2004). Secondly, in becoming a product distributor of a multinational firm, a domestic company often has to make a series of improvements, such as employee training, to meet the standards to be a retailer for the multinational.

Markusen and Venables (1999) develop a model with two imperfectly competitive industries which are linked by an input–output relationship. It is assumed that foreign investment takes place in the final goods sector, thus creating backward linkages to intermediate goods suppliers in the upstream sector. Multinational firms can help domestic firms in upstream sectors improve productivity via backward linkages. Domestic firms in downstream sectors can then also benefit from the improved intermediate products supplied by domestic suppliers. This benefit can outweigh the competition effect which multinational firms impose on domestic firms in downstream sectors, thus leading to the development of local industry.

Exports of MNE affiliates

To export involves sunk costs incurred for market research, advertising, distribution networks, etc., which might deter entry. Trade models with heterogeneous firms predict, and evidence from firm-level datasets confirm, that entry into exporting is a self-selection process in which more productive firms become exporters while less productive firms serve domestic markets only (Clerides *et al.* 1998; Melitz 2003). But even when some domestic firms are productive enough to enter export markets, they may lack information on overseas markets and foreign consumers may be unfamiliar with Chinese products. As large multinationals have well-established international trade networks and have extensive knowledge of international markets, their presence can help lower information barriers facing domestic firms and help acquaint foreign consumers with Chinese products (Aitken *et al.* 1997; Greenaway and Kneller 2008).

For domestic export candidates not currently productive enough to find exporting profitable, the success of multinational firms in international markets can stimulate domestic candidates to emulate them (Alvarez and López 2005). To achieve this goal, they have to improve their productivity and product quality to meet international standards.

There is little evidence of exporting itself improving firm productivity in developed countries (e.g. Greenaway and Kneller 2004, 2007). However, this does not necessarily imply that such productivity improvements may not occur in emerging markets, such as China. East Asian economies have transferred their labour-intensive, export-oriented assembly centres via FDI to the coastal provinces in China (Deng *et al.* 2007), and the export of FIEs accounts for more than 50 per cent of national total export volume in the last ten years. During 1980–2006, the commodity export volume of China has increased dramatically (by a factor of 53.5), while in the same period, the commodity export volumes of the UK and US have only increased by factors of 3.9 and 4.7, respectively.[1]

Horizontal effects: Demonstration, competition and resource reallocation

Demonstration is probably the "most evident" spillover channel (Crespo and Fontoura 2007, p. 411), especially in transition economies such as China which are transforming from a centrally planned economy, dominated by SOEs, into a market economy with a variety of ownerships in a short time span. Foreign-invested firms with technological and managerial advantages open a fresh "window" of high productivity, and showcase their superior practices in production, management and services to their indigenous counterparts. Domestic firms can thus imitate the production of foreign firms through "reverse engineering" (Das 1987).

Increased competition in a host economy created by the entry of MNEs constrains the market power of monopolistic domestic firms, forcing them to make more efficient use of existing resources.

Resource reallocation is a channel via which the presence of FDI can help the host economy relocate resources towards the most productive firms and increase industry-level and national productivity. The entry of foreign firms can intensify the competition for labour resources in host countries. Even for large transition economies with a huge hidden surplus labour supply like China (Fu and Balasubramanyam 2005), the price of non-skilled labour in export-intensive sectors will inevitably rise (Ceglowski and Golub 2007) due to the factor price convergence effect of international trade (Falvey and Kreickemeier 2005). The rising labour cost will make the least productive domestic firms unprofitable and drive them out of the market. Then resources will be relocated to more productive firms, allowing them to increase in production scale. Therefore the industry-level and aggregate-level productivity can be raised. This resource reallocation effect driven by FDI is consistent with that effect driven by trade which is modelled by Melitz (2003). This spillover via resource reallocation does not necessarily improve the productivity of any individual firm. But it helps explain why industry-level econometric analyses of FDI productivity spillovers tend to generate significantly positive results.

Determinant factors of FDI productivity spillovers

FDI intensity and technology intensity

It is found that there exists a threshold effect in FDI productivity spillovers – if the FDI volume is too low, the productivity spillover will be limited (Aitken and Harrison 1999). It is also generally acknowledged that the more FDI in an industry, the higher will be the possibility of productivity spillovers. However, the spillover effect also depends on the technology intensity of FDI. For foreign firms with mature and standardised rather than state-of-the-art technologies, their productivity spillover effect exhibits an inverted U curve trajectory as their presence becomes higher.

Koizumi and Kopecky (1977) were the first to explicitly specify the spillover effect of foreign capital. In their model, the total capital stock K in a host country is divided into K_F and K_N (i.e. $K = K_F + K_N$), which represent the portion owned by foreigners and domestic nationals, respectively. K_F and K_N are heterogeneous in that the former can trigger technology spillover.

The production function of the only domestic commodity X is

$$X = \psi(K_F/L)G[(K_F + K_N), L]$$

where $\psi(K_F/L)$ is the technology transfer function and K_F/L denotes foreign capital per capita. It is assumed that a host country always experiences technological improvement from contact with foreigners, so that $\psi(K_F/L) > 1$ for any $K_F/L > 0$.

Then technology spillover is denoted by the partial differentiations

$$\frac{\partial X}{\partial K_N} = \psi G_K, \quad \frac{\partial X}{\partial K_F} = \psi G_K + \left(\frac{\partial \psi}{\partial K_F}\right) G$$

Therefore the marginal product of foreign capital is greater than that of domestic capital by $(\partial\psi/\partial K_F)G$, which represents the productivity spillover embodied in foreign capital. When $\partial^2\psi/\partial K_F^2 > 0$, $(\partial\psi/\partial K_F)G$ is an increasing function of K_F. By linking domestic production to foreign capital intensity, the model indicates the importance of foreign capital in influencing the path of economic development.

In a dynamic model, Findlay (1978) hypothesises that the rate of technical efficiency change in the backward countries is an increasing function of the technology gap between advanced and backward regions.

The ratio of foreign capital stock $K_f(t)$ to domestic capital stock $K_d(t)$ is used to measure the foreign presence at time t. $A(t)$ and $B(t)$ represent the levels of technical efficiency in the advanced and backward regions at period t, respectively. We have

$$x \equiv \frac{B(t)}{A(t)}, \quad y \equiv \frac{K_f(t)}{K_d(t)}$$

$\partial \dot{x}/\partial y$ is assumed to be positive, i.e. the technological gap between the relatively backward and advanced countries will decrease as foreign capital intensity in the relatively backward country increases. The model shows that, under this assumption, (x, y) can cnoverge to a long-term steady state (x^*, y^*).

Das (1987) examines the optimal behaviour of a multinational firm's subsidiary in a host country when technology spillover takes place between it and its local rivals. Let parameter A denote the productivity of local firms. Then the advancement of A in any period is positively and linearly correlated with Q_m, the amount of output of the MNE's subsidiary during that period:

$$\dot{A} = \alpha Q_m, \quad \alpha > 0$$

This will intensify the competition and lower the price of the MNE's products. Assuming MNEs need to maximise their discounted profit, the model also finds that the best response of MNEs is to lower the rate of increase of domestic enterprises ($\dot{A}$) by lowering their own production scale (Q_m).

Buckley *et al.* (2002, 2007a) emphasise how the technology intensity of foreign investment affects the productivity spillover effect. In mainland China, the enterprises invested in by FDI from overseas Chinese in Hong Kong, Macau, and Taiwan tend to engage in labour-intensive manufacturing with standardised rather than state-of-the-art technologies. Their studies show that the spillover from HMT FDI falls beyond a certain critical point of foreign presence as the productivity spillover is mitigated by the competition with domestic enterprises for limited resources. The findings of Buckley *et al.* (2002, 2007a) are echoed by Wei and Liu (2006), who find that OECD-invested firms play a much greater role in inter-industry spillovers than overseas Chinese firms from HMT.

Proximity and participation

Geographic proximity matters in FDI productivity spillovers due to the limited spatial scope of labour mobility and the importance of face-to-face communication (Halpern and Murakozy 2007). Similarly, the entry modes of FDI (i.e. M&A or greenfield) also matter. Joint ventures involve a higher degree of local participation and a higher possibility of linkages with local firms, which could generate more productivity spillover.

Using data from Hungarian manufacturing firms, Halpern and Murakozy (2007) examine the role of geographic distance between where foreign-invested firms are located and domestic firms in productivity spillovers. They weight the spillover variables with functions of distance of foreign firms to domestic firms so that the spillover variables will be larger when the distance is smaller. For example, one of the weighting functions they employ is $f(d_{i,m}) = 1/(1 + d_{i,m}/100)$, where $d_{i,m}$ denotes the distance from the ith indigenous firm to the mth multinational affiliate. Their econometric analysis results show a significantly negative relationship between the foreign–domestic firm distance and spillover.

Their conclusion is consistent with those of Greenaway and Kneller (2008). As industrial or locational agglomeration might offer opportunities for lowering sunk costs, industrial or locational proximity to export-oriented multinational firms can help non-exporters become exporters. Using firm-level data from UK manufacturing sectors, they find that exporters have a strong positive and significant impact on the export decision of potential exporters in the same industry, and similarly from the same region. No significant impact is found on entry from exporting firms located in other regions or industries.

Using Romanian firm-level data, Javorcik and Spatareanu (2008) find M&A FDI has a greater productivity spillover effect on domestic firms than greenfield FDI does. First, affiliates in the form of joint ventures are likely to face lower costs of finding local suppliers of intermediates. Thus they should be more likely to source inputs locally, which in turn leads to more vertical productivity spillover to firms in upstream sectors, i.e. backward spillover (Javorcik 2004). Second, multinational headquarters tend to transfer medium advanced technologies to their partially owned affiliates and transfer state-of-the-art technologies to wholly owned subsidiaries. The medium advanced technologies could be easier to absorb after they spill over to domestic firms.

Absorptive capacity

Absorptive capacity includes both macro-level characteristics such as infrastructure, economic development and human capital, and micro-level indicators such as R&D expenditure, education of employees, employee training and flexibility of labour turnover. Theoretical models have shown that a firm with a stronger absorptive capacity can reap more benefit from FDI productivity spillover (Keller 1996; Lai *et al.* 2006).

Aitken and Harrison (1999) find that the economy of Venezuela is not sufficiently developed to accommodate the positive externalities of FDI. Their appreciation of macro-level absorptive capacity is echoed by research on the productivity spillover of international trade (e.g. Falvey *et al.* 2007a).

Studies of China also justify absorptive capacity as a necessary condition of FDI productivity spillover. With industrial survey data of 1995, Buckley *et al.* (2002) find that SOEs could reap no spillover from the presence of foreign firms while non-SOEs could get positive benefits from FDI spillover. This is not unusual as Chinese SOEs were tightly controlled by the government and operated "bureaucratically mandated plans" in the 1990s (Buckley *et al.*, p. 641).

Girma and Gong (2008a) examine the adjustment of Chinese SOEs' total factor productivity (TFP) to the presence of multinational firms using the following empirical model:

$$TFP_{it} = \alpha_i + \boldsymbol{\beta}'\mathbf{X}_{it} + \boldsymbol{\gamma}_1'\mathbf{RFDI}_{it} + \boldsymbol{\gamma}_2'\mathbf{OUTFDI}_{it} + \boldsymbol{\delta}'\mathbf{D}_{it} + \varepsilon_{it}$$

where i and t index SOEs and time respectively, ε represents a random error term and **X** is a vector of variables measuring absorptive capacity (employee training, market share, intangible assets, and exporting activity) hypothesised to impact on SOEs' TFP. **RFDI** and **OUTFDI** are two vectors consisting of variables capturing foreign presence in the firm's region and outside the region, respectively. The vector **D** consists of the full set of time, sectoral and regional dummy variables which control for economy-wide productivity shocks and the fact that FDI flow is endogenous in the sense of being partly determined by sectoral and regional productivity levels. They find that foreign presence is generally negatively associated with TFP level of SOEs. However, there is a positive effect of FDI on SOEs that export, invest in human capital or R&D, or have prior innovation experience. These findings confirm that absorptive capacity is indeed a necessary condition of FDI spillover.

Protection of intellectual property rights

How the protection of intellectual property rights (IPR) affects FDI productivity spillover is largely dependent on the channels via which the spillover takes place.

On the one hand, knowledge of multinational affiliates spills over, via labour mobility and demonstration, to domestic enterprises more quickly in a host country where the IPR protection system is not well established. Suppose that know-how is protected by patent in the UK, but that it is very time-consuming to apply for a patent for this know-how in a host country. Then, as the employees in the host country come to know the details of the patent, there exist risks that these employees will join local companies, taking with them this sensitive technology. This technology spillover is not illegal as the know-how has not been protected in the host country.

However, a poor IPR protection environment usually discourages FDI, especially in the form of joint ventures (Saggi 2002; Falvey *et al.* 2006; Gattai and Molteni 2007). This will decrease the magnitude of productivity spillover.

On the other hand, better protection of IPR can promote transfer of technology from multinational headquarters to overseas affiliates and also increase the local R&D expenditures of multinational affiliates (Branstetter *et al.* 2006). This may help FDI productivity spillover take place at a higher magnitude via vertical input–output linkages, although the chances of spillover via labour mobility or demonstration are greatly restricted. Furthermore, legal reform of IPR in the host country will also stimulate indigenous R&D activities, which can enhance domestic firms' capacity to absorb FDI productivity spillover.

Learning cost

There are numerous reasons why spillover is neither free nor automatic. First, domestic firms need to pay higher salaries to attract employees with work experience in MNE affiliates. Second, domestic enterprises need to make extra investments to improve their product standard to become qualified supplier candidates of MNE affiliates (Wang and Blomström 1992). Third, after observing the export success of MNE affiliates, domestic firms also need to do costly overseas market investigations in preparation for their own exports. Thus it is often found that the perceived effect of spillovers over a short time span is often negative, although the long-term productivity growth induced by FDI spillover is positive (Liu 2008).

Wang and Blomström (1992) acknowledge the cost of transferring technology within an MNE and the cost that native firms incur in learning from MNE affiliates. The technology capability of MNE, A_f, is augmented by resources (I_f) devoted to transferring technology: $\dot{A}_f = I_f A_f$.

The technology level of a domestic firm is an increasing function of its learning investment (I_d) and the investment exhibits a diminishing return as it increases. Let υ depict the rate of costless (i.e. when $I_d = 0$) technology spillover. Thus,

$$\dot{A}_d = \varphi(I_d) A_f$$
$$\varphi' > 0, \quad \varphi'' < 0, \quad \varphi(0) = \upsilon > 0$$

Then the transfer-absorption process can be derived:

$$\frac{d}{dt}\left(\frac{A_f}{A_d}\right) = \left[I_f - \varphi(I_d)\left(\frac{A_f}{A_d}\right)\right]\left(\frac{A_f}{A_d}\right) \tag{2.2}$$

Wang and Blomström (1992, p. 149) also note the externalities among the learning efforts of domestic firms themselves: "once a domestic firm has adopted or modified foreign technologies, it is generally easier and cheaper for other firms to do the same". Therefore, another specification is constructed to capture these intra-ownership externalities among domestic firms. Suppose there are n identical domestic firms and each of them is engaged in a learning investment I_i, $i = 1, 2, \ldots, n$. Let E_i be the effective learning investment in firm i:

$$E_i = I_i + \sum_{j \neq i}^{n} \beta I_j, \quad \beta \in (0, 1)$$

where β is an intra-ownership externality coefficient. Then equation (2.2) can be transformed to capture both an inter-ownership and an intra-ownership productivity spillover:

$$\frac{d}{dt}\left(\frac{A_f}{A_i}\right) = \left[I_f - \varphi(E_i)\left(\frac{A_f}{A_i}\right)\right]\left(\frac{A_f}{A_i}\right)$$

Sembenelli and Siotis (2008) employ Spanish firm-level panel data and examine how FDI affects the mark-ups of domestic firms as a proxy of firm performance. Their research shows that FDI has a positive long-run effect on the mark-ups of domestic firms in R&D intensive sectors. However, foreign presence dampens the mark-ups of domestic firms in the short run. This contrast reflects the negative and significant effect of short-run learning cost.

Empirical methodologies

Econometric methodologies

Almost all empirical research on FDI productivity spillover is conducted with econometric models. A typical econometric model of FDI productivity spillovers regresses the productivity of individual local firms on FDI presence in the local market, and a vector of control variables (**V**):

$$TFP_{i,j,t} = \alpha_1 + \beta_1 FDI_{j,t} + \boldsymbol{\gamma}\mathbf{V}_{j,t} + \varepsilon_{i,j,t}$$

where i, j, t index firm, industry, and time, respectively. If it is assumed that the production of value added takes the form of a Cobb–Douglas function, then this regression can be applied interchangeably with another similar type of model that replaces the dependent variable with the value added ($Y_{i,j,t}$) of local firms and adds labour ($L_{i,j,t}$) and capital ($K_{i,j,t}$) inputs to the right-hand side of the above equation:

$$Y_{i,j,t} = \alpha_2 + \beta_2 K_{i,j,t} + \beta_3 L_{i,j,t} + \beta_4 FDI_{j,t} + \boldsymbol{\delta}\mathbf{V}_{j,t} + \zeta_{i,j,t}$$

The above two regressions can be run with either firm-level or industry-level data (by suppressing firm index i).

As for variable selections, foreign presence can be measured by total FDI, proportion of foreign firms' output or employment, total output or employment of foreign firms; backward and forward linkage can be measured by either equation (2.1) or sectoral FDI weighted by input–output coefficients; absorptive capacity can be measured by local firms' R&D expenditure or labour training hours; and various dummy variables are usually adopted to control for the factors related to industry, time and export status.

Capital (K) is usually measured as the value of fixed assets deflated by industry (or GDP) deflator (e.g. Javorcik and Spatareanu 2008), or by constructing a capital stock from investment data using a certain depreciation rate (e.g. Aitken and Harrison 1999). Various measures of labour input (L) have been employed in the literature, including (a) the total number of employees, which is the most straightforward and most commonly adopted measure (e.g. Girma and Gong 2008a; Girma *et al.* 2008; Javorcik and Spatareanu 2008; Liu 2008); (b) employees broken down into skilled labour and unskilled labour (e.g. Aitken and Harrison 1999); (c) employees broken down into production workers and non-production workers (e.g. López 2008); (d) efficiency units, calculated by dividing total wages by the minimum wage (e.g. Javorcik 2004); or if high-quality data are available, (e) human capital, constructed by weighting workers in different categories by their relative wages to adjust for quality (e.g. Kugler 2006).

It is found that how the FDI presence variables are defined affects the results. For example, empirical studies with either the share of employment in foreign-owned firms or the share of output produced by these firms as a proxy for the foreign presence tend to get a higher spillover effect than those with other measures (e.g. the share of foreign equity participation), *ceteris paribus* (Görg and Strobl 2001).

Panel data analyses are preferred to cross-sectional analyses when it is necessary to control for time-invariant effects and to permit investigation of the development of domestic firm's productivity over a period of time rather than at a fixed point in time.

It is found that on the basis of firm-level studies, the empirical results of FDI spillover effects are controversial, while with industry-level data, empirical studies usually support the view that the FDI spillover promotes the productivity of host countries (Saggi 2002). One reason is that sector-level analyses also include the effects of resource allocation triggered by FDI, as previously discussed.

Computable general equilibrium modelling

FDI productivity spillover is a nation-wide and cross-industry phenomenon. It can be captured by computable general equilibrium models which attach due importance to the interdependency between industries, government and household activities. Therefore, a CGE model can also be tailored to evaluate FDI policies with respect to productivity spillovers.

Currently there is little literature on CGE models for FDI spillover. Several CGE models are constructed with trade-embodied technology spillover (Van Meijl and Van Tongeren 1998; Robinson *et al.* 2002; Das 2007), but no FDI spillover is incorporated in these models.

Robinson *et al.* (2002) build a ten-region, eleven-sector global CGE model that focuses on the services sectors. Links between trade performance and total factor productivity are introduced into the model by connecting a region's TFP growth with its imports of capital and technology-intensive products and professional services, especially from advanced industrial countries:

$$ITFP_{ir} = 1 + ims_{ir} \times \frac{NX_{ir}}{NX_{ir} + VA_{ir}} \times \left(\left[\frac{\sum_{j \in IM} \sum_{s \in R} X_{jsr}}{\sum_{j \in IM} \sum_{s \in R} X_{0,jsr}} \right]^{\sigma} - 1 \right)$$

where $ITFP_{ir}$ denotes the TFP shift variable; ims_{ir} is the share of imported products and services that are embodied with advanced technology used as firms' intermediate inputs in total imports of such products and services; NX_{ir} and VA_{ir} are intermediate inputs and value added respectively; $X_{0,jsr}$ and X_{jsr} are the base year and current trade flows, respectively; IM is the subset referring to those products embodied with advanced technology; R is the subset referring to those technologically backward countries; and σ is an exogenous parameter.

They compare the effects of trade liberalisation under two assumptions on the source of advanced technology, namely imports of intermediate and durable manufactures, and imported service intermediate inputs. They found that under the former assumption, service sector liberalisation has only a limited impact on each region's TFP growth, and such growth is relatively concentrated in the intermediate and durable sectors. However, under the second assumption, the impacts are quite significant and spread to more sectors through forward linkages.

Van Meijl and Van Tongeren (1998) also employ a global CGE model to address international technology spillovers. Their spillover hypothesis is summarised as:

$$\frac{a_{jis}}{a_{jir}} = E_{jirs}^{1-\delta_{irs}}, \quad \text{where } 0 \leq \delta_{irs} \leq 1; 0 \leq E_{jirs} \leq 1; \delta_{irs} = \delta_{irs}(H_{irs}, D_{irs})$$

in which a_{jir} and a_{jis} denote input-specific productivity growth rates of input j in activity i in the regions of origin r and destination s, respectively, and δ_{irs} indicates the effectiveness of this amount of knowledge. It is a function of an absorption capacity index H_{irs}, and an index of structural similarity D_{irs}. E_{jirs} is an index of the amount of knowledge embodied in commodity j which is used in activity i:

$$E_{jirs} = \frac{X_{jirs}/Y_{is}}{Y_{jir}^{d}/Y_{ir}}$$

where X_{jirs} represents the bilateral trade flows of input j that are used in sector i and which are exported from the source country r to the destination country s, Y_{is} production of sector i in country s, and Y_{jir}^{d} domestic inputs of sector j delivered to sector i in country of origin r.

The potential benefits from trade liberalisation with the above embodied technology spillovers are analysed by taking Chinese barriers against North American imports as a case study. The results show that its negative impact on the welfare of China (measured by equivalent variation) can be more than counterbalanced by the gains from technology spillovers.

Very similar specifications are employed by Das (2007) to explore the role of absorptive capacity and socio-institutional factors for the capture of information technology and biotechnology. Das finds that regions perform better with higher human capital, better governance and superior technological expertise.

Lejour *et al.* (2008) explicitly incorporate FDI productivity spillover into a world CGE model with FDI supply and demand endogenised. Suppose we have a sectoral production function $y = Af(k^F, k^D, l)$, where A, k^F, k^D and l denote TFP, foreign capital, domestic capital and total labour, respectively. Then FDI oductivity spillovers can be modelled as an externality:

$$A_t = A_0(1+\mu^{TFP})^t \exp\left(\gamma \frac{k^F_{t-1}}{k^F_{t-1}+k^D_{t-1}}\right)$$

where μ^{TFP} is exogenous TFP growth rate and γ is a productivity spillover coefficient estimated from the literature. The results show that opening up the services market to FDI in European countries with the above productivity spillovers can lead to twice marginal GDP growth (e.g. with an extra 0.8 per cent) compared to without productivity spillovers (e.g. with an extra 0.4 per cent). Lejour *et al.* allow the magnitude of the spillover to vary with the size of FDI. However, they take the value of the key parameter γ from the literature to link the FDI presence and its influence on the economy, and γ was not particularly estimated for the European Union economies in question, but for the US economy.

Conclusions

This chapter has reviewed the literature on the origin and channels of FDI productivity spillover, factors governing FDI productivity spillover effects, and empirical methodologies to quantify FDI productivity spillovers.

The theories constructed in the "ownership, location, internalisation" paradigm assume that firms engaging in FDI activities are homogeneous and more productive than their domestic rivals so that they can overcome the cost disadvantages of overseas business operations. The latest theories built on the assumption of "firms with heterogeneous productivity" find that firms engaging in FDI are more productive than firms which only export, while the latter are more productive than firms which only serve the domestic market. The above two generations of FDI theories both imply that multinational enterprises are the most productive, implying the possibility of FDI productivity spillovers.

The review also shows that possible channels of FDI productivity spillovers include labour mobility and vertical input–output linkages between multinational affiliates and domestic enterprises, export of MNEs, demonstration, increased competition, and resource reallocation.

Various factors determine the effects of FDI productivity spillovers. They include FDI intensity and technology intensity, geographic proximity to multinational affiliates, absorptive capacity of domestic enterprises, legal environment on intellectual property rights in host countries, and learning costs.

Available empirical methodologies include econometric models and computable general equilibrium models. The former are more widely adopted for firm-level and industry-level analysis, while the latter are more suitable for economy-wide analysis.

Part II

Econometric analyses for quantification of spillover effects

3 The interplay between foreign and domestic enterprises

Firm-level analysis

Introduction

There has been a rich emerging literature, both theoretical and empirical, on FDI productivity spillover channels since the 1990s. Empirical results show that the effectiveness of the different spillover channels also depends on various properties of the potential local recipients, such as their export propensity, research and development expenditure, geographic proximity to foreign firms, and employee training. The sources of FDI are also found to have an impact on spillover effects. This literature indicates that FDI productivity spillovers are complex phenomena, whose investigation requires detailed firm-level data.

There have been several firm-level studies on FDI productivity spillovers in the Chinese economy, and these are reviewed in Chapter 2. However, none of these studies has integrated all four spillover channels into a single empirical model. Given the extraordinarily high export propensity of foreign invested enterprises in China, their exports are potentially an important source of spillovers, yet this channel has been generally underestimated in the literature. Similarly, a lack of data availability means inter-ownership labour turnover has not been investigated.

We use a dataset derived from a sample of 998 Chinese firms in five manufacturing industries. This dataset has the advantage of including information on whether workers had previously been employed in foreign-owned firms, which allows us to investigate all four spillover channels in a single regression equation. We are particularly interested in how labour transfer between FIEs and local firms affects the productivity of local firms which employ foreign-trained workers.

Our results indicate that the absorptive capacity of local firms is important in determining the extent to which spillovers are effective in raising their productivity. Exports by MNE affiliates have positive spillovers for all local firms that export. Labour transfers and foreign firm presence in an industry (horizontal effects) also generate spillovers, but only to state-owned firms. Backward and forward linkages do not appear to generate spillovers.

Methodology

The roles of different channels in FDI spillovers are compared in a single equation which regresses the total factor productivity of domestic firms against spillover channel variables, controlling for a number of other covariates. To do this, we proceed in two steps. First, we estimate firm TFP in a standard fashion by regressing firm value added (VA) on capital (K) and labour (L) inputs:

$$\ln VA_i = \alpha_0 + \alpha_1 \ln K_i + \alpha_2 \ln L_i + \varepsilon \qquad (3.1)$$

where K is the book value of fixed assets, and L is measured in three alternative ways, to allow for the human capital embodied in the workforce – total employment, employment weighted by workers' years of schooling, and employment weighted by the economy-wide average wage for each type of employment ($\sum_i employment_i \times wage_i$).

Second, the total factor productivities obtained (i.e. $\ln(TFP_i) = \alpha_0 + \varepsilon$) will be regressed against spillover channel variables and other control variables:

$$\ln TFP_i = \beta_0 + \beta_1 \mathbf{SPILL}_i + \beta_2 \mathbf{SPILL}_i \mathbf{F}_i + \beta_3 \mathbf{F}_i + \beta_4 \mathbf{D}_j + \varsigma \qquad (3.2)$$

where i and j index domestic firms and sectors, respectively. The vector $\mathbf{D}_j$ denotes industry dummy variables, vector $\mathbf{SPILL}_i$ denotes the spillover channel variables, and $\mathbf{F}_i$ is a vector of firm characteristics. Specifically the independent variables that we use are as follows:

(1) Labour turnover, LT_i, is the share of employees with FIE work experience in total firm employment.
(2) Horizontal demonstration, $HZDS_j$, is the FIE share in industry output. As the literature suggests, it is likely that this spillover effect will depend on the absorptive capacity of local firms. We therefore form its interaction with firm-level R&D expenditure, RND_i.
(3) Export concentration, $EXCO_j$, denotes the proportion of FIE exports in total industry exports. While both exporting and non-exporting local firms can benefit through spillovers from the exports of MNEs, as discussed in Chapter 2, it is expected that local exporters will benefit more. We therefore form the interaction of $EXCO_j$ with the firm's export propensity, $EXPP_i$, i.e. the proportion of exports in a firm's total sales.
(4) Backward linkages, BL_j, and forward linkages, FL_j, are intended to capture local firm interactions with FIEs as purchasers and suppliers. The specifications of these two variables are similar to those of Javorcik (2004):

$$BL_j = \sum_k \alpha_{j,k} HZDS_k, \qquad FL_j = \sum_k \beta_{k,j} HZDS_k$$

where $\alpha_{j,k}$ and $\beta_{k,j}$ are input–output coefficients taken from *2002 Input–Output Tables of China* (National Bureau of Statistics of China 2006b). $\alpha_{j,k}$ is the proportion of sector j's output supplied to sector k, with $\sum_k \alpha_{j,k} = 1$; $\beta_{k,j}$ is the proportion of sector k's output supplied to sector j, with $\sum_k \beta_{k,j} = 1$. We form the interaction of BL_j and FL_j with the average training per employee

(TRN_i) to capture the potential importance of training in FDI spillovers via vertical linkages. Foreign-invested firms provide technical support and tutorials for their local upstream suppliers and downstream users or distributors, and subsequently these local firms need to train their employees to utilise this information. Thus the resources which local firms put into training are likely to determine the extent to which these spillovers are absorbed.

Data

Our firm-level data are derived from a survey conducted by Asia Market Intelligence. The database contains detailed information on 998 manufacturing firms in the year 2000. These firms were randomly selected from five manufacturing sectors in China, namely apparel and leather goods, consumer products, electronic components, electronic equipment, and vehicles. They are located in five large cities in China – the capital (Beijing), the municipalities in the fast-growing eastern coastal provinces (Shanghai, Tianjin and Guangzhou) and the western region (Chengdu). These cities are among the top cities in attracting FDI (Madariaga and Poncet 2007).

The ownership composition of these 998 firms is given by Table 3.1. Firms in the database can be categorised into FIEs (with at least 25 per cent of the equity invested by foreign institutions or individuals), state-owned enterprises with the government as their largest shareholder, and private firms which are purely invested by domestic private capital. FIEs, SOEs, and private firms account for 18.2 per cent, 19.4 per cent and 62.3 per cent of the total number of firms, respectively. The percentage of workers with work experience in FIEs is very low, averaging 0.2 per cent. The export propensity of each ownership class is given by Table 3.2. As can be seen, the average export propensity of FIEs is the highest, while that of SOEs is the lowest. The composition of average employees by work type and by technical qualifications is shown in Table 3.3. As we can see, the average employment of SOEs is largest, while that of private firms is smallest. FIEs and SOEs have equivalent shares of workers with technical qualifications (about 18 per cent), while this figure for the private firms is only 15.3 per cent.

Table 3.1 Ownership information

Industries	*Total no. of firms*	*No. of FIEs*	*No. of SOEs*	*No. of private firms*	*Workers in local firms with foreign experience (%)*
Apparel and leather goods	222	21	50	151	0.1
Consumer products	165	21	18	126	0.1
Electronic components	203	48	37	118	0.2
Electronic equipment	192	44	39	109	0.6
Vehicles and vehicle parts	216	48	50	118	0.1
Total	998	182	194	622	0.2

Source: Asia Market Intelligence.

Table 3.2 Export propensity (%)

Industries	*FIEs*	*SOEs*	*Private*
Apparel and leather goods	58.2	24.5	38.8
Consumer products	30.4	1.0	13.1
Electronic components	56.5	8.7	35.4
Electronic equipment	36.7	6.6	15.2
Vehicles and vehicle parts	19.1	3.6	11.0
Average	39.1	10.3	23.5

Source: As Table 3.1.

Table 3.3 Average composition of employees

	FIEs		*SOEs*		*Private*	
	No.	*%*	*No.*	*%*	*No.*	*%*
Classified by work type						
Basic production workers	414	58.0	336	36.6	287	53.7
Auxiliary production workers	73	10.2	93	10.1	60	11.2
Engineering and technical personnel	77	10.8	76	8.3	47	8.8
Managerial personnel	88	12.3	96	10.4	67	12.5
Service personnel	37	5.2	47	5.1	20	3.7
Other employees	25	3.5	119	12.9	42	7.9
Classified by technical titles						
Advanced technical titles	8	1.1	14	1.5	8	1.5
Intermediate technical titles	40	5.6	62	6.7	29	5.4
Preliminary technical titles	79	11.1	90	9.8	45	8.4
Total	714	100.0	919	100.0	534	100.0

Note: Some employees were counted in two or three categories in the survey.

Empirical results

Productivity comparison between ownerships

The TFP of firms is estimated using equation (3.1) and the results for firms in different ownership classes are compared in Table 3.4. Regardless of how the labour input is measured, it is clear that in this dataset, FIEs are generally more productive than SOEs, while private firms are the least productive. This productivity hierarchy indicates that SOEs and private firms may differ in their absorptive capacity, which may affect their ability to take advantage of potential productivity spillovers from FIEs (Girma 2005).

FDI productivity spillovers

With the TFP obtained from the previous estimates, we can then employ equation (3.2) to examine the roles of different spillover channels. The results are

Table 3.4 A comparison of natural logarithm of TFP

	No. of firms	*All five sectors (pooled)*		
		L	*HC*	*HW*
FIEs	182	2.91 (3.00)	2.41 (2.95)	1.85 (3.03)
SOEs	194	2.59 (2.21)	1.96 (2.23)	1.56 (2.49)
Private	622	2.47 (2.51)	1.80 (2.53)	1.42 (2.75)

Notes:

a Estimation specification is equation (3.1).

b "L" means the TFP data are estimated with capital and labour input data; "HC" means the TFP data are estimated with data on capital and human capital (calculated using schooling years); "HW" means the TFP data are estimated with data on capital and human capital (calculated using economy-wide wages);

c Standard deviations in parentheses.

presented in Table 3.5, and lead to the following conclusions. First, the broad picture of the firm results is consistent across the different measures of labour input. The signs are the same, though statistical significance can vary. Second, MNE exports have a significantly positive spillover effect on all domestic firms. Third, backward and forward linkages do not appear to be significant spillover channels. Fourth, while labour transfer generally has a significant negative impact on local firms combined, when they are separated into their component classes we find that labour transfer has a significant positive impact on the productivity of SOEs. When considered along with the productivity hierarchy shown in Table 3.4, this suggests that more productive firms (SOEs on average in this case) are in a better position to take advantage of the knowledge embodied in the transferred workers. The negative impact of labour transfer on private local firms might be explained by fact that those employees with foreign work experience are more expensive to recruit, but do not bring the expected benefits due to these firms' low absorptive capacity. Similar arguments apply to the horizontal demonstration (*HZDS*) which generally has a negative impact on local firms, but a significant positive impact on the productivity of SOEs. This implies that the SOEs in this sample not only effectively combat the competition posed by MNEs in the same industry but also absorb the productivity spillover from MNEs. Private firms are less successful.

Finally, we perform a robustness check on our labour transfer results by retaining labour turnover as the only spillover channel, and adding other firm-related control variables, such as employee training and R&D expenditure. The results are shown in Table 3.6. Again, we find that spillovers via labour transfer are generally negative, but that the SOEs have gained positive benefits from recruiting those people with work experience in multinational firms. Similar results arise when we

Table 3.5 FDI productivity spillover channels

	L	*HC*	*HW*	*L*	*HC*	*HW*
Constant	2.1	1.3	1.3	2.1	1.23	1.3
	(0.45)*	(0.45)	(0.45)	(0.45)**	(0.45)	(0.45)
$LT_{d,j}$	−6.5	−6.8	−7.0	−7.9	−8.2	−8.3
	(3.76)*	(3.76)*	(3.74)*	(3.86)**	(3.87)**	(3.84)**
$LT \times SOE$				26.0	25.7	24.4
				(15.66)*	(15.67)*	(15.59)
$BL \times TRN$	0.1	0.1	0.1	0.1	0.1	0.1
	(0.14)	(0.14)	(0.14)	(0.14)	(0.14)	(0.14)
$FL \times TRN$	0.0	0.0	0.0	0.0	0.0	0.0
	(0.02)	(0.02)	(0.02)	(0.02)	(0.02)	(0.02)
$HZDS \times RND$	−0.0	−0.0	−0.0	−0.0	−0.0	−0.0
	(0.00)**	(0.00)***	(0.00)***	(0.00)***	(0.00)***	(0.00)***
$HZDS \times RND \times SOE$				0.0	0.0	0.0
				(0.01)*	(0.01)*	(0.01)*
$EXCO \times EXPP$	0.6	0.6	0.73	0.60	0.63	0.78
	(0.33)*	(0.33)*	(0.33)**	(0.33)*	(0.33)*	(0.33)**
No. of observations	74	727	730	741	727	730
R-squared	0.02	0.03	0.03	0.03	0.03	0.03

*Statistically significant at 10%; **significant at 5%; ***significant at 1%.

Notes:

a Only local firms are included.
b The dependent variable is the logarithm of total factor productivity, $\log(TFP_{i,j})$, which is estimated using equation (3.2).
c "L", "HC" and "HW" have the same meaning as in Table 3.4.
d *SOE* is a dummy variable which is equal to 1 if the corresponding firm is an SOE, and 0 otherwise.
e Standard errors in parentheses.
f Each regression includes industry dummies.

restrict attention to firms in electronic component and product industries, which have the highest proportions of previously foreign-employed workers.

Our support for spillovers that favour SOEs differs from the previous empirical literature which largely finds that SOEs are negatively affected by FDI presence (e.g. Girma and Gong 2008a). The main reason for this difference probably lies in sample selection. The SOEs in this sample are located in five large cities in China, have large scale (see Table 3.3) and relatively high TFP (see Table 3.4). However, the clear message from this research is that only those domestic firms with higher productivity and better absorptive capacity are likely to benefit from FDI productivity spillovers.

Conclusions

This chapter is the first to encapsulate all potentially important spillover channels into a single micro-econometric model with firm-level data. These channels include inter-ownership labour turnover, vertical input–output linkages, export

Table 3.6 FDI productivity spillover via labour turnover

	All five sectors (pooled)			*Electronic industry only*		
	L	*HC*	*HW*	*L*	*HC*	*HW*
Constant	3.1	2.3	1.8	2.8	1.4	0.6
	(0.11)***	(0.11)***	(0.12)***	(0.14)***	(0.14)***	(0.14)***
$LT_{d,j}$	−28.7	−33.3	−36.2	−27.9	−27.7	−28.8
	(8.85)***	(9.24)***	(9.52)***	(8.70)***	(8.73)***	(8.74)***
$TRN_{d,j}$	0.0	−0.1	−0.2	0.0	−0.0	−0.0
	(0.10)	(0.10)	(0.10)*	(0.12)	(0.11)	(0.11)
$RND_{d,j}$	−0.0	−0.0	−0.0	0.0	0.0	−0.0
	(0.00)**	(0.00)**	(0.00)**	(0.00)	(0.00)	(0.00)
$LT_{d,j} \times SOE$	93.5	89.8	87.2	180.8	177.7	170.7
	(42.76)**	(44.65)**	(45.95)*	(51.66)***	(51.85)***	(51.90)***
$TRN_{d,j} \times SOE$	0.0	0.2	0.2	0.0	0.1	0.1
	(0.11)	(0.12)	(0.12)*	(0.12)	(0.12)	(0.12)
$RND_{d,j} \times SOE$	0.0	0.0	0.0	0.0	0.0	0.0
	(0.01)	(0.01)	(0.01)	(0.01)	(0.01)	(0.01)
No. of observations	743	732	732	409	401	402
R-squared	0.03	0.03	0.04	0.05	0.05	0.05

Notes: see Table 3.5.

of MNEs, and horizontal effects. Our results suggest the following. First, the extent to which spillover channels can play their role does depend on local firm characteristics, particularly R&D expenditure per capita and export status. Second, export spillovers from MNEs seem to have a particularly important role in China, perhaps reflecting the extraordinarily high export propensity of MNEs. Third, labour turnover transmits positive productivity spillover to SOEs but not to private firms, reflecting the greater ability of SOEs to absorb FDI productivity spillover. Fourth, horizontal demonstration and competition also bring SOEs positive spillover effects for similar reasons.

In brief, more productive enterprises (SOEs in this study) are more likely to benefit from spillovers due to the presence of foreign investment. The main policy message of this paper is therefore that policy-makers need to be aware that the strategy of "swapping market access for technology" (Long 2005) does not automatically lead to success. Measures should to be taken to encourage all domestic firms to increase their absorptive capacity.

4 What do the aggregate data tell us?

Industry-level analysis

Productivity decomposition

We use industry-level data to examine the roles of four possible productivity spillover channels: backward linkages, forward linkages, exports of FIEs and horizontal effects (including demonstration, competition, and resource reallocation). The spillover channel of labour turnover between FIEs and domestic enterprises is omitted from the model because such industry-level data are not available.

Suppose $VA_{i,t} = TFP_{i,t} \times G(K_{i,t}, L_{i,t})$, where $K_{i,t}$ and $L_{i,t}$ denote capital and labour, respectively. $G(K_{i,t}, L_{i,t})$ takes Cobb–Douglas rather than constant elasticity of substitution functional forms here, which is consistent with the literature. Then total factor productivity can be decomposed into

$$TFP = TFP_{\text{indigenous}} + TFP_{\text{spillover}} \tag{4.1}$$

where $TFP_{\text{indigenous}}$ captures all indigenous factors that contribute the TFP of a firm (e.g. R&D, employee education level, employee training hours and management skills), while $TFP_{\text{spillover}}$ measures the FDI productivity spillover effects.

The TFP and spillover effects can be estimated with a two-stage approach:

$$\ln(VA_{i,t}) = \alpha_0 + \alpha_K \ln K_{i,t} + \alpha_L \ln L_{i,t} + \varepsilon_{i,t} \tag{4.2a}$$

$$TFP_{i,t} = \exp(\alpha_0 + \varepsilon_{i,t}) = \alpha_1 + \boldsymbol{\beta} \times \mathbf{SPL} + \zeta_{i,t} \tag{4.2b}$$

where the vector **SPL** collectively denotes three FDI spillover channels. It contains four variables: horizontal demonstration, $HZDS_{i,t}$; backward linkages, $BL_{i,t}$; forward linkages, $FL_{i,t}$; and export concentration of multinational enterprises, $EXCO_{i,t}$. $HZDS_{i,t}$ is the share of FIEs in the gross output in sector j at time t. $BL_{i,t}$ and $FL_{i,t}$ are horizontal demonstrations weighted by input–output coefficients. They are designed to capture local firm interactions with FIEs as purchasers and suppliers, respectively. The specifications of BL and FL follow the practice adopted in the literature (Javorcik 2004; Kneller and Pisu 2007; Girma and Gong 2008a; Girma *et al.* 2008):

$$BL_{i,t} = \sum_{j} (\delta_{i,j,t} HZDS_{j,t}) \tag{4.3a}$$

$$FL_{j,t} = \sum_{i} (\delta_{i,j,t} HZDS_{i,t}) \tag{4.3b}$$

The $\delta_{i,j}$ are input–output coefficients measuring the percentage of output of industry i provided to industry j in the total output of industry i: $\delta_{i,j} = Y_{i,j}/Y_i$.

For example, assume the foreign presences in industry 1, 2, 3 are 10 per cent, 20 per cent, and 30 per cent, respectively. Industry 1 provides 40 per cent of its products to itself, 35 per cent to industry 2 and 25 per cent to industry 3. Then the coefficient of backward linkage is

$$BL = 40\% \times 10\% + 20\% \times 35\% + 30\% \times 25\% = 0.185$$

The development of the above two input–output linkage variables as a measure of FDI spillovers has three merits. Firstly, they have been widely applied in many country contexts (e.g. China, Lithuania and the UK) in the econometric studies in the literature mentioned above, to examine the correlation between the productivity of domestic enterprises and the FIEs in downstream and upstream sectors. Secondly, as *BL* and *FL* are both weighted measures of *HZDS* across a large number of sectors, the independence of *BL*, *FL* and *HZDS* is always observed in the literature. Third, in the subsequent CGE modelling to be discussed in detail in Chapter 7, both *BL* and *FL* can be modelled as endogenous variables and whole values can change endogenously in counterfactual simulations.

Finally, $EXCO_i$ is the ratio of the export of FIE sector i to the total export in sector i, which measures "export concentration" as another spillover channel.

Equations (4.2a) and (4.2b) are estimated with an industry-level panel dataset. As discussed by Görg and Strobl (2001), panel data analyses are superior to cross-sectional studies in their ability to capture time-invariant sector-specific factors which may impact on the relationship between foreign presence and the performance of domestic enterprises. Ignorance of such time-invariant factors usually leads to an overestimation of FDI productivity spillovers.

There are three issues regarding the above econometric model that merit discussion. The first one is the measurement of the labour input. It would be ideal to measure L with employment weighted by years of schooling. Unfortunately, data on years of schooling by ownership sector are not available.

The second issue is whether or not to include industry dummies to control for potential fixed industry effects. If industry dummy variables are included, equation (4.2b) can be transformed into

$$TFP_{i,t} = \exp(\alpha_0 + \varepsilon_{i,t}) = \alpha_1 + \boldsymbol{\beta} \times \mathbf{SPL} + \alpha_i \times DUMMY_i + \zeta_{i,t} \tag{4.2c}$$

Then the decomposition of TFP as specified by (4.1) and (4.2b) will not be confined to being uniform across all industries. In other words, the indigenous part of productivity could vary across industries ($TFP_{\text{indigenous}} = \alpha_1 + \alpha_i \times DUMMY_i + \zeta_i$), while the spillover part of productivity takes a uniform specification across industries ($TFP_{\text{spillover}} = \boldsymbol{\beta} \times \mathbf{SPL}$). Unfortunately, this option was not available for two reasons. (a) As we will discuss shortly, while for SOEs we have 31 (industries) × 5 (years) = 155 observations, for private enterprises we only have 31 (industries) × 2 (years) = 62 observations. The latter rules out including 30 industry dummies. (b) While our spillover variables (*HZDS, EXCO, BL* and *FL*, collectively denoted by the vector **SPL**) for the CGE modeling can change endogenously in counterfactual simulations (to be discussed shortly), we cannot allow for endogenous changes in industry fixed effects.

The third issue is whether or not to include year dummy variables to control for the effect of CGE benchmark year (2002). Again the limited data on private enterprises (for two years only, 2005 and 2006) preclude this.

Thus we can employ econometric regression to obtain the share of TFP caused by spillovers in total TFP:

$$\frac{TFP_{\text{spillover}}}{TFP_{\text{total}}} = \frac{\hat{\boldsymbol{\beta}} \times \mathbf{SPL}}{\hat{\alpha}_1 + \hat{\boldsymbol{\beta}} \times \mathbf{SPL}} \tag{4.4}$$

where $\hat{\boldsymbol{\beta}} \times \mathbf{SPL} \equiv \hat{\beta}_1 BL_{i,t} + \hat{\beta}_2 FL_{i,t} + \hat{\beta}_3 HZDS_{i,t} + \hat{\beta}_4 EXCO_{i,t}$.

In the CGE modelling to be discussed in Chapter 7, the share of FIEs in sectoral output ($HZDS_i$) and the share of FIEs in sectoral export ($EXCO_i$) will both be endogenously determined in counterfactual experiments. Backward linkages (BL_i) and forward linkages (FL_i) are also endogenously determined by equations (4.3a) and (4.3b), respectively. Therefore, the share of productivity spillovers is also endogenous, as specified by equation (4.4). Thus we can transform the value-added production equation into

$$VA_{i,t} = \Theta_i \times TFP_{i,t} \times K_{i,t}^{\alpha_K} L_{i,t}^{\alpha_L} \tag{4.5}$$

where

$$\Theta_i = \frac{TFP_i}{\overline{TFP0_i}}$$

in which $\overline{TFP0_i}$ denotes the benchmark TFP ($\hat{\alpha}_1 + \hat{\boldsymbol{\beta}} \times \overline{\mathbf{SPL}}$) and TFP_i denotes endogenous TFP value ($\hat{\alpha}_1 + \hat{\boldsymbol{\beta}} \times \mathbf{SPL}$). In this way we can model the FDI productivity spillovers endogenously. In the benchmark scenario, $\Theta_i = 1$, so that the above equation simplifies to

$$VA_{i,t} = TFP_{i,t} \times K_{i,t}^{\alpha_K} L_{i,t}^{\alpha_L}$$

Table 4.1 Available data for industry-level panel data analysis

Variables	*Symbols*	*Source*	*Years*
Value added	VA	CIESY	2001–2003, 2005–2006
Net fixed assets	K	CIESY	2001–2003, 2005–2006
Total employment	L	CIESY	2001–2003, 2005–2006
Input–output coefficients	$\delta_{i,j}$	I/O	2002
Backward linkages	$BL_{i,t} = \sum_j (\delta_{i,j,t} HZDS_{j,t})$	CIESY, I/O	2002
Forward linkages	$FL_{j,t} = \sum_i (\delta_{i,j,t} HZDS_{i,t})$	CIESY, I/O	2002
Horizontal demonstrations	$HZDS$	CIESY	2001–2003, 2005–2006
Export concentration	$EXCO$	CIESY	2001–2003, 2005–2006

Notes: CIESY is the acronym of China Industrial Economy Statistical Yearbook (2001–2003 and 2005–2006); I/O denotes the Input–Output Table of China in 2002. Value added VA and intermediate input M will be deflated with an "ex-factory or wholesale price index". Net fixed assets K will be deflated with a "fixed asset investment price index". Both indexes are obtained from *China Statistical Yearbook*. (National Bureau of Statistics of China, 2007.)

Econometric estimations of spillover parameters

The CGE model in this book is built on the Input–Output Table of China in 2002, so the FDI spillover parameters $\boldsymbol{\beta}$ have to be estimated for the years around 2002. The main data sources for estimation are the China Industrial Economy Statistical Yearbook (CIESY) and the Input–Output Table, both released by the National Bureau of Statistics of China (NBS). The available CIESYs around the year 2002 are for the years of 2001–2003 and 2005–2006. NBS releases input–output tables every 5 years and the latest one is for 2002. So the input–output table of 2002 will be employed to calculate all the input–output coefficients $\delta_{i,j,t}$ (thus t can be suppressed) for 2001–2003 and 2005–2006.

The available data sources are summarised in Table 4.1. There are 31 (industries) $\times$ 5 (years) = 155 observations (panel data) for estimations of SOEs. But the data for private enterprises are only available in 2005 and 2006, so there are only 62 observations for the private sectors.

Table 4.2 Estimation of value added

Firm types	*Constant*	*K*	*L*	*Obs.*	R^2
SOEs	0.13	0.91	0.09	155	0.99
	(0.04)***	(0.02)***	(0.03)***		
Private	1.01	0.39	0.70	62	0.97
	(0.19)***	(0.06)***	(0.04)***		

Notes:

a Estimation of equation (4.2a).

b Standard errors in parentheses. *, **, *** denote statistical significance at 10%, 5%, and 1% level, respectively.

c SOEs are state-owned enterprises and "Private" means domestic private enterprises.

Table 4.3 Estimation of productivity spillovers

Firm types	*Constant*	*BL*	*FL*	*HZDS*	*EXCO*	*Obs.*	R^2
SOEs	0.91	0.40	0.29	0.33	0.04	155	0.31
	(0.05)***	(0.42)	(0.15)*	(0.17)*	(0.07)		
Private	2.21	0.15	2.58	2.88	−1.74	62	0.30
	(0.32)***	(2.73)	(0.97)***	(1.11)***	(0.47)***		

Notes:

a Estimation of equation (4.2b).

b Standard errors in parentheses. *, **, *** denote statistical significance at 10%, 5%, and 1% level, respectively.

c SOEs are state-owned enterprises and "Private" means domestic private enterprises.

d Similar to the results in the literature, the correlation coefficients of *BL*, *FL* and *HZDS* are reasonably low (both below 0.30), so that their independence is justified.

The TFP estimated ($TFP_{i,t} = \exp(\alpha_0 + \varepsilon_{i,t})$) from equation (4.2a) – see Table 4.2 – is further regressed against spillover variables as specified by equation (4.2b).

As shown by Table 4.3, there is a significant relationship between the productivity of domestic enterprises and presence of FDI. Both SOEs and private domestic firms benefit from spillovers from FIEs in upstream and horizontal sectors, and the coefficients for private enterprises are larger and more statistically significant. This difference could be caused by the relatively weak absorptive capacity of SOEs that undertake less R&D activity and employee training, as suggested by Girma and Gong (2008a). Neither SOEs nor private enterprises benefit from the contacts with the FIEs in downstream sectors (*BL* coefficients are not significant). The reason for this could be that the potential benefit of backward linkages is counterbalanced by the increased competition among domestic enterprises in the upstream sectors triggered by the FIEs in the downstream sectors.

Finally, it seems that the export of MNE affiliates has no effect on improving the productivity of SOEs. Private enterprises are even negatively affected by the MNE exports. The latter makes little sense as an "export spillover" and may reflect industry characteristics – i.e. FIEs have a higher share of exports in industries where domestic firms have relatively lower TFP.[1] Because this effect can vary endogenously in our simulations, we retain it but note that it may not be picking up a spillover as such.

Based on the above econometric estimation, we calculate that the average contributions of FDI productivity spillovers to the overall TFP (estimated from equation (4.2a)) of SOEs and private enterprises (calculated with equation (4.4)) are 22 per cent and 20 per cent, respectively. The estimated significant and insignificant, and positive and negative spillover coefficients (denoted by the vector $\boldsymbol{\beta}$) will be carried forward as specified by equation (4.4) into the CGE modelling.

Part III

A general equilibrium framework for quantification of spillover effects

5 Computable general equilibrium modelling

Theoretical foundations

Basics of general equilibrium

The theory underpinning computable general equilibrium (CGE) modelling is Walrasian general equilibrium theory, which shows that the demand and supply in an economy can achieve a general equilibrium with the interaction and interdependence of individual markets and agents. Compared to general equilibrium theory, a partial equilibrium analysis considers the determination of prices for some products only, assuming that the prices for other products are constant.

A general equilibrium in an open economy can be depicted by a circular flow of goods, services, factors and payments as shown in Figure 5.1. There are three types of active agents in the economy: firms, households and government. Firms employ the endowment of households in factor markets, and produce goods and services, which will be bought by households in the product markets. The income of households comes from the rental of their endowments including labour, capital and land. The government collects taxes from households and firms and disburses the tax revenue to firms and households in the forms of subsidies and transfer payments.

An exchange economy with Walrasian general equilibrium

In a pure exchange economy, a Walrasian general equilibrium is characterised by a vector of prices that makes the excess demand for each good in the economy zero.

Suppose there are D consumers and N types of goods in the economy. The consumer agent needs to solve a utility maximisation problem:

$$\max\ U_d(\mathbf{X}_d) \quad \text{s.t. } \mathbf{P}\cdot\mathbf{X}_d \leq \mathbf{P}\cdot\mathbf{E}_d, \quad d = 1, 2, \ldots, D$$

where $\mathbf{P}$ is the price vector; $\mathbf{X}_d$ is the vector of demand for goods; and $\mathbf{E}_d$ denotes the vector of goods (endowments) of the dth consumer. The solution $\mathbf{X}(\mathbf{P}, \mathbf{P}\cdot\mathbf{E}_d)$ to this utility maximisation problem subject to the income constraint is the consumer's Marshallian demand bundle, which is homogeneous of degree 0 in prices.

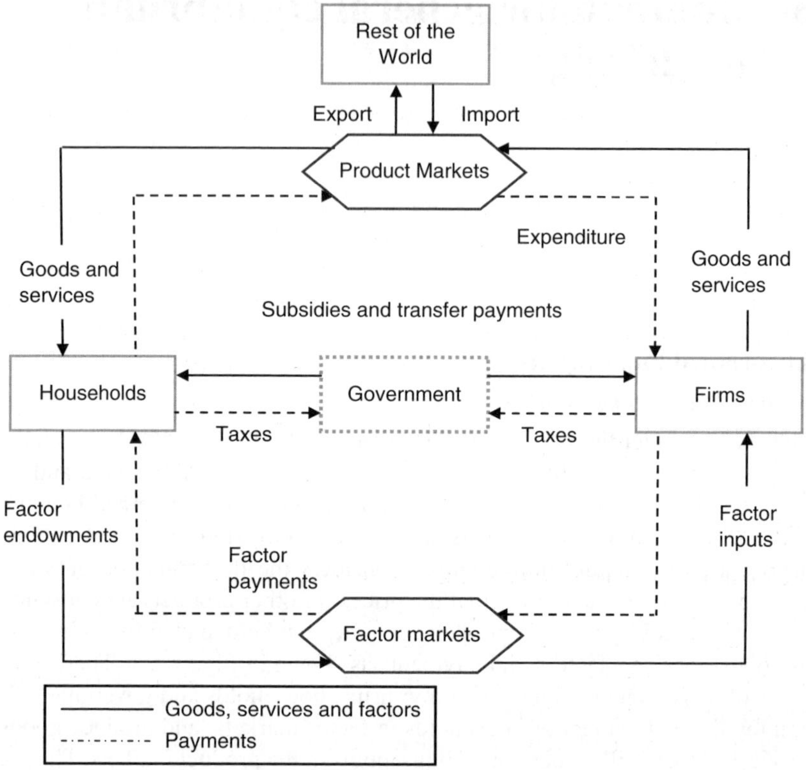

Figure 5.1 Circular flows in an open economy.

Source: Adapted version of the models of Sue Wing (2004) and Dervis *et al.* (1982).

Then for the ith good, the aggregate excess demand can be specified as

$$Z_i(\mathbf{P}) = \sum_{d=1}^{D} X_{i,d}(\mathbf{P}, \mathbf{P} \cdot \mathbf{E}_d) - \sum_{d=1}^{D} E_{i,d}, \quad i = 1, 2, \ldots, N$$

When $Z_i(\mathbf{P}) > 0$, the aggregate demand for the ith commodity exceeds the aggregate endowment of the ith commodity. When $Z_i(\mathbf{P}) < 0$, there is an excess supply of commodity i.

In vector form, the aggregate excess demand function for the whole set of commodities can be specified as

$$\mathbf{Z}(\mathbf{P}) = (Z_1(\mathbf{P}), \ldots, Z_N(\mathbf{P}))$$

Since the endowment vector $\mathbf{E}_d$ is exogenous variables independent of prices, $\mathbf{Z(P)}$ is also homogenous of degree 0 in prices.

Walrasian general equilibrium occurs when the aggregate excess demand for each commodity in the whole economy is zero. That is to say, a price vector $\mathbf{P}^*$ is called a Walrasian general equilibrium price vector if $\mathbf{Z}(\mathbf{P}^*) = \mathbf{0}$. Furthermore, the aggregate excess demand function must satisfy Walras' law: for any price vector $\mathbf{P}$, we have $\mathbf{P} \cdot \mathbf{Z(P)} = \mathbf{0}$.

The existence of a general equilibrium in the economy was controversial until it was proved by McKenzie (1954) and Arrow and Debreu (1954) with fixed point theorems. The general equilibrium is named after Walras only because "Walras was the first to attempt to an answer to the question of existence by reducing it to a question of whether simultaneous equations of market supply and market demand have a solution" (Jehle and Reny 2001, pp. 191–192).

Since the aggregate excess demand function is homogeneous of degree 0 in commodity prices, if $\mathbf{P}_0^* = [P_1, P_2, \ldots, P_N]$ is a solution, then $\mathbf{P}_1^* = [1, (P_2/P_1) \ldots, (P_N/P_1)]$ is also a solution to this exchange equilibrium, i.e. equilibrium determines relative prices, so we can choose the price of one good as numéraire.

A closed economy with competitive general equilibrium

The pure exchange economy can be extended to a competitive market with firms and production but no government. Now the general equilibrium in this economy has four important properties: good market clearance, factor market clearance, zero profit, and income balance.

Suppose there are N representative producers, each producing an idiosyncratic type of good or service. Suppose that there exists a representative household owning F types of endowments. The household rents its members' endowments, E_f, and consumes goods and services, X_j. Let indices $j = \{1, 2, \ldots, N\}$ denote the set of producers and their associated commodities, and $f = \{1, 2, \ldots, F\}$ denote the set of primary inputs. $\mathbf{P} = (P_1, P_2, \ldots, P_N)$ is the vector of market prices for goods, services, and $\mathbf{R} = (R_1, R_2, \ldots, R_F)$ is the vector of market prices for endowments.

Market clearance

Firstly, an equilibrium of economic flows implies that any product produced in a certain industry should be exhausted by firms in other industries as intermediate products, or consumed by households as final products, i.e. commodity market clearance; and all the endowments of households are fully employed by firms, i.e. factor market clearance.

Commodity market clearance implies that the supply of the jth commodity, Y_j, must be equal to the sum of the ith producer's demand for this commodity, $G_{j,i}$, indexed by $i = 1, 2, \ldots, N$, and the consumer's demand of this commodity, X_j:

$$Y_j = \sum_{i=1}^{N} G_{j,i} + X_j \tag{5.1}$$

In a similar way, factor market clearance implies that the quantity of the fth endowment is equal to sum of this particular endowment employed by the N industries:

$$E_f = \sum_{j=1}^{N} E_{f,j} \tag{5.2}$$

Zero profit

Another property of general equilibrium is that every representative firm makes zero profit. The reason for this property in competitive markets is that otherwise firms would enter the profit-making industries so that we cannot be in equilibrium. This implies that the revenue of gross output of the jth sector, $P_j Y_j$, should be equal to the sum of the total cost of the intermediate inputs plus the total cost of the primary factors which are employed for the production of the jth industry:

$$P_j Y_j = \sum_{i=1}^{N} P_i G_{j,i} + \sum_{f=1}^{F} R_f E_{j,f} \tag{5.3}$$

Income balance

The income balance implies that, for the representative household, all its members' income M should come from the return on their primary inputs into the production of goods and services:

$$M = \sum_{f=1}^{F} R_f E_f \tag{5.4}$$

All the income of the consumer should be exhausted in consuming the goods and services to satisfy his/her demand:

$$\sum_{i=1}^{N} P_i X_i = M = \sum_{f=1}^{F} R_f E_f \tag{5.5}$$

Model construction

Constant elasticity of substitution functions

CGE modelling uses standard functional forms to solve the production and consumption decisions which are captured by nonlinear optimality conditions. Most widely adopted forms of functions for production and utility are constant elasticity of substitution (CES) functions and their special cases, namely, Cobb–Douglas, Leontief and constant elasticity of transformation (CET) functions.

Various combinations of these four functional forms are employed in different scenarios in CGE modelling to capture different production technologies and consumption preferences. The choice of functional forms largely depends on availability of the parameter data, and also on the amount of effort the modeller is willing to invest in econometric estimation (Ginsburgh and Keyzer 1997).

A CES function takes the form

$$Y_j = A_j \left[\sum_{i=1}^{N} \delta_{j,i} X_{j,i}^{\rho_j} \right]^{1/\rho_j} \tag{5.6}$$

To derive the elasticity of substitution of this production function, the technical rate of substitution (TRS) between two inputs needs to be found first:

$$\frac{\partial Y_j}{\partial X_{j,s}} = A_j \cdot \frac{1}{\rho_j} \cdot \left[\sum_{i=1}^{N} \delta_{j,s} X_{j,s}^{\rho_f} \right]^{\frac{1}{\rho_j}-1} \cdot \delta_{j,s} \cdot \rho_j \cdot X_{j,s}^{\rho_j - 1}$$

$$\frac{\partial Y_j}{\partial X_{j,t}} = A_j \cdot \frac{1}{\rho_j} \cdot \left[\sum_{i=1}^{N} \delta_{j,t} X_{j,t}^{\rho_f} \right]^{\frac{1}{\rho_j}-1} \cdot \delta_{j,t} \cdot \rho_j \cdot X_{j,t}^{\rho_j - 1}$$

$$TRS_{j,s,t} = -\frac{\partial Y_j / \partial X_{j,s}}{\partial Y_j / \partial X_{j,t}} = -\frac{\delta_{j,s}}{\delta_{j,t}} \left(\frac{X_{j,s}}{X_{j,t}} \right)^{\rho_j \;\; 1}$$

The logarithm of the TRS is then

$$\ln |TRS_{j,s,t}| = \ln \left(\frac{\delta_{j,s}}{\delta_{j,t}} \right) + (\rho_j - 1) \ln \left(\frac{X_{j,s}}{X_{j,t}} \right)$$

Finally, the value of the elasticity of substitution (hereafter σ) can be calculated and turns out to be a constant:

$$\sigma_j = \frac{d \ln(X_{j,t}/X_{j,s})}{d \ln |TRS_{j,s,t}|} = \frac{d \ln(X_{j,t}/X_{j,s})}{\ln(\delta_{j,s}/\delta_{j,t}) + (\rho_j - 1) \cdot d \ln(X_{j,s}/X_{j,t})} = \frac{1}{1-\rho_j}$$

As $\rho \to 0$, i.e. $\sigma \to 1$, we can prove, using L'Hôspital's rule, that equation (5.6) becomes a Cobb–Douglas function. The logarithm form of equation (5.6) is

$$\ln \left(\frac{Y_j}{A_j} \right) = \frac{\ln[\sum_{i=1}^{N} \delta_{j,i} X_{j,i}^{\rho_f}]}{\rho_j},$$

so that

$$\lim_{\rho_j \to 0} \ln\left(\frac{Y_j}{A_j}\right) = \lim_{\rho_j \to 0} \frac{\ln[\sum_{i=1}^{N} \delta_{j,i} X_{j,i}^{\rho_f}]}{\rho_j} = \lim_{\rho_j \to 0} \frac{\sum_{i=1}^{N} \delta_{j,i} X_{j,i}^{\rho_f} \ln X_{j,i}}{\sum_{i=1}^{N} \delta_{j,i} X_{j,i}^{\rho_f}}$$

$$= \sum_{i=1}^{N} \delta_{j,i} \ln X_{j,i} = \ln\left[\prod_{i=1}^{N} X_{j,i}^{\delta_{f,i}}\right]$$

That is, when $\rho \to 0$ (i.e. $\sigma \to 1$), we get a Cobb–Douglas function $Y_j = A_j \prod_{i=1}^{N} X_{j,i}^{\delta_{f,i}}$, which also implies that any Cobb–Douglas function has unit elasticity of substitution. Compared to the unit elasticity of substitution of the Cobb–Douglas functions, the elasticity (σ) of a CES function offers CGE modellers greater flexibility because they can choose different parameter values for σ to capture a vast spectrum of production technology.

Another special case of CES is the Leontief form. As $\rho \to -\infty$, i.e. $\sigma \to 0$, the Leontief form is generated, as any Leontief function has zero substitutability among its inputs:

$$Y_j = \min(\eta_1 X_{j,1},\ \eta_2 X_{j,2}, \ldots, \eta_N X_{j,N})$$

CET functions have identical functional forms to CES functions. However, while CES functions specify an output as a function of inputs, CET functions state the input as a function of various outputs. This functional form is useful, for example, in disaggregating domestic output into exports and domestic sales on the assumption that the producers maximise their profits, subject to imperfect substitution between exports and domestic sales:

$$X_i = A_i \left[\sum_{j=1}^{N} \xi_{i,j} Y_{i,j}^{\tau_f}\right]^{1/\tau_f} \tag{5.7}$$

CES, Cobb–Douglas, Leontief and CET functions are all homogeneous of degree 1.

In CGE modelling, it is a common practice to combine several different functions in a nested form, with the upper-level function using as its input the output of the lower-level functions. Figure 5.2 provides a nested form of production. Total output is defined as a Cobb–Douglas function of an intermediate good bundle and a value-added bundle, which implies that the elasticity of substitution between these two bundles is 1. The intermediate good bundle is a Leontief, or linear, combination of N intermediate products, $X_{j,1}, \ldots, X_{j,N}$, so that the elasticity of substitution between any two alternative inputs is specified as zero. The value-added nest comprises a CES transformation of primary inputs such as labour and capital.

In a similar way, Figure 5.3 provides a nested utility function. The utility function is a Cobb–Douglas function of savings (future consumption) and

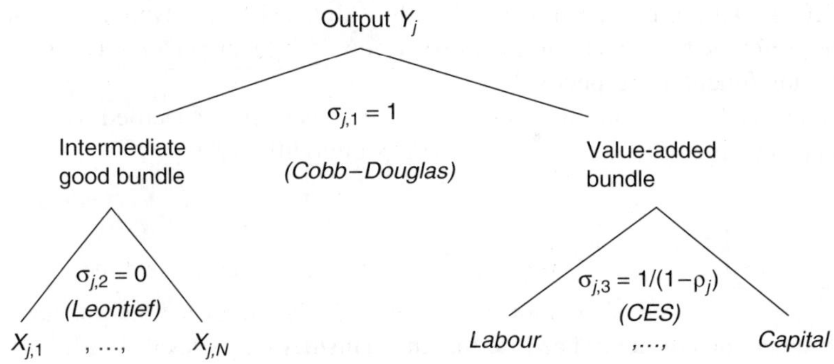

Figure 5.2 A nested production function.

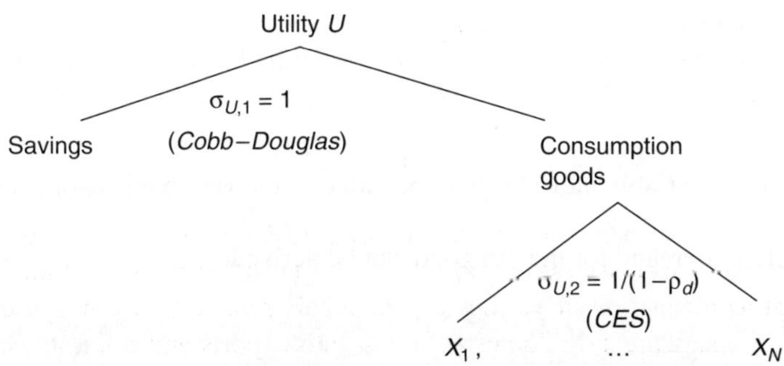

Figure 5.3 A nested utility function.

goods (current consumption), so that the elasticity of substitution is 1. Current consumption of goods is a CES function of N goods.

Nesting allows various production technologies and consumption preferences to be combined into a single model. Theoretically, infinite layers of nesting can be selected in a single CGE model, but the more layers the less tractable the model would be. Should a counterintuitive simulation result emerge, it would be difficult to pinpoint the precise source, thus forcing modellers to turn to less informative explanations (Blake 1998; Sue Wing 2004). Therefore, a feasible option would be to have two or three layers of nesting.

Algebraic framework

A CGE model consists of a system of core equations of production and consumption which need to be solved simultaneously, with benchmark data obtained from an input–output table or social accounting matrix, to identify the equilibrium price and output set in accordance with the principles of general equilibrium, namely, market clearance, zero profit and income balance. The algebraic framework of CGE modelling can be illustrated within a closed Cobb–Douglas economy, where preference and technology are represented by Cobb–Douglas utility and production functions, respectively.

The utility level of the only representative consumer is specified as a Cobb–Douglas function of the consumption of N commodities (X):

$$U = A\prod_{j=1}^{N} X_j^{\alpha_f}, \quad \text{with} \sum_{j=1}^{N} \alpha_j = 1$$

Assume that the consumer needs to maximise his/her utility level:

$$\begin{aligned} \max \quad & U = A\prod_{j=1}^{N} X_j^{\alpha_f} \\ \text{s.t.} \quad & \sum_{j=1}^{N} P_j X_j \leq \overline{M} \end{aligned}$$

where a bar over a variable indicates that the value of the variable is exogenously given.

The quantity of demand for the jth good can be derived:

$$X_j = \frac{\overline{M}}{P_j} \times \frac{\alpha_j}{\sum_{j=1}^{N} \alpha_j} = \frac{\alpha_j \overline{M}}{P_j}$$

This can be rewritten as $\alpha_j = P_j X_j / \overline{M}$. Therefore α_j is the share of the jth commodity in the total expenditure. Constant expenditure shares is also an important property of a Cobb–Douglas utility function.

The production function can be defined in a similar way. Assume that the jth producer needs to produce the jth good or service using N types of intermediate inputs g and F types of primary inputs E with a Cobb–Douglas function:

$$Y_j = A_j \prod_{i=1}^{N} G_{j,i}^{\beta_{j,i}} \prod_{f=1}^{F} E_{j,f}^{\gamma_{j,i}}, \quad \text{with} \sum_{i=1}^{N} \beta_{j,i} + \sum_{f=1}^{F} \gamma_{j,f} = 1$$

This producer needs to minimise its total cost:

$$\begin{aligned} \min \quad & C_j = \sum_{i=1}^{N} P_i G_{j,i} + \sum_{f=1}^{F} R_f E_{j,f} \\ \text{s.t.} \quad & Y_j \leq A_j \prod_{i=1}^{N} G_{j,i}^{\beta_{j,i}} \prod_{f=1}^{F} E_{j,f}^{\gamma_{j,i}}, \quad \text{with} \sum_{i=1}^{N} \beta_{j,i} + \sum_{f=1}^{F} \gamma_{j,f} = 1 \end{aligned}$$

The quantity of demand for the ith intermediate input and fth primary input are:

$$G_{j,i} = \frac{Y_j \beta_{j,i}}{A_j P_i} \prod_{i=1}^{N} \left(\frac{P_i}{\beta_{j,i}}\right)^{\beta_{j,i}} \prod_{f=1}^{F} \left(\frac{R_f}{\gamma_{j,f}}\right)^{\gamma_{j,f}}$$

$$E_{j,f} = \frac{Y_j \gamma_{j,f}}{A_j P_f} \prod_{i=1}^{N} \left(\frac{P_i}{\beta_{j,i}}\right)^{\beta_{j,i}} \prod_{f=1}^{F} \left(\frac{R_f}{\gamma_{j,f}}\right)^{\gamma_{j,f}}$$

With the solutions to consumption demand and intermediate and primary inputs in production, the four central conditions of a general equilibrium specified by equations (5.1)–(5.4) can be reformulated.

Commodity market clearance condition (5.1) can be transformed into an N-dimensional excess demand vector which measures the gap between supply and demand in the market for the jth commodity:

$$\begin{aligned}\mathbf{\Delta}_j^C &= \sum_{i=1}^{N} G_{j,i} + X_j - Y_j \\ &= \sum_{i=1}^{N} \left[\frac{Y_j \beta_{j,i}}{A_j P_i} \prod_{i=1}^{N} \left(\frac{P_i}{\beta_{j,i}}\right)^{\beta_{j,i}} \prod_{f=1}^{F} \left(\frac{R_f}{\gamma_{j,f}}\right)^{\gamma_{j,f}}\right] + \frac{\alpha_j \overline{M}}{P_j} - Y_j \qquad (5.8)\end{aligned}$$

Primary input market clearance condition (5.2) can be transformed into an F-dimensional excess demand vector which measures the gap between supply and demand in the market for the fth primary input:

$$\begin{aligned}\mathbf{\Delta}_f^F &= \sum_{j=1}^{N} E_{f,j} - \overline{E}_f \\ &= \sum_{f=1}^{N} \left[\frac{Y_j \gamma_{j,f}}{A_j P_f} \prod_{j=1}^{N} \left(\frac{P_i}{\beta_{j,i}}\right)^{\beta_{j,i}} \prod_{f=1}^{F} \left(\frac{R_f}{\gamma_{j,f}}\right)^{\gamma_{j,f}}\right] - \overline{E}_f \qquad (5.9)\end{aligned}$$

The zero-profit condition in equation (5.3) can be transformed into an N-dimensional vector which measures the gap between the costs incurred in production and total revenue for the jth commodity:

$$\begin{aligned}\mathbf{\Delta}_j^\pi &= P_j Y_j - \sum_{i=1}^{N} P_i G_{j,i} - \sum_{f=1}^{F} P_f E_{j,f} \\ &= P_j Y_j - \frac{Y_j}{A_j} \prod_{i=1}^{N} \left(\frac{P_i}{\beta_{j,i}}\right)^{\beta_{j,i}} \prod_{f=1}^{F} \left(\frac{R_f}{\gamma_{j,f}}\right)^{\gamma_{j,f}} \qquad (5.10)\end{aligned}$$

Finally, the income balance condition in equation (5.4) can be transformed into the excess income which measures the difference of total expenditure and the scalar income $\overline{M}$ of the representative consumer:

$$\Delta^m = \sum_{f=1}^{F} R_f E_f - \overline{M} \tag{5.11}$$

Vectors (5.8)–(5.11) formulate $2N + F + 1$ equations in $2N + F$ unknowns: N industry output levels, $\mathbf{Y} = [Y_1, Y_2, \ldots, Y_N]$, N commodity prices, $\mathbf{P} = [P_1, P_2, \ldots, P_N]$, and F primary factor prices, $\mathbf{R} = [R_1, R_2, \ldots, R_F]$. The general equilibrium is therefore the joint solution to these $2N + F + 1$ equations. This process can be reformulated as solving a mixture of the following complementarity problem (as defined in Table 5.1):

$$\begin{aligned} &\mathbf{V} \geq 0 \\ &\text{s.t.} \quad \psi(\mathbf{V}) \leq 0, \mathbf{V}'\psi(\mathbf{V}) = 0 \end{aligned} \tag{5.12}$$

where $\mathbf{V} = [\mathbf{Y}, \mathbf{P}, \mathbf{R}]'$ is the vector of commodity prices, primary input prices, quantities of commodity and income levels. $\psi(V) = [\mathbf{\Delta}^C, \mathbf{\Delta}^F, \mathbf{\Delta}^\pi \, \Delta^m]$ is a system of equations from (5.8)–(5.11). This complementarity problem is summarised in Table 5.2.

Therefore, problem (5.12) is an extended representation of Walras' law with the presence of firms and production. As the system of equations (5.8)–(5.11) is homogeneous of degree 0 in prices, once a nominal vector (**P**, **R**) is identified to solve the problem (5.12), then (λ**P**, λ**R**) should also be the solution to it for any constant λ. Therefore, only relative nominal values matter in solving a general equilibrium model. In other words, the model displays "neutrality of money" (Robinson and Lofgren 2005).

Table 5.1 Complementarity problem

A general equilibrium model can be formulated as a square system of weak inequalities, each with an associated non-negative variable. This is referred to as a **complementarity problem** in mathematics, and the associated variables are referred to as complementary variables.

For example, if a zero-profit condition holds as a strict inequality in equilibrium, profits for that activity are negative, thus that good will not be produced. So the complementary variable to a zero-profit condition is the quantity of the activity level. Take the profit of the jth product as an example as shown in equation (5.10):

Inequality: $\Delta_j^\pi = P_j Y_j - \sum_{i=1}^{N} P_i G_{j,i} - \sum_{f=1}^{F} R_f E_{j,f} \leq 0$

Associated **complementary variable**: Y_j

Complementary form: $Y_j \Delta_j^\pi = 0$

Table 5.2 A sketch of the complementarity problem (5.12)

Inequality	*Variable*	*Dimension*
$\Delta_j^C = \sum_{i=1}^{N}\left[\frac{Y_j\beta_{j,i}}{A_jP_i}\prod_{i=1}^{N}\left(\frac{P_i}{\beta_{j,i}}\right)^{\beta_{j,i}}\prod_{f=1}^{F}\left(\frac{R_f}{\gamma_{j,f}}\right)^{\gamma_{j,f}}\right]+\frac{\alpha_j M}{P_j}-Y_j$	P_j	N
$\Delta_f^F = \sum_{j=1}^{N}\left[\frac{Y_j\gamma_{j,f}}{A_jP_f}\prod_{i=1}^{N}\left(\frac{P_i}{\beta_{j,i}}\right)^{\beta_{j,i}}\prod_{f=1}^{F}\left(\frac{R_f}{\gamma_{j,f}}\right)^{\gamma_{j,f}}\right]-\overline{E}_f$	R_f	F
$\Delta_j^\pi = P_jY_j - \frac{Y_j}{A_j}\prod_{i=1}^{N}\left(\frac{P_i}{\beta_{j,i}}\right)^{\beta_{j,i}}\prod_{f=1}^{F}\left(\frac{R_f}{\gamma_{j,f}}\right)^{\gamma_{j,f}}$	Y_j	N

So when the price for a certain good or primary factor is chosen as a numéraire, e.g. $P_1 = 1$, all other nominal variables can be defined relative to the numéraire, e.g. $P_2' = P_2/P_1, \ldots, P_N' = P_N/P_1$. In CGE modelling, if a numéraire is not specified, prices obtained from different simulations are not directly comparable as they can be the base values (**P**, **R**) simultaneously multiplied by an arbitrary scalar ($\lambda\mathbf{P}$, $\lambda\mathbf{R}$). To avoid this problem, one must specify a price as numéraire and fix it at a constant value (normally 1) throughout all simulations, so that simulation results can be compared.

Theoretically any price can be taken as the numéraire, e.g. labour wage, nominal exchange rate and domestic price index. Prices obtained from a simulation may be different dependent on the choice of the numéraire, but no quantities are affected by it. Choosing the exchange rate as the numéraire does not imply a fixed exchange rate regime. Similarly, choosing the domestic consumer's price as the numéraire does not imply zero inflation. To design a fixed real exchange rate we have to put one more constraint on the exchange rate, i.e. fix the ratio of exchange rate to domestic price index.

Labour and capital markets

Classic CGE models usually assume full employment of primary factors of production (labour and capital) so that the economy always functions at full capacity. The product prices and factor prices adjust so that all factor markets clear, i.e. there is no excess supply or demand of factors.

The supply of various types of labour (e.g. skilled and unskilled) can be assumed to be fixed in a static model so that the total labour supply as a sum of these is also fixed. Constrained by their sector-specific skills and experience, labour can also be assumed to be imperfectly mobile across sectors in the short run, subject to certain constant elasticity of transformation functions.

Similarly, the total supply of capital can also be assumed fixed in a static model. Usually capital is treated as a homogenous factor and does not need to be further disaggregated into different types. But as capital is associated with ownership, entrepreneurship and sector-specific factors in the real economy, capital can also be assumed imperfectly mobile across sectors in the short run. Foreign direct investment can be introduced into a CGE model as an increment to the capital stock invested by a representative agent for multinational enterprises.

There are also two alternatives in terms of capital supply (Bussolo and Round 2003). The first is to fix the savings rate so that the change in capital stock will be proportionate to the change in GDP ("savings-driven"). The second is to keep the savings rate endogenous, so that a target real return on capital is achieved and maintained ("investment-driven"). These two options concern the relationship between investment and savings, and will also soon be addressed in this chapter.

The above full-employment and imperfect-mobility assumptions are suitable in the short run only. In the long run, it is usually more appropriate to assume that both capital and labour are freely mobile across sectors and that there exists slack capacity in the economy so that wage and capital rental are maintained at stable levels (Bussolo and Round 2003).

Model closure

In CGE modelling, modellers often need to incorporate macroeconomic mechanisms (e.g. government activities, international trade and foreign exchange) into general equilibrium models by including some variables that are central to policy considerations. Closure rules refer to how endogenous microeconomic price and quantity variables are constrained by exogenous macroeconomic balances.

Sen (1963) was the first economist to identify the necessity of closure rule in applied general equilibrium modelling with macroeconomic variables. He found that it would be impossible to warrant the *ex post* identity between savings and investment if some market equilibrium conditions have to be imposed on the model simultaneously. Therefore, in order to find a reasonable solution for a CGE model with macroeconomic variables, one of the conditions must be relaxed. Choosing a "closure rule" means deciding which of the conditions should be relaxed. In other words, a closure rule is a modified balancing constraint that does not necessarily represent a market equilibrium condition (Ginsburgh and Keyzer 1997). The design of closure rules is crucial to CGE modelling, in that it affects the model structure, simulation results and policy conclusions (Whalley and Yeung 1984; Dewatripont and Michel 1987; Bussolo and Round 2003; Robinson and Lofgren 2005).

Generally there are three types of macroeconomic closure rules that need to be designed by CGE modellers: government closure dealing with government behaviour; savings–investment closure for the determination of savings and investment; and external closure for current account and exchange rate regime. Each of the above three types of closure rules contains a variety of alternatives, the most commonly applied of which are outlined in Table 5.3.

Government closure

Government is generally modelled in CGE models as an agent collecting taxes, allocating transfer payments, and purchasing goods and services. There are a

Table 5.3 Alternative macroeconomic closures

Government	*Savings–investment*	*External*
• Fixed government savings or spending • Fixed government savings rate with respect to GDP • Fixed real government consumption and subsidy • Utility-maximising agent	• Savings-driven • Investment-driven	• Large/small open economy • Current account balance • Floating or fixed exchange rate

Source: Löfgren *et al.* (2002).

variety of choices to deal with government revenue and expenditure as well as government savings (surplus) or borrowing (deficit).

The first option is that the ratio of fiscal expenditure to GDP is maintained at a fixed level by introducing an endogenous tax variable. This policy design would reflect the government's target of maintaining a relatively stable level of economic intervention.

The target magnitude of fiscal savings (borrowings) can also be taken into consideration in the the government closure. For example, it could also be desirable to fix the level of government savings (borrowings), by forcing government spending and revenue to move in tandem. More realistically, we can also fix the fiscal savings (borrowings) rate with respect to GDP at a target level. This closure rule is pertinent to some countries whose political stability is easily threatened by inflationary pressure. For example, all European Union member states must abide by the Stability and Growth Pact, which requires the annual budget deficit no higher than 3 per cent of GDP. The above two "fiscal neutral" settings on fiscal savings (borrowings) will transmit any pressure of external shock impacting government expenditure directly to taxpayers.

There are also alternative government balance closure rules related to poverty-relieving policies. For example, both government consumption and subsidy can be fixed in real terms to guarantee stable poverty-relieving efforts, and government revenue comes from fixed tax rates. Thus the government savings (borrowings) are determined as a residual which is equal to the difference between variable government expenditure and revenue.

Finally, we can also treat government as analogous to a private representative utility-maximising agent (Shoven and Whalley 1992). In this case the government has a utility function determining government demand and the government meets its demand subject to its fiscal constraint.

The instrument by which the government reaches its closure target is also important. With any of the above fixed savings and/or consumption targets, the government can balance its budget by a variety of measures. Using a non-distortionary lump-sum transfer is often suitable if the distortionary costs of tax changes need to be separated from the costs or benefits of the simulation being imposed. Using a tax rate (e.g. an income tax) to meet the government's budget balance is often more suitable in practice.

Savings–investment closure

Savings–investment closure refers to the mechanism for generating savings and investment. It is either savings-driven (the value of investment adjusts endogenously) or investment-driven (the value of savings adjusts endogenously). Savings-driven closure fixes all non-government saving rates and scales investment demand so that investment spending equals savings. A standard investment-driven closure fixes real investment quantities and adjusts the savings rate of households endogenously.

External closure

External closure for CGE models with export and import activities concerns three basic questions: (a) whether the country modelled is large; (b) how the current account balance (foreign savings) is treated; and (c) whether the foreign exchange rate is flexible.

For a small open economy, its economy scale is so small that it has no monopolistic power to influence its export or import prices. Under such an assumption, we need to fix the export and import prices at which this country engages in transactions with the rest of the world. But under the large open economy assumption, the export and import prices on the world market need to change endogenously with the changes of the economy's exports and imports.

As for the current account balance, the most widely adopted solution for the current account balance is to fix the balance as an exogenous parameter in the modelling. This implies that modellers need to force both exports and imports to change with the same magnitude, and in the same direction (Robinson and Lofgren 2005).

Another equilibrium variable which is also integral to open economy modelling is foreign exchange rate, which is the relative price of commodities in international markets and commodities consumed in the domestic market. Fixed exchange rate closure means that this price has to be fixed relative to a certain domestic price index, while the flexible exchange rate closure lets this price be freely determined by the current account balance. Under a flexible exchange rate regime, an increase in current account surplus suggests a relatively higher demand for domestically manufactured commodities. This raises the relative prices of domestic commodities and leads to an appreciation (decrease) in real exchange rate (Robinson and Lofgren 2005).

Data

Input–output table

An input–output table contains information on transactions within and between production sectors and non-production sectors. It represents the value of transactions in a given year. The demand for marketed goods and services is disaggregated into two blocks, namely intermediate demand by producers and final demand by households, government and external markets. On the input side, total input is divided into intermediate input and value added. The value-added items include, *inter alia*, employment compensation, net taxes and depreciation. As Table 5.4 shows, an input–output table can be broken down into three blocks. Block $\overline{\mathbf{G}}$ captures the detailed intermediate input and demand presented by $N \times N$ inter-industry and intra-industry transactions. The entry $\overline{G}_{i,j}$ measures how much output of sector i is used by sector j. Block $\overline{\mathbf{X}}$ displays the final demand for each of the N industries, while block $\overline{\mathbf{E}}$ contains the value-added items for each of the N industries.

An input–output table provides an ideal dataset for CGE modelling as it represents a "balanced" economy characterised by goods and factor market clearance, zero profit and income balance. In Table 5.3, the row sum of any sector i in block $\overline{\mathbf{G}}$ and $\overline{\mathbf{X}}$ is equal to the total output in the corresponding sector, $\overline{Y}_j$. This stands for the goods market clearance, which is what equation (5.1) conveys. The column sum of block $\overline{\mathbf{E}}$ is equal to the total factor endowment of the corresponding factor supplier, E_f, which implies the factor market clearance condition as shown in equation (5.2). The sum for any column in block $\overline{\mathbf{G}}$ and $\overline{\mathbf{E}}$ is the total value of intermediate inputs and value added from primary inputs. This is equal to the gross value of output, which is exactly the zero-profit condition in equation (5.3). Finally, the sums of all the elements of block $\overline{\mathbf{X}}$ and $\overline{\mathbf{E}}$ should be equal, which means that the total factor endowment should be exhausted. This implies income balance, as stated in equation (5.5).

Social accounting matrix

While an input–output table only shows the relationship between production accounts and non-production accounts, an extended form of input–output table, the social accounting matrix (SAM), includes information on all transactions within and between all accounts. That is to say, the blank area below block $\overline{\mathbf{X}}$ in Table 5.4 can be filled in with new information on transactions among non-production sectors in a SAM.

Table 5.5 provides an example of the standard form of a SAM. Apart from the addition of transactions among non-production sectors, a SAM has two more special features. Firstly, there is a distinction between "activities" and "commodities". While the "activities" accounts represent the production sectors, the "commodities" accounts combine domestic supply with imports to generate a total supply to the domestic market, usually following the Armington assumption which specifies product differentiation by country of origin (Armington 1969), as illustrated in Figure 5.4. Secondly, there is a separate "capital" account which can be treated as an investment bank collecting savings from households, government and the rest of the world, and spending them on investment goods.

There is an important analogy of a balanced input–output table and SAM. For a balanced input–output table, the row sum is always equal to the column sum for

Table 5.4 Basic structure of an input–output table

Total inputs	*Total demand*								*Total output*
	Intermediate demand			*Final demand*					
	Industry 1	. . .	*Industry N*	*Households*	*Government*	*Export*	. . .	*Change in inventories*	
Intermediate input									
Industry 1									$\overline{Y}_1$
. . .		$\overline{\mathbf{G}}$				$\overline{\mathbf{X}}$	⋮		
Industry N									$\overline{Y}_N$
Value added									
Net taxes									$\bar{E}_1$
Wages									
. . .		$\overline{\mathbf{E}}$							⋮
Depreciation									
Operating surplus									$\bar{E}_F$
Total inputs	$\overline{Y}_1$	. . .	$\overline{Y}_N$	$\overline{X}_1$	. . .			$\overline{X}_D$	

Table 5.5 Basic structure of a social accounting matrix

Receipts	*Expenditures*							
			Factors		*Institutions*		*Capital account*	*Rest of the world*
	Commodities	*Activities*	*Labour*	*Capital*	*Households*	*Government*		
Activities		Domestic commodity supply				Export subsidy		
Commodities	Intermediate inputs				Private consumption	Government consumption	Investment	
Factors								
Labour	Wages							
Capital	Rentals							
Institutions								
Households			Labour income	Capital income		Transfers		Capital flow
Government	Indirect taxes	Tariffs			Direct taxes			
Capital account					Private saving	Government saving		
Rest of the world		Imports				Reserve accumulation		
Totals	Total costs	Total absorption	Factor income	Factor income	Household income	Government expenditure	Investment	Foreign exchange flow

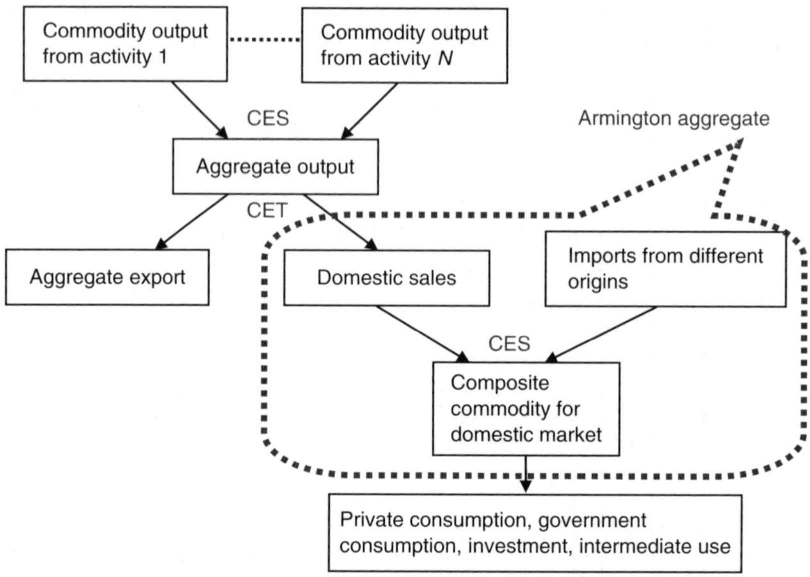

Figure 5.4 Flows of commodities and Armington aggregation.
Source: Löfgren *et al.* (2002).

each production sector, which represents the balance between production input and output. In a balanced SAM, the row sum for every "activity", "commodity", "factor", "institution" and "capital account" is equal to the associated column sum respectively, perfectly reflecting the goods and value flows at equilibrium.

The choice between an input–output table and a SAM is dependent on data availability and the purpose of the CGE research. For research focused on consumption, poverty, or any phenomenon directly related to household behaviour, a SAM is integral to the modelling, as the SAM has information on the transactions among non-production sectors. However, for multinational or global economic research where a full set of information on transactions among non-production sectors is not available, input–output tables can be used in place of SAMs. For example, the core datasets of the widely employed Global Trade Analysis Project database (Hertel 1997) are mainly input–output tables rather than SAMs (Walmsley and Lakatos 2008). Input–output tables are also suitable for other types of CGE models whose main concern is with the production rather than the consumption side.

Calibration and "calibrated forms" of a CES economy

Calibration of a CES economy

Calibration is an essential step in CGE modelling to make sure that the model equations designed can replicate a balanced benchmark economy (Mansur and

Whalley 1984; Shoven and Whalley 1984). Apart from selecting existing parameters from the econometric estimates from the same time period, this requires calculation of other necessary parameters with the model equations and benchmark dataset.

In calculating the parameters, all prices should be treated as unity and thus all value flows in the input–output table or SAM can be regarded as benchmark quantities. With these parameters and those selected from econometric estimates in the literature, solving problem (5.12) will then make the quantities of variables equal to the corresponding values in the benchmark dataset, thus replicating the benchmark equilibrium.

For a CES function as specified by equation (5.6), or equivalently by denoting $\sigma_j = 1/(1-\rho_j)$:

$$Y_j = A_j \left(\sum_{i=1}^{N} \delta_{j,i} X_{j,i}^{(\sigma_j - 1)/\sigma_j} \right)^{\sigma_j/(\sigma_j - 1)}, \quad \text{with} \sum_{i=1}^{N} \delta_{j,i} = 1 \tag{5.6a}$$

only A_j and $\delta_{j,i}$ can be calibrated. The elasticity of substitution σ_j should be exogenously selected by estimation or directly from the literature since an economy at the benchmark equilibrium only has information on price and quantity levels (Shoven and Whalley 1984).

The marginal revenue product (MRP) of the ith input $X_{j,i}$ in the jth output Y_j is then equal to the price of the ith input:

$$\begin{aligned} P_j \times \frac{\partial Y_j}{\partial X_{j,i}} &= P_j \times A_j \frac{\sigma_j}{\sigma_j - 1} \left(\sum_{i=1}^{N} \delta_{j,i} X_{j,i}^{(\sigma_j - 1)/\sigma_j} \right)^{1/(\sigma_j - 1)} \\ &\quad \times \alpha_{j,i} \frac{\sigma_j - 1}{\sigma_j} X_{j,i}^{-1/\sigma_j} \\ &= P_j \times Y_j^{1/\sigma_j} \alpha_{j,i} X_{j,i}^{-1/\sigma_j} A_j^{\rho_j - 1/\sigma_j} \\ &= P_j \times A_j^{(\sigma_j - 1)/\sigma_j} \delta_{j,i} \left(\frac{Y_j}{X_{j,i}} \right)^{1/\sigma_j} = P_i \end{aligned} \tag{5.13}$$

Similarly, the *MRP* of Y_j of the kth input $X_{j,k}$ is equal to the price of $X_{j,k}$:

$$P_j \times A_j^{(\sigma_j - 1)/\sigma_j} \delta_{j,k} \left(\frac{Y_j}{X_{j,k}} \right)^{1/\sigma_j} = P_k \tag{5.14}$$

Dividing (5.13) by (5.14) gives the quantity of one input in terms of the other:

$$X_{j,k} = X_{j,i} \left(\frac{\delta_{j,k} P_i}{\delta_{j,i} P_k} \right)^{\sigma_j} \tag{5.15}$$

Equation (5.15) can be transformed with benchmark values $(\overline{X}, \overline{P})$ from the input–output table (in Table 5.3):

$$\overline{X}_{j,k} = \overline{X}_{j,i}\left(\frac{\delta_{j,k}\overline{P_i}}{\delta_{j,i}\overline{P_k}}\right)^{\sigma_j}$$

$$\delta_{j,k} = \delta_{j,i}\frac{\overline{P_k}}{\overline{P_i}}\left(\frac{\overline{X}_{j,k}}{\overline{X}_{j,i}}\right)^{1/\sigma_j}$$

Since $\sum_{k=1}^{N}\delta_{j,k} = 1$,

$$\sum_{k=1}^{N}\delta_{j,i}\frac{\overline{P_k}}{\overline{P_i}}\left(\frac{\overline{X}_{j,k}}{\overline{X}_{j,i}}\right)^{1/\sigma_j} = \delta_{j,i}\frac{\sum_{k=1}^{N}\overline{P_k}(\overline{X}_{j,k})^{1/\sigma_j}}{\overline{P_i}\,\overline{X}_{j,i}^{1/\sigma_j}} = 1$$

$$\delta_{j,i} = \frac{\overline{P_i}\,\overline{X}_{j,i}^{1/\sigma_j}}{\sum_{k=1}^{N}\overline{P_k}(\overline{X}_{j,k})^{1/\sigma_j}} \tag{5.16}$$

With the calibrated value of $\delta_{j,i}$, A_j can then be derived by rearranging equation (5.6a):

$$A_j = \frac{\overline{Y_j}}{(\sum_{i=1}^{N}\delta_{j,i}\overline{X}_{j,i}^{(\sigma_j-1)/\sigma_j})^{\sigma_j/(\sigma_j-1)}} \tag{5.17}$$

With the calibrated parameter values of $(A_j, \delta_{j,i})$ and selected parameter values of (σ_j), a CGE model can solve the counterfactual results of $(X_{j,i}, Y_j, P_j, P_{j,i})$ when an external policy shock is introduced into the model.

"Calibrated forms" of CES functions

In CGE counterfactual simulations, an alternative algorithm, the "calibrated form" of CES functions, can be employed to replace the complicated and error-prone calibration procedures with more elegant and intuitive specifications (Rutherford 1995; Blake *et al.* 1999).

We need to specify a certain input as a function of the total output first. With the zero-profit condition:

$$P_jY_j = \sum_{k=1}^{N}P_kX_{j,k} = \sum_{k=1}^{N}P_kX_{j,i}\left(\frac{\delta_{j,k}P_i}{\delta_{j,i}P_k}\right)^{\sigma_j}$$

$$= X_{j,i}\left(\frac{P_i}{\delta_{j,i}}\right)^{\sigma_j}\sum_{k=1}^{N}P_k\left(\frac{\delta_{j,k}}{P_k}\right)^{\sigma_j} = X_{j,i}\left(\frac{P_i}{\delta_{j,i}}\right)^{\rho_j}\sum_{k=1}^{N}\delta_{j,k}^{\sigma_j}P_k^{1-\sigma_j}$$

$$X_{j,i} = P_j Y_j \left(\frac{\delta_{j,i}}{P_i}\right)^{\sigma_j} \Big/ \sum_{k=1}^{N} \delta_{j,k}^{\sigma_j} P_k^{1-\sigma_j} = P_j Y_j \left(\frac{\delta_{j,i}}{P_i}\right)^{\sigma_j} \Big/ \sum_{i=1}^{N} \delta_{j,i}^{\sigma_j} P_i^{1-\sigma_j} \tag{5.18}$$

Since equation (5.18) only contains four variables – the prices and quantities of an input and total output – if we replace the $X_{j,i}$ in equation (5.18) with that in equation (5.6a) and eliminate Y_j, we can derive the relationship between input price and output price. With equations (5.6a) and (5.18):

$$\begin{aligned}
Y_j &= A_j \left(\sum_{i=1}^{N} \delta_{j,i} \left(\frac{P_j Y_j (\delta_{j,i}/P_i)^{\sigma_j}}{\sum_{i=1}^{N} \delta_{j,i}^{\sigma_j} P_i^{1-\sigma_j}} \right)^{(\sigma_j-1)/\sigma_j} \right)^{\sigma_j/(\sigma_j-1)} \\
&= A_j \left(\left(\frac{P_j Y_j}{\sum_{i=1}^{N} \delta_{j,i}^{\sigma_j} P_i^{1-\sigma_j}} \right)^{(\sigma_j-1)/\sigma_j} \times \sum_{i=1}^{N} \delta_{j,i} \left(\frac{\delta_{j,i}}{P_i} \right)^{(\sigma_j-1)} \right)^{\sigma_j/(\sigma_j-1)} \\
&= A_j \frac{P_j Y_j}{\sum_{i=1}^{N} \delta_{j,i}^{\sigma_j} P_i^{1-\sigma_j}} \left(\sum_{i=1}^{N} \delta_{j,i}^{\sigma_j} P_i^{1-\sigma_j} \right)^{\sigma_j/(\sigma_j-1)} \\
&= A_j P_j Y_j \left(\sum_{i=1}^{N} \delta_{j,i}^{\sigma_j} P_i^{1-\sigma_j} \right)^{1/(\sigma_j-1)}
\end{aligned}$$

By eliminating Y_j from both sides, we get a unit cost function:

$$P_j = \frac{1}{A_j} \left(\sum_{i=1}^{N} \delta_{j,i}^{\sigma_j} P_i^{1-\sigma_j} \right)^{1/(1-\sigma_j)} \tag{5.19}$$

Calibrated form of quantity

With equation (5.17),

$$Y_j = A_j \left(\sum_{i=1}^{N} \delta_{j,i} X_{j,i}^{(\sigma_j-1)/\sigma_j} \right)^{\sigma_j/(\sigma_j-1)} = \frac{\left(\sum_{i=1}^{N} \delta_{j,i} X_{j,i}^{(\sigma_j-1)/\sigma_j}\right)^{\sigma_j/(\sigma_j-1)}}{\left(\sum_{i=1}^{N} \delta_{j,i} \overline{X}_{j,i}^{(\sigma_j-1)/\sigma_j}\right)^{\sigma_j/(\sigma_j-1)}} \overline{Y}_j$$

With equation (5.16), the above equation can be transformed into

$$\begin{aligned}
Y_j &= \overline{Y}_j \left(\frac{\sum_{i=1}^{N} \delta_{j,i} X_{j,i}^{(\sigma_j-1)/\sigma_j}}{\sum_{i=1}^{N} \delta_{j,i} \overline{X}_{j,i}^{(\sigma_j-1)/\sigma_j}} \right)^{\sigma_j/(\sigma_j-1)} \\
&= \left(\frac{\sum_{i=1}^{N} \left(\frac{\bar{P}_i \bar{X}_{j,i}^{1/\sigma_j}}{\sum_{k=1}^{N} \bar{P}_k (\bar{X}_{j,k})^{1/\sigma_j}} X_{j,i}^{(\sigma_j-1)/\sigma_j} \right)}{\sum_{i=1}^{N} \left(\frac{\bar{P}_i \bar{X}_{j,i}^{1/\sigma_j}}{\sum_{k=1}^{N} \bar{P}_k (\bar{X}_{j,k})^{1/\sigma_j}} \bar{X}_{j,i}^{(\sigma_j-1)/\sigma_j} \right)} \right)^{\sigma_j/(\sigma_j-1)} \times \overline{Y}_j
\end{aligned}$$

$$= \overline{Y}_j \left(\frac{\sum_{i=1}^{N} (\overline{P}_i \overline{X}_{j,i}^{1/\sigma_j} \times X_{j,i}^{(\sigma_j-1)/\sigma_j})}{\sum_{i=1}^{N} (\overline{P}_i \overline{X}_{j,i}^{1/\sigma_j} \times \overline{X}_{j,i}^{(\sigma_j-1)/\sigma_j})} \right)^{\sigma_j/(\sigma_j-1)}$$

$$= \overline{Y}_j \left(\frac{\sum_{i=1}^{N} (\overline{P}_i \overline{X}_{j,i}^{1/\sigma_j} \times (X_{j,i}/X_{j,i})^{1/\sigma_j} \times X_{j,i}^{(\sigma_j-1)/\sigma_j})}{\sum_{i=1}^{N} \overline{P}_i \overline{X}_{j,i}} \right)^{\sigma_j/(\sigma_j-1)}$$

$$= \overline{Y}_j \left(\frac{\sum_{i=1}^{N} (\overline{P}_i (\overline{X}_{j,i}/X_{j,i})^{1/\sigma_j} \times X_{j,i})}{\sum_{i=1}^{N} \overline{P}_i \overline{X}_{j,i}} \right)^{\sigma_j/(\sigma_j-1)}$$

$$= \overline{Y}_j \left(\frac{\sum_{i=1}^{N} (\overline{P}_i \times (\overline{X}_{j,i}/\overline{X}_{j,i}) \times (\overline{X}_{j,i}/X_{j,i})^{1/\sigma_j} \times X_{j,i})}{\sum_{i=1}^{N} \overline{P}_i \overline{X}_{j,i}} \right)^{\sigma_j/(\sigma_j-1)}$$

$$= \overline{Y}_j \left(\frac{\sum_{i=1}^{N} (\overline{P}_i \overline{X}_{j,i} \times (X_{j,i}/\overline{X}_{j,i})^{(\sigma_j-1)/\sigma_j})}{\sum_{i=1}^{N} \overline{P}_i \overline{X}_{j,i}} \right)^{\sigma_j/(\sigma_j-1)}$$

$$= \overline{Y}_j \left(\sum_{i=1}^{N} \left(\frac{\overline{P}_i \overline{X}_{j,i}}{\sum_{i=1}^{N} \overline{P}_i \overline{X}_{j,i}} \times \left(\frac{X_{j,i}}{\overline{X}_{j,i}} \right)^{(\sigma_j-1)/\sigma_j} \right) \right)^{\sigma_j/(\sigma_j-1)}$$

$$= \overline{Y}_i \left(\sum_{i=1}^{N} \left(\theta_{j,i} \times \left(\frac{X_{j,i}}{\overline{X}_{j,i}} \right)^{(\sigma_j-1)/\sigma_j} \right) \right)^{\sigma_j/(\sigma_j-1)}$$

where $\theta_{j,i}$ denotes the cost share of the ith input in product value. Replace the upper case variables with lower case ones which represent the ratios to the benchmark quantities (i.e. $y_j = Y_j/\overline{Y}_j$ and $x_j = X_{j,i}/\overline{X}_{j,i}$):

$$y_j = \left(\sum_{i=1}^{N} \theta_{j,i} x_{j,i}^{(\sigma_j-1)/\sigma_j} \right)^{\sigma_j/(\sigma_j-1)} \tag{5.6b}$$

With equation (5.6b), it would be faster to solve for the values of y_j and $x_{j,i}$ in counterfactual scenarios. Then new values of outputs and inputs can be obtained by multiplying these ratios with the associated benchmark values. We can see that there is no need to calibrate the parameters here. Equation (5.6b) exhibits elegance and conciseness compared to equation (5.6a).

Calibrated form of prices

Substituting $\alpha_{j,i}$, A_j in equation (5.19) with the specifications in equations (5.16) and (5.17) and follow similar procedures, we can obtain the relationship between multiples of output price and input price:

$$p_j = \left(\sum_{i=1}^{N} \theta_{j,i} p_i^{1-\sigma_j} \right)^{1/(1-\sigma_j)} \tag{5.19a}$$

This specification also applies to the CET production functions specified as (5.7).

Calibrated form of input demand

Using equation (5.16), we can obtain an equation to capture the relationship between output and input demand from equation (5.19) as well:

$$x_{j,i} = y_j \left(\frac{p_j}{p_i} \right)^{\sigma_j} \tag{5.18a}$$

For a CET production function specified by equation (5.7), the calibrated share form of output supply is similar to equation (5.18a):

$$y_{j,i} = x_j \left(\frac{p_j}{p_i} \right)^{1/(1-\tau_j)} \tag{5.18b}$$

Extensions with $\sigma_j \to 1$

Nonetheless, for the case of $\sigma_j = 1$, an extension to equations (5.6b) and (5.19a) with calibrated form is necessary. Otherwise they will collapse as $1/(1-\sigma_j)$ is undefined when $\sigma_j = 1$.

We can obtain a logarithmic form of equation (5.19a),

$$\ln p_j = \frac{\ln(\sum_{i-1}^{N} \theta_{j,i} p_i^{1-\sigma_j})}{1-\sigma_j}$$

When σ_j approaches 1, both numerator and denominator of the equation above approach zero. L'Hôspital's rule therefore applies:

$$\begin{aligned}
\lim_{\sigma_j \to 1} (\ln p_j) &= \lim_{\rho_j \to 0} \frac{\partial(\ln(\sum_{i-1}^{N} \theta_{j,i} p_i^{1-\sigma_j}))/\partial\sigma_j}{\partial(1-\sigma_j)/\partial\sigma_j} \\
&= \lim_{\rho_j \to 0} \frac{\sum_{i-1}^{N} \theta_{j,i} p_i^{1-\sigma_j} (\ln p_i) \times (-1)}{(-1) \times \sum_{i-1}^{N} \theta_{j,i} p_i^{1-\sigma_j}} \\
&= \frac{\sum_{i-1}^{N} \theta_{j,i} \ln p_i}{\sum_{i-1}^{N} \theta_{j,i}} = \sum_{i=1}^{N} \ln p_i^{\theta_{j,i}} = \ln \prod_{i=1}^{N} p_i^{\theta_{j,i}}
\end{aligned}$$

Thus, when $\sigma_j \to 1$, equation (5.19a) is transformed onto its "Cobb–Douglas counterpart":

$$p_j = \prod_{i=1}^{N} p_i^{\theta_{j,i}} \tag{5.19b}$$

For equation (5.6b), when $\sigma_j \rightarrow 1$, we can get its "Cobb–Douglas form" with L'Hôspital's rule as well:

$$y_j = \prod_{i=1}^{N} x_{j,i}^{\theta_{j,i}/\sigma_j} \tag{5.6c}$$

With equations (5.6b), (5.18a), (5.19a) and (5.19b), most equations of a CGE model can be listed succinctly. Actually, all of the generalised "production" functions (e.g. Armington aggregate, export and import, labour and capital disaggregation) can be expressed in (5.18a) and (5.19a, 5.19b) forms. These functions, together with the associated variables and parameters, can then be used to derive the income balance equations, demand–supply equilibrium equations and zero-profit conditions, which provide a more parsimonious specification of a general equilibrium analysis. These "calibrated forms" will be heavily used in Chapter 7 where a benchmark CGE model for the Chinese economy is constructed.

A flowchart of CGE modelling

CGE model construction typically consists of a sequence of steps such as model design, data collection and compilation, model benchmark checking and counterfactual simulation (see Figure 5.5).

First of all, a reasonable and feasible model framework should be built up. Besides the basic equations for standard production and consumption, special specifications should be designed to accommodate different features of the research project. The model should be flexibly designed so that the efforts can be focused on the major research topic. For example, a CGE model designed to examine the productivity spillover effects in manufacturing sectors should avoid using complex nested production functions for services sectors.

Then basic datasets for a benchmark year should be collected. These include an input–output table or SAM, tax data and trade data. After the data have been manipulated for mutual consistency, they can be used in computer programming to calibrate the benchmark equilibrium.

Counterfactual policy shocks are simulated to estimate the impact on the whole economy, the results of which need to be compared with the benchmark scenario for policy appraisal.

Software

More and more powerful computer software has helped CGE modellers to be able to solve problems and arrive at insights that they would have not been able to achieve otherwise. It has dramatically changed, extended and deepened the research agenda of CGE modellers (Markusen 2002b, p. 346). Among many software packages such as GEMPACK, MATLAB, C++ and EViews with which a CGE model can be coded and implemented, GAMS (General Algebraic Modeling System) and its subsystem MPSGE (Mathematical Programming System for

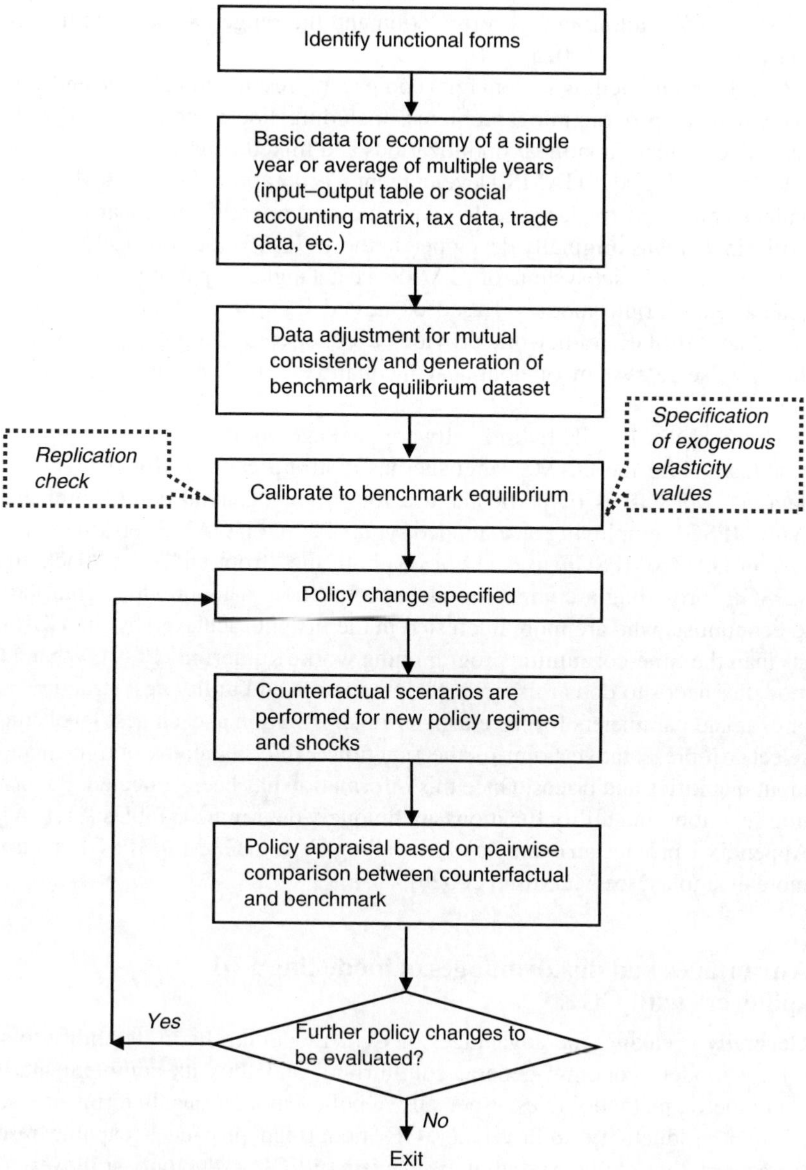

Figure 5.5 A flowchart of CGE modelling.

Source: Modified from Shoven and Whalley (1984).

General Equilibrium Analysis) help CGE economists focus on the model design work with a higher-level programming platform. Software packages other than GAMS/MPSGE generally do not allow the user to solve complementarity problems, greatly limiting model formulation and the range of questions that can be analysed (Markusen 2002a, p. 4).

GAMS is a modelling system for a compact representation of large and complex mathematical programming problems, including linear, nonlinear, mixed integer, mixed integer nonlinear optimizations and mixed complementarity problems (McCarl *et al.* 2007; GAMS Development Corporation 2008). GAMS has been widely employed for large-scale economic and operational research modelling work since it was originally developed in the 1970s (Rutherford 1999).

MPSGE, as a subsystem of GAMS, is a language particularly tailored for general equilibrium models. Based on nested CES production and utility functions, an MPSGE framework provides a concise modelling representation for the large-scale system of nonlinear inequalities which are the core of a CGE model.

The GAMS/MPSGE hybrid software package combines the strength of both systems. While the GAMS language has a strong capacity for managing large datasets, MPSGE is of particular use for solving general equilibrium models. With MPSGE employing an extended syntax based on GAMS sets, the integrated system GAMS/MPSGE uses GAMS as both the "front end" and "back end" to MPSGE, providing a compact model specification. This provides great benefits to economists who are more interested in the insights achieved by the CGE models than the time-consuming programming work (Rutherford 1999). What a CGE modeller needs to do is to specify the production and utility nest structure, select or estimate parameters for the elasticity of substitution at each nest level and then select a representative point of the functions which contains output quantities, input quantities and prices. Once this information has been collected, the production functions and utility functions are uniquely determined. Tables A1.1–A1.5 in Appendix 1 provide an example of modelling CGE in GAMS/MPSGE syntax (for more examples, see Markusen 2002b).

Advantages and disadvantages of modelling FDI spillovers with CGE

Generally speaking, the advantages of CGE modelling lie in its ability to structurally model economic general equilibrium, and thus its complementarity to econometric methodologies, especially in policy simulations. In terms of research on FDI productivity spillover, a CGE model can provide a capable research framework thanks to the conduit mechanism of FDI productivity spillovers.

First, the input–output table used in a CGE model captures the vertical linkages which generate productivity spillovers. As discussed in Chapter 2, the importance of vertical linkages in FDI productivity spillover are theoretically modelled (e.g. Markusen and Venables 1999; Fosfuri *et al.* 2001) and empirically evident (Javorcik 2004; Girma *et al.* 2008).

Second, export activities of MNE affiliates in host countries, which also provide possibilities for productivity spillover, can be readily explored with a CGE model. The export pattern of FIEs in China merits special attention in studying FDI productivity spillover. FIEs' share of exports in total foreign trade in China has gradually increased from 4 per cent in the early 1980s to over 50 per cent after 2000. These export-oriented MNE affiliates exert a vital demonstration effect on the boom of labour-intensive exporting firms in China, especially in the coastal provinces. A CGE model for China can comprehensively incorporate MNEs' export characteristics.

Third, FDI productivity spillover takes place via many other direct and indirect channels, including labour turnover, demonstration, competition, and induced resource reallocation towards the most productive enterprises. These channels can also be captured by CGE modelling with incorporation of corresponding endogenous variables.

Finally, a CGE model can be constructed to assess FDI spillover effects by examining not only industry-level performance (e.g. output, export and price changes) but also macroeconomic changes (e.g. GDP and national welfare). As a structural model, CGE can also be used to address more interesting issues which other methodologies rarely deal with, such as the impact of FDI policy reforms on FDI productivity spillover effects.

On the other hand, we also need to understand the weakness of CGE in applying a CGE model to doing research on FDI productivity spillover. First, as discussed in Chapters 1 and 2, FDI productivity spillovers are subject to various macro- and micro-level constraints. However, CGE models each industry as a representative agent and can only convey information on these constraints implicitly, in an aggregated way. For example, due to data limitations, the CGE model developed in this research cannot disaggregate the data on FIEs by the origin of FDI, i.e. from Hong Kong, Macau and Taiwan (HMT), or from other economies. However, as suggested in the literature (Buckley *et al.* 2007b), the difference between spillover effects of the FDI from the above two types of countries of origin is not trivial.

Second, the perceived magnitude of FDI spillover effect gauged by a CGE model, by and large, relies on the spillover coefficients selected from the existing econometric literature or based on new econometric estimates. Such a reliance on parameters can pose a dilemma for researchers. The parameters in the literature are usually not estimated for the economies being modelled in the CGE. For example, Lejour *et al.* (2008) had to employ a spillover coefficient value estimated for the USA rather than the EU countries examined in their research. However, if researchers want to estimate spillover parameters with their own econometric models, such an ambition will require further investment in data collection and analysis.

The last drawback is related to the fact that the CGE model in this book is based on the Chinese input–output table of 2002 which is indeed the latest one, yet still somewhat dated. This constraint makes it unlikely to exclude the impact of long-term business cycle on the FDI inflows and the performance of domestic firms. More importantly, since China's accession into WTO in December 2001, the market barriers to foreign commodities and investment have been effectively lowered. The Chinese government has also continued to use policy to channel resources into certain activities, with a view to "promoting investment in high technology, encouraging innovation, and protecting the environment" (World Trade Organization 2008, p. xi).

Conclusions

CGE modelling involves designing a large-scale general equilibrium model across all the industries and implementing computer-based simulations of counterfactual scenarios. CGE models are a class of models that explore the overall economic impact of policy, technology or other external "shocks". The microeconomic foundation for CGE models is Walrasian general equilibrium theory. A CGE model consists of: (a) a series of equations of production, consumption, utility and so on, which cover the whole economy, including the activities of all industries, governments, and households; and (b) a detailed database consistent with the model equations.

As a general-equilibrium model, a CGE model is inappropriate for the analysis of small-scale, sector-specific changes, but is well tailored to the investigation of broadly based policy innovations where inter-region and inter-industry feedbacks and interdependences are important. Most of the applications of CGE fall into the categories of tax and trade policy research and, more recently, resource and environment research.

The simulation work in a CGE model is based on a social accounting matrix or input–output table in a base year. A SAM expands a cross-industry input–output table by incorporating non-production sectors (e.g. households and government) in a more comprehensive way. A SAM or input–output table statistically represents flows of all economic transactions that take place within an economy.

GAMS provides a tailored and powerful higher-level coding platform for CGE modellers. MPSGE, as a subsystem of GAMS, is specially designed for a mix of complementarity problems that are most frequently met in general equilibrium models.

CGE modelling provides a structural research framework on the topic of FDI productivity spillovers and the associated FDI policy assessment. A CGE model can decompose FDI spillovers effects into benefits obtained through different channels, namely vertical linkages, export of MNEs and horizontal demonstration. However, due to the data constraint and the fact that a single year has to be taken as the benchmark year, the reliability of CGE modelling needs to be subject to sensitivity tests.

6 Data compilations

Data sources

Statistical standards in China

The data used in our CGE modelling follow two different statistical standards, making it necessary to identify the mapping between these standards. While version 1994 was the industrial classification adopted in Chinese official statistics between 1994 and 2002, version 2002 is the latest one (see Table 6.1) adopted by the National Bureau of Statistics (NBS) of China after 2002. Version 2002 is convertible to version 3.0 of the International Standard Industrial Classification (ISIC).

Both version 1994 and version 2002 follow the ISIC practice of differentiating industries into four hierarchies: section, division, group, and class. The difference (Table 6.2) between versions 1994 and 2002 mainly lies in the classification of services. As an interim classification standard, version 1994 has a similar structure to version 2002, but is less compatible with ISIC.

Data sources

As Table 6.3 shows, the FDI inflow to sectors of mining, manufacturing and utilities (MMU) in the benchmark year of 2002 accounted for 73.5 per cent of the total FDI inflow to China. The FDI inflow to the manufacturing sector alone accounted for 69.8 per cent of total FDI. According to *China Statistical Yearbook 2003* (CSY: National Bureau of Statistics of China 2003b), MMU contributed 44.4 per cent of GDP of China in 2002. Given the importance of these three sectors and the data availability on FIEs and SOEs in these sectors, special attention is paid to MMU in the following data disaggregation and CGE modelling.

One point merits special attention. Statistics on FDI to China have been greatly contaminated by "round-tripping" FDI, i.e. fake FDI. Round-tripping FDI refers to cross-border investment motivated by the more favourable treatment of foreign as opposed to domestic capital in a host country. In China a large number of domestic investors have transferred their capital out of China, only to reinvest it on the Chinese market under the banner of "foreign capital". Enterprises with such round-tripping investment are listed as "foreign invested enterprises" instead

Table 6.1 Chinese industrial classification (version 2002)

Section	*Division*	*Group*	*Class*
A: Agriculture, forestry, animal husbandry and fishing	5	18	38
B: Mining	6	5	33
C: Manufacturing	30	169	482
D: Utilities (production of electricity, gas and water)	3	7	10
E: Construction	4	7	11
F: Traffic, transport, storage and post	9	24	37
G: Information transfer, computer services and software	3	10	14
H: Wholesale and retail trade	2	18	93
I: Accommodation and restaurants	2	7	7
J: Finance	4	16	16
K: Real estate	1	4	4
L: Tenancy and business services	2	11	27
M: Scientific research, technical service and geologic perambulation	4	19	23
N: Management of water conservancy, environment and public establishment	3	8	18
O: Resident services and other services	2	12	16
P: Education	1	5	13
Q: Sanitation, social security and social welfare	3	11	17
R: Culture, sports and entertainment	5	22	29
S: Public management and social organisation	5	12	24
T: International organisations	1	1	1
Total: 20	95	396	913

Source: Zhao (2004).

Table 6.2 Comparison between Chinese industrial classification versions 1994 and 2002

	2002	*1994*	*Difference*
Sections	20	16	4
Divisions	95	92	3
Groups	396	368	28
Classes	913	846	67

Source: Zhao (2004).

of "domestic enterprises" in the Chinese economic census. By 2003, about a quarter of FDI in China was round-tripping FDI (United Nations Conference on Trade and Development 2003, p. 45).

Round-tripping investments are unlikely to generate the same productivity spillovers as the "authentic" foreign investments originating from successful Western entrepreneurs or institutions with advanced technology and mature management skills. Due to data availability, this research cannot differentiate round-tripping FDI from authentic FDI. It is also extremely difficult to establish the exact countries of origin of round-tripping FDI, and the industry distribution of fake FIEs in China. This problem may mean that later analyses underestimate the

Table 6.3 Foreign direct investment by sector in 2002

Sector	*Amount ($m)*	*Share (%)*
Farming, forestry, animal husbandry and fishing	1,028	1.9
Mining and quarrying	581	1.1
Manufacturing	36,800	69.8
Electric power, gas and water production and supply	1,375	2.6
Construction	709	1.3
Geological perambulation and water conservancy	7	0.0
Transport, storage, post and telecommunication services	913	1.7
Wholesale and retail trade and catering services	933	1.8
Banking and insurance	107	0.2
Real estate	5,663	10.7
Social services	2,943	5.6
Health care, sports and social welfare	128	0.2
Education, culture and arts, radio, film and television	38	0.1
Scientific research and polytechnic services	198	0.4
Other sectors	1,321	2.5
Total	52,743	100.0

Source: National Bureau of Statistics of China (2003b). "Amount" denotes utilised amount rather than contracted amount.

real magnitude of productivity spillovers of "authentic" FDI, especially in some sectors with a relatively concentrated presence of round-tripping FDI. However, aggregating both types of FDIs and then examining the actual spillover effects of such "blended" FDIs rather than "purified" FDI in China, can at least serve the purpose of reflecting the reality in the Chinese economy context.

The benchmark year of this CGE modelling exercise is 2002. The main data sources for that year include CSY, *China Industry Economy Statistical Yearbook 2003* (CIESY: National Bureau of Statistics of China 2003a), and *2002 Input–Output Tables of China* (I/O, in the format of Table 5.4: National Bureau of Statistics of China 2006a).

Two supplementary data sources are *China Economic Census Yearbook 2004* (CECY: National Bureau of Statistics of China 2006a) and the paper by Girma and Gong (2008a) which employs Chinese firm-level industrial survey data to evaluate FDI spillovers.

In CSY, disaggregated data on total output and value added at ownership level are available for foreign-invested enterprises (FIEs)[1] and state-run and state-holding enterprises (SOEs)[2] in MMU. Section-level data on FDI inflows are provided in CSY as well (Table 6.4). Disaggregated data on FDI in MMU at division level are also available on the Investment in China project website of the Ministry of Commerce of China (MOFCOM, http://www.fdi.gov.cn).

The data on FIEs and SOEs in MMU were originally collected by NBS officials from (1) all state-controlled industrial enterprises, which account for 36.3 per cent of gross output and 48.3 per cent of value added of all theenterprises surveyed; and (2) non-state-owned industrial enterprises with annual sales above RMB

Table 6.4 Available data

CSY	*CIESY*	*I/O*
1. For FIEs, SOEs and private enterprises in MMU: (a) Total output (b) Value added (c) Annual average employees 2. Amount of utilised FDI by section 3. GDP 4. Total export and import	1. For FIEs, SOEs and private enterprises in mining, manufacturing, and utilities: (a) Total output (b) Value added (c) Annual average employees (d) Export	1. Total intermediate inputs 2. Total value added (a) Compensation of employees (b) Net taxes on production (c) Depreciation of fixed capital (d) Operating surplus 3. Total input 4. Total intermediate use 5. Total final use (a) Rural household consumption (b) Urban household consumption (c) Government consumption (d) Gross fixed capital formation (e) Change in inventories (f) Exports 6. Imports 7. Gross output

5 million.[3] The enterprises surveyed account for 68 per cent of total industrial output and 69 per cent of total value added in MMU in 2002.

Similar to any input–output table, the I/O shows the interdependence of the economy's various productive sectors, as it contains information on transactions within and between production sectors and non-production sectors. The I/O also provides data on value added, private consumption, export, import and investment.

Data compilation strategy

There are many steps necesaary in transforming the original I/O into a tailored input–output table for our CGE modelling exercise (see Figure 6.1). The first step is to check data consistency, bearing in mind the different statistical standards. While the compilation of CSY and CIESY follows the old Chinese industry classification standard (version 1994), the I/O follows the new one (version 2002). As will shortly be discussed, a data consistency check shows that the data on two sectors in the I/O are inconsistent with those in CSY and CIESY. This problem can be addressed aggregating the data on the sectors in question with those of other similar sectors.

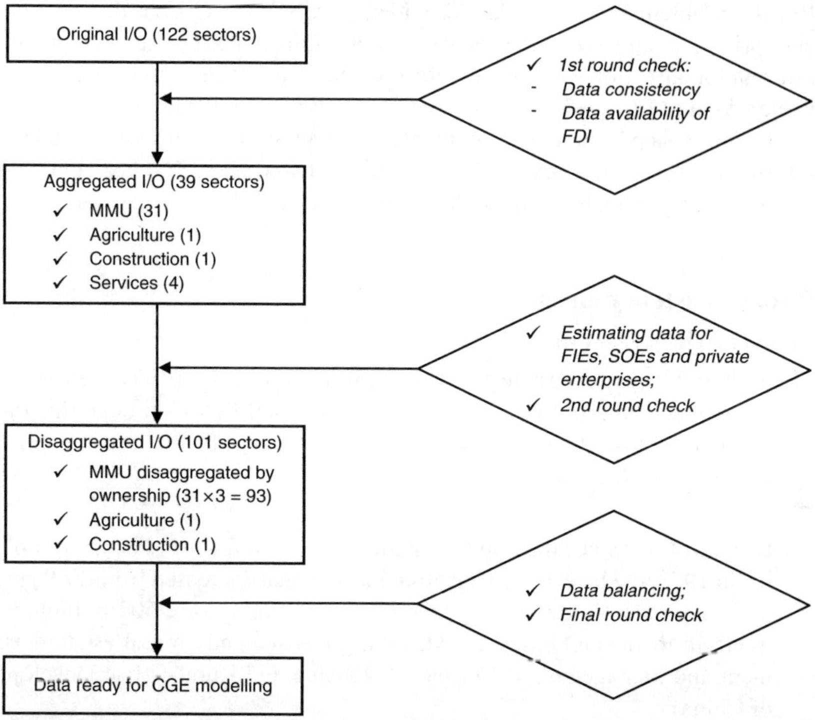

Figure 6.1 Transformations of the input–output table.

The second step is to reconcile the data availability of FDI inflows. MOFCOM only releases data on FDI at section level (see Table 6.1). The only exception is manufacturing. As FDI in manufacturing accounts for about 70 per cent of total FDI in recent years, MOFCOM also releases disaggregated data on FDI to manufacturing at division level (see Table 6.1), although data on some of these 30 divisions are missing. Thus an FDI shock introduced to the CGE model (see Chapter 7) can only take the values at a relatively aggregated level. This problem requires relevant data aggregation of some sectors in the I/O, which will shortly be discussed in detail.

The third step involves estimating data on FIEs, SOEs and other domestically invested (private) enterprises, as will shortly be discussed. As the main function of our CGE model is to analyse the effects of FDI productivity spillovers on Chinese domestic enterprises, it would be essential to expand the dimensions of I/O by disaggregating each of 31 MMU sectors into three ownership sectors. The textile sector, for example, can to be disaggregated into three individual sectors: the FIEs textile sector, SOEs textile sector, and private textile sector. This procedure can help explicitly model FDI productivity spillovers from FIEs to SOEs and private enterprises.

This can be done with the supplementary information from CSY and CIESY. But the problem is that the data provided by CSY and CIESY do not cover all enterprises, as already stated; however, our CGE modelling needs input–output information at national level. Therefore we need to estimate the total output and value added of FIEs, SOEs and private enterprises with certain techniques.

The fourth step is then to disaggregate the input–output table with the additional information on ownerships, which will be discussed later. The last step involves data balancing and a final-round data consistency check.

Data consistency check

Data on FDI in real estate

FDI in the Chinese real estate sector in 2002 and recent years has been extraordinarily high, accounting for about 10 per cent of total FDI. Although this ratio is higher than in most other countries, it is not unusual in the context of China due to following four factors:

(1) Urbanization. Since the implementation of the "Reform and Opening-up" policy in 1978, the level of urbanization in China has increased from 17.9 per cent to 39.1 per cent in 2002. By the end of 2002 there were 502 million people living in towns and cities, resulting in great demand on real estate development and management (Ministry of Housing and Rural-Urban Development of China).
(2) Policy incentives. Real estate is among the industries where non-resident investment is always encouraged by China's FDI policies, as is explicitly stated in the Guiding Directory on Industries Open to Foreign Investment, although 136 out of 184 IMF member countries have various controls on non-resident investment on real estate (International Monetary Fund 2004, pp. 12, 225).
(3) Macroeconomic prospects. As one of the most rapidly growing economies in the world, China has attracted a very high amount of FDI in real estate.
(4) Speculative investment. As a high-profit industry, real estate in China is very attractive to foreign institution investors (Jiang *et al.* 1998). Encouraged by the expectation of reminbi revaluation, FDI in real estate soared dramatically after 2004.

Tobacco processing sector

The total output (RMB 172 billion) and value added (RMB 131 billion) for the tobacco processing sector in the I/O are smaller than the figures in CSY for 2002 (RMB 204 billion and RMB 136 billion, respectively). As previously introduced, the total output of each sector in CSY only covers (1) all SOEs and (2) enterprises of other ownerships with annual sales above RMB 5 million. So the CSY figures should have been smaller than the corresponding I/O figures.

The causes of this problem could be the fact that the industry classifications adopted in I/O and CSY are different. Some sub-sectors might be classified as tobacco processing in CSY but not in I/O.

To solve this problem, we can aggregate tobacco processing with related sectors, namely food processing, food manufacturing and beverage manufacturing.

Production of electric power, steam and hot water sector

According to CSY, the total output of all SOEs and other above-scale enterprises in this sector is RMB 5,889 billion. The figure for SOEs is RMB 4,930 billion, and for other above-scale enterprises RMB 1,080 billion. This means the national output level is even smaller than the sum of the ownership-disaggregated enterprises, RMB 6,010 billion.

This problem is caused by double-counting of some enterprises with multiple ownerships. There is a possibility that some enterprises fall into both categories of FIE and SOE. If a firm's foreign share accounts for more than 25 per cent, the threshold to register as an FIE, then it is an FIE. However, if state agencies own a larger portion of it than anyone else, then it is also an SOE.

Therefore, to avoid double-counting, we need to purify the SOEs by excluding FIEs from them. The paper of Girma and Gong (2008a) provides a useful reference. They provide the shares of FIEs and SOEs in the total output of each sector in 2002. Their dataset and the CSY dataset come from precisely the same source – NBS data on (1) all SOEs and (2) all above-scale enterprises (with annual sales of RMB 5 million) of other ownership.

Girma and Gong's definition of FIEs is exactly the same as that adopted by CSY. However, their definition of SOEs is slightly different from that in CSY. In Girma and Gong (2008a), "SOEs" includes state-owned enterprises, state joint-ownership enterprises, joint state–collective ownership enterprises (dominated by state-owned funds), and sole state-funded enterprises. However, in CSY, "SOEs" only consists of state-owned enterprises, state joint-ownership enterprises, and sole state-funded enterprises. Joint state–collective ownership enterprises (dominated by state-owned funds) are categorised into state-holding enterprises in the CSY. Girma and Gong's definition of SOEs will be adopted here.

Data aggregation

Prior to our CGE modelling exercise, we aggregated the original China I/O from 122 sectors to 39. This aggregation reconciles the difference between industry classifications used in I/O and FDI data so that one and only one FDI inflow figure corresponds to each model section. The list of sectors after aggregation is given by Table 6.5.

Estimating data on FIEs, SOEs and private enterprises

Total output

With Girma and Gong's data on share of SOEs by sector, and the CSY data on total output for each sector, we can estimate the total output of SOEs in manufacturing

Table 6.5 I/O aggregation

Category	*Model sector*	*NBS version 2002*	*Name of model sectors*
Mining*	1	06, 07	Resource manufacturing (coal, petroleum and gas)
	2	08	Ferrous metals mining
	3	09	Non-ferrous metals mining
	4	10, 11	Mining of non-metals, other minerals and other ores
Manufacturing*	5	13–16	Food, beverage and tobacco manufacturing
	6	17	Textile industry
	7	18	Garments and other fibre products
	8	19	Leather, furs, down and related products
	9	20	Timber processing, bamboo, cane, palm fibre, etc.
	10	21	Furniture manufacturing
	11	22	Papermaking and paper products
	12	23	Printing and record medium reproduction
	13	24	Cultural, educational and sports goods
	14	25	Petroleum processing and coking
	15	26	Raw chemical materials and chemical products
	16	27	Medical and pharmaceutical products
	17	28	Chemical fibre
	18	29	Rubber products
	19	30	Plastic products
	20	31	Non-metal mineral products
	21	32	Smelting and pressing of ferrous metals
	22	33	Smelting and pressing of non-ferrous metals
	23	34	Metal products
	24	35	Ordinary machinery
	25	36	Special purpose equipment
	26	37	Transport equipment
	27	39, 40	Electronic and electric products
	28	41	Instruments, meters, cultural and office machinery
Utilities*	29	44	Production of electric power, steam and hot water
	30	45	Production of gas
	31	46	Production of tap water
Agriculture	32	01–05	Farming, forestry, animal husbandry and fishing

Table 6.5 Continued

Category	*Model sector*	*NBS version 2002*	*Name of model sectors*
Other Manufacturing	33	42	Manufacture of artwork and other manufacturing
	34	43	Recycling and disposal of waste
Construction	35	47–50	Construction
Banking and Insurance	36	68–71	Banking and insurance
Real Estate	37	72	Real estate
Other services	38	51–63;	Geological perambulation and water conservancy;
		65–67;	Transport, storage, post and telecommunication services;
		73–92	Wholesale and retail trade and catering; social services; healthcare, sports and social welfare; education, culture and arts, radio, films and television; scientific and technical services
	39	93–98	Public administration and other services

Notes:

a Categories marked with an asterisk are further disaggregated by ownership into FIEs, SOEs and private.

b In the NBS statistical standard version 2002, there are 98 two-digit sectors in total. Some of these are disaggregated into three-digit sectors in the I/O 2002, so that the I/O contains 122 sectors.

sectors by "reverse engineering":

$$Q^i_{SOEs} = Ratio^i_{SOEs} \times Q^i_{(CSY)All}, \quad i \in Manufacturing$$

where $Ratio^i_{SOEs}$ is the share of total output of each manufacturing sector (with SOE ownership) obtained from Girma and Gong (2008a). Thus, we can get total output value for "pure" SOEs.

The next step is to estimate the output level for SOEs in MMU based on the data on the output level of "pure" SOEs in MMU and manufacturing alone. Assuming that

$$\frac{Q^{MMU}_{SOEs}}{Q^{Manufacturing}_{SOEs}} = \frac{Q^{MMU}_{(CSY)SOEs}}{Q^{Manufacturing}_{(CSY)SOEs}}$$

we get

$$Q_{SOEs}^{MMU} = Q_{SOEs}^{Manufactuing} \times \frac{Q_{(CSY)SOEs}^{MMU}}{Q_{(CSY)SOEs}^{Manufactuing}}$$

Then the output level for each sector in mining and utilities can be estimated by allocating the difference between Q_{SOEs}^{MMU} and $Q_{SOEs}^{Manufacturing}$ with sector shares of corresponding SOEs and state-holding enterprises (SHEs) in CSY in each sector as a proxy for the share of sole SOEs:

$$Q_{SOEs}^{i} = (Q_{SOEs}^{MMU} - Q_{SOEs}^{Manufacturing}) \times Share_{SOEs+SHEs}^{i}, \quad i \in Mining, Utilities$$

Now we can augment (with a multiplier $Ratio_{FIEs}^{Q}$) the output value of above-scale FIEs in CSY to estimate an output value for all the FIEs:

$$Ratio_{FIEs}^{Q} = \frac{Q_{Total}^{I/O} - Q_{SOEs}^{I/O}}{Q_{Total}^{CSY} - Q_{SOEs}^{CSY}} = 1.59$$

As there are only three categories of ownership in our CGE modelling – FIEs, SOEs and private – the total output value of all private enterprises can be obtained by subtracting total output values of FIEs and SOEs from the total output values of corresponding sectors.

Value added

The value added of SOE sectors in MMU is estimated by the total output of each sector multiplied by a certain ratio. The ratio is obtained by dividing total value added by total output of SOEs in all manufacturing sectors (29.22 per cent). Then, with a similar estimation, we can augment (with a multiplier $Ratio_{FIEs}^{VA}$) the value added of above-scale FIEs in CSY to get the actual value added for all the FIEs:

$$Ratio_{FIEs}^{VA} = \frac{VA_{Total}^{IO} - VA_{SOEs}^{IO}}{VA_{Total}^{CSY} - VA_{SOEs}^{CSY}} = 1.52$$

As there are only three categories of ownership in the present CGE modelling – FIEs, SOEs and private – the total value added of private enterprises is obtained by subtracting the total value added of FIEs and SOEs from the total value added of corresponding sectors.

Disaggregation of input–output table by ownership

The CGE model constructed in this research is used to estimate the productivity spillover effects of FIEs on SOEs and other enterprises. It is necessary, therefore, to differentiate the ownership of enterprises and disaggregate the input–output

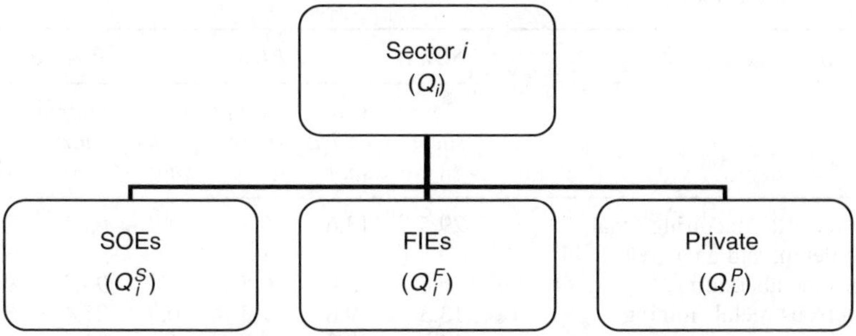

Figure 6.2 Disaggregating output and value added by ownership.

Note: $Q_i = Q_i^S + Q_i^F + Q_i^P$, $i = 1, \ldots, 31$; and Q represents total output or value added.

table (Gillespie *et al.* 2001, 2002). As ownership-disaggregated data on total output and value added are only available for sectors 1–31 in MMU, we disaggregate each of those 31 sectors into three separate sectors by ownership (FIEs, SOEs and private, as mentioned earlier), while the other eight sectors remain intact (Figure 6.2). We thus get $31 \times 3 = 93$ ownership-disaggregated sectors plus 8 other non-disaggregated sectors. In other words, there will be $(31 \times 3) + 8 = 101$ sectors in all: 31 foreign industry sectors, 31 SOE industry sectors, 31 private industry sectors, and 8 non-industry sectors.

Disaggregation of output by ownership

With the estimated ratios of output and value added by ownership (FIEs, SOEs and private) to total output and value added by industry as shown in Table 6.6, we can, at the first step, divide the total output of each sector (see Table 6.7) into output by ownership (see Table 6.8). For example, the nonferrous metals sector purchases 11,819 units of output from the coal, petroleum, and gas sector. As shown in Table 6.7, FIEs, SOEs and private companies provide output levels of 611, 3,490, and 7,718, respectively. The export propensity, i.e. the portion of export in total output, of FIEs, SOEs, and private companies are distinct from each other according to CIESY. As MNE exports are one of the channels of productivity spillover effects due to FIEs, we need to incorporate this distinction and make minor adjustments to the export values:

$$Export_i^{FIEs} = Q_i^{FIEs} \times e_i^{FIEs}, \qquad i = 1, \ldots, 31$$

$$Export_i^{SOEs} = Q_i^{SOEs} \times e_i^{SOEs+SHEs}, \qquad i = 1, \ldots, 31$$

$$Export_i^{Others} = Q_i^{Others} \times e_i^{SOEs+SHEs}, \qquad i = 1, \ldots, 31$$

Here e_i^j is the export propensity obtained from CIESY, whose industrial statistical data are from the same source as CSY. Due to the data availability of CIESY, the

Table 6.6 Shares of output and value added of SOEs, FIEs and private enterprises in MMU (%)

Division	*SOEs*		*FIEs*		*Private*	
	Output share	*Value added share*	*Output share*	*Value added share*	*Output share*	*Value added share*
Resource manufacturing (coal, petroleum, and gas)	29.5	13.6	5.2	3.9	65.3	82.5
Ferrous metals mining	6.0	3.8	0.5	0.3	93.5	95.9
Non-ferrous metals mining	13.3	9.8	1.3	0.9	85.4	89.3
Mining of non-metals, other minerals and other ores	4.7	2.9	1.7	1.0	93.7	96.0
Food, beverage and tobacco manufacturing	21.0	19.7	34.8	31.8	44.2	48.4
Textile industry	8.2	9.7	24.8	24.2	67.0	66.1
Garments and other fibre products	1.4	1.5	51.2	47.5	47.4	51.0
Leather, furs, down and related products	0.9	1.3	60.1	72.5	39.0	26.1
Timber processing, bamboo, cane, palm fibre, etc.	2.1	2.2	12.7	11.0	85.2	86.8
Furniture manufacturing	0.7	0.8	29.2	29.2	70.1	70.1
Papermaking and paper products	5.7	5.6	30.5	28.8	63.9	65.6
Printing and record medium reproduction	8.4	5.8	20.0	15.1	71.7	79.1
Cultural, educational and sports goods	1.2	1.2	53.0	44.0	45.7	54.8
Petroleum processing and coking	27.3	46.4	12.7	15.9	60.0	37.8
Raw chemical materials and chemical products	15.1	17.5	24.0	25.5	60.9	57.0
Medical and pharmaceutical products	15.9	12.0	29.7	28.4	54.4	59.7
Chemical fibre	11.8	16.0	38.2	39.6	50.0	44.4
Rubber products	11.1	11.8	39.0	39.8	49.8	48.5
Plastic products	1.5	1.8	30.5	32.1	68.0	66.1
Non-metal mineral products	10.0	8.9	23.4	20.8	66.5	70.3
Smelting and pressing of ferrous metals	24.6	27.6	6.8	5.9	68.5	66.5
Smelting and pressing of non-ferrous metals	15.9	23.5	13.1	13.0	71.0	63.5
Metal products	3.0	3.7	31.3	31.9	65.7	64.5
Ordinary machinery	9.9	10.2	19.8	19.1	70.3	70.7
Special purpose equipment	14.1	14.9	17.4	17.7	68.4	67.4
Transport equipment	25.8	28.8	43.7	45.2	30.4	26.0
Electronic and electric products	6.4	8.5	81.5	78.7	12.1	12.8
Instruments, meters, cultural and office machinery	5.5	6.3	63.3	51.4	31.1	42.3
Production of electric power, steam and hot water	32.2	18.8	21.7	22.9	46.1	58.3
Production of gas	22.5	32.2	27.7	14.0	49.9	53.8
Production of tap water	29.5	17.2	3.9	3.0	66.7	79.8

Source: National Bureau of Statistics of China (2003b, 2006b); Girma and Gong (2008a).

Note: The sum of output shares across SOEs, FIEs, and private in each division is equal to 100%. The same rule applies to the value added shares.

export values for SOEs and private companies can only be estimated by multiplying the corresponding output level by the export propensity values of SOEs plus SHEs.

But the sum of the estimated export values is larger than the sum of original export values of these 31 industry sectors. To make the adjusted I/O as close to the original one as possible, it is necessary to make a further adjustment. We can get a ratio of total original export value in the sum of estimated total export value of these 31 sectors:

$$Ratio = \frac{\sum_{i=1}^{31} \sum_j Export_{ij}^{Original}}{\sum_{i=1}^{31} \sum_j Export_{ij}^{Estimated}} = 0.79, \quad j = FIEs, SOEs, Others$$

The estimated export values can be multiplied by this ratio to make them "shrink" to new values, whose sum is equal to the sum of the original total export for these 31 sectors.

Disaggregation of value added by ownership

We also need to disaggregate the value added for sectors 1–31 by ownership. The original value added matrix for industrial sectors 1–31 is shown in Table 6.9. With the portions of value added for each type of ownership (see Table 6.6), we can disaggregate each item in the upper panel into three items, as shown in Table 6.10. For example, total value added for sector 1 is 46,012,251. After disaggregation, the corresponding total value added for FIEs, SOEs and private companies is 1,773,282, 6,276,175 and 37,962,794, respectively.

Further disaggregation of intermediate inputs by ownership

We can further disaggregate the matrix in the upper left panel in Table 6.8 under a simplistic hypothesis: the more a sector produces, the more it purchases from other sectors. But the disaggregation is not as straightforward as that used in constructing Table 6.8. In the first step, as total input is equal to total output for each ownership-disaggregated sector, if we transpose the "total output" column in the lower panel of Table 6.8, we get a row of "total input". In the second step, we can estimate the ratio of input in total intermediate input (TII) for each category of ownership by:

$$Ratio_{ij} = \frac{Total\ Output_{ij} - TVA_{ij}}{TII_i}, \quad i = 1, \ldots, 39;\ j = FIEs, SOEs, \text{private}$$

For example, the ratio for partitioning the input value for "all" categories of ownerships to get the input value for FIEs in sector 1 can be obtained as

$$Ratio_{1j} = \frac{Total\ Output_{1j} - TVA_{1j}}{TII_1} = \frac{3{,}761{,}858 - 1{,}773{,}282}{26{,}729{,}892} = 0.074$$

Table 6.7 I/O prior to disaggregation by ownership

		1: Coal, petroleum, gas			*Section i* ($i = 2, \ldots, 30$)			*31: Non-ferrous metals*		
		All	–	–	*All*	–	–	*All*	–	–
1: Coal, petroleum, gas	All	1,530,390	–	–	...	–	–	11,819	–	–
	–	–	–	–	...	–	–	–	–	–
	–	–	–	–	...	–	–	–	–	–
Section *i* ($i = 2, \ldots, 30$)	All	0	–	–	...	–	–	0	–	–
	–	–	–	–	...	–	–	–	–	–
	–	–	–	–	...	–	–	–	–	–
31: Non–ferrous metals	All	86,257	–	–	...	–	–	234,702	–	–
	–	–	–	–	...	–	–	–	–	–
	–	–	–	–	...	–	–	–	–	–
32	All	305,261	–	–	...	–	–	15	–	–
Sector *j* ($j = 33, \ldots, 38$)	All	...	–	–	...	–	–	...	–	–
39	All	0	–	–	...	–	–	0	–	–
TII	All	26,729,892	–	–	...	–	–	2,829,596	–	–

Note: "all" means that the aggregate value is the sum of all three ownerships (SOEs, FIEs and private).

Table 6.7 Continued

		Non-industry sectors			*Final use*			*Other*		
		32: Agriculture	…	*39: Private*	*Rural consumption*	…	*Export*	*Import*	*Error*	*Total output*
1: Coal, petroleum, gas	All	896,766	…	275,332	725,778	…	2,785,896	11,244,793	4,222,156	72,742,143
	–	–	…	–	–	…	–	–	–	–
	–	–	…	–	–	…	–	–	–	–
Section *i* ($i = 2, \ldots, 30$)	All	…	…	…	…	…	…	…	…	…
	–	…	…	…	…	…	…	…	…	…
	–	…	…	…	…	…	…	…	…	…
31: Non-ferrous metals	All	87,588	…	105,509	217,195	…	10,558	1,367,136	–36,903	5,664,668
	–	–	…	–	–	…	–	–	–	–
	–	–	…	–	–	…	–	–	–	–
32	All	46,368,196	…	0	49,328,792	…	4,741,965	6,811,579	7,141,077	285,787,423
Sector *j* ($j = 33, \ldots, 38$)	All	…	…	…	…	…	…	…	…	…
39	All	0	…	0	0	…	304,817	371,087	–7,147,553	95,754,579
TII	All	119,482,762	…	47,076,127						

Note: $TII = \sum_{i=1}^{39} input_i$ is total intermediate input.

Table 6.8 The first step of disaggregation by ownership

		1: Coal, petroleum, gas			*Section i* $(i=2,\ldots,30)$			*31: Non-ferrous metals*		
		All	–	–	*All*	–	–	*All*	–	–
1: Coal, petroleum, gas	FIEs	79,144	–	–	...	–	–	611	–	–
	SOEs	451,888	–	–	...	–	–	3,490	–	–
	Private	999,358	–	–	...	–	–	7,718	–	–
Section i $(i=2,\ldots,30)$	FIEs	...	–	–	...	–	–	...	–	–
	SOEs	...	–	–	...	–	–	...	–	–
	Private	...	–	–	...	–	–	...	–	–
31: Non-ferrous metals	FIEs	3,359	–	–	...	–	–	9,139	–	–
	SOEs	2,540	–	–	...	–	–	69,134	–	–
	Private	57,490	–	–	...	–	–	156,429	–	–
32	All	305,261	–	–	...	–	–	15	–	–
Sector j $(j=33,\ldots,38)$	All	...	–	–	...	–	–	...	–	–
39	All	0	–	–	...	–	–	0	–	–
TII	All	26,729,892	–	–	...	–	–	2,829,596	–	–

Table 6.8 Continued

		Non-industry sectors			*Final use*			*Other*		
		32: Agriculture	...	*39: Private*	*Rural consumption*	...	*Export*	*Import*	*Error*	*Total output*
1: Coal, petroleum, gas	FIEs	46,376	...	14,239	37,534	...	1,158,936	581,524	−796,515	3,761,858
	SOEs	264,794	...	81,299	214,305	...	1,018,944	3,320,323	1,050,369	21,479,046
	Private	585,596	...	179,794	473,939	...	608,016	7,342,945	3,968,302	47,501,240
Section i ($i = 2, \ldots, 30$)	FIEs	...	...	...	...	...	...	...	...	...
	SOEs	...	...	...	...	...	...	...	...	...
	Private	...	...	...	...	...	...	...	...	...
31: Non-ferrous metals	FIEs	3,411	...	4,108	8,457	...	0	53,234	−1,026	220,575
	SOEs	25,800	...	31,079	63,977	...	259	402,704	−8,019	1,668,587
	Private	58,377	...	70,322	144,761	...	585	911,198	−18,144	3,775,507
32	All	46,368,196	...	0	49,328,792	...	4,741,965	6,811,579	7,141,077	285,787,423
Sector j ($j = 33, \ldots, 38$)	All	...	...	...	...	...	...	...	...	...
39	All	0	...	0	0	...	304,817	371,087	−7,147,553	95,754,579
TII	All	119,482,762	...	47,076,127						

Note: $TII = \sum_{i=1}^{39} input_i$ is total intermediate input.

Table 6.9 Value added matrix prior to disaggregation by ownership

	1: Coal, petroleum, gas			*Section i* ($i = 2, \ldots, 30$)			*31: Non-ferrous metals*		
	All	–	–	*All*	–	–	*All*	–	–
CP	18,695,996	–	–	...	–	–	1,272,821	–	–
NT	4,344,716	–	–	...	–	–	387,779	–	–
DP	5,285,208	–	–	...	–	–	1,200,874	–	–
OP	17,686,331	–	–	...	–	–	−26,402	–	–
TVA	46,012,251	–	–	...	–	–	2,835,072	–	–

Note: CP = Compensation to employees; NT = Net taxes on production; DP = Depreciation of fixed capital; OP = Operating surplus; TVA = Total value added.

Table 6.10 Value added matrix after disaggregation by ownership

	1: Coal, petroleum, gas			*Section i* ($i = 2, \ldots, 30$)			*31: Non-ferrous metals*		
	FIEs	*SOEs*	*Private*	*FIEs*	*SOEs*	*Private*	*FIEs*	*SOEs*	*Private*
CP	720,531	2,550,176	15,425,288	...	...	...	37,953	218,892	1,015,975
NT	167,443	592,629	3,584,645	...	...	...	11,563	66,688	309,528
DP	203,688	720,914	4,360,605	...	...	...	35,808	206,519	958,547
OP	681,620	2,412,456	14,592,256	...	...	...	−787	−4,540	−21,074
TVA	1,773,282	6,276,175	37,962,794	...	...	...	84,537	487,559	2,262,976

Note: See Table 6.9.

where j = FIEs, SOEs, private. The three numbers in the above calculation (3,761,858, 1,773,282 and 26,729,892) come from Tables 6.8, 6.10 and 6.8, respectively.

With 0.074 as the share of input value for FIEs in sector 1, we can get all 101 input values for FIEs in sector 1, as shown in the third column of Table 6.12. With the value of each ownership in every sector, we can sum up all the inputs by columns and get all the TII values, as shown in the third last row in Table 6.12.

Negative data and data balancing

The operating surplus in the production of tap water sector is negative (see Table 6.13). This negativity is not acceptable in coding the CGE model. To solve this problem, we need to “smooth” the values for all the utilities by ownership whilst keeping the net taxes on production (NT) row unchanged.

The first step is to sum CP, DP, and OP for the three utilities sectors by ownership, as shown in Table 6.14. NT is excluded here to keep its values unchanged, as this variable is important for tax reform analysis in Chapter 7. The second step is to calculate the percentage of CP, DP, and OP in their sums (see the lower panel in Table 6.14). With these weighted shares, we can then “redistribute” CP, DP, and

Table 6.11 Intermediate input–output matrix by ownership (prior to further disaggregation)

		1: Coal, petroleum, gas			*Section i* $(i = 2, \dots, 30)$			*31: Non-ferrous metals*		
		All	–	–	*All*	–	–	*All*	–	–
1: Coal, petroleum, gas	FIEs	79,144	–	–	…	–	–	611	–	–
	SOEs	451,888	–	–	…	–	–	3,490	–	–
	Private	999,358	–	–	…	–	–	7,718	–	–
Section i	FIEs	…	–	–	…	–	–	…	–	–
$(i = 2, \dots, 30)$	SOEs	…	–	–	…	–	–	…	–	–
	Private	…	–	–	…	–	–	…	–	–
31: Non–ferrous	FIEs	3,359	–	–	…	–	–	9,139	–	–
metals	SOEs	25,408	–	–	…	–	–	69,134	–	–
	Private	57,490	–	–	…	–	–	156,429	–	–
32	All	305,261	–	–	…	–	–	15	–	–
Sector j $(j = 33, \dots, 38)$	All	…	–	–	…	–	–	…	–	–
39	All	0	–	–	…	–	–	0	–	–
TII	All	26,729,892	–	–	…	–	–	2,829,596	–	–
TVA	All	1,773,282	6,276,175	37,962,794	…	…	…	84,537	487,559	2,262,976
Total input	All	3,761,858	21,479,046	47,501,240	…	…	…	220,575	1,668,587	3,775,507

Table 6.12 Intermediate input–output matrix by ownership (after further disaggregation)

		1: Coal, petroleum, gas			*Section i* ($i = 2, \ldots, 30$)			*31: Non-ferrous metals*		
		FIEs	*SOEs*	*Private*	*FIEs*	*SOEs*	*Private*	*FIEs*	*SOEs*	*Private*
1: Coal, petroleum, gas	FIEs	5,888	45,014	28,242	...	...	...	29	255	327
	SOEs	33,618	257,016	161,254	...	...	...	168	1,457	1,865
	Private	74,347	568,394	356,616	...	...	...	371	3,221	4,125
Section *i* ($i = 2, \ldots, 30$)	FIEs	...	...	...	...	...	...	...	...	...
	SOEs	...	...	...	...	...	...	...	...	...
	Private	...	...	...	...	...	...	...	...	...
31: Non-ferrous metals	FIEs	250	1,910	1,199	...	...	...	439	3,814	4,885
	SOEs	1,890	14,451	9,067	...	...	...	3,324	28,855	36,955
	Private	4,277	32,698	20,515	...	...	...	7,521	65,291	83,617
32	All	22,710	173,620	108,931	...	...	...	1	6	8
Sector *j* ($j = 33, \ldots, 38$)	All	...	–	–	...	...	...	...	–	–
39	All	0	0	0	...	...	...	0	0	0
TII	All	1,988,576	15,202,871	9,538,446	...	...	...	136,038	1,181,028	1,512,530
TVA	All	1,773,282	6,276,175	37,962,794	...	...	...	84,537	487,559	2,262,976
Total input	All	3,761,858	21,479,046	47,501,240	...	...	...	220,575	1,668,587	3,775,507

Table 6.13 Old dataset for utilities sectors

	Production of electric power, steam and hot water			*Production of gas*			*Production of tap water*		
	FIEs	*SOEs*	*Private*	*FIEs*	*SOEs*	*Private*	*FIEs*	*SOEs*	*Private*
CP	1,953,597	1,607,695	4,986,182	42,187	96,651	161,472	37,953	218,892	1,015,975
NT	1,814,021	1,492,832	4,629,940	19,388	44,417	74,206	11,563	66,688	309,528
DP	2,481,278	2,041,945	6,332,986	42,570	97,528	162,937	35,808	206,519	958,547
OP	2,807,624	2,310,509	7,165,923	22	50	83	−787	−4,540	−21,074

Note: As Table 6.9.

Table 6.14 Sum of value added (NT excluded) of three "utilities" sectors

	FIEs	*SOEs*	*Private*
Sum of three utility sectors			
CP	2,033,738	1,923,238	6,163,630
NT	–	–	–
DP	2,559,656	2,345,992	7,454,469
OP	2,806,859	2,306,019	7,144,932
Sum	7,400,253	6,575,249	20,763,031
Shares			
CP	27.5%	29.2%	29.7%
NT	–	–	–
DP	34.6%	35.7%	35.9%
OP	37.9%	35.1%	34.4%
Sum	100%	100%	100%

Note: As Table 6.9.

Table 6.15 New dataset for "utilities" sectors

	Production of electric power, steam and hot water			*Production of gas*			*Production of tap water*		
	FIEs	*SOEs*	*Private*	*FIEs*	*SOEs*	*Private*	*FIEs*	*SOEs*	*Private*
CP	1,990,384	1,743,324	5,487,410	23,299	56,811	96,327	20,055	123,103	579,893
NT	1,814,021	1,492,832	4,629,940	19,388	44,417	74,206	11,563	66,688	309,528
DP	2,505,091	2,126,530	6,636,629	29,324	69,299	116,501	25,241	150,163	701,339
OP	2,747,024	2,090,296	6,361,052	32,156	68,118	111,664	27,678	147,605	672,217

Note: As Table 6.9.

OP within each ownership. The results are shown in Table 6.15. A comparison of Tables 6.13 and 6.15 shows that the values of NT do not change and that the values of OP in the production and supply of tap water sectors are now positive.

The error column in the I/O table needs to be removed and the remaining I/O matrix needs to be balanced using certain data manipulation techniques. Usually this job can be done by nonlinear programming (NLP). However, this balancing technique generated big discrepancies between the old unbalanced dataset and the new balanced dataset. An explanation for this is that many observations in the change in inventories column are negative. Forcing all the data in the new estimated SAM to be positive in NLP leads to an impairment of the the overall quality of the data.

To avoid the problem caused by NLP, we have to do the data balancing manually. We can augment each entry in the final demand columns with a multiplier so that the new final demand data plus the intermediate demand for each sector is equal to the gross output. The multiplier is obtained as

$$\alpha_i = \frac{FD_i + ER_i}{FD_i}, \quad i = 1, 2, \ldots, 101$$

where FD_i and ER_i represent the final demand and error of the ith industry, respectively.

Final-round data consistency check

Before importing the new ownership-disaggregated input–output table into our CGE modelling exercise, it is very important to do a final round of data validity checking to make sure that the table is balanced in an accounting sense.

The first step is to check whether the sum of ownership-disaggregated intermediate inputs is equal to the corresponding disaggregated total intermediate inputs. For example, for FIEs in sector 1, we need to check whether

$$\sum_{i=1}^{31} input_{1i}^{FIEs} + \sum_{i=32}^{39} input_{1i}^{FIEs} = TII_{1i}^{FIEs} = 1{,}988{,}576$$

The second step is to check whether the sum of disaggregated value added is equal to the corresponding disaggregated total value added (*TVA*). For example, for FIEs in sector 1, we need to check whether

$$CP_1^{FIEs} + NT_1^{FIEs} + DP_1^{FIEs} + OP_1^{FIEs} = TVA_1^{FIEs} = 1{,}773{,}282$$

The third step is to check whether the sum of disaggregated intermediate use is equal to the corresponding disaggregated total intermediate use (*TIU*). For example, for FIEs in sector 1, we need to check whether

$$\sum_{i=1}^{31} use_{1i}^{FIEs} + \sum_{i=32}^{39} use_{1i}^{FIEs} = TIU_{1i}^{FIEs} = 1{,}988{,}576$$

The final step is to check whether the sum of disaggregated final use (*FU*), export (*EX*) and error (*ERR*) with import excluded is equal to the corresponding disaggregated gross output (*GO*). For example, for FIEs in sector 1, we need to check whether

$$FU101_1^{FIEs} + FU102_1^{FIEs} + FU103_1^{FIEs} + FU201_1^{FIEs} + FU202_1^{FIEs} + EX_1^{FIEs} - IM_1^{FIEs} = GO_1^{FIEs} = 3{,}761{,}858$$

Conclusions

The transformation of the original input–output table involves a complex data manipulation process, which mainly involves three types of work: (1) aggregating the original 122 × 122 input–output table into a 39 × 39 table; (2) disaggregating the 39 × 39 table into a 101 × 101 table with information on different ownership, which enables the CGE model constructed on this input–output table to address issues regarding ownership (i.e. spillovers from FIEs to domestic enterprises); (3) data balancing and consistency checking.

Data employed are mainly from *China Statistical Yearbook 2003*, *China Industry Economy Statistical Yearbook 2003* and *China Input–Output Table 2002*. Data on several sectors are aggregated to reconcile different statistical standards. Data on agriculture, construction, and services are also aggregated to a great extent to cater for the data availability on FDI inflows. By doing so, we obtain a 39 × 39 input–output table. With data estimated for FIEs, SOEs, and private enterprises, 31 out of the 39 sectors can be further disaggregated into 31 × 3 = 93 ownership sectors. Data balancing techniques are used to balance the transformed input–output table. In the data manipulation process, three rounds of data consistency checks are carried out.

7 A benchmark CGE model for the Chinese economy and its extensions

Introduction

This book on the productivity spillover effects of FDI in China is concerned with a static single-country CGE model with 101 sectors. The basic framework of the benchmark model will be discussed first. Three extensions to the benchmark model are also presented. In the first extension, endogenous variables are constructed to capture the FDI productivity spillovers. FDI productivity spillover parameters are estimated by econometric analysis. The second extension incorporates monopolistic competition into the CGE model with FDI spillovers. Then the model is further extended to examine the effects of FDI spillovers under monopolistic competition among firms with heterogeneous productivity.

CGE model structure

The CGE model structurally encapsulates the productivity spillover effects of FDI on domestic firms by endogenising four spillover channels – backward linkages, forward linkages, export of MNEs, and horizontal impact (demonstration, competition and resource reallocation). The model is focused on the manufacturing sectors in that almost 70 per cent of FDI flows into China go into manufacturing. The research has been carried out in the context of the Chinese economy, considering the fact that China has been the largest FDI host among the developing countries since 1993. In China, as a country in transition from a centrally planned economy to a market economy, the potential impact of FDI productivity spillovers on state-owned enterprises and the emerging private sectors is of special interest.

The circular flows of the Chinese economy are depicted in Figure 5.1. Commodity aggregation and disaggregation are sketched in Figure 5.4.

As discussed in Chapter 6, 31 out of 39 industries (i.e. manufacturing and utilities industries) are disaggregated into $31 \times 3 = 93$ sectors by ownership, namely foreign-invested sectors, state-owned sectors and domestic private sectors. The data on the other eight agricultural and services industries remain unchanged. Thus a 101×101 input–output table is constructed as the basis of this CGE model on FDI productivity spillovers.

In this model, the national composite demand for products and services is satisfied through a nested aggregation structure, each nesting level of which can be represented by a CES function, as shown in Figure 7.1 and by equations (7.1)–(7.4).

The lowest level (level 4) aggregates the commodity across firms in the same industry with the same ownership, e.g. the products of SOEs in the textile industry:

$$Y_{i,j,k} = \left[\sum_{f=1}^{N_f} \varphi_{i,j,k,f} Q_{i,j,k,f}^{(\sigma_4-1)/\sigma_4} \right]^{\sigma_4/(\sigma_4-1)} \tag{7.1}$$

where i, j, k, f index the hierarchy of this composite aggregation from the top to the bottom. f indexes individual firms. The number of firms $(N_{i,j,k,f})$ in each ownership sector is rather different, ranging from 2 to 15,305. (National Bureau of Statistics of China 2003a). k indexes ownership and takes values 1, 2, 3, representing FIEs, SOEs and domestic private enterprises. j represents sources of commodities and takes values 1 and 2, denoting domestically produced and imported commodities, respectively. Finally, $i = 1, 2, \ldots, 101$ stands for the sectors: 93 of which are ownership-disaggregated and 8 ownership-mixed. While $Q_{i,j,k,f}$ denotes firm-level output, $Y_{i,j,k}$ denotes aggregate production of FIEs, SOEs and private enterprises.

The second last level of aggregation is a CES aggregation across three ownerships:

$$DI_{i,j} = \left[\sum_{k=1}^{3} \gamma_k Y_{i,j,k}^{(\sigma_3-1)/\sigma_3} \right]^{\sigma_3/(\sigma_3-1)} \tag{7.2}$$

At the second level is Armington aggregation (AR_i) of domestically manufactured goods and imported goods:

$$AR_i = \left[\sum_{j=1}^{2} \beta_j DI_{i,j}^{(\sigma_2-1)/\sigma_2} \right]^{\sigma_2/(\sigma_2-1)} \tag{7.3}$$

At the top level, a further aggregation is applied:

$$AG = \left[\sum_{i=1}^{101} \alpha_i AR_i^{(\sigma_1-1)/\sigma_1} \right]^{\sigma_1/(\sigma_1-1)} \tag{7.4}$$

The sum over the shares parameters at each aggregation level is assumed to be equal to unity:

$$\sum_{i=1}^{101} \alpha_i = \sum_{j=1}^{2} \beta_{i,j} = \sum_{k=1}^{3} \gamma_{i,j,k} = \sum_{f=1}^{N_f} \varphi_{i,j,k,f} = 1$$

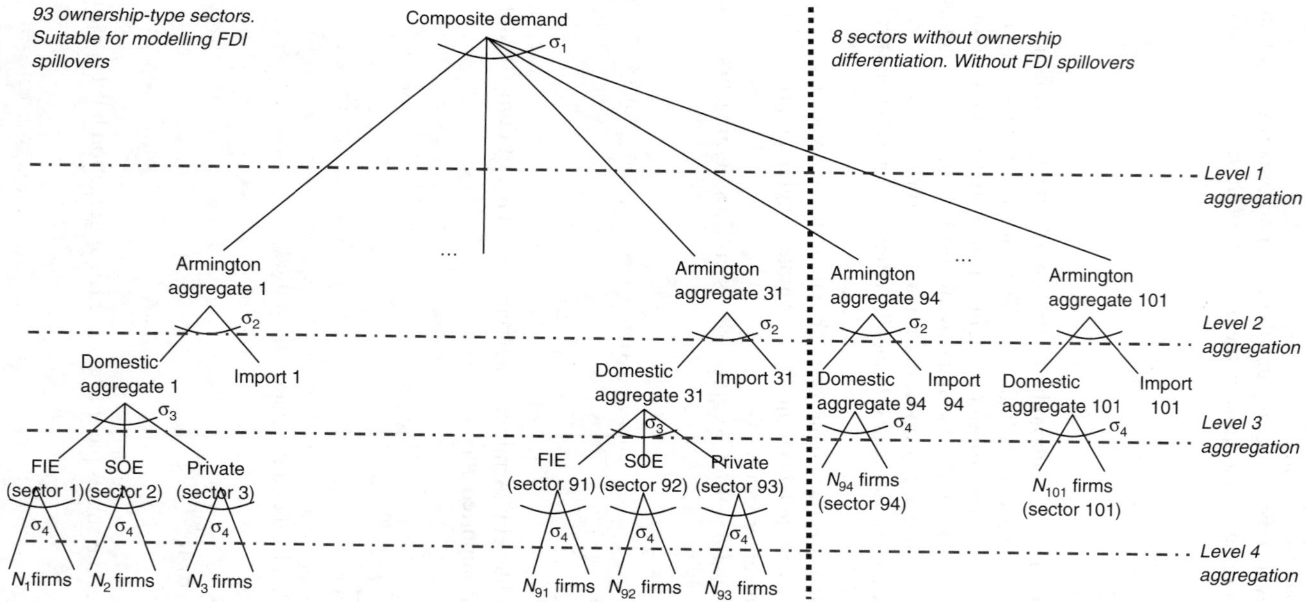

Figure 7.1 Consumption aggregation (101 sectors).

A benchmark CGE model

In this section, we will discuss the framework, closure rules and numéraire of the benchmark model. Tables A2.1–A2.13 in Appendix 2 list the MPSGE declaration, equations, variables and parameters of the benchmark model.

Model characteristics

In the model, there exist many production activities (denoted by "SECTOR" in Appendix 2) that convert inputs (including primary and intermediary inputs) into outputs (COMMODITY). The complementary variable associated with a sector is the activity level, while the complementary variable associated with a commodity is its price.

Consumers are represented by a domestic representative agent (RA). He or she receives the returns on the labour and capital and the balance of current account, and then purchases investment and private consumption. The government is also designated to be a representative agent (GOV). In an imperfect competitive market where mark-ups or profits exist, a representative enterprise can also be denoted as a representative agent (ENTRE) to collect mark-up and pay its fixed cost. Finally, a foreign representative agent (FDI) is designed to allocate foreign investments into different sectors and collects earnings on foreign capital in each sector.

The production of a value-added composite is the starting point for the core model. Value added is produced by means of a Cobb–Douglas function from two primary inputs, labour (WL) and capital (RK). The elasticity of substitution is thus equal to 1 (S:1). The choice of Cobb–Douglas functions, rather than CES or Leontief forms, is consistent with Chow and Lin (2002) who employ Cobb–Douglas to estimate the TFP in China, and Fan *et al.* (2007) who find non-zero substitution between labour and capital in the Chinese economy. This choice is also echoed by Balistreri *et al.* (2003) who fail to reject the Cobb–Douglas specification in 20 of the 28 industries in the USA.

FDI productivity spillovers are modelled as an economic externality taking place during the production of value added, which will be discussed in detail in this chapter. The productivity spillovers take the form of "increment" to the value added, with an increment rate of NTFP. This extra increase in value added exists due to the presence of foreign enterprises, but it does not "borrow" resources from any of the agents in the economy. In coding productivity spillover in the CGE modelling, the incremental part (i.e. the spillover part) of the value added is "transferred" by the government (GOV). But this does not change the government budget balance at all – in the event of productivity spillover, there is always an exact match of extra government expenditure for spillover and extra government revenue (i.e. extra "endowment") to offset the "spillover expenditure".

The value-added composite and intermediate products are employed for production of commodities with a Leontief production function (S:0). *Ad valorem* tax is levied on the output at a rate of NTP(A) and is redistributed to the government (GOV). The change in production tax rate (TDIFF1(A)) can be added to the existing tax rates to perform simulations on FDI tax reforms which will be analysed in Chapter 9.

The production block will also be used to capture the effect of monopolistic competition and firm heterogeneity, theoretical models of which will be constructed.

Outputs of each sector are disaggregated into two portions with a CET function, one for export and the other for domestic use. The elasticity of transformation takes values from the Global Trade Analysis Project database version 6.

The total supplies of labour and domestic capital are both fixed, and the economy is assumed to in full employment. Extra capital can be introduced to the stock of foreign capital in the form of an FDI shock, which will be discussed in detail in the next chapter. The purpose of imposing the assumption of fixed domestic capital supply is to simplify the model so that we can focus on the pure effects of an FDI shock with spillovers.

The assumption of fixed total labour supply is consistent with the economic environment in China since around 2007–2008. It was argued in the literature that China was in the process of fast urbanisation and industrialisation, and it had a huge amount of hidden unemployment in both urban and rural areas, which provided a large pool of extra labour supply to the economy (Fu and Balasubramanyam 2005). However, this "excess labour supply" story is no longer true. Since early 2006 China's export-concentrated provinces have begun to face mounting pressure from labour shortage, partly because massive rural tax cuts have helped keep people working on farms, and also because the "one-child policy" has started to affect the supply of young Chinese workers (Barboza 2006).

Both capital and labour are first disaggregated across 39 industries at an upper nesting level first, subject to constant elasticity of transformation. For each of the 31 mining, manufacturing and utilities (MMU) industries, both primary inputs will be further allocated to the three ownership-disaggregated sectors, namely FIEs, SOEs, and domestic private sectors, also subject to CET.

Both labour and capital can move imperfectly across industries and ownerships within each of the 31 MMU industries. The elasticity of transformation for the upper nesting CET function is set to be 1, while the elasticity for the lower nesting CET function takes the form of a parameter (`TAU_L` for labour and `TAU_K` for capital), the value of which will be subject to sensitivity tests in the next chapter.

There are two nesting levels here in the generation of Armington aggregate goods. At the lower nesting level, domestically produced goods are aggregated across ownerships in each industry. Then at the higher nesting level, domestically produced goods in each industry are aggregated with imported goods. The elasticity of substitution between domestic and imported goods takes values from the Global Trade Analysis Project database version 6.

In the export block, exported goods generate a special output, foreign currency (`PFX`), while in the import block foreign currency is exchanged for imported goods.

The representative domestic agent (`RA`) is endowed with primary factors – labour and capital. Using the returns on the labour and capital and the balance of the current account, the agent purchases investment goods, which include fixed asset formation and change of inventory. The remaining part is expended over private consumption.

An agent representing multinational firms (`FDI`) added here to capture the capital flow of FDI. This agent manipulates its capital and redirects the earnings worldwide. Its investment stock in China was approximately RMB 200 billion in 2002, which is denoted as an endowment of foreign exchange. An increment of total capital in the form of worldwide earnings will take the form of new FDI. This FDI flows to each foreign-invested sector and will thus boost the production of these sectors. This agent also earns returns on capital since the agent has its presence in every industry. With these endowments and earnings, the agent spends RMB 200 billion in foreign currency on investment plus the returns on its presence.

Closure rules and numéraire

As for the government closure, tax revenue is less than government consumption demand, suggesting a fiscal deficit. The deficit is financed by private households in the form of "direct taxes". In this model, direct taxes are measured by a fixed quantity of consumed commodities multiplied by the endogenous commodity prices. In other words, this model assumes a fiscal-neutral deficit, which is fixed in terms of the quantity of consumed commodities.

The government consumes a variable quantity of commodities, and their prices may also vary endogenously. The fiscal revenue comes from the collection of indirect taxes (i.e. "net taxes on production" which will be introduced in Chapter 9) at fixed tax rates.

In counterfactual simulations the fiscal revenue collected from indirect taxes will vary with the change of tax bases (production). Thus the government has to adjust its consumption demand given its variable indirect tax revenue and fixed amount of deficit in terms of commodity quantity. This fiscal-neutral closure therefore "insulates" the external shock from the amount of commodities to be consumed by private households, as the government can only borrow a fixed amount of commodities from the households. So this closure provides a reasonable environment for the analysis of welfare changes caused purely by the shock of FDI productivity spillover in the next chapters.

As for the savings–investment closure, this is a static model and there is no intertemporal savings–investment transformation. The model is based on input–output table data, so data on savings and investment are determined by gross domestic fixed capital formation. The investment demand of the representative agent is fixed and includes fixed asset formation and changes of inventories. The representative agent receives income from labour and capital and makes (fixed) purchases of foreign exchange (net transfers and foreign savings) and investment. The remainder of his or her income is spent on private consumption.

As for the external closure, the nominal exchange rate is selected as the numéraire[1] and a flexible real exchange rate regime is adopted. Alternatively, we could set a fixed real exchange rate by fixing the ratio of exchange rate to domestic price index and allowing the government to sell and buy foreign exchange to maintain this price ratio. However, the Chinese government switched to a managed floating exchange rate regime in July 2005 and had let the renminbi exchange rate gradually appreciate 19.5 per cent by December 2010. Therefore it is preferable not to fix the real exchange rate in the model.

The model adopts a small open economy assumption, which suggests that changes in export and import volumes in each sector in counterfactual simulations are not large enough to affect the export and import prices in international markets. The quantity of exports and imports change endogenously, but the current account balance is fixed.

Extension 1: FDI spillovers under monopolistic competition

Incorporating monopolistic competition into the CGE model

The CGE model constructed in previous sections assumes that the Chinese economy is a perfectly competitive market. However, perfect competition is only one among various possible market structures and it is important to further examine the effects of FDI productivity spillovers in an alternative scenario, "monopolistic competition" (Dixit and Stiglitz 1977). Monopolistic competition refers to a market structure where a relatively large group of firms produce different varieties of a particular product. The product of one firm within the group is highly, but not perfectly, substitutable for the product of another firm. Therefore each firm has a limited monopoly power and faces a downward rather than horizontal demand curve. Entry barriers are low so that entry occurs in a monopolistically competitive group when a new firm introduces a new product. In the long run, every surviving firm makes zero profit due to the assumption of free entry and exit.

The scenario of monopolistic competition has been applied widely in the analysis of trade liberalisation (e.g. Harrison *et al.* 1994, 1995, 1997; Francois and Roland-Holst 1997; Blake *et al.* 1999). Their analyses conclude that the benefits of trade liberalisation under monopolistic competition include consumption of a greater product variety, lower product price and higher production efficiency due to increased competition.

However, FDI productivity spillovers in this scenario have not yet been studied. This section aims to fill this gap. The key to modelling monopolistic competition in the CGE model on FDI productivity spillovers is to find the mark-up rate (to be defined by equation (7.11)).

For a firm with a certain market power, its total revenue is

$$TR = P(Q) \times Q$$

where product price (P) is a function of total output (Q). Marginal revenue (MR) is

$$MR = \frac{\partial TR}{\partial Q} = P + \frac{\partial P}{\partial Q} Q = P\left(1 - \frac{1}{|\varepsilon|}\right) \tag{7.5}$$

where

$$|\varepsilon| = -\frac{P}{Q}\frac{\partial Q}{\partial P}$$

denotes the price elasticity of demand. Also

$$MR = MC \Rightarrow \frac{1}{|\varepsilon|} = \frac{P - MC}{P} \equiv markup(\%) \tag{7.6}$$

where MC denotes marginal cost. As discussed, in the long run, every surviving firm makes zero profit due to the assumption of free entry and exit, so that $TR = P \times Q = TC$. Therefore the mark-up rate is also equal to the proportion of fixed cost in total cost:

$$markup(\%) = \frac{P - MC}{P} = \frac{(P - MC) \times Q}{P \times Q} = \frac{TC - VC}{P \times Q} = \frac{FC}{P \times Q} = \frac{FC}{TC}$$

where TC, VC, and FC denote total cost, variable cost and fixed cost, respectively.

This indicates that in a monopolistic competitive market, each firm has to collect a mark-up to pay the fixed cost. This transformed zero-profit condition, together with market clearance and income balance conditions, is an important property of a general equilibrium (see Chapter 5), and the mark-up rate is crucial to modelling monopolistic competition in a CGE model.

In the FDI spillover model, the representative agent has a nested consumption structure, which can be represented by a CES function, as shown by equations (7.1)–(7.4). With FDI productivity spillovers specified by equations (5.8) and (5.9), we know that $Y_{i,j,k}$, as ownership-type products, is a function of FDI productivity spillovers, so that we write $Y_{i,j,k}(\Theta_{i,j,k})$, where

$$\Theta_{i,j,k} = \frac{NTFP_{i,j,k}}{NTFP_{0,i,j,k}}$$

Such spillovers are assumed to take place between FIEs and domestic firms, so that $NTFP_{i,j,k} = NTFP_{0,i,j,k}$ and $\Theta_{i,j,k} = 1$ for $k = 1$ (FIEs).

The associated demand functions of CES equations (7.1)–(7.4) can be derived: for bottom-level aggregation,

$$Q_{i,j,k,f} = \left(\frac{P_{Y(i,j,k)}}{P_{Q(i,j,k,f)}}\right)^{\sigma_4} \times Y_{i,j,k} \tag{7.1a}$$

for third-level aggregation,

$$Y_{i,j,k} = \left(\frac{P_{DI(i,j)}}{P_{Y(i,j,k)}}\right)^{\sigma_3} \times DI_{i,j} \tag{7.2a}$$

for second-level aggregation,

$$DI_{i,j} = \left(\frac{P_{AR(i)}}{P_{DI(i,j)}}\right)^{\sigma_2} AR_i \tag{7.3a}$$

and for top-level aggregation,

$$AR_i = \left(\frac{P_{AG}}{P_{AR(i)}}\right)^{\sigma_1} AG \tag{7.4a}$$

Starting from the bottom-level aggregation, we transform (7.1a) as

$$\begin{aligned} P_{Q(i,j,k,f)} &= \left(\frac{Y_{i,j,k}}{Q_{i,j,k,f}}\right)^{1/\sigma_4} \times P_{Y(i,j,k)} \\ &= (Q_{i,j,k,f}^{-1})^{1/\sigma_4} \times (Y_{i,j,k}^{-1})^{1/\sigma_4} \times (P_{Y(i,j,k)}) \end{aligned} \tag{7.1b}$$

All three terms in brackets on the right-hand side of equation (7.1b) are functions of $Q_{i,j,k,f}$. So we can differentiate equation (7.1b) with respect to $Q_{i,j,k,f}$ following the product rule:

$$\begin{aligned} \frac{\partial P_{Q(i,j,k,f)}}{\partial Q_{i,j,k,f}} &= -\frac{1}{\sigma_4}\frac{P_{Q(i,j,k,f)}}{Q_{i,j,k,f}} + \frac{1}{\sigma_4}\frac{P_{Q(i,j,k,f)}}{Y_{i,j,k}}\frac{\partial Y_{i,j,k}}{\partial Q_{i,j,k,f}} \\ &\quad + \frac{P_{Q(i,j,k,f)}}{P_{Y(i,j,k)}}\frac{\partial P_{Y(i,j,k)}}{\partial Q_{i,j,k,f}} \end{aligned} \tag{7.7}$$

Unitary "conjectural variation" (Kamien and Schwartz 1983) is assumed here, i.e. each firm assumes that an increase of one unit of its own product value will bring exactly the same increase of total value of the product aggregate of its group. In other words, no other firm changes its output:

$$P_{Y(i,j,k)} \times \Delta Y_{i,j,k} = P_{Q(i,j,k,f)} \times \Delta Q_{i,j,k,f},$$

so that

$$\frac{\Delta Y_{i,j,k}}{\Delta Q_{i,j,k,f}} = \frac{P_{Q(i,j,k,f)}}{P_{Y(i,j,k)}} \tag{7.8}$$

The term $\partial P_{Y(i,j,k)}/\partial Q_{i,j,k,f}$ in (7.7) can thus be transformed using equation (7.8):

$$\frac{\partial P_{Y(i,j,k)}}{\partial Q_{i,j,k,f}} = \frac{\partial P_{Y(i,j,k)}}{\partial Y_{i,j,k}}\frac{\partial Y_{i,j,k}}{\partial Q_{i,j,k,f}} = \frac{\partial P_{Y(i,j,k)}}{\partial Y_{i,j,k}}\frac{P_{Q(i,j,k,f)}}{P_{Y(i,j,k)}} \tag{7.9}$$

Substituting (7.8) and (7.9) back into (7.7) and multiplying both sides of (7.7) by $Q_{i,j,k,f}/P_{Q(i,j,k)}$ gives

$$\begin{aligned}\frac{1}{\varepsilon_{Q(i,j,k,f)}} &= \frac{\partial P_{Q(i,j,k,f)}}{\partial Q_{i,j,k,f}}\frac{Q_{i,j,k,f}}{P_{Q(i,j,k)}} \\ &= -\frac{1}{\sigma_4}+\frac{1}{\sigma_4}\frac{P_{Q(i,j,k,f)}}{P_{Y(i,j,k)}}\frac{Q_{i,j,k,f}}{Y_{i,j,k}} \\ &\quad +\left(\frac{P_{Q(i,j,k,f)}}{P_{Y(i,j,k)}}\frac{Q_{i,j,k,f}}{Y_{i,j,k}}\right)\left(\frac{\partial P_{Y(i,j,k)}}{\partial Y_{i,j,k}}\frac{Q_{i,j,k,f}}{P_{Y(i,j,k)}}\right) \\ &= -\frac{1}{\sigma_4}+\frac{1}{\sigma_4}\varphi_{i,j,k,f}+\varphi_{i,j,k,f}\times\frac{1}{\varepsilon_{Y(i,j,k)}} \qquad (7.10)\end{aligned}$$

where $\varphi_{i,j,k,f}$ denotes the market share of the fth firm in the kth sector.

From equation (7.10) we find that the inverse of elasticity of demand of the fth firm's products is a function of the inverse elasticity of demand of the kth sector, which can be derived following a similar procedure:

$$\frac{1}{\varepsilon_{Y(i,j,k)}} = -\frac{1}{\sigma_3}+\frac{1}{\sigma_3}\gamma_{i,j,k}+\gamma_{i,j,k}\times\frac{1}{\varepsilon_{DI(i,j)}} \qquad (7.11)$$

$$\frac{1}{\varepsilon_{DI(i,j)}} = -\frac{1}{\sigma_2}+\frac{1}{\sigma_2}\beta_{i,j}+\beta_{i,j}\times\frac{1}{\varepsilon_{AR(i)}} \qquad (7.12)$$

$$\frac{1}{\varepsilon_{AR(i)}} = -\frac{1}{\sigma_1}+\frac{1}{\sigma_1}\alpha_i+\alpha_i\times\frac{1}{\varepsilon_{AG}} \qquad (7.13)$$

where α_i, $\beta_{i,j}$ and $\gamma_{i,j,k}$ are market share parameters of AR_i, $DI_{i,j}$, and $Y_{i,j,k}$ respectively:

$$\alpha_i = \frac{AR_i\times P_{AR(i)}}{AG\times P_{AG}},\quad \beta_{i,j}=\frac{DI_{i,j}\times P_{DI(i,j)}}{AR_i\times P_{AR(i)}},\quad \gamma_{i,j,k}=\frac{Y_{i,j,k}\times P_{Y(i,j,k)}}{DI_{i,j}\times P_{DI(i,j)}}$$

As $Y_{i,j,k}$ is a function of the endogenous FDI productivity spillover terms $\Theta_{i,j,k} = NTFP_{i,j,k}/\overline{NTFP}_{0,i,j,k}$, its market share $\gamma_{i,j,k}$ is also a function of $\Theta_{i,j,k}$.

For the aggregate product AG, assume $P_{AG}\cdot AG = E$, where E denotes the consumer's fixed expenditure. Then $AG = E/P_{AG}$. Thus we can get the elasticity of demand for this aggregate product:

$$\varepsilon_{AG} = \frac{\partial AG}{\partial P_{AG}}\frac{P_{AG}}{AG} = \left(-\frac{E}{P_{AG}^2}\right)\left(\frac{P_{AG}}{E/P_{AG}}\right) = -1 \qquad (7.14)$$

Substitute (7.14) back into (7.13), and then substitute (7.13) into (7.12), and so on until we get the final expression of the firm-level inverse elasticity of demand, which is also the firm-level mark-up rate:

$$\begin{aligned}
mk_{i,j,k,f}(\%) &= \left|\frac{1}{\varepsilon_{Q(i,j,k,f)}}\right| \\
&= \frac{1}{\sigma_4} + \varphi_{i,j,k,f}\left(\frac{1}{\sigma_3} - \frac{1}{\sigma_4}\right) + \varphi_{i,j,k,f}\gamma_{i,j,k}\left(\frac{1}{\sigma_2} - \frac{1}{\sigma_3}\right) \\
&\quad + \beta_{i,j}\gamma_{i,j,k}\varphi_{i,j,k,f}\left(\frac{1}{\sigma_1} - \frac{1}{\sigma_2}\right) \\
&\quad + \alpha_i\beta_{i,j}\gamma_{i,j,k}\varphi_{i,j,k,f}\left(\frac{1}{\sigma_1} - 1\right)
\end{aligned} \tag{7.15}$$

In the model which examines the FDI productivity spillovers in a new market structure, i.e. monopolistic competition among firms with heterogeneous productivities (in short, "firm heterogeneity"), a firm's market share $\varphi_{i,j,k,f}$ will be determined by its productivity within each group (Melitz 2003). We will then replace equation (7.15) with alternative specifications containing richer information on the new scenario.

But in the current "representative producer" CGE model, only the ownership-level aggregate mark-up rate matters. Suppose each "ownership group" (indexed by k) is populated by N_f firms of identical size but producing differentiated products. Thus their market share $\varphi_{i,j,k,f}$ is simply equal to $1/N_f$. This size symmetry also implies that the mark-up rate of each group is equal to that of its representative firm:

$$\begin{aligned}
mk_{i,j,k}(\%) = mk_{i,j,k,f}(\%) &= \left|\frac{1}{\varepsilon_{Q(i,j,k,f)}}\right| \\
&= \frac{1}{\sigma_4} + \frac{1}{N_{i,j,k,f}}\left(\frac{1}{\sigma_3} - \frac{1}{\sigma_4}\right) + \frac{\gamma_{i,j,k}}{N_{i,j,k,f}}\left(\frac{1}{\sigma_2} - \frac{1}{\sigma_3}\right) \\
&\quad + \frac{\beta_{i,j}\gamma_{i,j,k}}{N_{i,j,k,f}}\left(\frac{1}{\sigma_1} - \frac{1}{\sigma_2}\right) + \frac{\alpha_i\beta_{i,j}\gamma_{i,j,k}}{N_{i,j,k,f}}\left(\frac{1}{\sigma_1} - 1\right)
\end{aligned} \tag{7.15a}$$

In equation (7.15a), the market share parameters (α_i, $\beta_{i,j}$, $\gamma_{i,j,k}$) are endogenously determined while the elasticities of substitution (σ_i, $i = 1, 2, 3, 4$) are exogenously chosen. $\gamma_{i,j,k}$ is of particular importance as it is a function of the term $\Theta_{i,j,k}$ and conveys information on FDI spillover.

FDI productivity spillovers under monopolistic competition

The impact of FDI productivity spillovers in a scenario of monopolistic competition can be illustrated by a variety-scale diagram (originally proposed by Francois and Roland-Holst, 1997, p. 349, in a trade model) for a certain domestic sector whose aggregate output is denoted by $Y_{i,j,k}$. As shown in Figure 7.2, $N_{i,j,k,f}$

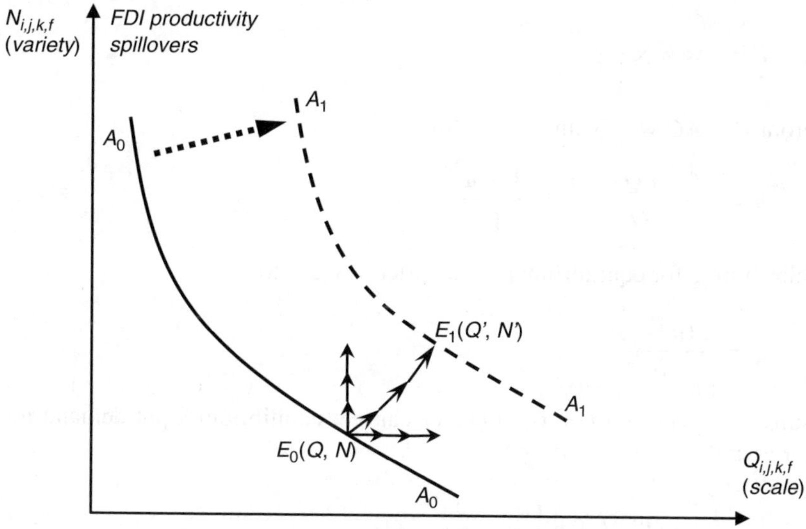

Figure 7.2 FDI productivity spillovers under monopolistic competition.

(variety, N for short) and $Q_{i,j,k,f}$ (scale, Q for short) are the vertical and horizontal axis, respectively. A downward-sloping curve A_0A_0 depicts the trade-off between variety and scale due to the resource constraint facing the producers in this sector. A_0A_0 can also be understood as a "variety-scale possibility frontier".

Now consider a case where the production capacity of this domestic sector expands from A_0A_0 to A_1A_1 due to FDI productivity spillovers, which helps the domestic producers in this sector produce more efficiently with the given resources. Suppose an initial production point is $E_0(Q, N)$. Then a production capacity enlargement can result in two dimensions of expansion, one along Q and the other along N, as shown in Figure 7.2.

This can be illustrated algebraically in a simple model (Krugman 1980). Suppose the composite input for each firm is denoted by l, and total factor supply is L. All firms have the same input function $l = f + vQ$, where f and v denote fixed cost and variable cost measured in units of input, respectively. Then the profit of any firm is $\pi = p(Q)Q - w(f + vQ)$, where p and w denote prices of output and input, respectively.

At long-run equilibrium with entry and exit, two conditions should be both satisfied: the first is profit maximisation, i.e. $MR = MC$; and the second is zero profits in long-run equilibrium, i.e. $P = AC$.

With equation (7.5), $MR = MC$ means

$$MR = P \times \left(1 - \frac{1}{|\varepsilon|}\right) = v \times w = MC$$

so that

$$P = v \times w \times \frac{|\varepsilon|}{|\varepsilon| - 1}$$

From $P = AC$ we obtain

$$P = \frac{(f + vQ) \times w}{Q} = \frac{f \times w}{Q} + v \times w$$

Substituting for equilibrium product price P leads to

$$Q = \frac{f(|\varepsilon| - 1)}{b}$$

Substituting Q into $l = f + vQ$, we can get equilibrium input demand for any variety:

$$l = f + vQ = f + v\frac{f(|\varepsilon| - 1)}{v} = f|\varepsilon|$$

Thus the number of varieties which can possibly be produced given the limited total supply of factor L is determined by the full employment condition $L = N \times l$, which implies that:

$$N = \frac{L}{l} = \frac{L}{f \times |\varepsilon|}$$

Given the equilibrium solution of scale and variety,

$$(Q, N) = \left(\frac{f(|\varepsilon| - 1)}{v}, \frac{L}{f \times |\varepsilon|}\right)$$

we can now examine how FDI productivity spillovers affect the parameter values of f and v, which in turn affect the solutions of (Q, N). In this context, both f and v are functions of FDI spillovers, i.e. $f(\Theta)$ and $v(\Theta)$. As FDI spillovers push both fixed cost and variable cost lower, i.e. $\partial f(\Theta)/\partial\Theta < 0$, and $\partial v(\Theta)/\partial\Theta < 0$, the number of varieties ($N = L/f|\varepsilon|$) produced in the economy will increase. When variable cost decreases faster than fixed cost does, i.e. $|\partial v(\Theta)/\partial\Theta| > |\partial f(\Theta)/\partial\Theta|$, then the production scale, $Q = f(|\varepsilon| - 1)/v$, will also increase with FDI spillovers.

The above two expansion possibilities (i.e. both Q and N increase with FDI productivity spillovers) jointly result in a new equilibrium point $E_1(Q', N')$ in Figure 7.2. An upward-sloping curve connecting E_0 and E_1 depicts the positive correlation between N and Q, and can be understood as a "sectoral variety-scale expansion path". Therefore under the assumption of monopolistic competition, if domestic firms receive productivity spillovers from foreign-invested firms, the new equilibrium $E_1(N', Q')$ will bring consumers welfare improvement thanks to more varieties and cheaper prices ($P = vw|\varepsilon|/(|\varepsilon| - 1)$). However, only the price benefits may be available if goods are homogeneous and markets are perfectly competitive.

Extension 2: FDI spillovers under firm heterogeneity

Firm heterogeneity and CGE modelling

The CGE model under monopolistic competition assumes a representative firm of each type in each sector. However, this assumption is at odds with reality. Recent empirical research has shown that firms differ a lot in productivity. For example, Girma *et al.* (2005) found that a productivity hierarchy exists and determines the behaviour of British firms – only the most productive firms can engage in FDI, and less productive firms export, while the least productive firms can only serve the domestic market.

Moreover, such pervasive productivity heterogeneity leads to firm size difference within each sector – the firm productivity is positively related to firm size, as shown by Melitz (2003). In his model explicitly considering the productivity heterogeneity among firms, Melitz theoretically analyses the impact of trade on intra-industry resource reallocations and aggregate industry productivity. The model shows that only the most productive firms can afford the sunk cost of exporting. Trade liberalisation can induce these firms to produce more and engage in export, leading to stronger competition for a common pool of labour. This can push up labour costs and drive the least productive firms to exit. So firms with higher productivity survive the trade liberalisation and grow larger by absorbing the resources released by the exiting firms. Thus aggregate industry productivity increases due to the resource reallocation effect of trade under firm heterogeneity. These conclusions are supported by Feenstra and Kee (2008), who find that export variety of firms accounts for the time-series variation in productivity. In brief, firm heterogeneity is an important theoretical assumption for explaining productivity growth caused by the endogenous self-selection of exporters.

In this research on FDI productivity spillovers, the assumption that firms have heterogeneous productivity is also important in accounting for the effects of potential FDI spillovers – the productivity improvement effect and resource reallocation effect. This will shortly be discussed in detail.

In each sector, firms are heterogeneous in that they produce differentiated goods and differ in productivity. Every firm incurs fixed and variable costs in production.

An option for incorporating heterogeneous firms into a standard "representative firm" CGE model is to decompose the whole CGE model into a partial equilibrium (PE) module and general equilibrium (GE) module (Balistreri *et al.* 2007). This option has been adopted here. Firm behaviour is determined in the PE module, while the aggregate economy is calibrated in the GE module. Key variables are selected to transmit information recursively between PE and GE modules. PE and GE modules recursively recalibrate to the new information. This sequential recalibration (SR) process will continue until all variables common to the PE and GE are consistent, i.e. the discrepancy between the variable values obtained from

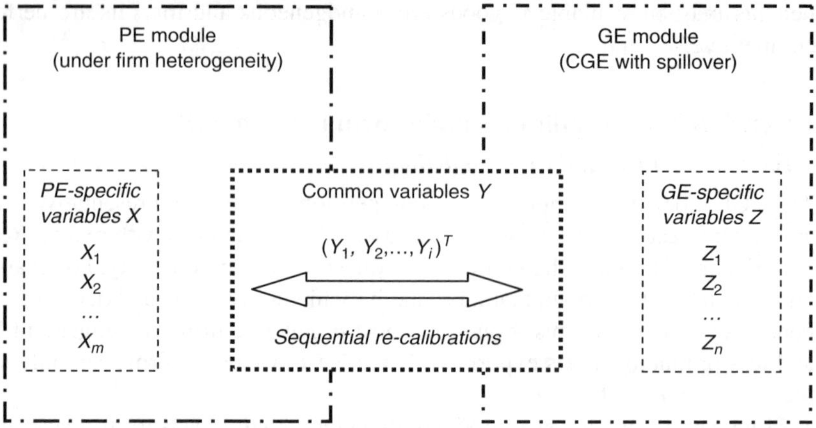

Figure 7.3 A decomposition of CGE model under firm heterogeneity.

the $(t-1)$th and tth iterations is at a trivial level. This SR has proven effective in achieving model convergence (Rutherford and Tarr 2008; Rausch and Rutherford 2010). The decomposition is sketched in Figure 7.3.

Model construction for firm heterogeneity (PE module)

The PE module is constructed to model the heterogeneity of firms in their productivity. Suppose there is a mass of M_i heterogeneous firms in the ith sector. These M_i firms produce highly, but not perfectly, substitutable products in that sector and have limited monopoly power, so that they can set their prices higher than their marginal costs, charge mark-ups to compensate fixed costs and earn possible profits. On entry each firm is assumed to take a free draw (i.e. no entry cost) of productivity φ_i from a Pareto distribution $g(\varphi_i) = (a/\varphi_i)(b/\varphi_i)^a$, setting a price $P_{i,f}(\varphi_i)$ and producing output $Q_{i,f}(\varphi_i)$. The values of parameters a and b can be taken from the literature (Bernard *et al.* 2003; Zhai 2008).

Firstly, we discuss the market structure. Suppose every firm in the ith sector needs to pay the same fixed cost F_i, which is assumed not to change to any external shock, e.g. productivity spillovers. Suppose firms in the ith sector face a market with a Dixit–Sliglitz style of preference (Dixit and Stiglitz 1977):

$$U_i = \left[\int_{\omega_i \in \Omega_i} Q(\omega_i)^{(\sigma-1)/\sigma}\, d\omega_i\right]^{\sigma/(\sigma-1)}, \quad \sigma > 1 \tag{7.16}$$

where ω_i indexes a continuum of variety of goods produced by the mass of M_i firms. The values of σ should be greater than 1 so that $\sigma(\sigma-1)/\sigma$ is greater than zero.

From the profit maximisation condition $MR = MC$, we know that each firm sets a price so that the mark-up rate equals the inverse of the absolute value of the elasticity of demand, i.e.

$$mk_{i,f}(\%) = \frac{1}{|\varepsilon_i|} = \frac{1}{\sigma} \tag{7.6a}$$

From the mark-up rule (7.6a), one can derive the optimal pricing rule for a firm with productivity $\varphi_{i,f}$:

$$mk_{i,f}(\%) = \frac{P_{i,f} - C_i/\varphi_{i,f}}{P_{i,f}} = \frac{1}{\sigma}$$

so that

$$P_{i,f} = \frac{\sigma}{\sigma - 1}\frac{C_i}{\varphi_{i,f}} \tag{7.17}$$

where C_i denotes the price of unit input cost in the ith sector, which is a weighted average of the intermediate input prices $(P_{i,j})$ and primary input prices $(P_{i,k})$:

$$C_i = \frac{\sum_z (PA_{i,z} \times \overline{IOD}_{i,z}) + PVA_i \times \overline{VA}_i}{\sum_z \overline{IOD}_{i,z} + \overline{VA}_i}$$

In this equation $\overline{IOD}_{i,z}$ denotes the zth intermediate input while $\overline{VA}_i$ denotes the primary input composite used for the production in the ith sector. The symbols for the prices of the two types of inputs ($PA_{i,z}$ and PVA_i) are identical to those in Tables A2.2–A2.3. The amount of these inputs also corresponds to the parameters in Tables A2.2–A2.3, i.e. $\overline{IOD}_{i,z} = \overline{IOD}(i, z)$ and $\overline{VA}_i = \overline{CP}(i) + \overline{DP}(i) + \overline{OP}(i)$.

The duality of CES preference (7.16) implies that the aggregate price is

$$\begin{aligned}
\hat{P}_i &= \left[\int_{\omega_i \in \Omega} P_{i,f}(\omega_i)^{1-\sigma}\, d\omega_i\right]^{1/(1-\sigma)} \\
&= \left[\int_0^{+\infty} P_{i,f}(\varphi_i)^{1-\sigma} \cdot M_i \cdot g(\varphi_i)\, d\varphi_i\right]^{1/(1-\sigma)} \\
&= \left[\int_0^{+\infty} \left(\frac{\sigma \cdot C_i}{(\sigma - 1)\varphi_i}\right)^{1-\sigma} \cdot M_i \cdot g(\varphi_i)\, d\varphi_i\right]^{1/(1-\sigma)} \\
&= \frac{\sigma \cdot C_i}{\sigma - 1} M_i^{1/(1-\sigma)} \left[\int_0^{+\infty} \varphi_i^{\sigma-1} g(\varphi_i)\, d\varphi_i\right]^{1/(1-\sigma)}
\end{aligned}$$

$$= \frac{(\sigma \cdot C_i/(\sigma-1))M_i^{1/(1-\sigma)}}{[\int_0^{+\infty} \varphi_i^{\sigma-1} g(\varphi_i)\, d\varphi_i]^{1/(\sigma-1)}}$$

$$= \left[\frac{\sigma \cdot C_i}{(\sigma-1)\tilde{\varphi}_i}\right] M_i^{1/(1-\sigma)} = P_i(\tilde{\varphi}_i) \cdot M_i^{1/(1-\sigma)} \tag{7.18}$$

where

$$\tilde{\varphi}_i \equiv \left[\int_0^{+\infty} \varphi_i^{\sigma-1} g(\varphi_i)\, d\varphi_i\right]^{1/(\sigma-1)} \tag{7.19}$$

denotes a weighted average of the firms' productivity levels φ.

For the sake of feasibility of computation, one needs information on the productivity distribution of corresponding sectors. In the literature, the Pareto distribution has been found "compelling" in approximating the real distribution of firm productivity (Helpman 2006, p. 597). For a Pareto distribution with probability density function $g(\varphi_i) = (a/\varphi_i)(b/\varphi_i)^a$, the corresponding cumulative distribution is:

$$G(\varphi_i) = \int_0^{\varphi_i} g(x)\, dx = \int_0^{\varphi_i} \frac{a}{x}\left(\frac{b}{x}\right)^a dx = \int_0^{\varphi_i} ab^a x^{-a-1}\, dx$$

$$= \frac{ab^a x^{-a}|_0^{\varphi_i}}{-a} = -\left(\frac{b}{x}\right)^a\Big|_0^{\varphi_i} = 1 - \left[-\left(\frac{b}{x}\right)^a\Big|_{\varphi_i}^{+\infty}\right]$$

$$= 1 + \left[0 - \left(\frac{b}{\varphi_i}\right)^a\right] = 1 - \left(\frac{b}{\varphi_i}\right)^a \tag{7.20}$$

Now we can have a definition of the "marginal firm". For any firm, the demand for its products from consumers is determined by the preference equation (7.16). Assuming the total expenditure on products in the ith sector is E_i, then

$$Q_{i,f} = \frac{E_i}{\hat{P}_i}\left(\frac{\hat{P}_i}{P_{i,f}(\varphi_{i,f})}\right)^\sigma \tag{7.21}$$

The profit function of a firm can be derived from (7.21) and (7.18):

$$\pi_{i,f}(\varphi_{i,f}) = P_{i,f}(\varphi_{i,f}) \times Q_{i,f}(\varphi_{i,f}) - C_i F_i$$

$$= E_i \times \hat{P}_i^{\sigma-1} \times [P_{i,f}(\varphi_{i,f})]^{1-\sigma} - C_i F_i$$

$$= E_i \times \hat{P}_i^{\sigma-1} \times \left[\frac{C_i \cdot \sigma}{(\sigma-1)\varphi_{i,f}}\right]^{1-\sigma} - C_i F_i$$

$$= E_i \times \left[\frac{C_i \cdot \sigma}{\hat{P}_i(\sigma-1)}\right]^{1-\sigma} \times \varphi_{i,f}^{\sigma-1} - C_i F_i \tag{7.22}$$

As can be seen from (7.22), since $\sigma > 1$, profit ($\pi_{i,f}$) is a monotonically increasing function of productivity ($\varphi_{i,f}$). Suppose there exists a productivity level φ_i^* which satisfies $\pi_i^*(\varphi_i^*) = 0$, i.e. "zero cut-off profit". Then for a firm whose $\varphi_{i,f} > \varphi_i^*$, $\pi_{i,f} > 0$ so that it can survive; while for other firms whose $\varphi_{i,f} < \varphi_i^*$, $\pi_{i,f} < 0$ so that they have to exit. A firm taking a productivity draw of φ_i^* can be called a "marginal firm". Therefore the probability of successful entry (those firms with productivity higher than the marginal one, φ_i^*) is

$$1 - G(\varphi_i^*) = \left(\frac{b}{\varphi_i^*}\right)^a \tag{7.23}$$

For the marginal firm, its mark-up equals the fixed cost, i.e.

$$C_i \cdot F_i = P_i(\varphi_i^*) \cdot Q_i(\varphi_i^*) \cdot \frac{1}{\sigma} \tag{7.24}$$

Secondly, we measure the aggregate productivity at industry level. The conditional distribution of $g(\varphi_i)$ on $[\varphi_i^*, +\infty)$ can be obtained with the information on the probability of successful entry (equation (7.23)):

$$\mu(\varphi_i) = \begin{cases} \dfrac{g(\varphi_i)}{1 - G(\varphi_i^*)} & \text{if } \varphi_i \geq \varphi_i^* \\ 0 & \text{otherwise} \end{cases}$$

Suppose $\tilde{\varphi}_i$ (defined by equation (7.19)) is the productivity of a firm pricing at $\tilde{P}_i$, then the weighted average of the firm productivity $\tilde{\varphi}_i$ can be "inflated" (with equation (7.23)) conditional on the successful entry:

$$\begin{aligned}
\tilde{\varphi}_i(\varphi_i^*) &\equiv \left[\int_{\varphi_i^*}^{+\infty} \varphi_i^{\sigma-1} \frac{g(\varphi_i)}{1 - G(\varphi_i^*)}\, d\varphi_i\right]^{1/(\sigma-1)} \\
&= \left[\frac{1}{1 - G(\varphi_i^*)} \int_{\varphi_i^*}^{+\infty} \varphi_i^{\sigma-1} g(\varphi_i)\, d\varphi_i\right]^{1/(\sigma-1)} \\
&= \left[\left(\frac{\varphi_i^*}{b}\right)^a \int_{\varphi_i^*}^{+\infty} \varphi_i^{\sigma-1} g(\varphi_i)\, d\varphi_i\right]^{1/(\sigma-1)} \\
&= \left[\left(\frac{\varphi_i^*}{b}\right)^a \int_{\varphi_i^*}^{+\infty} \varphi_i^{\sigma-1} \frac{a}{\varphi_i}\left(\frac{b}{\varphi_i}\right)^a d\varphi_i\right]^{1/(\sigma-1)} \\
&= \left[a(\varphi_i^*)^a \int_{\varphi_i^*}^{+\infty} \varphi_i^{\sigma-a-2}\, d\varphi i\right]^{1/(\sigma-1)} = \left[\frac{a(\varphi_i^*)^a}{\sigma - a - 1} \varphi_i^{\sigma-a-1}\Big|_{\varphi_i^*}^{+\infty}\right]^{1/(\sigma-1)}
\end{aligned}$$

If $\sigma - a - 1 > 0$, $\tilde{\varphi}_i$ approaches to infinity. When $\sigma - a - 1 < 0$ (consistent with the results of Bernard *et al.* 2003), a solution can be obtained:

$$\tilde{\varphi}_i(\varphi_i^*) = \left(\frac{a}{a+1-\sigma}\right)^{1/(\sigma-1)} \varphi_i^* \tag{7.25}$$

Thus the weighted aggregate productivity in sector $i(\tilde{\varphi}_i)$ is denoted as a function of the cut-off productivity (φ_i^*). This facilitates the interaction of the GE and PE modules in the CGE model. In the PE module, the values of cut-off productivity (φ_i^*) are simulated, then the values of aggregate productivity $(\tilde{\varphi}_i)$ can be obtained with equation (7.25), summarising the productivity distribution of the firms in sector i. A virtual "quasi-representative" firm with a productivity level of $\tilde{\varphi}_i$ can be assumed here to represent the whole mass of firms in that sector. Such a "quasi-representative" firm takes the place of the conventional "representative" firm in each sector in the GE module, enabling the CGE model to capture how firm behaviour (e.g. productivity spillovers) affects macroeconomic performance.

Thirdly, we identify the zero cut-off profit condition. From the model of Melitz (2003, p. 1700), we know that the ratio of any two firms' revenues depends on the ratio of their productivity levels, so that, using equation (7.25):

$$\frac{P_i(\tilde{\varphi}_i)Q_i(\tilde{\varphi}_i)}{P_i(\varphi_i^*)Q_i(\varphi_i^*)} = \left(\frac{\tilde{\varphi}_i}{\varphi_i^*}\right)^{\sigma-1} = \left[\left(\frac{a}{a+1-\sigma}\right)^{1/(\sigma-1)}\right]^{\sigma-1} = \frac{a}{a+1-\sigma}$$

and

$$P_i(\varphi_i^*)Q_i(\varphi_i^*) = \tilde{P}_i(\tilde{\varphi}_i)\tilde{Q}_i(\tilde{\varphi}_i)\left(\frac{a+1-\sigma}{a}\right) \tag{7.26}$$

Substituting equation (7.26) into equation (7.24), we obtain a new condition dependent on the weighted average productivity $\tilde{\varphi}_i$:

$$C_i \cdot F_i = P_i(\tilde{\varphi}_i)Q_i(\tilde{\varphi}_i)\left(\frac{a+1-\sigma}{a\sigma}\right) \tag{7.27}$$

Fourthly, we derive the firm-level demand. The duality of CES preference also implies that the demand for the output of the "quasi-representative firm" is determined by

$$\tilde{Q}_i = \frac{E_i}{\hat{P}_i}\left(\frac{\hat{P}_i}{\tilde{P}_i(\tilde{\varphi}_i)}\right)^{\sigma} = \frac{E_i}{\hat{P}_i}\left(\frac{\hat{P}_i}{\tilde{P}_i(\varphi_i^*)}\right)^{\sigma} \tag{7.28}$$

where $\hat{P}_i$ and E_i are the composite output price and expenditure level for the ith sector.

Fifthly, we obtain input partial equilibrium. Finally, one more equation is needed to link the PE module to the GE module. This equation concerns the cost of total input for each sector:

$$M_i \cdot C_i \cdot \left(F_i + \frac{\tilde{Q}_i(\tilde{\varphi}_i)}{\tilde{\varphi}_i} \right) = \sum_z (PA_{i,z} \times \overline{IOD}_{i,z}) + PVA_i \times \overline{VA}_i \tag{7.29}$$

where, again, $\overline{IOD}_{i,z}$ denotes the zth intermediate input while $\overline{VA}_i$ denotes the primary input composite used for the production in the ith sector. With the information of key price variables from the GE module (output price vector, **P**, and input price vector **C**), the above system of five equations (7.17), (7.25), (7.27), (7.28), and (7.29) can be solved to obtain the values of five endogenous variables, $(M_i, \tilde{Q}_i, \tilde{P}_i, \tilde{\varphi}_i, \varphi_i^*)$. Then the information on computed productivity level $\tilde{\varphi}_i$ is passed back to the GE module, and the GE module recalibrates to this new information. This sequential recalibration process continues until the values of the above three key variable vectors ($\mathbf{P}$, $\mathbf{C}$, $\boldsymbol{\varphi}$) obtained from the recalibrations in the PE and GE modules are mutually consistent, i.e. the discrepancy between the variable values obtained from the $(t-1)$th and tth iterations is at a trivial level. With the PE module constructed above, we can thus extend the CGE model from a representative-firm model to one capable of analysing firm-level changes caused by productivity shocks.

FDI productivity spillovers under firm heterogeneity

If the FDI productivity spillovers occur, then two effects arise. The first one is the productivity improvement effect, i.e. SOEs and private domestic enterprises can improve their productivity accordingly. As shown in Figure 7.4, the probability density function $g_1(\varphi)$ of the productivity distribution will be shifted to the right from $g_1(\varphi)$ to $g_2(\varphi)$. Another effect is resource reallocation effect. The domestic firms are now generally more productive than before, and the market becomes more competitive. As a higher productivity enables a firm to reduce its price and to sell more, this will increase the demand for limited resources and thus lift input costs. The least productive enterprises can no longer afford the higher costs and will be forced to exit. Thus the cut-off productivity level φ^* will be lifted from the original level φ_1^* (without spillovers) to a new level φ_2^* (with spillovers). With the above two effects combined, the productivity of existing firms improves, as does the distribution from which new entrants draw productivity.

Therefore the cut-off productivity level φ^* is a function of the variable measuring FDI productivity spillovers, i.e. $\varphi^*(\Theta)$ (defined before). If we assume that the $g(\varphi)$ will be shifted by the same magnitude as φ^* is, then a Pareto distribution function of domestic firms' productivity can be transformed into

$$g(\varphi - \Delta\varphi^*) = \frac{ab^a}{(\varphi - \Delta\varphi^*(\Theta))^{a+1}} = \frac{ab^a}{(\varphi - (\varphi_2^*(\Theta) - \varphi_1^*(\Theta)))^{a+1}}$$

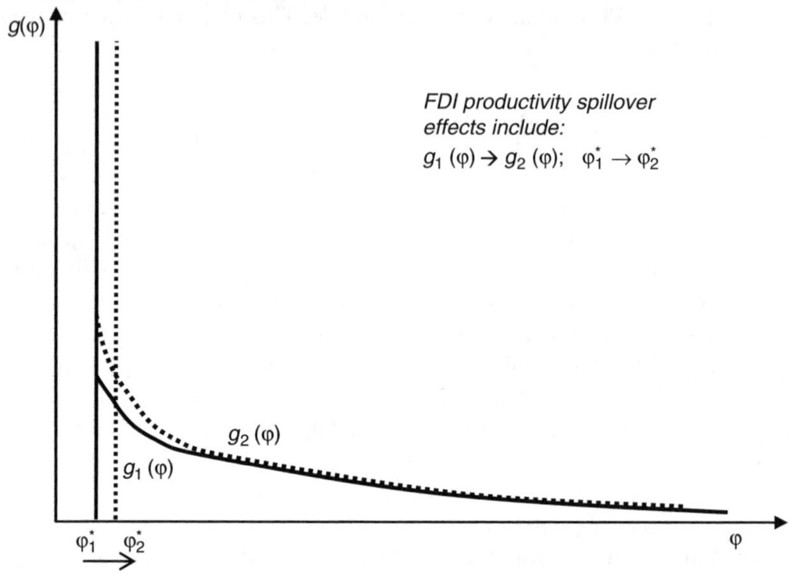

Figure 7.4 FDI spillovers under firm heterogeneity.

In computer programming, we can calibrate the benchmark value of $\varphi_1^*(\Theta)$ first. Then in counterfactual scenarios with FDI productivity spillovers, a new cutoff productivity value $\varphi_2^*(\Theta)$ is endogenously determined.

We will discuss the results obtained in computer simulations in the next chapter.

Conclusions

A benchmark CGE model for the Chinese economy has been presented with the original forms and "calibrated duality forms" of CES functions. The model contains blocks for value-added production, output production, CET transformation into export and domestic consumption, labour and capital disaggregation, Armington aggregation, export and import, representative domestic agent, representative agent for multinational enterprises, and government. Equations for equilibria of factor markets, Armington markets, aggregate export and import are also presented.

We model the FDI productivity spillovers in an alternative market structure – monopolistic competition with homogeneous firms. In this scenario, the markup rate of a representative firm of each sector is derived, which is essential to extending a CGE model to incorporate monopolistic competition. A CGE model to study FDI spillovers under monopolistic competition can also reflect the changes of product varieties and quantities caused by the spillovers.

We also model the FDI productivity spillovers in another alternative market structure, i.e. monopolistic competition with heterogeneous firms. This market structure is a newly explored one in the literature, and is potentially important in explaining the productivity change of domestic firms. A CGE model under firm heterogeneity is composed of a general equilibrium module and a partial equilibrium module. The former is a model with FDI spillovers under perfect competition. The latter deals with firm heterogeneity, assuming a virtual "quasi-representative" firm and "summarising" the distribution of firm productivity in each sector. The CGE model in this scenario can provide an alternative perspective on the effects of spillovers by examining productivity improvement under FDI productivity spillovers in a more direct way.

In the next chapter, the effects of an FDI shock to the economy under three market structures (perfect competition assumption, monopolistic competition with homogeneous firms and heterogeneous firms) will be evaluated and compared. The effects of the 2008 corporate income tax reform on the above three market structures will then be analysed and compared in Chapter 9.

8 Magnitude and pattern of productivity spillovers

An FDI shock to the benchmark economy (without spillovers)

An FDI shock without spillovers is introduced into the economy by increasing the capital stock in each foreign-invested sector. The investment data actually take the amount of FDI inflows in 2003, the year after the benchmark year 2002. As shown in Table 8.1, FDI into the manufacturing sectors accounts for almost 70 per cent of total FDI. Among manufacturing sectors, the top five sectors in attracting FDI are electronic products (11.9% of total FDI), textile (7.1%), raw chemical materials and chemical products (4.9%), garments and other fibre products (4.4%), and transport equipment (4.4%).

When the above FDI shock is introduced into the CGE model by changing the values of $\overline{DELTAFDI}(A)$ in equation (A2.13.1), the changes in sectors of different ownerships are as shown in Table 8.2. The table shows that an FDI shock to the benchmark economy enables the output of FIEs in the manufacturing, mining and utilities (MMU) sectors to surge by 20.8 per cent, while domestic enterprises (both SOEs and private) are negatively affected. This negative impact is caused by the expansion of foreign-invested firms which attract labour away from the domestic enterprises in the same industries. Nonetheless, the overall impact of FDI on total output, GDP and welfare is positive.

Table 8.3 shows how FDI affects the performance of enterprises of different ownership in the top five FDI recipient industries. The changing patterns of output, value added and export are consistent with those exhibited by Table 8.2, i.e. the outputs of FIEs increase dramatically, while the outputs of domestic enterprises contract.

The price of capital is generally pulled down by the influx of foreign capital. Due to the imperfect transformability of capital between foreign-invested and domestic enterprises (with a benchmark elasticity of 2), the price of capital in domestic sectors does not decrease with a magnitude as large as in foreign-invested sectors.

The price of labour in foreign-invested sectors is generally higher as more foreign capital is pursuing the limited amount of labour. Due to the very low transformability of labour between foreign-invested and domestic enterprises (with an benchmark elasticity of 0.5), a contraction of domestic sectors will lead to less demand for labour and pull down the price of labour.

Table 8.1 FDI in China by sectors, 2003 ($ million)

Groups	*Sectors*	*FDI*	*%*
Mining	Coal, petroleum and gas	2,779	0.6
	Ferrous metals mining	0	0.0
	Non-ferrous metals mining	0	0.0
	Mining of non-metal, other minerals, and other ores	0	0.0
Manufacturing	Food, beverage and tobacco manufacturing	11,206	2.5
	Textile industry	22,591	5.1
	Garments and other fibre products	19,653	4.4
	Leather, furs, down and related products	14,344	3.2
	Timber processing, bamboo, cane, palm fibre, etc.	3,252	0.7
	Furniture manufacturing	4,438	1.0
	Papermaking and paper products	9,807	2.2
	Printing and record medium reproduction	4,268	1.0
	Cultural, educational and sports goods	7,083	1.6
	Petroleum processing and coking	2,354	0.5
	Raw chemical materials and chemical products	21,518	4.9
	Medical and pharmaceutical products	7,864	1.8
	Chemical fibre	3,595	0.8
	Rubber products	5,966	1.3
	Plastic products	16,201	3.7
	Non-metal mineral products	13,615	3.1
	Smelting and pressing of ferrous metals	10,809	2.4
	Smelting and pressing of non-ferrous metals	5,836	1.3
	Metal products	16,635	3.8
	Ordinary machinery	12,906	2.9
	Special purpose equipment	10,128	2.3
	Transport equipment	19,622	4.4
	Electronic and electric products	52,490	11.9
	Instruments, meters, cultural and office machinery	13,671	3.1
Utilities	Production of electric power, steam and hot water	4,549	1.0
	Production of gas	3,919	0.9
	Production of tap water	2,244	0.5
Agriculture	Farming, forestry, animal husbandry and fishing	8,278	1.9
Construction	Construction	5,061	1.1
Banking and insurance	Banking and insurance	1,919	0.4
Real estate	Real estate	43,302	9.8
Other services	Geological perambulation and water conservancy; transport, storage, post and telecommunication services; wholesale and retail trade and catering; social services; healthcare, sports and social welfare; education, culture, radio, films and television; scientific and technical services	60,578	13.7
	Public administration and other services	0	0.0
Subtotal	All manufacturing	309,852	69.9
Total	All sectors	442,481	100.0

Source: Ministry of Commerce of China; National Bureau of Statistics of China (2004). Compilations by the author.

Table 8.2 Effects of an FDI shock to the benchmark economy (without spillovers)

Variables	*Change (%)*
National output	5.9
GDP	5.7
Output of FIEs in MMU	20.8
Output of domestic enterprises (SOEs + private) in MMU	−1.9
– SOEs	−0.6
– private enterprises	−2.3
Output of non-MMU sectors (both foreign and domestic)	6.3
Welfare (equivalent variation)	2.5

Notes:
a MMU is composed of mining, manufacturing and utilities.
b Welfare level (or equivalent variation) denotes the scale of total consumption by the representative consumer.
c Elasticity of transformation of capital and labour $(\tau_K, \tau_L) = (2.0, 0.5)$.

Table 8.3 Impacts of FDI on enterprises with different ownerships in the top five recipient sectors in manufacturing (%), without spillovers

		Export	*Output*	P_L	P_K
Textile	FIEs	46.1	39.9	7.7	−39.3
	SOEs	−7.9	−4.0	−4.6	−1.3
	Private	−8.8	−4.7	−5.4	−2.4
Garments	FIEs	43.4	31.9	5.2	−34.4
	SOEs	−5.9	−9.1	−9.0	−4.6
	Private	−5.9	−9.1	−9.0	−4.6
Chemicals	FIEs	41.6	32.7	6.5	−29.2
	SOEs	−5.5	−3.2	−2.6	−0.5
	Private	−6.0	−3.6	−3.0	−1.2
Transport	FIEs	31.0	16.1	−2.2	−24.6
	SOEs	0.5	−4.6	−7.5	−2.3
	Private	−0.9	−5.5	−8.5	−3.7
Electronicals	FIEs	15.7	12.0	4.7	−12.5
	SOEs	−5.2	−4.6	−0.8	0.0
	Private	−5.3	−4.7	−0.9	−0.1

Source: As Table 8.2.

The elasticity of transformation of labour between ownerships is lower than that of capital because inter-ownership labour mobility is still very low in China. According to a recent firm-level survey conducted by Asia Market Intelligence (see Table 8.4), in the 1,500 firms surveyed, only about 0.2 per cent of the employees had FIE work experience in 2000. Labour mobility in the other direction, from domestic firms to foreign-invested firms, should be higher given the higher salaries (Zhao 2002) and more vibrant work environment in the latter. In brief, the labour mobility between ownerships is rather one-directional, if any. Knight and Yueh (2004) also argue that the inter-firm labour mobility in urban areas in China was

Table 8.4 Employees with employment history in foreign firms, 2000

Industries	*Number of firms surveyed*	*(%)*
Accounting and related services	104	0.5
Advertising and marketing	89	0.4
Apparel and leather goods	222	0.1
Business logistics services	110	0.0
Communication services	71	0.0
Consumer products	165	0.1
Electronic components	203	0.2
Electronic equipment	192	0.6
Information technology services	128	0.6
Vehicles and vehicle parts	216	0.1
Total	1,500	0.2

Source: Asia Market Intelligence.

still very low in 1999. Therefore it is reasonable to set a relatively low benchmark parameter value for the elasticity of transformation of labour.

However, as a robustness check, we can also try different parameter values for the elasticities of capital (τ_K) and labour (τ_L) transformation and see what effect this has on the results. In the experiments, τ_K and τ_L take 10 different values ($\tau_K = 0.1, 0.4, 0.7, \ldots, 2.8$). While some studies (e.g. Springer 1998; Lejour *et al.* 2008) take 3 or 4 as the elasticity of capital transformation, 3 is taken here as the upper limit given the idiosyncratic characteristics of foreign capital, state capital and private capital in the Chinese economy in transition. A value of 3 is also set as the upper limit for the elasticity of labour transformability, for the reasons discussed earlier. Therefore there are in total $10 \times 10 = 100$ combinations of (τ_K, τ_L). The CGE model is run for each of these parameter combinations to give 100 simulation results, as shown in the three-dimensional diagrams in Figure 8.1. The horizontal plane shows the parameter values, while the vertical axis represents the percentage changes in output. A "value net" has 100 "knots", each corresponding to a (τ_K, τ_L) combination.

Figure 8.1(a) shows that total output always increases. The magnitude of changes gradually increases as the combination of (τ_K, τ_L) moves from one corner (2.8, 0.1) towards the other (0.1, 2.8). This implies that a higher degree of labour mobility will be beneficial to the economy. The changes in GDP and national welfare are all positive and their patterns (not reported here) are very similar to that of national total output shown in Figure 8.1(a).

In Figure 8.1(b) and (c), it is evident that the changes in SOEs and private enterprises' total output are ambiguous. For example, in Figure 8.1(b), the output change gradually turns positive as the combination of (τ_K, τ_L) moves from one corner (0.1, 2.8) towards the other (2.8, 0.1). One can also see in Figure 8.1(d) that when $(\tau_K, \tau_L) = (0.1, 2.8)$, i.e. when the foreign enterprises can attract away labour from their domestic rivals most easily yet without losing much capital, the change in foreign enterprises' output reaches the highest level.

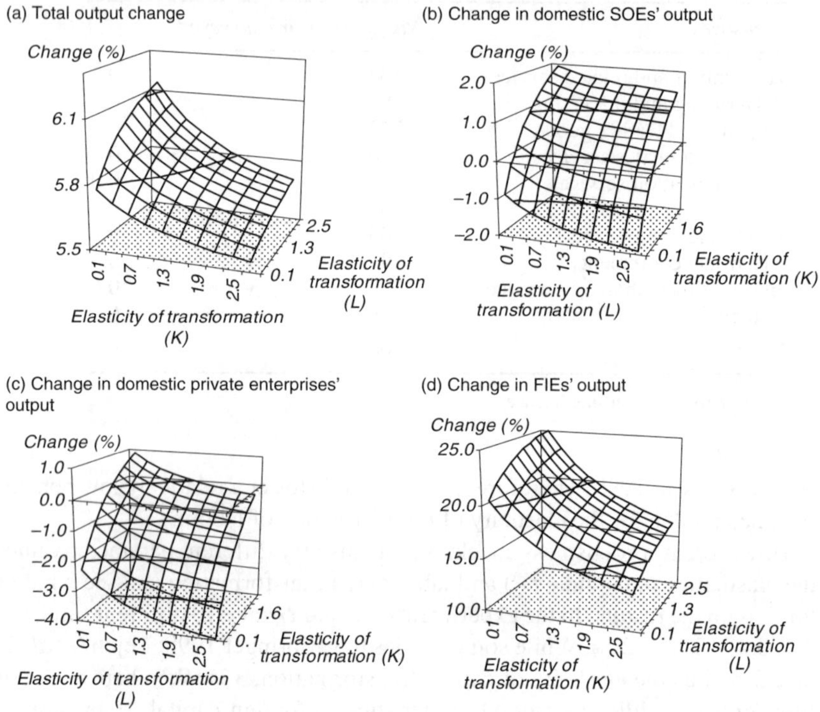

Figure 8.1 Impact of FDI shock on output under perfect competition (without spillovers).

FDI spillovers under perfect competition

This section examines the effects of FDI spillovers under perfect competition. The same FDI shock is introduced into the economy as in the previous section. The only difference is that the FDI shock is accompanied by endogenous productivity spillovers. The purpose of illustrating the effects of an FDI shock with as well as without spillovers is to facilitate the comparison between these two scenarios.

Figure 8.2 summarises the percentage changes in total output of the whole economy (a), SOEs only (b), private enterprises only (c) and FIEs only (d). A comparison of the corresponding panels of Figures 8.1 and 8.2 exhibits highly similar effects of FDI shock with or without FDI productivity spillovers. When (τ_K, τ_L) moves from the (low, high) corner to the (high, low) corner, SOEs and private enterprises benefit more from the FDI shock. However, the FIEs will lose more as (τ_K, τ_L) moves towards the (high, low) corner, because capital is more easily attracted away to SOEs and private enterprises, while labour is more difficult to attract to the FIEs. Collectively, national total output benefits more as (τ_K, τ_L) moves from corner (high, low) to (low, high).

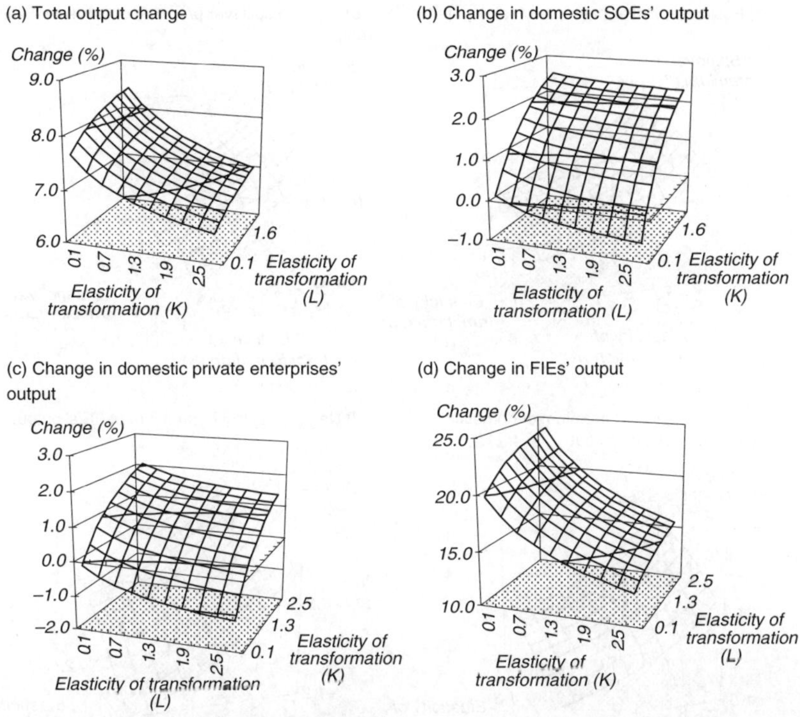

Figure 8.2 Impact of FDI shock on output under perfect competition (with spillovers).

The changes in GDP and national welfare are all positive and their patterns are very similar to that of total output shown in Figure 8.2(a). So the relevant graphs are omitted here.

Although Figures 8.1 and 8.2 look very similar, there are differences between them. For example, the rates of increase in national total output are higher in the scenario with FDI productivity spillovers than those in the scenario without. That is to say, the "value net" in Figure 8.2(a) is at a position higher than that in Figure 8.1(a). The magnitude of this difference between Figures 8.1(a) and 8.2(a) is shown in Figure 8.3(a). Such a difference caused by FDI productivity spillovers is referred to as a "spillover premium" throughout this chapter.

Nonetheless, the rate of increase in FIEs' output is lower than that in the scenario without FDI productivity spillovers given the same combination of (τ_K, τ_L), i.e. a negative spillover premium occurs (see Figure 8.3(d)). This contrast has important implications, i.e. FDI productivity spillovers are beneficial to promoting the host country's total output, GDP and national welfare, although the total output of foreign-invested sectors will show a smaller increase. In other words, the lower rate of increase for FIEs is outweighed by the even better performance of domestic enterprises thanks to FDI productivity spillovers.

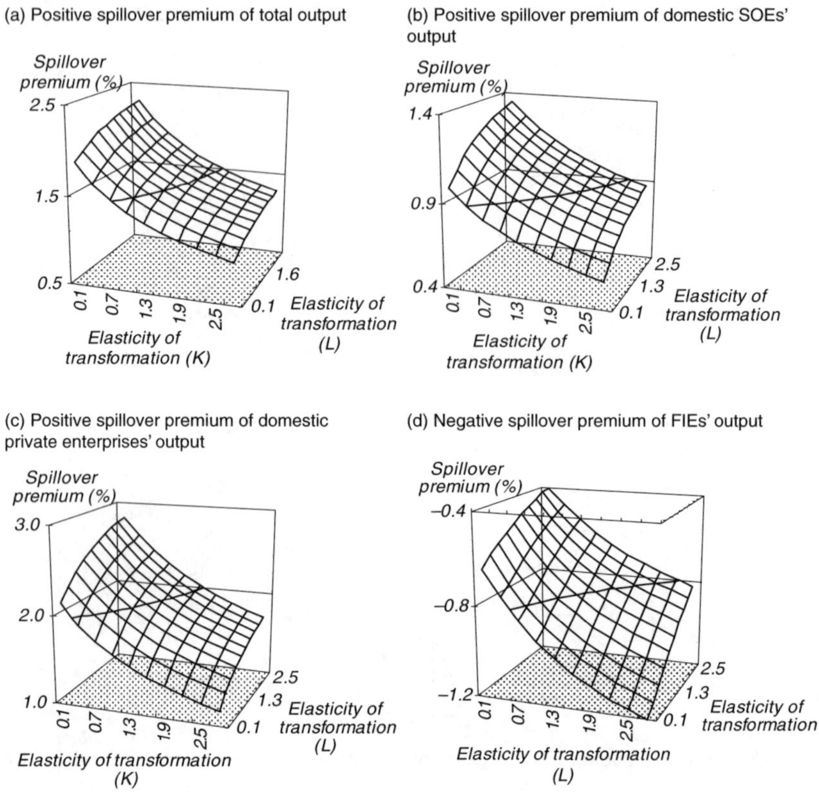

Figure 8.3 Impact of FDI shock on output under perfect competition: spillover premium.

Tables 8.5 and 8.6 provide detailed illustrations of how the FDI shock has affected the performance of SOEs and private firms. The FDI column measures the FDI of each sector as a percentage of total FDI. The *BL*, *FL*, *HZDS* and *EXCO* columns respectively show the percentage changes in the four spillover variables, namely backward linkages, forward linkages, horizontal demonstrations and export concentration of FIEs. As shown in Tables 8.5 and 8.6, almost all four spillover variables have increased due to the FDI shock.

As introduced in Chapter 7, the changes in the values of the above spillover variables will affect the productivity spilt over from foreign firms to domestic firms. The contribution of FDI productivity spillovers to the total productivity measured by equation (4.4) will also change endogenously. This change is shown in the *NTFP* column. For both SOEs and private firms in almost all industries, the contribution of FDI spillovers to their productivity has increased. For SOEs, the production of tap water gains the most from the FDI spillovers. This is probably because the FDI volume in this industry was relatively low. For private enterprises,

Table 8.5 Changes (%) of SOEs with an FDI shock under perfect competition

	*FDI**	*BL*	*FL*	*HZDS*	*EXCO*	*NTFP*	*TFP*	*Export*	*Import*	*Output*	*P*
Coal, petroleum and gas	0.6	7.8	7.6	6.8	9.6	6.7	0.8	−4.5	8.8	1.3	2.0
Ferrous metals mining	0.0	7.2	18.0	−2.6	NA	11.2	1.2	−3.9	9.1	1.8	1.9
Non-ferrous metals mining	0.0	8.8	19.7	−2.0	−2.9	12.3	1.3	−6.4	15.4	3.5	3.4
Mining of non-metal, other minerals, and other ores	0.0	9.6	13.9	−1.9	−2.5	9.6	0.8	−4.2	7.7	0.6	1.6
Food, beverage and tobacco manufacturing	2.5	4.7	3.0	0.8	1.4	1.4	0.2	−16.2	22.2	0.0	6.1
Textile industry	5.1	14.0	12.6	16.6	21.0	11.8	2.6	0.6	7.8	2.0	0.4
Garments and other fibre products	4.4	14.8	9.6	9.9	9.2	8.7	2.4	6.6	−7.5	0.3	−1.6
Leather, furs, down and related products	3.2	9.5	10.4	10.2	10.5	7.1	2.8	5.7	4.0	4.2	−0.4
Timber processing, bamboo, cane, palm fibre, etc.	0.7	13.3	13.9	17.4	23.6	13.3	1.6	−1.6	3.1	−0.6	0.3
Furniture manufacturing	1.0	13.5	8.9	17.4	17.3	13.6	2.3	6.4	−7.6	−0.3	−1.7
Papermaking and paper products	2.2	12.4	9.3	13.8	9.2	9.4	2.4	5.0	−3.0	−1.6	−2.2
Printing and record medium reproduction	1.0	12.9	7.6	11.9	9.3	10.0	1.7	5.7	−8.3	−3.6	−3.1
Cultural, educational and sports goods	1.6	10.5	8.7	9.8	8.5	7.6	2.3	4.3	−5.1	0.7	−0.9
Petroleum processing and coking	0.5	7.2	11.0	6.6	8.6	7.2	0.7	−1.9	6.9	1.8	1.8
Raw chemical materials and chemical products	4.9	10.7	10.9	13.3	16.5	9.4	2.2	2.6	3.5	1.7	−0.3
Medical and pharmaceutical products	1.8	9.8	9.9	10.2	14.3	8.4	1.6	−1.6	−3.6	−5.2	−1.1

Continued

Table 8.5 Continued

	*FDI**	*BL*	*FL*	*HZDS*	*EXCO*	*NTFP*	*TFP*	*Export*	*Import*	*Output*	*P*
Chemical fibre	0.8	11.0	11.8	10.1	12.8	8.1	2.5	9.4	−1.1	2.5	−2.0
Rubber products	1.3	12.2	7.8	12.4	14.3	8.7	2.3	1.5	0.3	−0.8	−0.7
Plastic products	3.7	12.7	7.0	14.1	12.3	8.5	2.5	7.7	−1.6	1.5	−1.8
Non-metal mineral products	3.1	10.9	6.8	14.7	14.2	10.2	1.7	8.0	−10.7	−3.9	−3.9
Smelting and pressing of ferrous metals	2.4	14.7	11.9	31.0	46.0	15.0	1.7	1.1	3.3	1.0	0.0
Smelting and pressing of non-ferrous metals	1.3	16.1	6.8	24.4	38.3	10.4	2.1	0.4	7.5	2.8	0.6
Metal products	3.8	15.8	7.8	13.7	15.4	10.2	2.2	9.2	−5.2	1.5	−1.9
Ordinary machinery	2.9	9.9	8.2	12.9	13.6	8.7	1.7	3.9	−0.7	0.8	−0.7
Special purpose equipment	2.3	10.7	12.9	19.7	14.8	13.0	1.8	7.9	−6.1	−0.3	−1.9
Transport equipment	4.4	7.9	6.1	5.6	5.7	4.9	1.5	9.7	−7.1	0.4	−2.0
Electronic and electric products	11.9	3.7	2.5	1.5	1.2	1.5	0.8	2.9	2.4	1.5	−0.3
Instruments, meters, cultural and office machinery	3.1	5.6	7.9	11.4	8.4	6.2	2.7	1.4	3.1	0.8	−0.2
Production of electric power, steam and hot water	1.0	6.2	11.4	1.4	0.1	4.5	0.8	−3.7	12.5	4.2	2.8
Production of gas	0.9	9.3	10.2	20.8	51.1	14.2	2.3	7.7	−8.5	−1.6	−3.2
Production of tap water	0.5	9.0	10.9	160.2	NA	26.3	2.9	−4.3	−8.2	−13.0	−3.3

Notes: (1) FDI, percentage of total FDI in corresponding sectors; *BL*, backward linkages; *FL*, forward linkages; *HZDS*, horizontal demonstration; *EXCO*, export concentration of FIEs; *NTFP*, share of TFP spillovers in total TFP, measured by equation (4.4); *TFP*, industry-level productivity, measured by the denominator of (4.4); Export, export of SOEs; Output, total output of SOEs; *P*, price of product; Variety, number of firms; Scale, production scale of each variety. (2) $(\tau_K, \tau_L) = (2.0, 0.5)$. (3) Data not available are marked "NA", as the initial values are zero and it is not possible to calculate the percentage changes.

Table 8.6 Changes (%) of private enterprises with an FDI shock under perfect competition

	FDI	*BL*	*FL*	*HZDS*	*EXCO*	*NTFP*	*TFP*	*Export*	*Import*	*Output*	*P*
Coal, petroleum and gas	0.6	7.8	7.6	6.8	9.6	6.0	1.5	−3.5	8.8	2.1	1.9
Ferrous metals mining	0.0	7.2	18.0	−2.6	NA	13.7	2.9	−1.9	9.1	3.5	1.8
Non-ferrous metals mining	0.0	8.8	19.7	−2.0	−2.9	14.1	3.2	−5.5	15.4	4.3	3.3
Mining of non-metal, other minerals, and other ores	0.0	9.6	13.9	−1.9	−2.5	10.1	1.5	−2.9	7.7	1.6	1.5
Food, beverage and tobacco manufacturing	2.5	4.7	3.0	0.8	1.4	1.2	0.6	−14.6	22.2	1.4	6.0
Textile industry	5.1	14.0	12.6	16.6	21.0	9.3	5.0	0.2	7.8	1.7	0.4
Garments and other fibre products	4.4	14.8	9.6	9.9	9.2	5.1	2.9	6.3	−7.5	0.1	−1.6
Leather, furs, down and related products	3.2	9.5	10.4	10.2	10.5	5.6	4.9	−6.1	4.0	−5.5	0.2
Timber processing, bamboo, cane, palm fibre, etc.	0.7	13.3	13.9	17.4	23.6	11.7	3.6	−0.1	3.1	0.6	0.2
Furniture manufacturing	1.0	13.5	8.9	17.4	17.3	10.9	3.9	6.1	−7.6	−0.6	−1.7
Papermaking and paper products	2.2	12.4	9.3	13.8	9.2	6.6	4.9	6.8	−3.0	−0.3	−2.3
Printing and record medium reproduction	1.0	12.9	7.6	11.9	9.3	7.8	2.7	11.6	−8.3	0.5	−3.5
Cultural, educational and sports goods	1.6	10.5	8.7	9.8	8.5	5.6	2.9	5.3	−5.1	1.5	−1.0
Petroleum processing and coking	0.5	7.2	11.0	6.6	8.6	6.5	1.8	−2.2	6.9	1.6	1.8
Raw chemical materials and chemical products	4.9	10.7	10.9	13.3	16.5	7.1	4.5	2.3	3.5	1.5	−0.2
Medical and pharmaceutical products	1.8	9.8	9.9	10.2	14.3	6.6	3.0	5.7	−3.6	0.2	−1.6

Continued

Table 8.6 Continued

	FDI	*BL*	*FL*	*HZDS*	*EXCO*	*NTFP*	*TFP*	*Export*	*Import*	*Output*	*P*
Chemical fibre	0.8	11.0	11.8	10.1	12.8	5.5	5.0	5.1	−1.1	−0.6	−1.7
Rubber products	1.3	12.2	7.8	12.4	14.3	5.9	4.2	0.4	0.3	−1.7	−0.6
Plastic products	3.7	12.7	7.0	14.1	12.3	5.7	4.5	6.9	−1.6	0.9	−1.7
Non-metal mineral products	3.1	10.9	6.8	14.7	14.2	7.9	3.5	13.2	−10.7	−0.2	−4.3
Smelting and pressing of ferrous metals	2.4	14.7	11.9	31.0	46.0	12.9	4.0	2.6	3.3	2.1	−0.1
Smelting and pressing of non-ferrous metals	1.3	16.1	6.8	24.4	38.3	7.0	4.3	−1.5	7.5	1.4	0.7
Metal products	3.8	15.8	7.8	13.7	15.4	6.6	4.0	7.2	−5.2	0.0	−1.8
Ordinary machinery	2.9	9.9	8.2	12.9	13.6	7.1	3.2	5.0	−0.7	1.6	−0.8
Special purpose equipment	2.3	10.7	12.9	19.7	14.8	13.4	3.9	9.5	−6.1	0.8	−2.0
Transport equipment	4.4	7.9	6.1	5.6	5.7	3.1	2.3	7.5	−7.1	−1.0	−1.9
Electronic and electric products	11.9	3.7	2.5	1.5	1.2	0.7	1.0	2.2	2.4	1.0	−0.3
Instruments, meters, cultural and office machinery	3.1	5.6	7.9	11.4	8.4	7.2	5.0	3.3	3.1	2.5	−0.2
Production of electric power, steam and hot water	1.0	6.2	11.4	1.4	0.1	3.4	1.5	−5.0	12.5	3.0	2.9
Production of gas	0.9	9.3	10.2	20.8	51.1	12.0	5.8	0.9	−8.5	−6.8	−2.8
Production of tap water	0.5	9.0	10.9	160.2	NA	40.7	8.1	21.3	−8.2	4.8	−5.1

Notes: See Table 8.5.

the instruments, meters, cultural and office machinery sector benefits most for a similar reason.

While the *NTFP* column measures the contribution rate of FDI spillovers to total productivity, *TFP* simply measures the total productivity as measured by $\hat{\alpha}_1 + \hat{\boldsymbol{\beta}} \times \mathbf{SPL}$ in equation (4.4). The FDI productivity spillovers also bring about an improvement in the total TFP of each industry. Almost all SOEs and private enterprises in all industries have a positive TFP change with the FDI shock. However, the top five FDI recipient industries are not necessarily among the top recipient industries of such FDI spillovers. The reason for this inconsistency is that FDI shock affects the productivity of domestic enterprises via four spillover channels, and the importance of these channels varies, as shown in Table 4.3.

Regarding the total output in the output column and product price in the price column, the results are mixed. The reasons are twofold. On the one hand, the FDI shock can generally improve the productivity of domestic enterprises (SOEs and private firms), which can potentially raise their total output. On the other hand, the FDI shock can attract away resources from domestic firms and pose a threat to the latter. The above two forces make the collective results ambiguous.

FDI spillovers under monopolistic competition

Impact of spillovers on output

Similar to the scenario of perfect competition, the FDI productivity spillovers in the scenario of monopolistic competition can also exert positive impacts on national total output, GDP, welfare and total output of domestic enterprises. Total production of FIEs will increase at a lower rate due to the fact that limited resources are attracted by domestic enterprises which become more productive with FDI productivity spillovers.

The initial number of firms, and also the number of varieties, is set to 8 in each ownership type in each industry in the benchmark economy. Figure 8.4 provides a summary of the findings. Figure 8.4(a) shows that the national total output with spillover increases, with the highest rate of increase at $(\tau_K, \tau_L) = (0.1, 2.8)$. The changes in GDP and national welfare (not shown) also exhibit the similar pattern of positive changes, i.e. when (τ_K, τ_L) approaches (0.1, 2.8), the rates of increase in GDP and welfare are the highest.

Both SOEs (Figure 8.4(b)) and private enterprises (Figure 8.4(c)) benefit the most from FDI spillovers if labour cannot easily be attracted away by foreign enterprises and they can easily absorb capital from the latter, i.e. when (τ_K, τ_L) approaches (2.8, 0.1). In contrast, the total output of FIEs (Figure 8.4(d)) increases the least when $(\tau_K, \tau_L) = (2.8, 0.1)$. However, Figure 8.4(a) shows that the national total output increases most when $(\tau_K, \tau_L) = (0.1, 2.8)$ because the increase for the foreign enterprises outweighs the loss incurred by the domestic enterprises.

The productivity "spillover premium" under monopolistic competition that exists between the effects of FDI shock with and without spillovers is shown

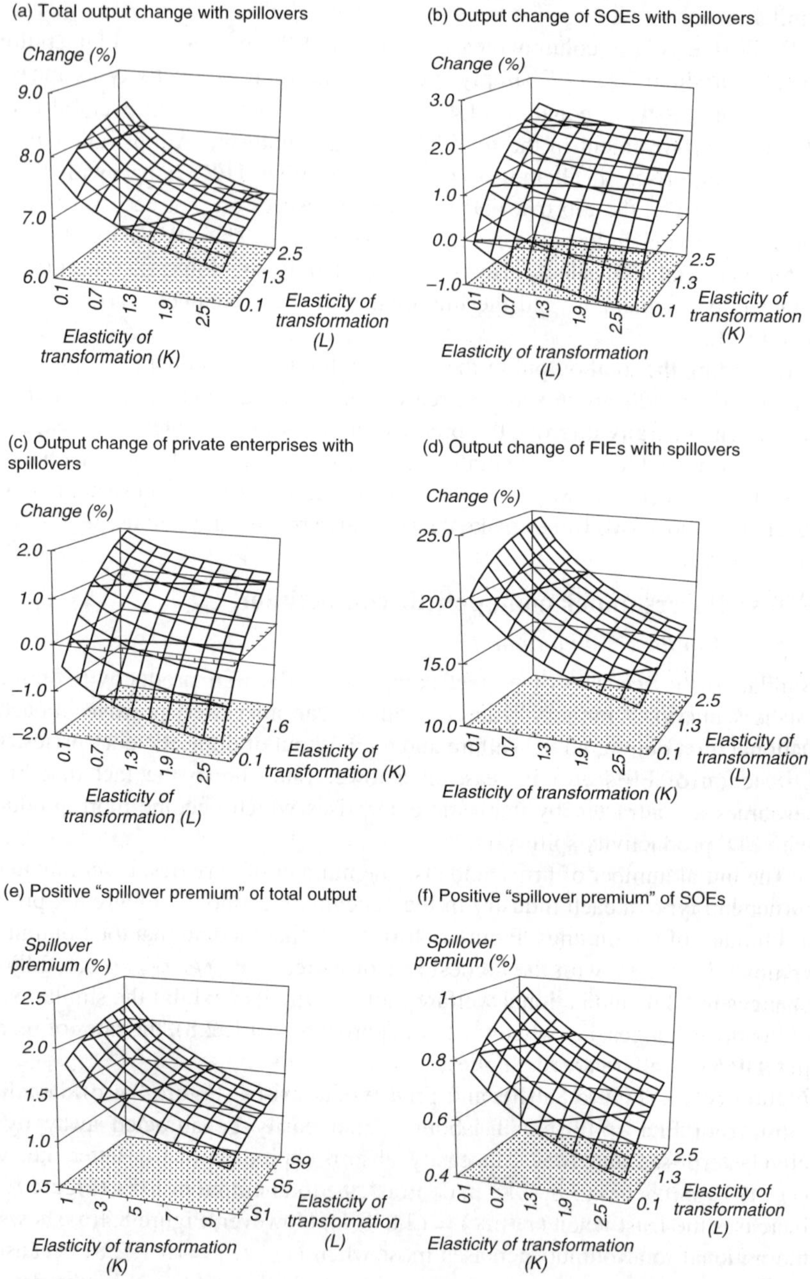

Figure 8.4 FDI spillover effects under monopolistic competition.

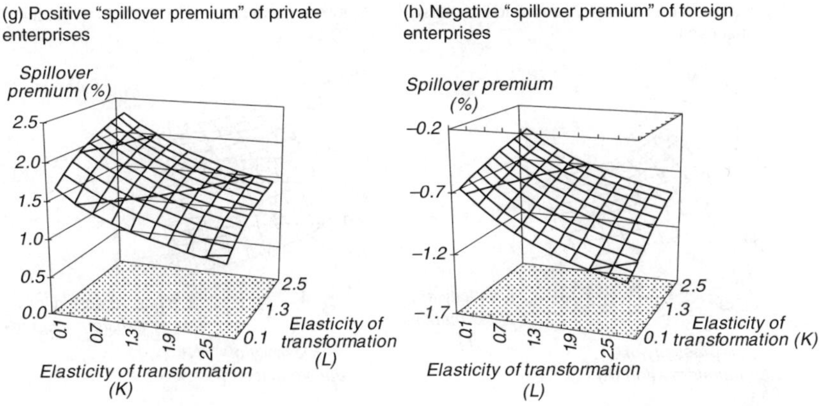

Figure 8.4 Continued.

in Figure 8.4(e)–(h). Domestic enterprises get a positive premium, while for foreign enterprises it is negative. But the overall premium is collectively positive, a conclusion similar to that obtained in the previous section.

Impact of spillovers on product varieties and scale

Another important impact of FDI productivity spillovers under monopolistic competition is reflected by the changes in varieties and scale of domestic enterprises. From Figure 8.5(b) and (c) one can see that, with FDI productivity spillovers under monopolistic competition, the number of varieties produced by domestic enterprises generally decreases. But the number of total varieties in each sector increases (see Figure 8.5(a)) thanks to more varieties being created by foreign-invested sectors.

Figure 8.5(e)–(g) indicates that there also exist positive "spillover premium" effects of FDI spillovers on the changes in variety, i.e. $\Delta N/N_0$ (with spillovers) $\Delta - \Delta N'/N_0'$ without spillovers) > 0.

Figure 8.6(a)–(d) shows how the FDI shock increases the production scale per variety of all enterprises, SOEs, private and foreign enterprises, respectively. Figure 8.6(e)–(h) indicates that the FDI productivity spillovers lead to a positive "spillover premium" in the changes in production scale, although such premium effects are very marginal. Similar to the results of Figures 8.4 and 8.5, when (τ_K, τ_L) approaches (2.8, 0.1), the production scale of the domestic enterprises benefits most, as they can attract the most capital from foreign enterprises while almost keeping their labour input unchanged.

Thus it may be concluded from Figures 8.5 and 8.6 that FDI spillovers can result in more product varieties produced by domestic enterprises, and can also help domestic enterprises increase their production scale for each product, although the net result of the FDI shock will be reduced domestic varieties when the values

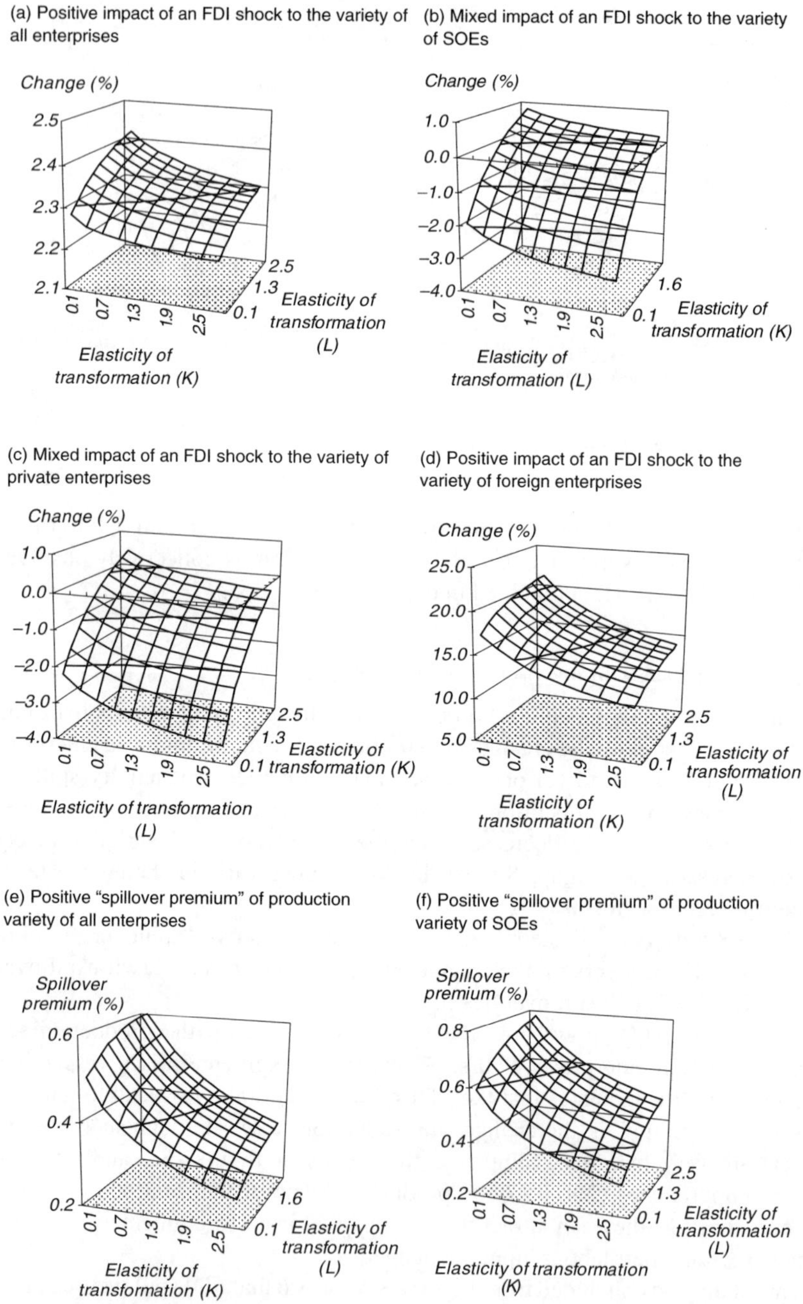

Figure 8.5 Variety changes with FDI productivity spillovers under monopolistic competition.

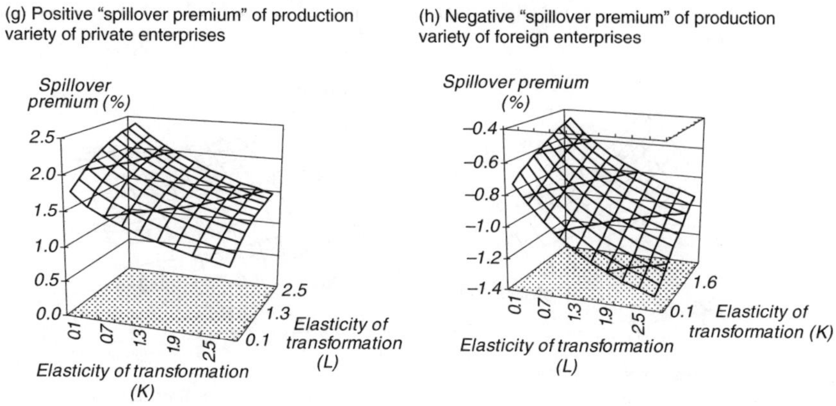

Figure 8.5 Continued.

of (τ_K, τ_L) move towards (low, high). This conclusion justifies the theoretical proposition derived in Chapter 7.

The "spillover premium" effects on variety and scale are briefly illustrated in Figure 7.2. Figure 8.7 compares how an FDI shock with and without productivity spillovers affects the domestic sectors. Figure 8.7(a) shows that an FDI shock without spillovers may lead to fewer varieties and a larger scale for each variety in every domestic sector. Collectively, the benchmark equilibrium E_0 will be shifted to either E_1 or E_2. Figure 8.7(b) (same as Figure 7.2 in nature) depicts how spillovers can affect these changes. The "spillover premiums" on both varieties and scale are positive, pushing A_1A_1 and A_2A_2 upwards, resulting in a new equilibrium at E_1' or E_2'.

Tables 8.7 and 8.8 illustrate the changes in key variables at industry level. Similar to Tables 8.5 and 8.6, the contribution rate of productivity spillovers to total spillovers of domestic enterprises (*NTFP*) increases, resulting in moderate productivity (*TFP*) improvement. Tables 8.7 and 8.8 also report the changes in varieties and scale of production in each industry. The results are consistent with those shown in Figures 8.5 and 8.6 – varieties decrease for both SOEs and private enterprises while scale per variety increases.

Comparison of an FDI shock under perfect and monopolistic competitions

The impacts of FDI productivity spillovers on macroeconomic variables with different initial degrees of monopolistic power are shown in Table 8.9. Two alternative values of the initial number of firms (N) and the number of varieties are chosen in each ownership type in each industry in the benchmark economy. N is an endogenous variable, the value of which may change in the counterfactual

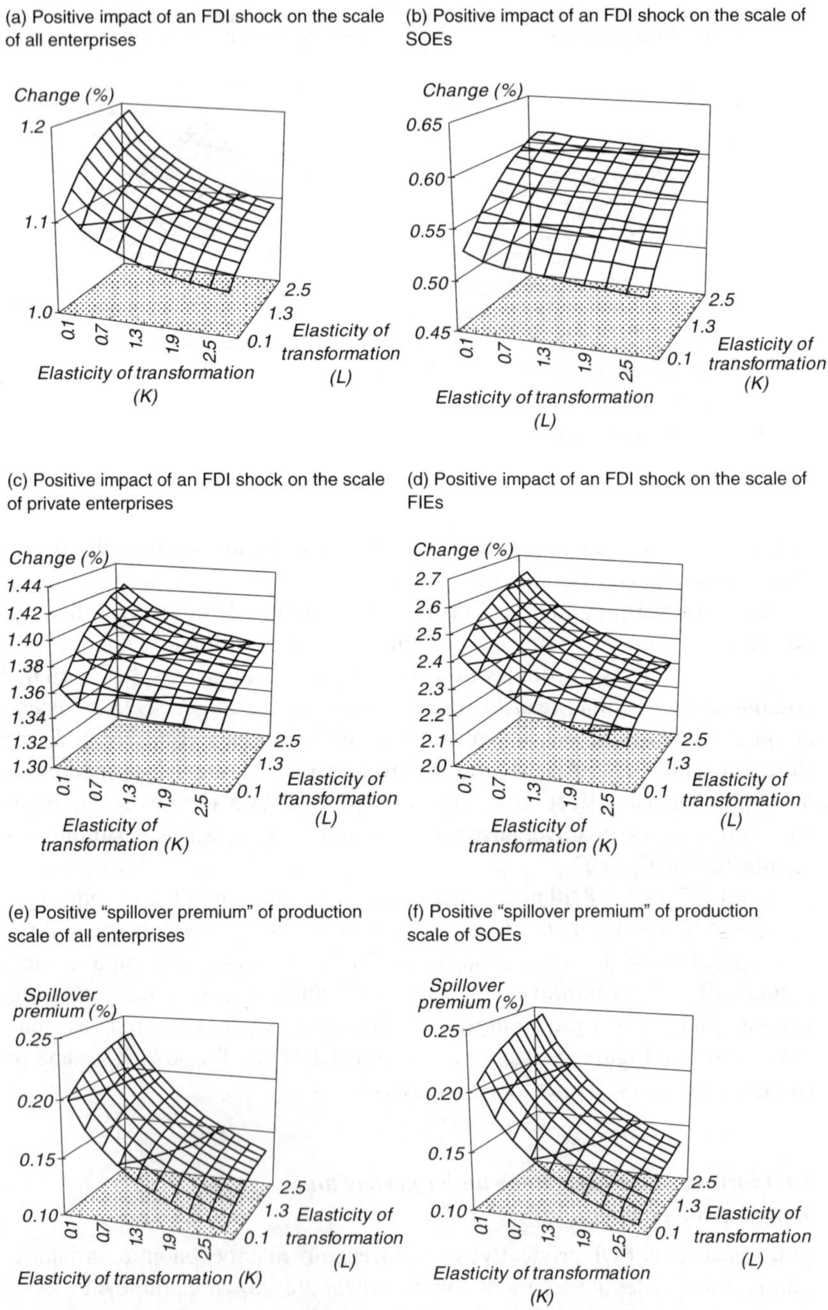

Figure 8.6 Scale per variety changes with FDI productivity spillovers under monopolistic competition.

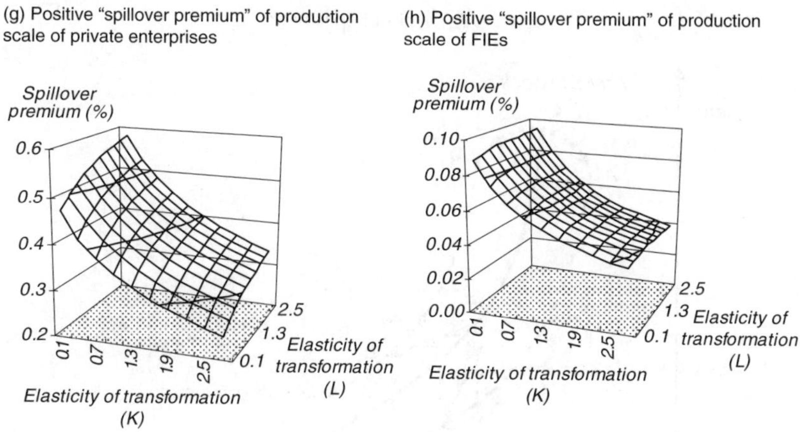

Figure 8.6 Continued.

simulations. For example, when $N = 10$, the change in total output under an FDI shock without spillovers is 6.0 per cent, while under the same FDI shock with spillover it is 7.2 per cent, suggesting a net 1.2 per cent FDI productivity spillover premium.

We also include the outcomes for perfect competition for comparison. It is evident that the reduction in the number of competitors increases the impact of an FDI shock, with or without FDI spillovers. For example, the rate of increase in GDP under perfect competition with spillovers is 7.1 per cent, but this figure becomes 7.8 per cent and 8.3 per cent when $N = 10$ and $N = 5$, respectively. Moreover, the FDI spillover premia are higher when the benchmark number of firms (varieties) is smaller. For example, the spillover premia of total output increase rate are 1.1 per cent, 1.2 per cent and 1.3 per cent, when the economy is competitive, $N = 10$ and $N = 5$, respectively. To conclude, the lower the degree of competition in the benchmark, the higher the returns to the FDI shock from competition.

The only exception is the total output of SOEs, whose spillover premium exhibits a relatively stable pattern, reflecting the balance of the benefits from the FDI shock (productivity spillovers and cheaper capital), and the negative impact of increased competition from foreign firms.

FDI spillovers under firm heterogeneity

Impact of spillovers on output

In the scenario of firm heterogeneity, firms are different in their productivities so that the least productive enterprises will be driven out of the market when input prices are higher. Similarly to the scenarios of perfect and monopolistic competition, the FDI productivity spillovers in the scenario of heterogeneous competition can also exert positive impacts on national total output, GDP, welfare and total

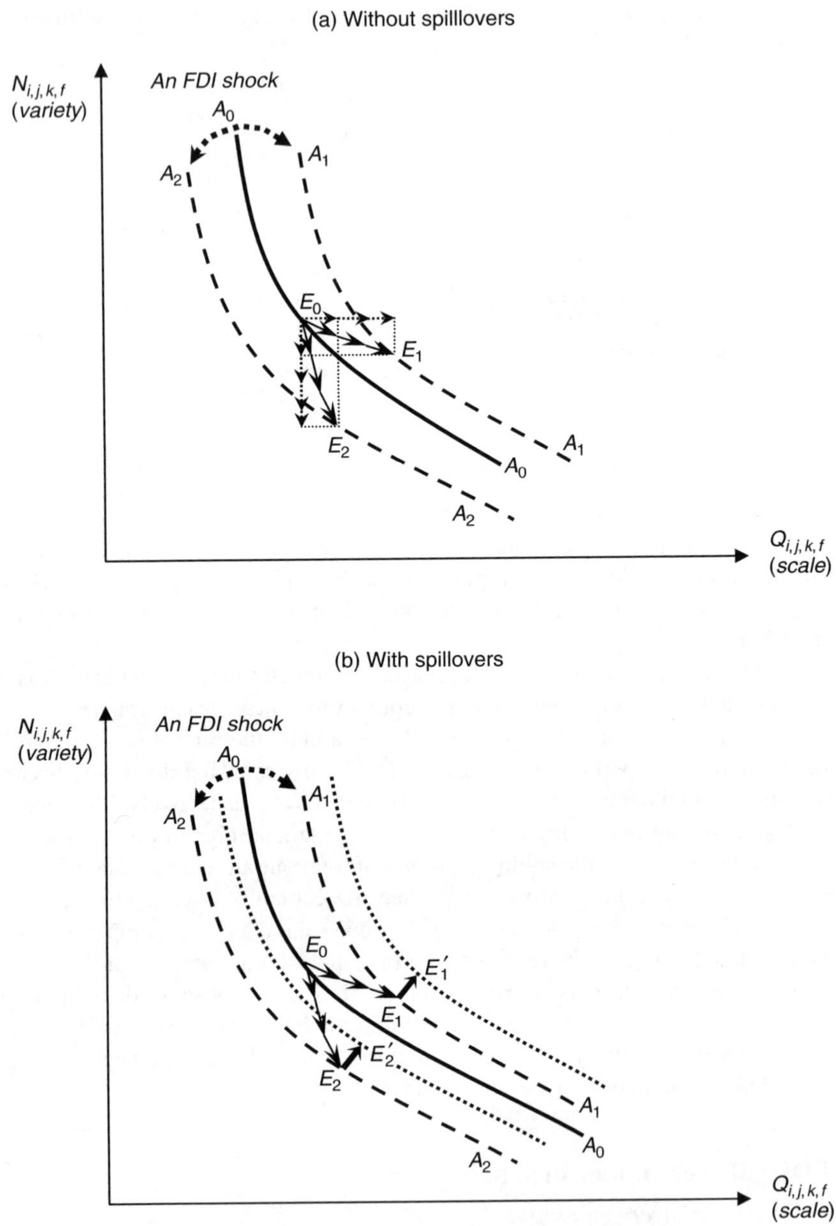

Figure 8.7 Variety and scale of domestic enterprises with an FDI shock.

Table 8.7 Changes (%) of SOEs with an FDI shock under monopolistic competition

	*FDI**	*BL*	*FL*	*HZDS*	*EXCO*	*NTFP*	*TFP*	*Export*	*Import*	*Output*	*P*	*VRT*	*SCL*
Coal, petroleum and gas	0.6	7.9	7.6	6.8	9.6	6.7	0.8	−5.1	9.3	1.1	2.1	0.7	0.4
Ferrous metals mining	0.0	7.2	18.0	−3.1	NA	11.2	1.2	−4.5	8.8	1.2	1.9	1.0	0.2
Non-ferrous metals mining	0.0	8.8	19.6	−2.5	−3.5	12.3	1.3	−6.7	15.2	3.1	3.4	2.5	0.6
Mining of non-metal, other minerals, and other ores	0.0	9.7	14.0	−2.1	−2.8	9.6	0.8	−4.7	7.8	0.3	1.7	0.2	0.1
Food, beverage and tobacco manufacturing	2.5	4.6	2.9	0.6	1.4	1.3	0.2	−18.2	26.0	0.2	7.1	−0.1	0.2
Textile industry	5.1	14.0	12.7	16.4	20.9	11.7	2.6	−0.2	7.8	1.3	0.5	0.6	0.6
Garments and other fibre products	4.4	14.7	9.7	10.0	9.3	8.7	2.4	5.2	−7.1	−0.7	−1.5	−0.9	0.2
Leather, furs, down and related products	3.2	9.7	10.7	10.6	10.8	7.2	2.9	4.1	4.3	3.0	−0.3	2.7	0.3
Timber processing, bamboo, cane, palm fibre, etc.	0.7	13.3	13.9	17.3	23.5	13.2	1.6	−2.8	3.4	−1.3	0.5	−1.3	0.0
Furniture manufacturing	1.0	13.6	9.0	17.3	17.1	13.5	2.3	5.1	−7.4	−1.3	−1.7	−1.3	0.0
Papermaking and paper products	2.2	12.5	9.4	13.9	9.3	9.4	2.4	4.3	−3.3	−2.4	−2.2	−2.7	0.3

Continued

Table 8.7 Continued

	*FDI**	*BL*	*FL*	*HZDS*	*EXCO*	*NTFP*	*TFP*	*Export*	*Import*	*Output*	*P*	*VRT*	*SCL*
Printing and record medium reproduction	1.0	13.0	7.7	11.9	9.3	10.0	1.7	5.3	−8.3	−4.0	−3.1	−4.0	0.1
Cultural, educational and sports goods	1.6	10.6	8.9	10.1	8.7	7.7	2.4	3.2	−4.9	−0.3	−0.9	−0.5	0.2
Petroleum processing and coking	0.5	7.2	11.0	6.5	8.5	7.2	0.7	−2.4	7.0	1.5	2.0	1.0	0.5
Raw chemical materials and chemical products	4.9	10.7	11.0	13.3	16.5	9.4	2.2	2.2	3.3	1.2	−0.2	0.4	0.8
Medical and pharmaceutical products	1.8	9.9	10.0	10.3	14.4	8.4	1.6	−3.1	−2.3	−5.5	−0.7	−5.7	0.2
Chemical fibre	0.8	11.1	11.8	10.3	13.1	8.2	2.6	9.4	−1.9	1.8	−2.1	0.9	0.8
Rubber products	1.3	12.3	7.9	12.6	14.5	8.8	2.3	0.6	0.5	−1.4	−0.5	−2.1	0.7
Plastic products	3.7	12.7	7.1	14.0	12.2	8.6	2.5	7.2	−2.5	0.4	−2.0	0.2	0.2
Non-metal mineral products	3.1	10.9	7.0	14.7	14.2	10.2	1.7	7.5	−10.7	−4.3	−3.9	−4.5	0.2
Smelting and pressing of ferrous metals	2.4	14.8	12.0	31.1	46.2	15.1	1.7	1.1	2.9	0.6	0.0	−0.2	0.8
Smelting and pressing of non-ferrous metals	1.3	16.0	7.0	24.3	38.1	10.4	2.1	0.4	7.0	2.3	0.6	1.5	0.8

Table 8.7 Continued

	*FDI**	*BL*	*FL*	*HZDS*	*EXCO*	*NTFP*	*TFP*	*Export*	*Import*	*Output*	*P*	*VRT*	*SCL*
Metal products	3.8	15.8	7.9	13.7	15.3	10.2	2.3	8.7	−5.7	0.7	−2.0	0.4	0.3
Ordinary machinery	2.9	10.0	8.3	12.8	13.4	8.8	1.7	3.7	−1.1	0.4	−0.7	−0.1	0.5
Special purpose equipment	2.3	10.8	13.0	19.7	14.8	13.0	1.9	7.7	−6.3	−0.7	−1.9	−1.3	0.6
Transport equipment	4.4	8.0	6.3	5.8	5.9	5.0	1.5	9.6	−7.1	0.2	−2.0	−0.6	0.9
Electronic and electric products	11.9	3.9	2.8	1.8	1.4	1.6	0.9	1.9	2.3	0.6	−0.3	0.1	0.5
Instruments, meters, cultural and office machinery	3.1	5.8	8.0	11.8	8.7	6.4	2.8	0.5	3.2	0.0	−0.1	−0.5	0.5
Production of electric power, steam and hot water	1.0	6.4	11.4	1.3	0.1	4.5	0.8	−4.0	13.3	4.4	3.2	3.3	1.0
Production of gas	0.9	9.5	10.4	21.6	53.3	14.7	2.4	7.2	−8.1	−1.9	−3.0	−2.5	0.6
Production of tap water	0.5	9.0	11.0	160.7	NA	26.4	2.9	−4.9	−7.8	−13.2	−3.1	−13.8	0.6

Notes: *VRT*, number of firms in the sector; *SCL*, production scale of each variety. Other variables are as in Table 8.5. The benchmark number of firms (under monopolistic competition) in each sector is set to 8. The values of elasticity of transformation are $(\tau_K, \tau_L) = (2.0, 0.5)$.

Table 8.8 Changes (%) of private enterprises with an FDI shock under monopolistic competition

	*FDI**	*BL*	*FL*	*HZDS*	*EXCO*	*NTFP*	*TFP*	*Export*	*Import*	*Output*	*P*	*VRT*	*SCL*
Coal, petroleum and gas	0.6	7.9	7.6	6.8	9.6	5.9	1.5	−4.1	9.3	1.9	2.1	1.3	0.6
Ferrous metals mining	0.0	7.2	18.0	−3.1	NA	13.7	2.9	−1.8	8.8	3.3	1.9	2.3	0.9
Non-ferrous metals mining	0.0	8.8	19.6	−2.5	−3.5	14.1	3.1	−5.2	15.2	4.2	3.4	2.9	1.2
Mining of non-metal, other minerals, and other ores	0.0	9.7	14.0	−2.1	−2.8	10.1	1.5	−3.1	7.8	1.5	1.6	1.1	0.4
Food, beverage and tobacco manufacturing	2.5	4.6	2.9	0.6	1.4	1.1	0.6	−16.7	26.0	1.6	7.0	1.3	0.4
Textile industry	5.1	14.0	12.7	16.4	20.9	9.2	5.0	0.6	7.8	1.7	0.6	−0.4	2.1
Garments and other fibre products	4.4	14.7	9.7	10.0	9.3	5.1	2.9	6.9	−7.1	0.3	−1.3	−2.7	3.1
Leather, furs, down and related products	3.2	9.7	10.7	10.6	10.8	5.8	5.1	−6.5	4.3	−6.0	0.5	−8.2	2.4
Timber processing, bamboo, cane, palm fibre, etc.	0.7	13.3	13.9	17.3	23.5	11.6	3.6	−0.5	3.4	0.4	0.5	−0.6	0.9
Furniture manufacturing	1.0	13.6	9.0	17.3	17.1	10.8	3.8	6.5	−7.4	−0.5	−1.4	−2.6	2.1
Papermaking and paper products	2.2	12.5	9.4	13.9	9.3	6.7	4.9	7.4	−3.3	−0.4	−2.2	−2.1	1.7

Table 8.8 Continued

	*FDI**	*BL*	*FL*	*HZDS*	*EXCO*	*NTFP*	*TFP*	*Export*	*Import*	*Output*	*P*	*VRT*	*SCL*
Printing and record medium reproduction	1.0	13.0	7.7	11.9	9.3	7.8	2.7	11.7	−8.3	0.4	−3.4	−0.5	1.0
Cultural, educational and sports goods	1.6	10.6	8.9	10.1	8.7	5.8	2.9	5.9	−4.9	1.5	−0.6	−2.0	3.6
Petroleum processing and coking	0.5	7.2	11.0	6.5	8.5	6.5	1.8	−2.3	7.0	1.6	2.0	0.8	0.7
Raw chemical materials and chemical products	4.9	10.7	11.0	13.3	16.5	7.2	4.5	2.7	3.3	1.5	−0.1	−0.2	1.6
Medical and pharmaceutical products	1.8	9.9	10.0	10.3	14.4	6.7	3.0	4.7	−2.3	0.2	−1.2	−0.8	1.0
Chemical fibre	0.8	11.1	11.8	10.3	13.1	5.6	5.0	5.7	−1.9	−0.9	−1.7	−2.5	1.7
Rubber products	1.3	12.3	7.9	12.6	14.5	6.0	4.3	0.3	0.5	−1.9	−0.4	−3.6	1.8
Plastic products	3.7	12.7	7.1	14.0	12.2	5.7	4.5	8.3	−2.5	0.9	−1.7	−1.3	2.2
Non-metal mineral products	3.1	10.9	7.0	14.7	14.2	7.9	3.5	13.5	−10.7	−0.2	−4.1	−1.4	1.2
Smelting and pressing of ferrous metals	2.4	14.8	12.0	31.1	46.2	12.9	4.0	3.1	2.9	2.1	−0.1	0.8	1.2
Smelting and pressing of non-ferrous metals	1.3	16.0	7.0	24.3	38.1	7.0	4.4	−0.6	7.0	1.5	0.8	−0.1	1.6

Continued

Table 8.8 Continued

	*FDI**	*BL*	*FL*	*HZDS*	*EXCO*	*NTFP*	*TFP*	*Export*	*Import*	*Output*	*P*	*VRT*	*SCL*
Metal products	3.8	15.8	7.9	13.7	15.3	6.6	4.0	8.3	−5.7	0.1	−1.7	−1.9	2.0
Ordinary machinery	2.9	10.0	8.3	12.8	13.4	7.1	3.2	5.7	−1.1	1.6	−0.7	0.2	1.5
Special purpose equipment	2.3	10.8	13.0	19.7	14.8	13.4	3.9	10.1	−6.3	0.8	−1.9	−0.7	1.5
Transport equipment	4.4	8.0	6.3	5.8	5.9	3.2	2.4	7.6	−7.1	−1.1	−1.8	−1.9	0.9
Electronic and electric products	11.9	3.9	2.8	1.8	1.4	0.9	1.2	1.5	2.3	0.2	−0.2	−0.6	0.8
Instruments, meters, cultural and office machinery	3.1	5.8	8.0	11.8	8.7	7.5	5.1	3.1	3.2	2.2	0.0	−0.4	2.6
Production of electric power, steam and hot water	1.0	6.4	11.4	1.3	0.1	3.4	1.5	−5.7	13.3	2.9	3.3	1.8	1.0
Production of gas	0.9	9.5	10.4	21.6	53.3	12.4	6.0	0.6	−8.1	−6.9	−2.6	−7.6	0.7
Production of tap water	0.5	9.0	11.0	160.7	NA	40.8	8.1	21.4	−7.8	4.8	−4.7	2.6	2.2

Notes: As Table 8.7.

output of domestic enterprises. Total products of FIEs will increase at a lower rate due to the fact that resources are attracted by domestic enterprises which become more productive with FDI productivity spillovers.

Table 8.10 shows how FDI shock affects the national total output with and without productivity spillovers. As we can see, the existence of FDI productivity spillovers helps the total output increase by a greater magnitude. This difference is reflected in the bottom panel titled "spillover premium".

Figure 8.8 presents the findings diagrammatically. Figure 8.8(a) shows that total output of all industries with spillovers increases, with the rate of increase highest at $(\tau_K, \tau_L) = (0.4, 2.8)$, where only labour is relatively mobile. SOEs (Figure 8.8(b)) benefit the most from the FDI shock with spillovers when $(\tau_K, \tau_L) = (2.8, 2.8)$. However, private domestic enterprises (Figure 8.8(c)) benefit the most from FDI spillovers if labour cannot easily be attracted away by foreign enterprises while they can easily absorb capital from the latter, i.e. $(\tau_K, \tau_L) = (2.8, 0.4)$. In contrast, the total output of FIEs increases least at $(\tau_K, \tau_L) = (2.8, 0.4)$.

Similar to the conclusions drawn under perfect competition and monopolistic competition, domestic enterprises get a positive productivity "spillover premium" (Figure 8.8(f) and (g)) while for foreign enterprises the premium is negative (Figure 8.8(h)). But the overall premium is positive (Figure 8.8(e)).

Table 8.9 An FDI shock under perfect and monopolistic competitions

	% change of	*Perfect competition*	*N = 10*	*N = 5*
With spillovers	Total output	6.8	7.2	7.5
	GDP	7.1	7.8	8.3
	Total output of SOEs	1.9	1.8	1.8
	Total output of private enterprises	1.2	1.3	1.4
	Total output of FIEs	14.9	15.3	15.6
	National welfare	3.6	4.4	5.0
Without spillovers	Total output	5.6	6.0	6.2
	GDP	5.6	6.2	6.6
	Total output of SOEs	1.3	1.3	1.3
	Total output of private enterprises	0.0	0.1	0.1
	Total output of FIEs	15.5	15.9	16.3
	National welfare	2.5	3.1	3.6
Spillover premium	Total output	1.1	1.2	1.3
	GDP	1.5	1.6	1.7
	Total output of SOEs	0.5	0.5	0.5
	Total output of private enterprises	1.2	1.2	1.3
	Total output of FIEs	−0.6	−0.6	−0.6
	National welfare	1.2	1.3	1.4

Note: Elasticity of transformation of capital and labour $(\tau_K, \tau_L) = (2.0, 0.5)$.

Table 8.10 Total output changes (%) with and without spillovers under firm heterogeneity

Total output change (%)	*Elasticity of labour transformation (τ_L)*								
	0.4	*0.7*	*1*	*1.3*	*1.6*	*1.9*	*2.2*	*2.5*	*2.8*
Elasticity of capital transformation (τ_K)									
Under firm heterogeneity (without spillovers)									
0.4	5.3	5.3	5.4	5.4	5.5	5.4	5.5	5.5	5.5
0.7	5.4	5.4	5.4	5.5	5.5	5.5	5.5	5.5	5.5
1	5.4	5.5	5.5	5.5	5.5	5.5	5.6	5.6	5.6
1.3	5.5	5.5	5.5	5.5	5.6	5.6	5.6	5.6	5.6
1.6	5.5	5.5	5.6	5.6	5.6	5.6	5.6	5.6	5.6
1.9	5.5	5.6	5.6	5.6	5.6	5.6	5.6	5.6	5.6
2.2	5.6	5.6	5.6	5.6	5.6	5.6	5.6	5.7	5.7
2.5	5.6	5.6	5.6	5.6	5.6	5.7	5.7	5.7	5.7
2.8	5.6	5.6	5.6	5.6	5.7	5.7	5.7	5.7	5.7
Under firm heterogeneity (with spillovers)									
0.4	6.8	7.0	7.1	7.2	7.3	7.4	7.4	7.4	7.5
0.7	6.8	6.9	7.0	7.1	7.1	7.2	7.2	7.3	7.3
1	6.7	6.8	6.9	7.0	7.0	7.1	7.1	7.2	7.2
1.3	6.6	6.7	6.8	6.9	6.9	7.0	7.0	7.1	7.1
1.6	6.5	6.7	6.7	6.8	6.9	6.9	7.0	7.0	7.0
1.9	6.5	6.6	6.7	6.8	6.8	6.9	6.9	6.9	7.0
2.2	6.5	6.6	6.6	6.7	6.8	6.8	6.8	6.9	6.9
2.5	6.4	6.5	6.6	6.7	6.7	6.8	6.8	6.8	6.9
2.8	6.4	6.5	6.6	6.6	6.7	6.7	6.8	6.8	6.8
Spillover premium									
0.4	1.5	1.7	1.8	1.8	1.9	1.9	1.9	1.9	2.0
0.7	1.4	1.5	1.5	1.6	1.7	1.7	1.7	1.8	1.8
1	1.3	1.4	1.4	1.5	1.5	1.6	1.6	1.6	1.6
1.3	1.1	1.2	1.3	1.3	1.4	1.4	1.4	1.5	1.5
1.6	1.0	1.1	1.2	1.2	1.3	1.3	1.4	1.4	1.4
1.9	1.0	1.0	1.1	1.2	1.2	1.2	1.3	1.3	1.3
2.2	0.9	1.0	1.0	1.1	1.1	1.2	1.2	1.2	1.2
2.5	0.9	1.0	1.0	1.0	1.1	1.1	1.1	1.2	1.2
2.8	0.8	0.9	0.9	1.0	1.0	1.1	1.1	1.1	1.1

Impact of spillovers on product varieties, scale and productivity

Another important impact of FDI productivity spillovers under firm heterogeneity is reflected by the changes in varieties and scale. From Figure 8.9(b) and (c) one can see that, with FDI productivity spillovers under firm heterogeneity, the number of varieties produced by domestic enterprises may increase or decrease, subject to the values of elasticities of capital and labour transformation. The total varieties in the whole country may also increase and decrease (Figure 8.9(a)). The impact on the variety of FIEs is negative. The "spillover premium" effects of FDI spillovers on the changes in variety for all types of enterprises are negative (Figure 8.9(f)–(h)), i.e. $\Delta N/N_0$ (with spillovers) $-\Delta N'/N_0'$ without spillovers) < 0.

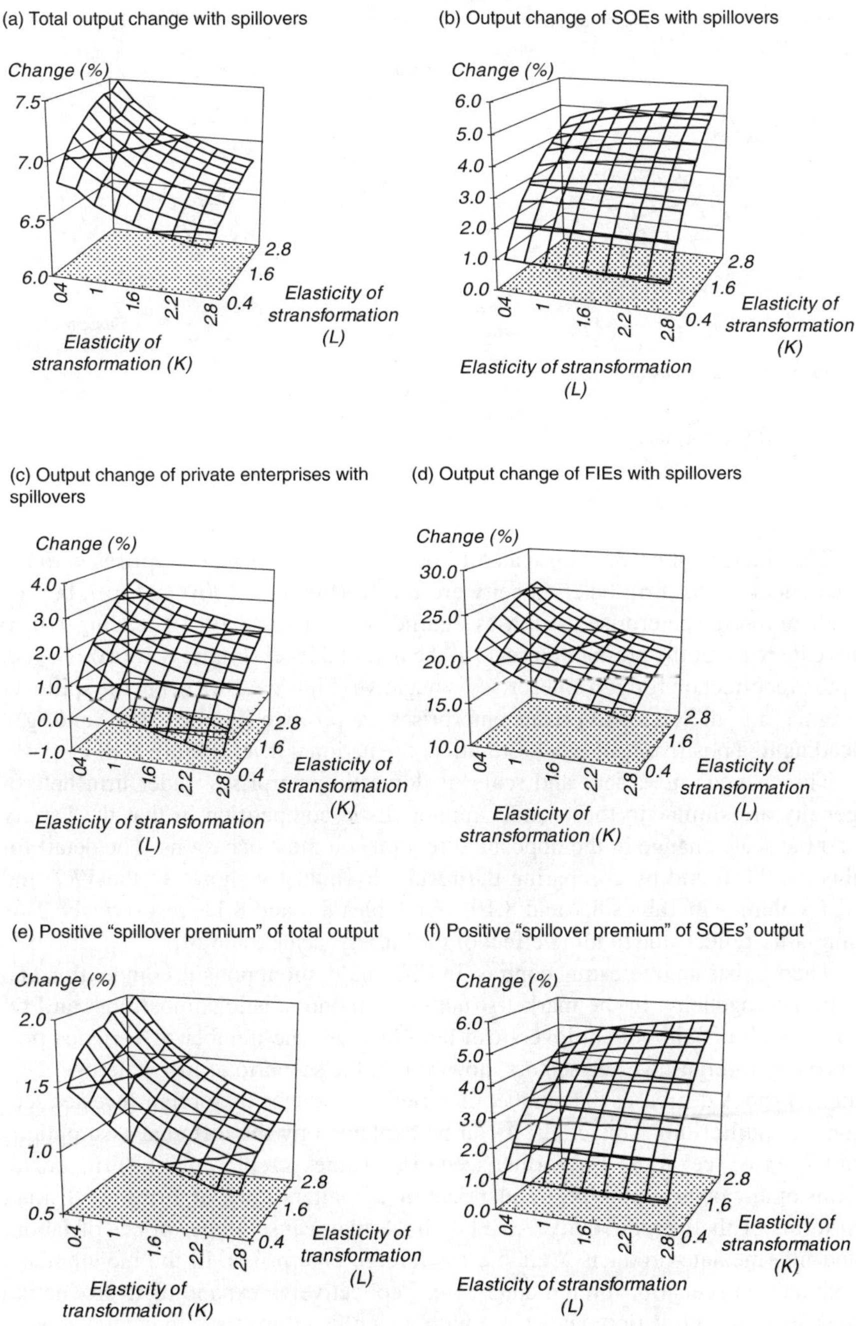

Figure 8.8 FDI spillover effects under firm heterogeneity.

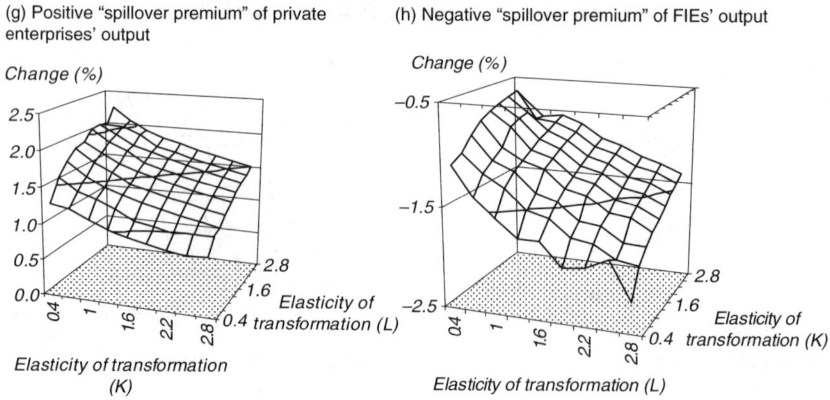

Figure 8.8 Continued.

The changes in production scale of both SOEs and private enterprises with the FDI shock under firm heterogeneity are mixed (Figure 8.10(b) and (c)), but the scale of foreign enterprises increases significantly (Figure 8.10(d)), leading to positive increase of the production scale at the national level (Figure 8.10(a)). The net spillover effect on foreign enterprises is negative (Figure 8.10(h)), but the spillover premia of both SOEs and private enterprises are positive (Figure 8.10(f) and (g)), leading to a positive spillover premium at the national level (Figure 8.10(e)).

The changes in variety and scale of domestic enterprises under firm heterogeneity are similar to those under monopolistic competition in that the variety and the scale change in the opposite directions on most occasions. The detail for this can be found by comparing the results by industry shown in the *VRT* and *SCL* columns in Tables 8.7 and 8.10, and Tables 8.8 and 8.11, respectively. This similarity reflects the binding effect of the variety–scale trade-off.

There exists an interesting contrast in FIEs under monopolistic competition and firm heterogeneity. In the market structure of monopolistic competition, an FDI shock with or without spillovers can help increase the number of varieties produced by foreign-invested sectors; however, in the scenario of firm heterogeneity, an FDI shock decreases the number of varieties produced by foreign-invested sectors in equilibrium. This contrast can be explained by the different assumptions of these two scenarios. The former scenario assumes a representative firm, i.e. all firms of any ownership type are identical; in the latter, however, firms are distinct in terms of their productivity. An FDI shock may cause higher prices of labour and intermediate products available for foreign enterprises. In the monopolistic competition scenario, foreign enterprises "collectively" expand their production presence (in both variety and scale) with a significant increase in capital supply, regardless of the higher input costs. Under firm heterogeneity, higher input costs cause the least productive foreign firms to exit and reduce the number of varieties

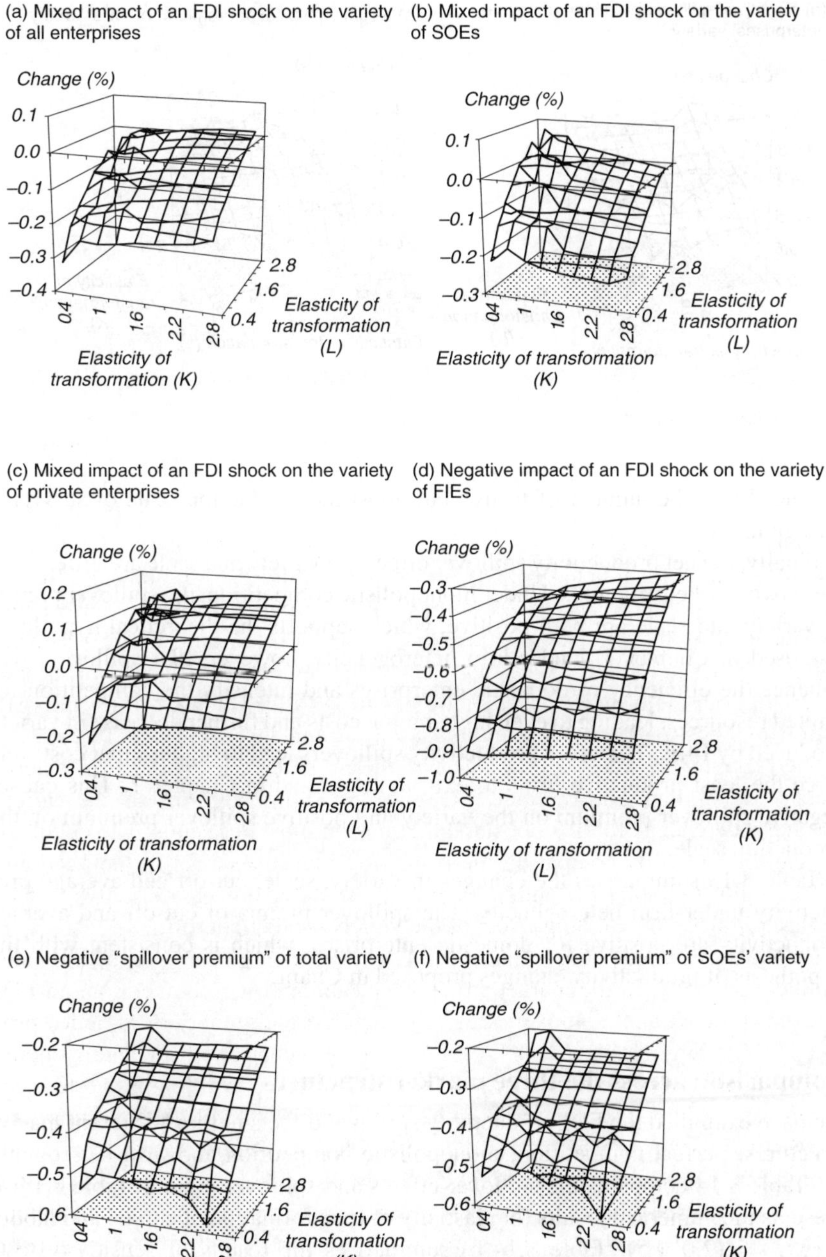

Figure 8.9 Variety changes with FDI productivity spillovers under firm heterogeneity.

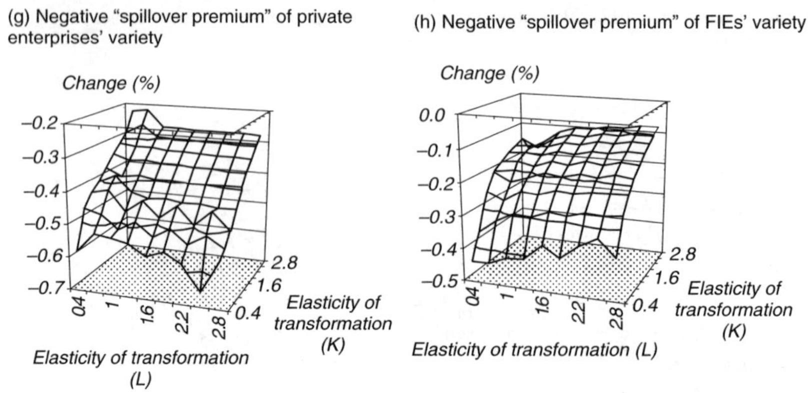

Figure 8.9 Continued.

produced (i.e. the number of firms), but boost the production scale of surviving foreign firms.[1]

Finally, the net productivity spillover effects on variety and scale are different in these two market structures. Under monopolistic competition, the spillover premia of variety and scale are both positive, which supports the theoretical hypothesis proposed in Chapter 7. Under firm heterogeneity, however, FDI spillovers will enhance the efficiency of domestic enterprises and intensify the competition for limited resources, leading to even higher input costs and further decrease in variety produced by FIEs. Therefore productivity spillovers lead to higher input costs and force the least productive firms to exit, as suggested in Chapter 7. This causes negative spillover premium on the variety and positive spillover premium on the production scale.

Table 8.13 summarises the changes in variety, scale, cut-off and average productivity under firm heterogeneity. The spillover premia of cut-off and average productivity are positive for domestic enterprises, which is consistent with the hypothesis of productivity changes proposed in Chapter 7.

Comparison across the three market structures

We have examined the FDI productivity spillover effects in three different market structures: perfect competition, monopolistic competition and firm heterogeneity. Table 8.14 compares the spillover effects and spillover premia. Table 8.14(a) presents the numerical results for elasticity of transformation of capital and labour $(\tau_K, \tau_L) = (2.0, 0.5)$. Table 8.14(b) summarises the results of sensitivity tests against changes in (τ_K, τ_L). The range of $\tau_K(\tau_L)$ is $0.1, 0.4, \ldots, 2.8$, the same range as adopted in the sensitivity experiments performed in previous sections. The results show that the spillover effects and premia are similar across the three market structures.

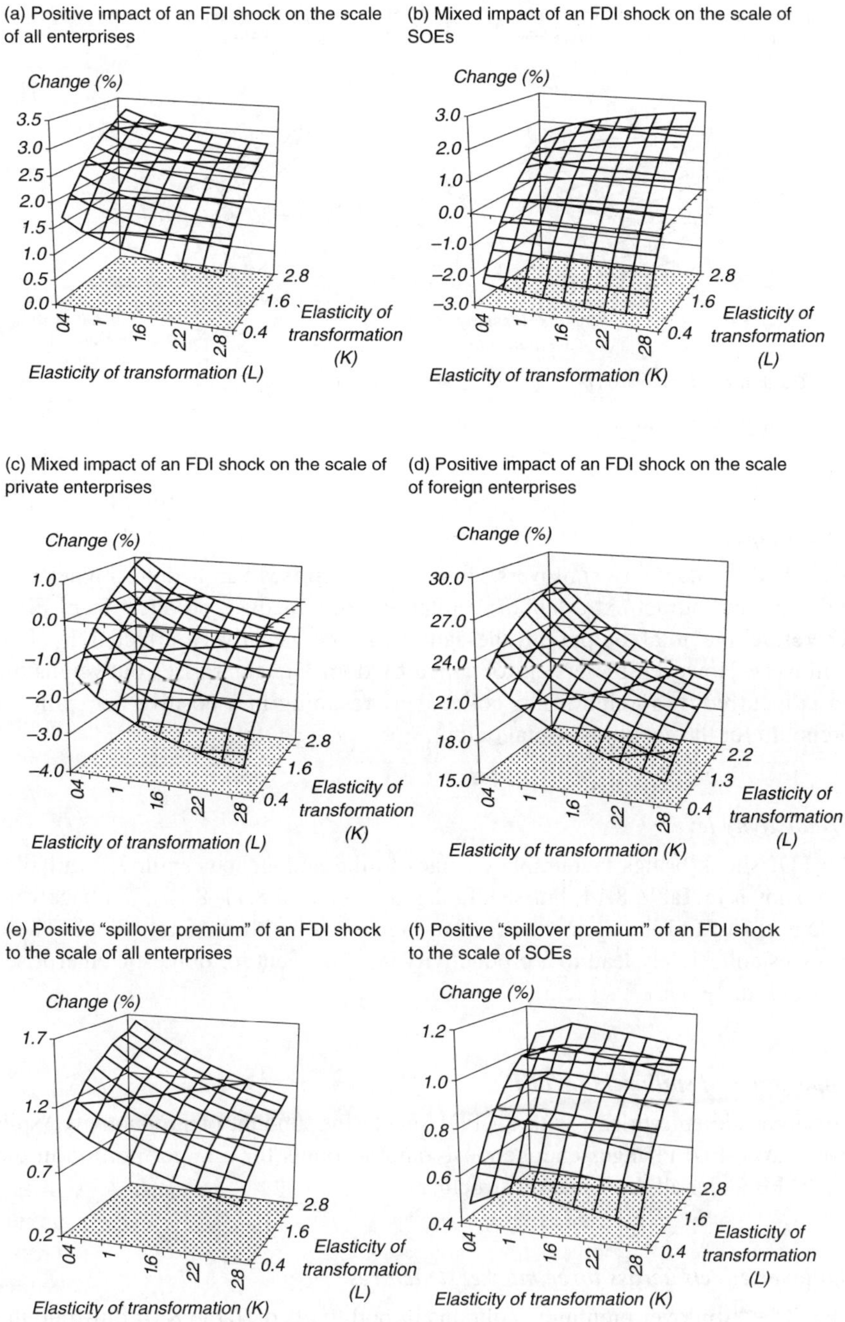

Figure 8.10 Scale per variety changes with FDI productivity spillovers under firm heterogeneity.

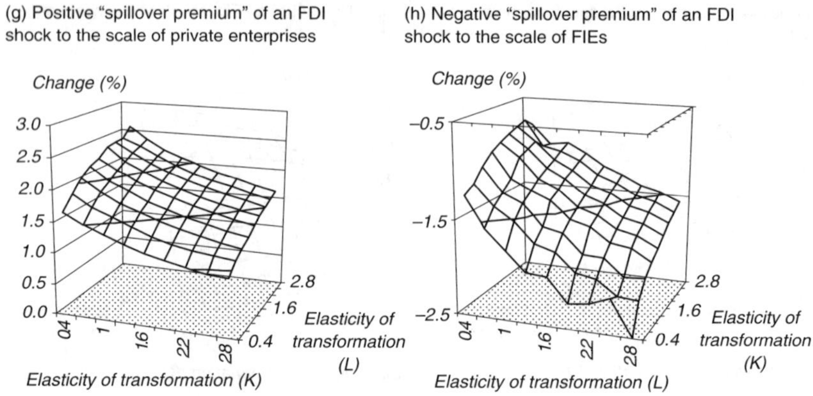

Figure 8.10 Continued.

Total output

With FDI productivity spillovers, domestic enterprises can acquire higher productivity and attract extra labour, capital and intermediate products from FIEs. Therefore the total output of the latter will be negatively affected by FDI spillovers. However, the benefit obtained by domestic enterprises outweighs the costs incurred by foreign firms, collectively resulting in a positive net spillover premium for the economy's total output.

Productivity level

An FDI shock brings favourable changes to the endogenous spillover variables (not shown in Table 8.14, but see Tables 8.5–8.8 and 8.11–8.12), i.e. backward linkages, forward linkages, export of foreign firms and horizontal effects. These changes collectively lead to a productivity improvement for domestic enterprises under all three market structures.

Importance of spillovers in TFP

For domestic enterprises, with an FDI shock, the amount of productivity "spilt over" from FDI changes endogenously and accounts for a larger portion in the total TFP under all three market structures.

Spillover effects across three market structures

The three "spillover premium" columns in both parts of Table 8.14 illustrate the distinct net effects brought about by the endogenous FDI productivity spillovers. The simulation results obtained from the monopolistic competition scenario are

Table 8.11 Changes (%) of SOEs under firm heterogeneity

	*FDI**	*BL*	*FL*	*HZDS*	*EXCO*	*NTFP*	*TFP*	*Export*	*Import*	*Output*	*P*	*VRT*	*SCL*
Coal, petroleum and gas	0.6	7.1	7.8	6.2	12.3	6.3	0.8	−31.0	36.8	−0.1	5.3	5.3	−5.2
Ferrous metals mining	0.0	6.6	16.0	−7.3	NA	10.0	1.0	−15.9	9.9	−4.0	1.9	1.9	−5.7
Non-ferrous metals mining	0.0	8.6	19.7	−11.8	−15.9	11.9	1.3	12.7	−29.2	−17.4	−4.3	−4.3	−13.7
Mining of non-metal, other minerals, and other ores	0.0	10.2	13.2	−2.9	−3.3	9.5	0.8	−7.4	9.0	0.2	1.1	1.1	−0.9
Food, beverage and tobacco manufacturing	2.5	7.3	5.6	4.9	0.8	4.8	0.9	42.0	−30.1	−5.8	−5.8	−5.8	0.1
Textile industry	5.1	14.6	13.2	16.7	20.8	12.2	2.7	19.2	5.4	11.8	−0.8	−0.8	12.7
Garments and other fibre products	4.4	14.9	9.4	11.3	8.0	10.2	2.8	46.7	−32.4	12.5	−3.2	−3.2	16.1
Leather, furs, down and related products	3.2	7.6	7.4	6.4	5.2	5.2	2.1	38.0	−6.4	19.3	−1.6	−1.6	21.3
Timber processing, bamboo, cane, palm fibre, etc.	0.7	13.9	14.3	19.5	24.2	14.5	1.8	40.4	−24.3	0.5	−4.2	−4.2	4.9
Furniture manufacturing	1.0	13.3	8.8	18.5	14.4	14.8	2.5	40.8	−28.9	5.9	−3.3	−3.3	9.6
Papermaking and paper products	2.2	9.8	7.7	9.1	7.8	6.8	1.7	−47.4	61.1	−2.8	9.3	9.3	−11.1

Continued

Table 8.11 Continued

	*FDI**	*BL*	*FL*	*HZDS*	*EXCO*	*NTFP*	*TFP*	*Export*	*Import*	*Output*	*P*	*VRT*	*SCL*
Printing and record medium reproduction	1.0	10.3	7.6	7.8	5.6	7.5	1.2	1.5	−16.2	−14.9	−2.5	−2.5	−12.6
Cultural, educational and sports goods	1.6	10.4	8.8	10.0	7.1	8.1	2.5	28.3	−21.1	11.9	−1.6	−1.6	13.7
Petroleum processing and coking	0.5	6.8	10.7	7.6	10.6	7.4	0.7	−29.9	40.7	5.6	8.2	8.2	−2.4
Raw chemical materials and chemical products	4.9	11.7	12.3	14.4	17.5	10.5	2.4	22.7	−5.1	6.2	−1.9	−1.9	8.2
Medical and pharmaceutical products	1.8	11.1	12.2	12.4	15.4	11.1	2.1	150.4	−61.8	−6.4	−12.2	−12.2	6.6
Chemical fibre	0.8	12.8	12.9	13.2	15.6	9.9	3.1	485.2	−70.7	16.9	−19.1	−19.1	44.5
Rubber products	1.3	12.2	7.4	12.2	12.3	9.0	2.4	35.3	−21.3	5.5	−3.3	−3.3	9.1
Plastic products	3.7	15.3	8.2	20.4	10.7	11.7	3.5	122.1	−46.4	5.3	−9.4	−9.4	16.2
Non-metal mineral products	3.1	9.8	6.2	12.1	12.5	8.7	1.5	−2.5	−4.1	−6.6	−0.7	−0.7	−6.0
Smelting and pressing of ferrous metals	2.4	13.7	10.1	29.6	45.3	13.6	1.5	−73.9	189.0	3.3	22.0	22.0	−15.3

Table 8.11 Continued

	*FDI**	*BL*	*FL*	*HZDS*	*EXCO*	*NTFP*	*TFP*	*Export*	*Import*	*Output*	*P*	*VRT*	*SCL*
Smelting and pressing of non-ferrous metals	1.3	15.9	6.2	24.8	40.1	9.9	2.0	−59.1	129.3	9.5	11.0	11.0	−1.4
Metal products	3.8	14.1	6.6	9.5	15.3	7.3	1.6	−41.9	73.0	4.4	7.1	7.1	−2.5
Ordinary machinery	2.9	9.0	7.2	9.3	14.1	6.9	1.4	−29.4	25.2	−5.8	3.2	3.2	−8.8
Special purpose equipment	2.3	9.4	11.8	16.2	16.3	10.9	1.5	−26.4	17.9	−5.7	2.7	2.7	−8.2
Transport equipment	4.4	7.9	6.5	6.2	6.6	5.2	1.5	7.2	−4.2	0.9	−0.6	−0.6	1.6
Electronic and electric products	11.9	3.6	2.2	1.3	0.9	1.4	0.8	17.5	−0.4	9.0	−0.8	−0.8	9.9
Instruments, meters, cultural and office machinery	3.1	5.2	7.1	9.0	5.9	5.3	2.3	20.5	1.6	15.5	−0.6	−0.6	16.2
Production of electric power, steam and hot water	1.0	5.5	11.1	1.9	0.2	4.4	0.8	−12.5	14.9	−0.9	4.6		
Production of gas	0.9	6.5	7.3	3.2	8.3	3.9	0.6	17.8	−4.9	9.9	−2.5		
Production of tap water	0.5	8.2	10.5	146.0	NA	24.2	2.6	−3.5	−17.9	−19.8	−6.4	−30.9	−29.6

Notes: Parameters of Pareto distribution for domestic firms $a = 3.4$, $b = 0.2$, $\sigma = 3.8$; parameters of Pareto distribution for foreign-invested firms $a = 3.4$, $b = 0.3$, $\sigma = 3.8$. Elasticity of transformation of capital and labour $(\tau_K, \tau_L) = (2.0, 0.5)$.

Table 8.12 Changes (%) of private enterprises under firm heterogeneity

	*FDI**	*BL*	*FL*	*HZDS*	*EXCO*	*NTFP*	*TFP*	*Export*	*Import*	*Output*	*P*	*VRT*	*SCL*
Coal, petroleum and gas	0.6	7.1	7.8	6.2	12.3	6.3	1.6	−27.3	36.8	3.7	5.1	5.1	−1.3
Ferrous metals mining	0.0	6.6	16.0	−7.3	NA	12.1	2.5	−8.7	9.9	1.9	1.5	1.5	0.4
Non-ferrous metals mining	0.0	8.6	19.7	−11.8	−15.9	13.5	3.0	34.7	−29.2	-5.8	−4.9	−4.9	−0.9
Mining of non-metal, other minerals, and other ores	0.0	10.2	13.2	−2.9	−3.3	9.5	1.4	−5.5	9.0	1.8	1.0	1.0	0.7
Food, beverage and tobacco manufacturing	2.5	7.3	5.6	4.9	0.8	1.8	1.0	49.0	−30.1	-2.3	−6.0	−6.0	3.9
Textile industry	5.1	14.6	13.2	16.7	20.8	8.5	4.6	22.6	5.4	14.3	−0.9	−0.9	15.3
Garments and other fibre products	4.4	14.9	9.4	11.3	8.0	0.0	0.0	40.6	−32.4	8.6	−3.1	−3.1	12.0
Leather, furs, down and related products	3.2	7.6	7.4	6.4	5.2	1.0	0.8	45.2	−6.4	24.4	−1.7	−1.7	26.6
Timber processing, bamboo, cane, palm fibre, etc.	0.7	13.9	14.3	19.5	24.2	11.0	3.4	42.3	−24.3	1.4	−4.3	−4.3	6.0
Furniture manufacturing	1.0	13.3	8.8	18.5	14.4	6.5	2.2	36.9	−28.9	3.6	−3.3	−3.3	7.1
Papermaking and paper products	2.2	9.8	7.7	9.1	7.8	5.2	3.8	−45.4	61.1	-0.1	9.2	9.2	−8.5

Table 8.12 Continued

	*FDI**	*BL*	*FL*	*HZDS*	*EXCO*	*NTFP*	*TFP*	*Export*	*Import*	*Output*	*P*	*VRT*	*SCL*
Printing and record medium reproduction	1.0	10.3	7.6	7.8	5.6	5.2	1.8	25.2	−16.2	−0.6	−3.3	−3.3	2.8
Cultural, educational and sports goods	1.6	10.4	8.8	10.0	7.1	1.7	0.8	26.2	−21.1	10.3	−1.6	−1.6	12.1
Petroleum processing and coking	0.5	6.8	10.7	7.6	10.6	7.5	2.1	−29.8	40.7	5.7	8.2	8.2	−2.3
Raw chemical materials and chemical products	4.9	11.7	12.3	14.4	17.5	7.5	4.7	19.7	−5.1	4.2	−1.8	−1.8	6.2
Medical and pharmaceutical products	1.8	11.1	12.2	12.4	15.4	1.0	0.5	173.9	−61.8	0.3	−12.4	−12.4	14.5
Chemical fibre	0.8	12.8	12.9	13.2	15.6	6.1	5.5	233.7	−70.7	−22.1	−17.4	−17.4	−5.6
Rubber products	1.3	12.2	7.4	12.2	12.3	3.6	2.6	31.7	−21.3	3.3	−3.2	−3.2	6.7
Plastic products	3.7	15.3	8.2	20.4	10.7	5.2	4.1	110.1	−46.4	1.0	−9.2	−9.2	11.3
Non-metal mineral products	3.1	9.8	6.2	12.1	12.5	6.8	3.0	4.3	−4.1	−1.7	−0.9	−0.9	−0.8
Smelting and pressing of ferrous metals	2.4	13.7	10.1	29.6	45.3	12.3	3.8	−74.9	189.0	0.3	22.2	22.2	−17.9

Continued

Table 8.12 Continued

	*FDI**	*BL*	*FL*	*HZDS*	*EXCO*	*NTFP*	*TFP*	*Export*	*Import*	*Output*	*P*	*VRT*	*SCL*
Smelting and pressing of non-ferrous metals	1.3	15.9	6.2	24.8	40.1	7.6	4.7	−74.5	129.3	−20.6	12.9	12.9	−29.7
Metal products	3.8	14.1	6.6	9.5	15.3	7.5	4.6	−52.0	73.0	−8.9	7.8	7.8	−15.5
Ordinary machinery	2.9	9.0	7.2	9.3	14.1	6.8	3.1	−29.1	25.2	−5.6	3.2	3.2	−8.5
Special purpose equipment	2.3	9.4	11.8	16.2	16.3	12.7	3.6	−28.0	17.9	−7.1	2.8	2.8	−9.6
Transport equipment	4.4	7.9	6.5	6.2	6.6	3.5	2.6	−5.5	−4.2	−7.4	−0.2	−0.2	−7.2
Electronic and electric products	11.9	3.6	2.2	1.3	0.9	0.3	0.4	11.8	−0.4	5.1	−0.7	−0.7	5.8
Instruments, meters, cultural and office machinery	3.1	5.2	7.1	9.0	5.9	4.5	3.0	23.4	1.6	18.0	−0.6	−0.6	18.8
Production of electric power, steam and hot water	1.0	5.5	11.1	1.9	0.2	3.5	1.6	−7.7	14.9	3.4	4.1		
Production of gas	0.9	6.5	7.3	3.2	8.3	2.7	1.2	0.4	−4.9	−3.6	−1.4		
Production of tap water	0.5	8.2	10.5	146.0	NA	37.6	7.4	42.6	−17.9	8.9	−9.2	−5.3	−17.6

Note: As Table 8.11.

Table 8.13 The impact of an FDI shock on variety, scale, cut-off (φ^*) and average ($\bar{\varphi}$) productivity under firm heterogeneity

	Variety			*Scale*			φ^*			$\bar{\varphi}$		
	A	*F*	*D*	*A*	*F*	*D*	*A*	*F*	*D*	*A*	*F*	*D*
Without spillovers	+/−	−	+	+/−	+	+/−	+	+	+/−	+	+	+/−
With spillovers	+/−	−	+/−	+	+	+/−	+	+	+/−	+	+	+/−
Spillover premium	−	−	−	+	−	+	+	−	+	+	−	+

Notes: (1) *A*, all enterprises' output; *F*, foreign-invested enterprises in manufacturing sectors only; *D*, refers to domestic-invested enterprises (including SOEs and private enterprises). (2) + and − denote positive and negative changes. (3) Some results can be positive or negative, depending on the values of capital and labour elasticities.

numerically comparable with those obtained from the perfect competition scenario with all parameter values controlled, because the former scenario is simply an extreme example of the latter when the number of firms in a sector approaches infinity. As discussed with regard to Table 8.9, the net spillover effects under monopolistic competition are larger than under perfect competition for domestic enterprises and for GDP, welfare and total output.

However, the net spillover effects obtained under firm heterogeneity are less comparable with those obtained under the other two alternative market structures, because the simulation results obtained under firm heterogeneity depend on the parameter values of the Pareto distribution of firm productivity taken from estimates for US firms (Bernard *et al.* 2003).

Table 8.14(a) shows that the spillover premia of output, GDP and welfare given the Pareto parameters under firm heterogeneity are very close to those obtained under monopolistic competition. Table 8.14(b) shows that the spillover premia exhibit a highly similar pattern across the three market structures, except for the changes in variety. The reason for the exception is the different theoretical assumptions for monopolistic competition and firm heterogeneity, as explained in Chapter 8.

Conclusions

This chapter discusses how an FDI shock to the benchmark economy together with productivity spillovers affects economic performance. Simulations are conducted under three different market structures: perfect competition, monopolistic competition and firm heterogeneity.

Results show that (1) in terms of national aggregate indicators, an FDI shock is beneficial to the economy, and FDI productivity spillovers are followed by positive spillover premiums under the three market structure assumptions; (2) for domestic enterprises (including SOEs and private enterprises), FDI productivity

Table 8.14 The effects of an FDI shock (percentage change)

		Perfect competition		*Monopolistic competition*		*Firm heterogeneity*	
		With spillovers	*Spillover premium*	*With spillovers*	*Spillover premium*	*With spillovers*	*Spillover premium*
(a) Elasticity of transformation of capital and labour $(\tau_K, \tau_L) = (2.0, 0.5)$							
Output	All	6.8	1.1	7.2	1.2	6.6	1.0
	FIEs	14.9	−0.6	15.3	−0.6	17.0	−0.8
	SOEs	1.9	0.5	1.8	0.5	4.2	0.5
	Private	1.2	1.2	1.3	1.2	2.8	1.1
Variety	All	Not applicable		2.4	0.3	−0.2	−0.3
	FIEs			13.3	−0.7	−0.5	−0.2
	SOEs			0.3	0.4	−0.2	−0.3
	Private			−0.2	1.3	−0.1	−0.3
Scale	All			1.0	0.1	2.9	0.8
	FIEs			2.0	0.0	18.4	−0.9
	SOEs			0.5	0.1	1.2	0.6
	Private			1.3	0.3	0.4	1.2
Productivity	SOEs	1.8	1.8	1.9	1.9	5.3	5.3
	Private	3.5	3.5	3.6	3.6	5.4	5.4
Spillovers	SOEs	8.7	8.7	8.7	8.7	10.3	10.3
	Private	7.3	7.3	7.4	7.4	8.3	8.3
Welfare		3.6	1.2	4.4	1.3	4.0	1.0
GDP		7.1	1.5	7.8	1.6	2.6	1.4
(b) Sensitivity test of the elasticity of transformation of capital and labour							
Output	All	+	+	+	+	+	+
	FIEs	+	−	+	−	+	−
	SOEs	+/−	+	+/−	+	+	+
	Private	+/−	+	+/−	+	+/−	+
Variety	All	Not applicable		+	+	+/−	−
	FIEs			+	−	−	−
	SOEs			+/−	+	+/−	−
	Private			+/−	+	+/−	−
Scale	All			+	+	+	+
	FIEs			+	−	+	−
	SOEs			+	+	+/−	+
	Private			+	+	+/−	+
Productivity	SOEs	+	+	+	+	+	+
	Private	+	+	+	+	+	+
Spillovers	SOEs	+	+	+	+	+	+
	Private	+	+	+	+	+	+
Welfare		+	+	+	+	+	+
GDP		+	+	+	+	+	+

Notes: (1) τ_K and τ_L take values $0.1, 0.4, \ldots, 2.8$, the same range as adopted in the sensitivity experiments performed in previous sections. (2) Productivity is given by equation (4.2b). (3) The spillovers rows measure how the importance of productivity spillovers in domestic enterprises' TFP changes, as denoted by equation (4.4). (4) The initial number of firms in each ownership sector is set to 10.

spillovers promote their performance and always outweigh the negative impact of an FDI shock; (3) for foreign-invested enterprises, FDI productivity spillovers cause resources to be attracted away by their rivals that are more productive thanks to the FDI spillovers, thus making the increase in FIEs' total output lower than otherwise; a finding which applies to all three market structures; (4) product variety and production scale per variety can both be improved by an FDI shock, and FDI productivity spillovers can exert positive "spillover premiums" under certain conditions; and (5) the experiments under the monopolistic competition assumption show that FDI productivity spillovers are more prominent in an industry with a lower initial degree of competition.

The simulation results obtained under the three market structures are generally consistent with the theoretical hypotheses derived in the previous chapter. Under any market structure, productivity spillovers enable domestic enterprises to attract more labour, capital and intermediate products from foreign enterprises. In this way FDI generates positive spillover premia for domestic enterprises and negative spillover premia for foreign enterprises.

Under monopolistic competition, we derive a theoretical hypothesis that both variety and production scale of domestic enterprises can increase due to the possibly lower input costs brought about by the FDI productivity spillovers. This hypothesis is justified by the simulation results presented in Figure 8.5.

Under firm heterogeneity, we further derive two theoretical hypotheses, namely the productivity improvement effect caused by the FDI spillovers from foreign to domestic enterprises, and the resource reallocation effect which transfers resources from the least productive firms (exiting the market due to the increased competition) to the remaining firms. Both effects boost the average productivity of the remaining firms. This proposition is also justified by the simulation results presented in Tables 8.13 and 8.14.

But there is one result seemingly counter to the theoretical hypotheses set out earlier. Under firm heterogeneity, the spillover premium of domestic enterprises' ouput is not significantly larger than that obtained under the other two alternative market structures. However, as the average productivity levels of both foreign and domestic enterprises can increase with an FDI shock (as hypothesised in Chapter 7 and justified by the simulation results presented in the "with spillovers" row in Table 8.13), it was anticipated that the spillover premium in terms of the change of domestic enterprises' output would be much more significant. This may reflect the parameters of the Pareto distribution of firm productivity, which were taken from values estimated for US rather than Chinese enterprises, as discussed in Chapter 8.

In brief, the simulated effects of the FDI productivity spillovers obtained under the three market structures generally support the theoretical hypotheses derived earlier in this book. The trivial deviation between expected and actual results arises mainly due to the selection of parameter values and model design.

Part IV

Significant impact of FDI productivity spillovers

9 Swapping market access for productivity spillovers?

An assessment of 2008 corporate income tax reform

China's FDI policies

China's FDI policies are mainly stated in two types of official documents, namely the Guiding Directory on Industries Open to Foreign Direct Investment (FDI Directory) and various laws and regulations (see Table 9.1), which were originally issued at the early stages of "Reform and Opening-up" policy implementation in the late 1970s and early 1980s. Although these official documents have been amended various times in the past three decades, one of the priority targets has never been changed: that FDI policies should provide foreign firms with preferential incentives (Prasad and Rajan 2006) aimed at swapping domestic market access for advanced foreign technology and productivity (Long 2005).

The FDI Directory lists three categories of industries, in which FDI is respectively "encouraged", "restricted" and "prohibited". It has been amended five times since its first release in 1995. As shown in Table 9.2, the proportion of "encouraged" industries gradually increased from 53.9 per cent in 1995 to 73.4 per cent in 2007, while the proportion of "restricted" industries decreased by half during that period.

Various preferential treatments used to be granted to foreign-invested enterprises[1] in manufacturing sectors, and such treatments were enforced by laws and regulations. The most controversial treatment was the differential corporate income tax rates. According to the Income Tax Law for Enterprises with Foreign Investment and Foreign Enterprises passed in 1991 (abolished in 2008), foreign-invested firms paid income tax at the rate of 30 per cent. However, any enterprise with foreign investment of a manufacturing nature scheduled to operate for a period of not less than 10 years was, from the year in which it began to make a profit, exempt from income tax in the first and second years and able to claim a 50 per cent reduction in the third to fifth years. That is to say, most FIEs only needed to pay income tax at an average rate of roughly 15 per cent in the first seven years of operation. In contrast, the corporate income tax rate for domestic firms was as high as 33 per cent.

The dual differential corporate income tax system was abolished by China's Parliament and the new tax rate for both domestic firms and FIEs was set at 25 per cent from January 2008. Nonetheless, FIEs established before 16 March 2007 can

Table 9.1 China's main FDI policies

Category	*Name*	*Last updated*
Directory	• Guiding Directory on Industries Open to Foreign Investment	2007
Laws	• Corporate Income Tax Law	2007
	• Law on Wholly Foreign-Owned Enterprises	2001
	• Law on Chinese–Foreign Joint Ventures	2000
	• Law on Chinese–Foreign Cooperative Enterprises	1988
	• Law on Protection of Investment by Compatriots from Taiwan	1994
Regulations	• Regulations for Encouraging Investment from Overseas Chinese and Compatriots from Hong Kong and Macao	1990
	• Regulations for Encouraging Investment from Compatriots from Taiwan	1988

Table 9.2 Three categories of industries listed in the FDI directory

Version	*Encouraged*		*Restricted*		*Prohibited*	
	Number	*%*	*Number*	*%*	*Number*	*%*
1995	172	53.9	116	36.4	31	9.7
1997	186	57.1	112	34.4	28	8.6
2002	262	71.0	75	20.3	32	8.7
2004	257	70.2	76	20.8	33	9.0
2007	351	73.4	87	18.2	40	8.4

Source: As Figure 1.1. Author's compilation.

still enjoy the tax exemption for a five-year interim period from 1 January 2008 until 31 December 2012.

Regardless of the above *de facto* dual tax system during the five-year interim period, both domestic enterprises and FIEs can also equally enjoy various nationwide tax incentives, such as the following:

(a) a reduced rate of 20 per cent may be applied to small or low-profit enterprises. The withholding tax[2] rate is 10 per cent on interest, royalties, capital gains and dividends;
(b) a reduced tax rate of 15 per cent applied to advanced technology enterprises;
(c) tax exemption or reduction for enterprises that engage in infrastructure projects, agriculture, forestry, fishery, energy and water preservation, environmental protection business and transfer of qualified technology;
(d) reduced taxable income in proportion to the investment of venture capital;
(e) tax reduction for R&D expenses for developing new technology, new products and new processes.

The objectives of China's FDI policies are mainly concerned with export promotion and technology transfer. Before China's accession into the World Trade Organization (WTO) in 2001, export promotion and technology transfer were among the most important targets of China's FDI policies. In the late 1970s when China began its transformation from almost an autarchy economy to an export-oriented one, the foreign exchange reserves it held were as little as US$0.2 billion, which was a trivial figure compared to the reserves it held by September 2010, $2648.3 billion (State Administration of Foreign Exchange of China, http://www.safe.gov.cn/). In desperate need of foreign exchange reserves to fund the import of intermediate products and advanced technology, China adopted a series of mercantilist measures to promote exports. The FDI policies on exports required that FIEs should keep a balance of exchange, or make sure the proportion of their domestically made products in the total number of products were maintained at a reasonable level, or a certain share of their products should be exported. Furthermore, any FIE exporting 70 per cent of its total products was entitled to claim 50 per cent cut in corporate income tax. However, since such requirements and incentives were inconsistent with the provisions of the WTO Agreement on Trade-Related Investment Measures (TRIMs), they were abolished in 2001 when China became a WTO member state.

The FDI policies were so effective in export promotion that the export propensity of FIEs and the contribution of FIEs to China's total exports have been astonishingly high. In 2004, the average ratio of exports to total sales of FIEs was 46.1 per cent in manufacturing, while the average ratio of other types of enterprises was only 10.2 per cent (National Bureau of Statistics of China 2006a). In 2007, the share of FIEs' exports in China's total export hit a record high, 60 per cent, which was much higher than the 4 per cent achieved in the early 1980s (Ministry of Commerce of China). The strong export performance of FIEs set a good example for Chinese indigenous enterprises to enter the international market.

China's laws on FIEs had specific technology requirements even after the removal (in 2001) of the clauses inconsistent with China's WTO commitments. According to the latest Law on Chinese–Foreign Joint Ventures, "the technology and equipment that serve as the investment of the foreign partner in a joint venture must be advanced technology and equipment that indeed suit China's needs". Both the Law on Wholly Foreign-Owned Enterprises and the Law on Chinese–Foreign Cooperative Enterprises also say that the state encourages the establishment of wholly foreign-owned enterprises and production-based Chinese–foreign cooperative enterprises with advanced technology.

Costs and benefits of preferential FDI treatment

As discussed, most FIEs only needed to pay corporate income tax at an average rate as low as 15 per cent in the first seven years of operation. In contrast, the income tax rate (i.e. corporate income tax divided by total profit) of domestic firms is as high as 33 per cent. Table 9.3 shows the actual corporate income tax rates for state-owned, private and foreign-invested enterprises in 2004. The tax rates are

Table 9.3 Corporate income tax rate by industry for state-owned, domestic, private and foreign-invested enterprises, 2004 (%)

Sectors	*SOEs*	*Private*	*FIEs*
Coal, petroleum and gas	12.8	21.1	1.4
Ferrous metals mining	19.6	27.2	15.5
Non-ferrous metals mining	20.8	19.1	9.8
Mining of non-metal, other minerals, and other ores	32.2	20.7	23.7
Food, beverage and tobacco manufacturing	30.3	14.9	14.5
Textile industry	NA	20.2	12.7
Garments and other fibre products	24.8	21.2	11.9
Leather, furs, down and related products	NA	14.7	13.3
Timber processing, bamboo, cane, palm fibre, etc.	29.6	15.2	14.3
Furniture manufacturing	10.0	17.3	8.7
Papermaking and paper products	45.4	20.6	13.2
Printing and record medium reproduction	26.7	23.8	12.4
Cultural, educational and sports goods	47.7	18.5	15.6
Petroleum processing and coking	24.5	20.3	12.4
Raw chemical materials and chemical products	21.3	17.5	10.1
Medical and pharmaceutical products	19.7	17.9	12.5
Chemical fibre	55.7	18.6	13.8
Rubber products	35.7	20.8	13.0
Plastic products	24.6	19.1	12.5
Non-metal mineral products	29.1	20.7	10.3
Smelting and pressing of ferrous metals	24.8	18.9	6.7
Smelting and pressing of non-ferrous metals	24.2	19.3	10.9
Metal products	28.2	20.6	11.1
Ordinary machinery	22.7	20.6	12.1
Special purpose equipment	29.2	21.3	9.4
Transport equipment	10.5	19.6	7.8
Electronic and electric products	22.6	19.6	10.3
Instruments, meters, cultural and office machinery	42.0	17.3	10.6
Production of electric power, steam and hot water	21.5	24.8	12.2
Production of gas	45.6	10.9	11.4
Production of tap water	NA	26.2	22.1
Average	19.5	19.3	10.4

Source: National Bureau of Statistics of China (2006a).

calculated with the data from China Economic Census Statistical Yearbook 2004, as the data for the benchmark year (2002) of our CGE model is not available. The average tax rates for SOEs and private enterprises were 19.5 per cent and 19.3 per cent, respectively. However, FIEs only paid income tax at 10.4 per cent, almost half of those of their domestic rivals.

It is observed that there is much variation in these rates. Such variation is caused by various tax exemptions applicable to some enterprises, as previously discussed. Domestic enterprises in some industries collectively pay tax at a rate higher than the upper limit of 33 per cent, which could be due to accounting and measurement errors.

The preferential tax treatment potentially encouraged foreign capital to flow to China, especially at the beginning of marketisation (1980s) when the Chinese market was relatively closed and unknown to the rest of the world. The foreign capital increased the foreign reserves of China and helped it to import advanced equipment and technology. FDI also helped break the monopoly of SOEs and create a more competitive market environment. More importantly, preferential tax treatment potentially promoted the productivity spillovers from foreign firms to domestic firms via backward and forward input–output linkages, cross-ownership labour mobility, the export of foreign firms, and horizontal effects.

However, the benefits of such a preferential tax treatment seem to have diminished gradually for the following two reasons. First, in recent years China's foreign reserves have been the highest in the world, reducing the necessity to accumulate reserves by attracting FDI (especially the export-oriented and labour-intensive foreign capital) simply with preferential tax treatment. Second, in manufacturing sectors, the monopoly power of the SOEs has already been greatly restricted, and a more competitive market environment has already been fostered with the emergence of a variety of ownerships. As shown in Table 9.4, by 2007 the SOEs, private enterprises, and FIEs account for 9 per cent, 23 per cent, and 31 per cent of national total output, respectively. So the benefit of the preferential tax treatment to the FIEs in breaking the monopoly of the SOEs is no longer so appealing.

At the same time problems related to such preferential treatments also emerged so that the costs of the differential tax system have increased in recent years. The most critical was "round-tripping" FDI – cross-border investment motivated by the more favourable treatment of foreign as opposed to domestic capital, as discussed in Chapter 6. By 2003, about a quarter of FDI in China was round-tripping FDI (United Nations Conference on Trade and Development 2003, p. 45). Those enterprises invested in by round-tripping FDI are not necessarily more productive

Table 9.4 A decomposition of national total output by ownership, 2007

	Total output (RMB bn)	*(%)*
Total	40,518	100
Domestic enterprises	27,755	69
– SOEs	3,639	9
– Limited liability company	9,034	22
– Stock company	4,016	10
– Private enterprises	9,402	23
– Others	1,664	4
Foreign-invested enterprises	12,763	31
– Joint venture	5,410	13
– Solely foreign-owned	6,425	16
– Others	928	2

Source: National Bureau of Statistics of China (2008).

Note: Statistics only cover the enterprises with annual sales above RMB 5 million in the mining, manufacturing and utilities sectors.

than firms registered as "domestic enterprises". However, the former were able to enjoy a much lower corporate income tax rate (15 per cent) for a maximum of seven years. After this initial seven-year period, the investors could deliberately claim "bankruptcy" and re-register their fund as a new "foreign-invested enterprise". By doing this, a domestic investor could circumvent the high corporate income tax forever. Such tax evasion behaviour jeopardises the market environment and constitutes unfair competition against domestic enterprises.

The second problem was related to the technology content and origin of FDI. FDI from Hong Kong, Macau, and Taiwan (HMT) tends to remain in labour-intensive, low-technology manufacturing sectors (e.g. textiles, toys, and clothing). Some of these FIEs did not have any advantage in productivity, and the only advantage they held to beat domestic enterprises was the favourable corporate income tax rate. Empirical evidence suggests that once the presence of FDI in a certain sector exceeds a optimal point, FIEs may impose a negative impact on the performance of their domestic rivals (Buckley *et al.* 2007a).

The third problem of the preferential taxes is linked to the survival of domestic firms in services in China. The expansion of service sectors normally accompanies the industrialisation process. The percentage of services in China's GDP grew from less than 25 per cent in late 1970s to around 40 per cent in 2006. Also, employment in services accounted for 32 per cent of total employment in China in 2006. These two figures for 2006 are still far below those in post-industrialisation economies, and indicate that the service sectors in the Chinese economy are far from well established. Facing the strong competition from mature foreign multinational firms in service industries (e.g. banking, insurance, retail and wholesale), domestic enterprises do need a fair competitive environment where they can survive and sustain. A differential corporate income tax system will, however, threaten the development of domestic enterprises in service sectors.

The fourth problem was the international competitiveness of Chinese domestic enterprises. The average corporate income tax rate is 28.6 per cent among all the 159 countries (or regions) around the world which have adopted a corporate income tax system. The average rate is 26.7 per cent among the 18 countries (or regions) neighbouring China mainland (State Administration of Taxation of China, http://www.chinatax.gov.cn, 27 March 2007.). A tax rate of 33 per cent on domestic enterprises undoubtedly reduced the international competitiveness of the domestic enterprises.

The final problem was related to fiscal revenue. Various empirical studies have found a negative relationship between corporate income tax and FDI inflows – with a lower corporate income tax rate on foreign firms, a country can generally attract more FDI (e.g. Grubert and Mutti 1991; Hines and Rice 1994; Cassou 1997; Wei 2000a, b; Choi 2003; Ang 2008). If FDI is very elastic to the preferential corporate income taxes, then a lower tax rate could raise the fiscal revenue from foreign enterprises' taxes. However attacted by the potential effectiveness of various tax incentives in attracting FDI, countries have "increasingly" relied on such policy instruments (United Nations Conference on Trade and Development 2000, p. 3). So compared with the corporate income tax rates (the *de facto* rates

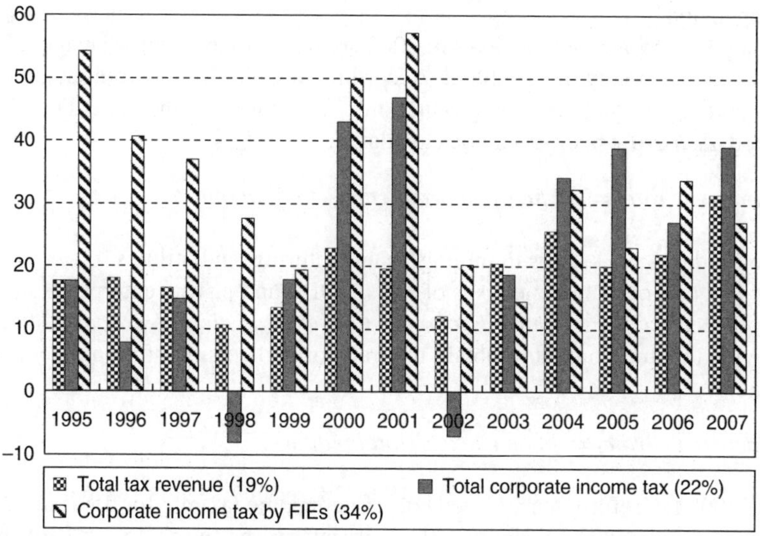

Figure 9.1 Growth rates of tax revenue in China, 1995–2007 (%).

Source: State Administration of Taxation of China (http://www.chinatax.gov.cn/).

may be lower than the average 26.7 per cent as discussed) in surrounding regions, the tax rate of 15 per cent in China might not appear so attractive. Moreover, if FDI is attracted to China more by the cheap labour and raw materials and the market potential in China rather than the low tax rate, then a low tax rate will cause a net loss of fiscal revenue. The total tax revenue, total corporate income taxes, and corporate income taxes paid by the foreign enterprises in China have grown very fast since early 1990s, as shown in Figure 9.1.

The average annual growth rates of total corporate income taxes and corporate income taxes paid by FIEs were 22 per cent and 34 per cent, respectively, both higher than that of total tax revenue (19 per cent). These figures indicated that the foreign enterprises performed well in the Chinese market, so a low corporate income tax on FIEs might have incurred a loss of fiscal revenue collected from foreign enterprises' income taxes.

In brief, the recent Chinese macroeconomic situation indicates that the costs of the dual corporate income tax system may have come to exceed the benefits in the recent years, thus yielding an optimal time to harmonise the tax rates.

Assessment of tax harmonisation

The aim of the experiments conducted in this section is to evaluate whether a removal of preferential corporate income tax treatment will hamper FDI productivity spillovers. The simulations are situated under three different market structure assumptions: perfect competition, monopolistic competition and firm heterogeneity.

Data on corporate income taxes in 2002 are not available, but we can use alternative data to remedy this problem. According to China's input–output table, the only tax data are "net taxes on production",[3] and based on the tax data and total output data, a gross tax rate can be calculated:

$$gross\ tax\ rate_i = net\ taxes\ on\ production_i / total\ output_i$$

where i indexes the sectors in mining, manufacturing, and utilities.

Data on corporate income taxes of FIEs, SOEs, and private enterprises in 2004 are collected from the *China Economic Census Statistical Yearbook 2004*, and are divided by total output to obtain the transformed version of corporate income tax rate:

$$income\ tax\ rate_i = income\ taxes_i / total\ output_i \quad (9.1)$$

The 2008 tax reform harmonised corporate income tax rate for domestic enterprises (previously 33 per cent) and foreign enterprises (up to 15 per cent) to 25 per cent. This reform formula can be modelled by deflating the corporate tax rate of domestic enterprises' output by 24.2% $[(25\%–33\%)/33\% = -24.2\%]$, while augmenting the tax rate of foreign enterprises' output by 66.7 per cent $[(25\%–15\%)/15\% = 66.7\%]$.

It is necessary to endogenise the FDI flows by linking FDI with such a tax reform.[4] Here a parameter is taken from Wei (2000b) who estimates the responsiveness of FDI inflows to the statutory corporate income tax with a gravity FDI model. The responsiveness of FDI to tax can be specified as:

$$\frac{\partial \ln(FDI)}{\partial (tax)} = \frac{\Delta(FDI)}{FDI \times \Delta(tax)} = -0.032 \quad (9.2)$$

Wei's work covers bilateral FDI data from 14 source countries to 53 host economies (including mainland China), while other papers only examine the relationship between corporate income tax and FDI flows of a single FDI source country or recipient country (e.g. Grubert and Mutti 1991; Hines and Rice 1994; Cassou 1997; Ang 2008). More importantly, this work is one of the very few papers which estimate tax responsiveness for the FDI flow to China. Another paper by Wei (2000a), which covers 12 FDI source countries and 45 host countries, and a paper by Choi (2003) employing the same database of Wei (2000b), have both obtained very close tax sensitivity values. Thus it is reasonable to employ the parameter (−0.032) in this model to capture the endogenous link between corporate income tax rate and FDI inflow amount in China.

Four types of tax reforms are simulated. In scenario A, single-sided reform without spillovers, there are no FDI productivity spillovers, and only the corporate income tax rate for foreign firms increases by 40 per cent. In scenario B, integrated reform without spillovers, there are no FDI productivity spillovers, the corporate income tax rate for foreign firms increases by 40 per cent, and the tax rate for domestic firms decreases by 24.2 per cent. In scenario C, single-sided reform with spillovers, there are FDI productivity spillovers, and only the corporate income tax rate for foreign firms increases by 40 per cent. In scenario D, integrated reform with spillovers, there are FDI productivity spillovers, the corporate income tax rate for foreign firms increases by 40 per cent, and the tax rate for domestic firms decreases by 24.2 per cent. The above tax rate changes will be captured by changing the values of parameter $\overline{TAXREF}(a)$ in equation (A2.3.1). For example, this parameter value for the foreign enterprises in the electronic and electric products sector can be obtained by calculating the income tax rate using equation (9.1), which gives 0.75 per cent, and then calculating the tax increment, $0.75\% \times 40\% = 0.3\%$.

All of the above reforms are accompanied by endogenous FDI inflow reduction. From equation (9.2) we know that the percentage change of FDI inflow is

$$\frac{\Delta(FDI)}{FDI} = -0.032 \times \Delta(tax) \qquad (9.3)$$

For example, in the electronic and electric products sector, FDI volume will decrease by 0.032 × [25 (%, new tax rate) – 10.3 (%, old tax rate)] = 0.47%. This reduces FDI inflow, and will result in a lower foreign presence in terms of the proportion of output produced by foreign firms in the total output produced by all types of firms. This will make the channels (i.e. backward and forward linkages, export of the foreign enterprises and horizontal effects) of FDI productivity spillovers shrink, and reduce the magnitude of FDI productivity spillovers, as captured by equation (4.4).

The domestic capital stock is assumed fixed in this static CGE model. As the output prices of products by foreign enterprises are higher after the reform, the cost of intermediate products used by domestic enterprises will also be higher. At the same time, facing higher corporate income taxes, the returns on capital and labour in foreign enterprises will be lower. This will lead to a lower price of primary inputs of domestic enterprises due to the transformability between foreign and domestic capital. Therefore, the impact of single-sided reform on domestic enterprises will be jointly determined by the above three possible effects, namely a smaller magnitude of FDI productivity spillovers, higher intermediate input costs, and lower primary input costs. But overall, single-sided reform will increase the average national tax rate level, and therefore reduce the welfare level. This model adopts a fiscal-neutral government closure rule (see Chapter 7), i.e. the fiscal deficit is financed by borrowing a fixed amount of commodities from households, and government spending is endogenously determined subject to the exogenous tax rate level (to be changed in counterfactual simulations in this section). Government closure is so designed that the change in welfare, measured by the total amount of consumption goods and services available for households and government, can be fully attributed to the tax reform.

An integrated tax reform not only raises the taxes of foreign enterprises but also reduces the taxes of domestic enterprises. This will complicate the net impact of the tax reform on the total output of domestic enterprises in that it can increase the returns to the capital and labour used by domestic enterprises. In terms of the FDI productivity spillovers, the impact of such a tax reform still tends to be negative for similar reasons. The sign of the national welfare change with an integrated tax reform cannot easily be predicted.

Fiscal revenue will also change accordingly. In the model, the other tax rates, i.e. the average output overall tax rates, denoted by NTP(a) in equation (A2.3.1), are assumed to be fixed. Due to the nonlinear relationship between tax rate and tax revenue suggested by the Laffer curve, the sign of tax revenue change cannot be predicted *ex ante* either, and the different changing directions of tax rates over domestic (up) and foreign (down) enterprises also leave this as an empirical problem.

Table 9.5 reports the numerical results from scenario A only. Table 9.6 reports the results from scenarios A–D. To make the results from fthe our scenarios more easily comparable, Table 9.6 reports only the signs of the results. A comparison of these results leads to four main findings.

(a) The difference between the scenarios with single-sided (A, C) and integrated (B, D) reforms. The economy before the tax reform is already distorted with corporate taxes. Single-sided reform simply raises the tax rate on foreign enterprises, leaves the economy even more distorted and reduces welfare. However, the integrated reform not only raises the tax rate on foreign enterprises, but also lowers the tax rate on domestic enterprises and improves national welfare. The production scale of SOEs and private enterprises is negatively impacted in the single-sided reforms, but positively affected in the integrated reforms.

(b) The difference between the scenarios with (C, D) and without (A, B) spillovers. The results are almost the same with or without spillovers. The only difference is the total output of private enterprises in Table 9.6(a) and (c). Their output is negatively affected in the scenario with spillovers while positively affected in the scenario without spillovers. This seemingly counterintuitive result can be explained by the competition between the SOEs and private enterprises. With a single-sided tax reform, the prices of intermediate inputs are higher while the prices of primary inputs become lower. When there are no productivity spillovers, private enterprises appear to benefit from such a reform. However, when there are spillovers, SOEs benefit more from these than the private enterprises do, so that SOEs attract resources from the private enterprises, making the latter lose from the spillovers.

(c) The comparison between the three alternative assumptions about industry structure. We need to keep in mind that any structure alone cannot reflect the whole picture of an economy: some industries tend to be perfectly competitive as they produce highly homogeneous products (e.g. petroleum processing and coking, and textile); some industries are more monopolistic competitive

Table 9.5 Effects of corporate income tax reform, scenario A (percentage changes, single-sided reform without spillovers)

		Perfect competition	*Monopolistic competition*	*Firm heterogeneity*
Output	All	−0.17	−0.18	−0.19
	FIEs	−0.72	−0.75	−0.83
	SOEs	0.04	0.04	0.02
	Private	0.05	0.04	0.06
Variety	All	Not applicable	−0.05	−0.10
	FIEs		−0.67	−0.40
	SOEs		0.09	−0.07
	Private		0.11	−0.05
Scale	All	Not applicable	−0.02	0.07
	FIEs		−0.11	−0.43
	SOEs		−0.01	0.12
	Private		−0.03	0.15
Productivity	All	Not applicable		0.02
	FIEs			0.01
	SOEs			0.02
	Private			0.02
Spillovers	SOEs	Not applicable		
	Private			
Total tax revenue		−0.19	−0.20	−0.21
Corporate income tax revenue		11.87	11.86	11.82
Welfare		−0.40	−0.42	−0.37
GDP		−0.14	−0.16	−0.14

Note: "Productivity" is industry-level productivity, measured by the denominator in equation (4.4); "spillovers" measures how the importance of productivity spillovers in domestic enterprises' TFP changes, as measured by equation (4.4). (2) Parameters of Pareto distribution for domestic firms are $a = 3.4$, $b = 0.2$, $\sigma = 3.8$, and for foreign-invested firms $a = 3.4$, $b = 0.3$, $\sigma = 3.8$. Elasticity of transformation of capital and labour $(\tau_K, \tau_L) = (2.0, 0.5)$. (3) "Not applicable" means that the values of the corresponding variables are not obtainable.

as their products are idiosyncratic and the number of firms is relatively small (e.g. transport equipment); and finally, some industries could be closer to the assumption of monopolistic competition with heterogeneous productivity, such as the "electronic and electric products" industry hosting a very high level of product variety and the largest number of firms in China. Therefore, the main purpose of spotting the difference between the above three alternative market structure assumptions is not to identify which assumption is "superior" to the others, but to get a sense of the range of possible outcomes.

Simulations under the scenario of perfect competition can provide results on output, productivity of domestic enterprises, spillovers, welfare and GDP. Simulations under the scenario of monopolistic competition can provide further details on variety and production scale. Simulations under the scenario of firm heterogeneity

Table 9.6 Effects of corporate income tax reform (%)

		Perfect competition	*Monopolistic competition*	*Firm heterogeneity*
(a) Single-sided reform without spillovers				
Output	All	–	–	–
	FIEs	–	–	–
	SOEs	+	+	+
	Private	+	+	+
Variety	All	Not applicable	–	–
	FIEs		–	–
	SOEs		+	–
	Private		+	–
Scale	All	Not applicable	–	+
	FIEs		–	–
	SOEs		–	+
	Private		–	+
Productivity	All	Not applicable		+
	FIEs			+
	SOEs			+
	Private			+
Spillovers	SOEs	Not applicable		
	Private			
Total tax revenue		–	–	–
Corporate income tax revenue		+	+	+
Welfare		–	–	–
GDP		–	–	–
(b) Integrated reform without spillovers				
Output	All	–	–	+
	FIEs	–	–	–
	SOEs	+	+	+
	Private	+	+	–
Variety	All	Not applicable	–	+
	FIEs		–	–
	SOEs		+	+
	Private		+	+
Scale	All	Not applicable	–	+
	FIEs		–	–
	SOEs		+	+
	Private		+	+
Productivity	All	Not applicable		+
	FIEs			+
	SOEs			+
	Private			+
Spillovers	SOEs	Not applicable		
	Private			

Table 9.6 Continued

		Perfect competition	*Monopolistic competition*	*Firm heterogeneity*
Total tax revenue		−	−	−
Corporate income tax revenue		−	−	−
Welfare		+	+	+
GDP		−	−	+
(c) Single-sided reform with spillovers				
Output	All	−	−	−
	FIEs	−	−	−
	SOEs	+	+	+
	Private	−	−	−
Variety	All	Not applicable	−	−
	FIEs		−	−
	SOEs		+	−
	Private		+	−
Scale	All	Not applicable	−	+
	FIEs		−	−
	SOEs		−	+
	Private		−	+
Productivity	All	Not applicable		+
	FIEs			+
	SOEs	−	−	+
	Private	−	−	+
Spillovers	SOEs	−	−	−
	Private	−	−	−
Total tax revenue		−	−	−
Corporate income tax revenue		+	+	+
Welfare		−	−	−
GDP		−	−	−
(d) Integrated reform with spillovers				
Output	All	−	−	+
	FIEs	−	−	−
	SOEs	+	+	+
	Private	+	+	−
Variety	All	Not applicable	−	+
	FIEs		−	−
	SOEs		+	+
	Private		+	+
Scale	All	Not applicable	−	−
	FIEs		−	−
	SOEs		+	+
	Private		+	+

Continued

Table 9.6 Continued

		Perfect competition	*Monopolistic competition*	*Firm heterogeneity*
Productivity	All	Not applicable		+
	FIEs			+
	SOEs	−	−	+
	Private	−	−	+
Spillovers	SOEs	−	−	−
	Private	−	−	−
Total tax revenue		−	−	−
Corporate income tax revenue		−	−	−
Welfare		+	+	+
GDP		−	−	+

Note: As Table 9.5.

can capture not only the above variables, but also the productivity changes of both domestic firms and foreign firms.

The results on the productivity of domestic firms, output, productivity spillovers, welfare and GDP are similar for the first two market structures. But the results under firm heterogeneity are different from those under the other two market structures to some extent. For example, in Table 9.6(a) and (c), the variety of SOEs and private enterprises are positively affected under monopolistic competition while negatively affected under firm heterogeneity. A similar contrast applies to the changes of scale under monopolistic competition and firm heterogeneity. However, the above contrasts are consistent with those reflected in Table 8.14.

Another difference between the scenario of firm heterogeneity and the other two market structures is the change in productivity of domestic firms under the above three scenarios. The productivity change is positive under firm heterogeneity but negative under the other two scenarios. Such an inconsistency can be explained by the different specifications of "productivity". Under perfect and monopolistic competition, productivity is denoted by $\hat{\alpha}_1 + \hat{\boldsymbol{\beta}} \times \mathbf{SPL}$ in equation (4.4), so that the productivity of domestic firms is directly dependent on the presence of foreign firms. Under firm heterogeneity, however, productivity is an endogenous variable denoted by equation (7.30) in the partial equilibrium module, and it is only indirectly linked with the foreign presence. In this sense, "productivity" denoted by $\hat{\alpha}_1 + \hat{\boldsymbol{\beta}} \times \mathbf{SPL}$ may not capture the actual information on domestic firms' productivity as fully as the "productivity" variable denoted by equation (7.25) under firm heterogeneity.

A comparison of Table 9.6(b) and (d) shows differences in total output and GDP. These two variables increase under firm heterogeneity while decreasing under the other two alternative market structures. This is also because the assumption of firm heterogeneity makes the model capture the productivity changes in a different way. When there are no spillovers (scenario B), firm productivity is endogenously modelled under firm heterogeneity and can affect the output and GDP explicitly, while productivity takes the benchmark value of 1 under perfect competition and monopolistic competition. When there are spillovers (scenario D), as discussed, the productivity of domestic firms will decrease under perfect competition and monopolistic competition as it is directly affected by the weaker presence of foreign firms. But the productivity of all firms improves under firm heterogeneity, which is beneficial to total output and GDP.

Finally, total government tax revenue unanimously decreases in the above four scenarios. Crporate income tax revenue decreases in integrated reforms, but increases in single-sided reforms. That is to say, given the model assumptions, a lower corporate income tax rate for foreign firms did indeed reduce the tax revenue collected from the foreign firms.

(d) The relationship between corporate income tax reform and FDI productivity spillovers, i.e. the soundness of the strategy of swapping market access for technology. As reflected by the "spillovers" rows in Table 9.6(c) and (d), neither single-sided nor integrated reform can increase the proportion of the productivity spilt over from foreign firms to domestic firms in total productivity of domestic enterprises, as denoted by equation (4.4). This is because, with a higher corporate income tax rate, the output of foreign firms decreases, so that their input–output linkages with domestic firms are also weakened. That is to say, all of the four spillover channels (backward linkages, forward linkages, export of foreign firms, and horizontal effects) shrink, via which FDI productivity spillovers take place. The above result also implies that the original dual corporate income tax system was indeed good for the FDI productivity spillovers to occur in that it helped strengthen the foreign presence, which is vital for FDI productivity spillovers.

However, the above conclusion derived from this static CGE model might need to be modified if we situate this problem in a dynamic perspective. First of all, with the integrated corporate income tax reform, the productivity of domestic firms is higher than before under firm heterogeneity in all of the four scenarios. This implies that the domestic firms have acquired better absorptive capacity to exploit the FDI productivity spillovers (Girma 2005; Blake *et al.* 2009). Secondly, in scenarios B and D, the average productivity of the foreign firms surviving the integrated tax reform is higher. This implies a greater likelihood of productivity spillovers. Therefore, taking into consideration the changing pattern of productivity under firm heterogeneity, the tax reform will only temporarily lower the FDI productivity spillover effects. They can promote the speed and magnitude of spillovers later, i.e. a "J-curve" effect of tax reform on productivity spillovers may exist.

Conclusions

This chapter simulates the impact of corporate income tax reform in 2008 on the FDI productivity spillover effect in China. It introduces the major tax incentives to attract FDI in China, and discusses the costs and benefits of such preferential FDI treatment. The results of the tax reform simulations show that the original dual corporate income tax system was indeed good for the FDI productivity spillovers to occur in that it helped strengthen the foreign presence which is vital for FDI productivity spillovers.

A higher corporate income tax levied on FIEs alone distorts the economy's structure and lowers total output, welfare and GDP. However, an integrated tax reform formula can do a better job by increasing the output level of domestic enterprises and by promoting national welfare. Under firm heterogeneity, the spillover benefit of integrated reform is even more prominent, because the reform can raise the average productivity of all existing enterprises, and raises the possibility of productivity spillovers and the absorptive capacity of domestic enterprises. This is more beneficial for the productivity spillovers from foreign-invested firms to domestic enterprises.

Neither single-sided nor integrated reform can increase the proportion of productivity spilt over from foreign to domestic firms in the total productivity of domestic enterprises. Taking into consideration the changing pattern of productivity under firm heterogeneity, the tax reform will only temporarily lower the FDI productivity spillover effects, However, it may promote the speed and magnitude of spillovers later.

10 Why was the Chinese banking system able to survive the global financial crisis?

The role of WTO accession and FDI efficiency spillovers

Introduction

Chinese banks used to be criticised for their tremendous non-performing loans (NPLs) and low efficiency. Some academics have even argued that the Chinese banking system was hardly able to survive competition from foreign banks (Lardy 2002). Other economists were not so pessimistic, but also expressed their deep concern over the pressure the Chinese domestic banks faced when the foreign banks were granted full national treatment in 2006 (Xu and Lin 2007). However, those seemingly vulnerable domestic banks have not only grown steadily, but also survived the global financial crisis so far. What has happened to the Chinese banking system and why was such a previously fragile system able to survive the tremendous shock posed by the crisis? In exploring the answer to this intriguing question, this study finds that the efficiency spillover of foreign banks in China has played an integral role.

In the literature there has been some research suggesting mixed relationships between foreign bank entry and the efficiency of domestic banks in host economies. The seminal work of Claessens *et al.* (2001), employing bank-level panel data, found that an increase in foreign presence is closely linked to a decrease in profitability, non-interest income and total operation costs of domestic banks. Their results suggest that opening up the banking sector can improve its market efficiency while a higher foreign presence also places stronger pressure on domestic banks. Lensink and Hermes (2004) introduce economic development level as a control variable into the empirical model of Claessens *et al.* (2001). They find that foreign entry can cause the operation costs and profit of domestic banks to rise if the host economy is relatively undeveloped. However, the impact of foreign presence on domestic banks is ambiguous in more developed host countries. In the more recent literature there have been some empirical studies on how domestic banks are affected by foreign investments in the form of mergers and acquisitions. Using data on 2095 banks from 105 countries (90 per cent of the world's banks), Lensink *et al.* (2008) employ stochastic frontier analysis to examine the above relation between foreign shares and the investment recipient banks. Their research indicates that foreign ownership generally has a negative impact on the efficiency of domestic banks. Furthermore, institutional factors (e.g. political stability, governance, regulation, legislation, and anti-corruption efforts) have also been incorporated as control variables. The results suggest that the above negative relationship can be alleviated in a host country with a relatively well-developed institutional framework. They also find that if the institutional frameworks of foreign direct investment in the home and host countries are similar, then foreign presence in a domestic bank can have a positive impact on the latter's efficiency. Berger *et al.* (2009) and Lin and Zhang (2009) have carried out a case study on the Chinese banking system, the former finding that the foreign ownership is positively linked to the improvement of the efficiency level of the invested banks, and the latter finding that state-owned banks only experience a marginal improvement in their efficiency after they absorb foreign investment and are listed on the stock market.

However, the cross-country analyses in the literature generally take fewer than 10 Chinese banks as a sample and thus ignore the particularity of the Chinese banking system, especially the potential efficiency improvement in the post-WTO era. The two single-country studies on China focus on the immediate impact of foreign ownership on domestic banks' efficiency only and thus greatly underestimate the cross-bank spillover effects on the whole banking system. The purpose of this study is to fill in this research gap by studying exactly how foreign presence can change the overall efficiency level of the whole banking system of a host country, taking China in the post-WTO era as a case study.

According to this study, the first to outline the micro-level channels via which FDI efficiency spillovers take place in a banking system, the efficiency spillover of foreign banks in China has occurred through the following five channels: (a) an increased degree of competition in the banking system stimulated the domestic banks to expedite their reforms unprecedentedly; (b) foreign banks exerted a very strong demonstration effect in high-end businesses (e.g. personal banking, credit cards and financial product innovation); (c) expert turnovers from foreign banks to domestic banks helped domestic banks to improve their efficiency; (d) collaborations with strategic investors have improved the corporate governance of domestic banks; (e) foreign banking shareholders have applied their financial innovation techniques in the Chinese banks.

This study empirically investigates the efficiency spillover in the banking system after China's accession into the WTO in 2001. Threatened by competition from foreign banks, domestic banks dramatically accelerated the restructuring process after 2001. By the end of 2006, when the post-WTO interim period was over, four of the five large state-owned banks (the "Big Five")[1] have all been transformed into listed companies. The reform of state-owned banks was accompanied by the restructuring reforms of other financial institutions, including medium and small-sized commercial banks, rural medium and small-sized financial institutions and other financial institutions. The overall risk of those financial institutions was significantly reduced, while the capital adequacy ratio and NPL provisioning coverage ratio improved to a higher benchmark.

In this empirical study, stochastic frontier analysis (SFA) is employed to analyse the efficiency of the Chinese banking sector in 2001 and 2007 with an unprecedented Bankscope dataset covering 126 banks operating in mainland China. This study suggests that the presence of foreign banks has indeed exerted prominent efficiency spillover – it has helped improve the overall profitability of the Chinese banking sector, and has also effectively constrained the scale of loans. Our results paper highlight the importance of efficiency spillovers which can be brought by cautious financial liberalisation to a transition economy.

The remainder of this chapter is organised as follows. The next section offers a retrospect on the entry of foreign banks into China after China's WTO accession in the end of 2001. The channels of efficiency spillovers from FDI in the Chinese banking system are outlined first. We discuss the methodology, variables and data employed for the research and the empirical results.

The entry of foreign banks into China after WTO accession

Greenfield investment: Business expansion by setting up new branches

Foreign banks started to enter the Chinese market in the early 1980s. The first foreign bank entity in China, the Export-Import Bank of Japan, established a representative office in Beijing in 1980. In the following year Nanyang Commercial Bank set up a branch in Shenzhen, the first foreign bank branch in China. By the end of 1993, there were 76 branches in 13 cities with total assets of US$8.9 billion.

The Chinese government issued the Regulatory Directory of Foreign Financial Institutions in 1994 which explicitly stated the market access threshold and regulatory standard and allowed foreign banks to operate in any area in China. Furthermore, the Central Bank of China licensed foreign banks to operate Renminbi (RMB) business with foreign-invested enterprises and foreign nationals in 1994. The above two steps greatly stimulated the business expansion of foreign banks in China. By the end of 2001 when China became a WTO member, there were 175 foreign bank branches with total assets of $27.0 billion.

In November 2006 when the five-year post-WTO interim period was over, the Chinese government issued a Regulatory Guide for Foreign Banks and fully opened up market access to foreign banks as promised during its WTO accession negotiations. Any foreign bank branches with a legal person status in China can operate exactly the same business as their domestic counterparts. Since then foreign banks have accelerated their expansion by setting up new branches, especially in large and medium-sized cities and costal regions. Beijing, Shanghai, Shenzhen and Tianjin are the top four cities hosting foreign bank branches.

By the end of 2008, 196 foreign banks from 46 countries had established 237 representative offices. Furthermore, 28 solely foreign-invested banks and 2 foreign–Chinese joint venture banks had also been set up. The value of total assets of foreign banks was RMB 1,345 billion, accounting for 2.16 per cent of the total assets of all financial institutions in China. The total loans and total deposits of foreign banks were RMB 7,309 billion and RMB 1,203 billion, accounting for 2.30 per cent and 2.05 per cent of total loans and total deposits of all commercial banks in China, respectively.[2] As shown by Table 10.1, the presence of foreign banks grew steadily after China's WTO accession in 2001. The number

Table 10.1 The share of foreign banks in Chinese banking system (%)

Year	*Total assets and liabilities*	*Total assets*	*No. of branches*
2001	0.7	1.3	1.0
2002	0.7	1.3	1.0
2003	0.7	1.3	1.1
2004	0.9	1.7	1.3
2005	1.1	1.8	1.5
2006	1.2	1.9	2.3
2007	1.7	2.5	5.2

Sources: *Almanac of China's Finance and Banking*, various issues. "Total assets and liabilities" refers to the total assets and liabilities of foreign banks and non-financial institutions. "No. of branches" refers to headquarters and branches of foreign banks.

of branches grew fastest, increasing from 1.0 per cent in 2001 to 5.2 per cent in 2007.

The foreign banks have been negatively impacted by the global financial crisis since January 2008. Particularly in the fourth quarter of 2008, the crisis deteriorated rapidly and spread to the Chinese economy. The Chinese economy, with its typical export orientation, experienced a rapid decline in growth.[3] The NPLs of foreign banks increased from RMB 3.6 billion in the first quarter of 2008 to RMB 7.4 billion in the first quarter of 2009, with a moderate decrease in the second quarter of 2009. The NPL ratio increased from 0.49 per cent in the first quarter of 2008 to 1.03 per cent as of June 2009.

Brownfield investment: business expansion as strategic investors

Foreign banks expanded their presence in China not only by establishing new headquarters and branches in China, but also by becoming strategic shareholders in domestic commercial banks. By the end of 2008, nine foreign financial institutions had invested in the four large commercial banks, 33 foreign financial institutions had invested in 24 small and medium-sized commercial banks, and three foreign financial institutions had invested in rural financial cooperative institutions, investing in excess of $32 billion.[4]

Such expansion had been fairly modest before China's WTO accession, as the Chinese government had imposed strict restrictions on the process of opening up of the banking sector. Any foreign strategic investment into the banking sector had to get direct approval from the central government. There were two foreign shareholding investments only in the Chinese banking system before 2001.

Upon WTO accession in 2001, the Chinese government explicitly promised to grant full access to foreign financial investors by the end of 2006, i.e. after a 5-year interim period. During that interim period, any individual foreign investor could invest in up to 15 per cent of the shares of a domestic bank, and the total foreign-owned shares in a domestic bank could be up to 20 per cent.

Those promises and opening-up measures greatly stimulated foreign investment. Compared to the strategy of branch expansion as a greenfield investment, the entry mode of shareholding expansion as a "brownfield" investment can take advantage of the local business networks of domestic banks.

In December 2003, the China Banking Regulatory Commission, which is affiliated to the State Council, raised the upper limit of foreign investment, so that any individual foreign investor could invest in up to 20 per cent of the shares of a domestic bank, and the total foreign-owned shares in a domestic bank could be up to 25 per cent. The new policies prompted a second round of investment expansion.

In the final two years of the 5-year interim period, domestic banks dramatically expedited their reforms and foreign banks also made massive strategic investments in order to obtain potential first-mover advantages. In 2005 and 2006 three mega-sized state-owned banks were transformed into listed companies, attracting huge amounts of strategic foreign investment: the China Construction Bank saw investments by Bank of America (9 per cent) and Asia Financial Holdings (5.1 per cent); the Bank of China saw investments by Royal Bank of Scotland (5 per cent), Temasek Holdings (5 per cent), UBS (1.61 per cent) and ADB (0.24 per cent); and Industrial and Commercial Bank of China saw investments by Goldman Sachs (4.9 per cent), Allianz (1.9 per cent) and American Express (0.4 per cent).

Meanwhile stock commercial banks (e.g. Bohai Bank, Hua Xia Bank, CITIC Bank, and Guangdong Development Bank) were also popular among foreign investors. Well-performing city commercial banks were also heavily invested in by foreign banks: Nanjing City Commercial Bank was invested in by BNP Paribas, Beijing Bank by ING Group and IFC, and Nanchong City Commercial Bank by DEG and SIDT.

Channels of efficiency spillovers from FDI in the banking system

The early empirical literature on FDI spillovers treats the spillover process as a "black box", treating foreign presence as an independent variable without much justification as to why and how spillovers take place. More recent literature started exploring the mechanisms and moderators of FDI spillover, which makes such studies more convincing. In this section we follow the trend of the broad literature on FDI spillovers and try to explore the five possible channels via which the spillovers could occur.

Intensified competition leading to reform of domestic banks

The introduction of the Regulatory Guide of Foreign Banks granted foreign banks national treatment in 2006. This posed a "credible threat" to domestic banks, forcing an unprecedented increase in the pace of reform. It is observed that some intrinsic problems in the Chinese banking system have been tackled at an accelerated pace. In 1979 there was only one bank in China, the People's Bank of China, with its dual functions of central banking and commercial banking. It took

15 years to abolish this centrally planned banking system and to establish four state-owned commercial banks. Then it took only 9 years to reform the commercial banking system and dump all the NPLs into state-owned specialist capital management companies. Under the pressure of competition from foreign banks, it took only another 5 years to transform the Big Five into joint-stock companies, to diffuse most of the chronic risks, and to initiate comprehensive restructuring in the whole commercial banking system after 2003. The total assets of the financial institutions in the banking sector increased from RMB 237 trillion in 2002 to RMB 624 trillion by the end of 2008. The amount of total NPLs was only RMB 568 billion, which was RMB 700 billion lower than at the beginning of 2008. The NPL ratio was only 2.45 per cent in December 2008, 3.71 per cent lower than in January 2008.[5]

Strong demonstration effect in high-end financial services

Foreign banks have introduced massive innovative financial products to China which exert a strong demonstration effect on domestic banks. For example, with the steady growth in GDP per capita in China, personal banking has been a very profitable business area for the likes of Citibank, AIG Private Bank, ABN, HSBC, Bank of East Asia, and Standard Chartered. Foreign banks have identified this market potential and introduced various personal finance products and lowered the minimum entry level to personal finance services. On the other hand, foreign banks (e.g. the Bank of East Asia) have introduced renminbi credit cards into the Chinese market backed by their rich experience in this business in the other countries.

Foreign banks have a strong demonstration effect on their domestic counterparts in the two products above, whose financial product innovation has been accelerated in recent years. Practically no Chinese consumers possessed a credit card before China's accession into the WTO, but since 2002 there has been a massive emergence of credit cards introduced by domestic banks, including Industrial and Commercial Bank of China, Merchants' Bank, and Construction Bank of China. In recent years, almost all of the major commercial banks have also introduced their own idiosyncratic personal financial products, such as the "Gold Key" introduced by the Agricultural Bank of China.

Competition for talent and its spillover

To fully localise themselves in the Chinese market, foreign banks need to recruit local financial talent familiar with the Chinese market, culture, legal system and business routine. Since 2001, foreign banks have attracted many talented people away from their domestic rivals as they can provide a highly competitive salary package, incentives, life-long training and job satisfaction. In contrast, domestic banks have lacked such an incentive mechanism. The human resource management in domestic banks have had a strong centrally planned flavour and usually no separate research and development team in charge of financial product innovation.

The fierce competition for talent has forced domestic banks to raise their salaries for medium and high-ranked managers and sales representatives. On the other hand, they have also reformed the existing human resource management system and provided various incentives to motivate their employees. More and more commonly, domestic banks attract high fliers from foreign banks with even more competitive salary packages and higher positions. It is highly likely that those elite managers can improve the domestic banks' management and improve their performance after they join domestic banks. As a matter of fact, similar efficiency spillover effects in manufacturing sectors have been widely observed as a result of the turnover of educated labour from multinational affiliates to their domestic counterparts (e.g. Görg and Strobl 2005; Blake *et al.* 2009; Todo *et al.* 2009).

Ownership diversification improves the corporate governance of domestic banks

Absorbing foreign investment can improve not only the capital adequacy ratio, but also, and more importantly, the corporate governance and managerial skills of domestic banks from a number of perspectives. First, share structure becomes more diversified so that the power of shareholders is more reasonably balanced. Minority shareholders such as institutional investors can improve the monitoring of managers and operation risks, so that the interests of shareholders can be better protected (Berger *et al.* 2009). Second, the institutional foundation becomes more solid. The introduction of foreign strategic investors can help to establish a well-functioning governance structure including the board of directors, board of supervisors, and management. Each level of the governance structure has clearly specified duties and responsibilities so that the decision-making process could become more efficient, transparent and scientific, and less error-prone. Third, information disclosure helps the management become more transparent. Information disclosure offers an effective way to get banks monitored by the public. When a joint-stock bank with foreign shareholders is listed, it will be not only monitored by the Chinese banking and securities regulatory bodies, and the Chinese public, but also closely watched by the overseas media and public. Such close surveillance can force commercial banks to disclose more details in greater depth, and thus managements will need to make every effort to improve the efficiency and performance of the banks whilst minimising risks.

But we have to admit that the efficiency spillover of foreign shareholders via improved corporate governance is still much constrained in the decision-making process for some key issues, including strategic investment and senior management recruitment. For example, state-owned banks usually tend to appoint a senior government official with China Communist Party membership as their senior manager-in-chief.

Foreign shareholders help design new products

For mature commercial banks in the industrialised countries, bank intermediaries have a significant contribution to revenue, and commercial banks have sound experience in developing intermediaries to cater for market demand. However, the bank intermediaries in China are still in their infancy. Foreign shareholders can introduce mature intermediary products (e.g. syndicated loans jointly set up by the Bank of China and Royal Bank of Scotland). Such a direct import of new products can help the domestic banks quickly expand their market share. For example, Allianz is focused on cooperation with the Industrial and Commercial Bank of China in banking insurance, while American Express is deepening its cooperation with the ICBC in issuing joint credit cards. Furthermore, foreign shareholders can also train domestic partners in how to perform market analysis, differentiate and target potential consumers, and invent new products for local Chinese customers.

Data and methodology

Both stochastic frontier analysis (SFA) and data envelope analysis (DEA) have been widely applied in analyses of bank efficiency in the literature (Yao *et al.* 2007; Lensink *et al.* 2008). SFA is a parametric estimation approach, while DEA is a non-parametric estimation method. This book employs SFA to examine the impact of foreign banks on domestic banks after China's accession into the WTO. SFA is more suitable than DEA for banking efficiency analysis in China, as a basic assumption of SFA is that the optimal efficiency of a firm (i.e. bank in this context) is a stochastic rather than a constant term. Since China's WTO accession in 2001, the Chinese banking system has seen a dramatic reshuffle. As discussed in the previous sections, most state-owned and well-performing commercial banks established partnerships with strategic investors; city credit cooperatives upgraded to commercial banks; and foreign banks increased the rate at which they expanded their market shares and established affiliated banks with legal person status. Under such circumstances, the efficiency frontier of all types of banks can be volatile, and thus SFA is more suitable for banking efficiency analysis in the post-WTO era.

SFA assumes that the optimal production capacity of a bank is stochastic, and the observed efficiency level may deviate from the stochastic optimal efficiency level due to the impact of internal and external shocks (e.g. efficiency spillover from its rivals). SFA can be applied to calculate the efficiency level of a firm in every year of the observation period. The calculated efficiency takes a value between 0 and 1. The closer it is to 1, the closer the efficiency level is to the optimal level.

A "one-step" estimation approach (Battese and Coelli 1995) is applied here to integrate the estimated efficiency and estimated efficiency spillover, the advantage of which is that we can obtain a more reliable result (Reifschneider and Stevenson 1991). The specification of the model is

$$Y_{it} = \boldsymbol{\beta}\mathbf{X}_{it} + (V_{it} - U_{it}), \quad i = 1, 2, \ldots, N;\ t = 1, 2, \ldots, T$$

Here Y_{it} is the bank's output of a bank, which can be represented by before-tax profit or loans. $\boldsymbol{\beta}$ is a parameter vector. $\mathbf{X}_{it}$ is the vector of bank inputs, including fixed assets, deposits and owner's equity. V_{it} is a random variable which follows a normal distribution with mean zero and variance σ_V^2, written $N(0, \sigma_V^2)$. U_{it} is a non-negative stochastic variable which is used to measure the "non-efficiency" of a bank, i.e. the distance of the real efficiency of a bank from its efficiency frontier. U_{it} follows a $N(m_{it}, \sigma_U^2)$ distribution, where $m_{it} = \boldsymbol{\delta}\mathbf{Z}_{it}$, the $\mathbf{Z}_{it}$ being the variables that affect bank non-efficiency. In this study, $\mathbf{Z}_{it}$ includes the equity–total asset ratio, percentage of state-owned shares, and the market shares of foreign banks. $\boldsymbol{\delta}$ is a vector of parameters to be estimated. If $\boldsymbol{\delta}$ is greater than zero (i.e. all its component parameters are greater than zero), the corresponding variable makes the bank efficiency deviate from its efficiency frontier. In other words, the corresponding variable lowers the bank efficiency.

An indicator to evaluate the goodness of a SFA model is

$$\gamma = \frac{\sigma_U^2}{\sigma_U^2 + \sigma_V^2}$$

If γ is close to 1, σ_U^2 is very large compared to σ_V^2, i.e. the "non-efficiency" term U_{it} is statistically significant and SFA is appropriately applied.

Thus the SFA model used in this bank efficiency study can be specified as follows:

$$\begin{aligned}\ln(\mathit{profit}_{it}) = {} & \beta_0 + \beta_1 \ln(\mathit{fixedasset}_{in}) + \beta_2 \ln(\mathit{deposit}_{in}) \\ & + \beta_3 \ln(\mathit{equity}_{it}) + V_{it} - U_{it}\end{aligned}$$

$$U_{it} = \delta_0 + \delta_1 \ln\left(\frac{E}{A}\mathit{ratio}_{it}\right) + \delta_2 SOE_{it} + \delta_3 FDI_t$$

Here the profit before tax (profit_{it}) can be substituted by bank loans. E/A ratio is the equity–asset ratio, an accounting measure of the risk preference of a bank. It can be used to reflect the connection between a bank's non-efficiency and its behaviour, especially its willingness of taking risks. Generally a bank with a low E/A ratio tends to take more risks in its operations and makes more profit. Therefore E/A ratio can have a negative impact on a bank's efficiency (Yao *et al.* 2007). SOE_{it} refers to the summed shares invested directly by the state and the state-owned institutions. FDI_t denotes the market share of foreign banks, which can be measured in three ways: (a) the market share of total assets and liabilities of foreign banks against non-financial institutions and households (FDI-1); (b) the share of total assets of foreign banks in the whole Chinese banking system (FDI-2); (c) the share of number of foreign banks with legal person status in the whole banking system (FDI-3). FDI_t is entered into the above regression model to measure how the entry of foreign banks affects the efficiency of domestic banks.

Empirical results

A comparison of the estimation results with different dependent variables

The dependent variable in Table 10.2 is the logarithm value of profit before tax. The difference between models 1, 2 and 3 lies in the measure of "foreign

Table 10.2 FDI and the efficiency of domestic banks (profit before tax as dependent variable)

Variables	*Model 1*	*Model 2*	*Model 3*
(A) Production function			
Intercept	−2.14	−2.16	−2.23
	(7.55)***	(7.48)***	(−7.7)***
Fixed assets	−0.04	−0.05	−0.07
	(−0.83)	(−0.97)	(−1.26)
Deposit	0.33	0.33	0.34
	(3.97)***	(4.00)***	(4.17)***
Owner's equity	0.71	0.72	0.73
	(8.01)***	(8.33)***	(8.25)***
(B) "Non-efficiency" function			
Intercept	−1.20	−0.27	−1.28
	(−1.50)*	(−0.34)	(−1.27)
E/A ratio	0.79	0.83	0.92
	(3.40)***	(3.47)***	(3.20)***
State share (%)	−0.02	−0.03	−0.03
	(−0.41)	(−0.47)	(−0.44)
FDI_{it}	−1.34	−1.98	−0.70
	(−4.13)***	(3.93)***	(−3.24)***
(C) Parameters			
δ^2	0.78	0.81	0.90
	(4.07)***	(4.05)***	(3.69)***
γ	0.84	0.84	0.85
	(17.80)***	(18.48)***	(19.58)***
(D) Other information			
No. of banks	126	126	126
Years	7	7	7
No. of observations	468	468	468
Average efficiency	0.57	0.58	0.59

Note: (1) Dependent variable is profit before tax; (2) all variables take logarithm values; (3) FDI_{it} in models 1, 2 and 3 is the market share of total assets and liabilities of foreign banks against non-financial institutions and households (FDI-1), the share of total assets of foreign banks in the whole Chinese banking system (FDI-2) and the share of number of foreign banks with legal person status in the whole banking system (FDI-3), respectively. (4) *t* statistics are given in parentheses; (5) *, ** and *** denote significant coefficients at 10%, 5% and 1% levels, respectively.

presence", for which we use FDI-1, FDI-2, and FDI-3 respectively. The dependent variable in Table 10.3 is the logarithm value of bank loans. Models 4, 5 and 6 respectively take FDI-1, FDI-2, and FDI-3 as the measure of "foreign presence".

The results of models 1, 2 and 3 suggest that the market share of foreign banks has a negative impact on the non-efficiency of domestic banks. In other words, the higher the market share of foreign banks, the smaller will be the deviation of the efficiency level of the Chinese banking system from its efficiency frontier, i.e. it is more efficient. This suggests a positive role played by the foreign banks in improving the overall efficiency level of the Chinese banking system.

Table 10.3 FDI and the efficiency of domestic banks (bank loans as dependent variable)

Variables	*Model 4*	*Model 5*	*Model 6*
(A) Production function			
Intercept	0.79	0.69	0.70
	(0.88)	(7.44)***	(8.10)***
Fixed assets	−0.04	0.04	0.04
	(0.30)	(2.54)***	(2.94)***
Deposit	0.68	0.70	6.91
	(4.28)***	(29.3)***	(29.0)***
Owner's equity	0.27	0.26	0.26
	(2.46)***	(14.2)***	(14.5)***
(B) "Non-efficiency" function			
Intercept	−0.51	−6.73	−6.18
	(−0.53)	(2.15)***	(−2.40)***
E/A ratio	−0.27	1.48	1.44
	(0.95)	(2.54)***	(2.77)***
State share (%)	0.01	0.26	0.25
	(0.07)	(2.73)***	(2.74)***
FDI_{it}	0.11	0.91	0.34
	(0.11)	(1.71)**	(2.06)***
(C) Parameters			
δ^2	0.13	0.59	0.56
	(0.48)	(2.45)***	(2.78)***
γ	0.87	0.96	0.96
	(2.45)***	(64.7)***	(58.1)***
(D) Other information			
No. of banks	126	126	126
Years	7	7	7
No. of observations	468	468	468
Average efficiency	0.78	0.84	0.84

Note: (1) Dependent variable is bank loans; (2) all variables take logarithm values; (3) FDI_{it} in model 4, 5 and 6 is the market share of total assets and liabilities of foreign banks against non-financial institutions and households (FDI-1), the share of total assets of foreign banks in the whole Chinese banking system (FDI-2) and the share of number of foreign banks with legal person status in the whole banking system (FDI-3), respectively. (4) t statistics are given in parentheses; (5) *, ** and ***denote significant coefficients at 10%, 5% and 1% levels, respectively.

The value of γ is about 0.84, and significantly different from zero, which indicates the appropriateness of applying SFA in this research. The average efficiency level is approximately 0.58, which suggests that the overall profitability level is still at a relatively low level. As predicted, the E/A ratio measures the risk preference and innovation ability of a bank, and that ratio is indeed negatively connected to a bank's efficiency. This finding is consistent with that of Yao *et al.* (2007). Finally, state shares have no significant impact on bank efficiency.

But if we change the dependent variable to bank loans, we can see that foreign presence has no significant impact over the bank efficiency at all in model 4.

Models 5 and 6 indicate that foreign presence has a negative impact on the bank loans, which suggests that the banking system becomes more prudent when the competition from foreign banks is intensified. The results of models 5 and 6 suggest that the E/A ratio again has a negative impact on the efficiency of granting bank loans, i.e. a bank with a lower operation risk tends to be more cautious in granting loans. Finally, in models 5 and 6 state participation ($SOE_{i,t}$) has a significant negative impact on the efficiency of granting bank loans. This result, coupled with the results presented in Table 10.2, suggests that the government intervention in the post-WTO era has made a dramatic "*U*" turn, which helped effectively to control bank loans.

Dynamics of bank efficiency

The efficiency of all banks has generally declined a little before recovering to a higher level. Space considerations prelude reporting the details of the changes here. This "*V*"-type efficiency dynamic pattern is consistent with recent banking reforms. After China's accession to the WTO, domestic banks were granted a five-year interim period to fully adjust to the coming competition from foreign banks' affiliates which can enjoy national treatment after that interim period. Most of the domestic banks made substantial investments to introduce comprehensive reforms and thus lowers the revealed efficiency temporarily. For example, Construction Bank of China, Bank of China, and Industrial and Commercial Bank of China had to extract part of their profit to improve their NPL provisioning coverage. Once such reforms were finished, their balance sheets were improved and their observed efficiency became even better than before. Moreover, the Chinese banking system is a typical cyclical sector whose performance is closely connected to the macroeconomic dynamics, because the financing of enterprises is heavily dependent on the banking system rather than stock market. Since early 2004, there was a strong investment boom in manufacturing and construction sectors, which also contributed to the recovery of bank efficiency.

State-owned banks

As discussed, the Chinese government has provided strong support to state-owned banks since China's WTO accession to improve their efficiency and performance. The results of this research suggest that the efforts of the government seem to have been effective. For example, the results of model 3 reveal that the average efficiency of the Big Five was 0.65, higher than the average efficiency in the whole banking system (0.59), during the sample period. If we exclude the least efficient of the five, Agricultural Bank of China, the average efficiency level of the remaining four banks was 0.72. The extraordinary performance of the Big Five, together with the previous finding that the state share has no positive impact on the overall efficiency of the banking system, implies that the state share plays a trivial or even negative role in non-Big-Five banks. The reason why the Big Five have become an exception is partially that they were "too big to fail", i.e. the Chinese central government had to mobilise tremendous resources to make sure they operated properly so as to minimise the macroeconomic risk.

Conclusions

Combining qualitative and quantitative analyses, this study is the first in the literature to explore how foreign presence can improve the overall efficiency level of the whole banking system in a host country. The Chinese banking system in the post-WTO era was chosen for a case study, with an unprecedentedly large Bankscope dataset of the Chinese banks employed.

The efficiency spillovers of foreign banks in China have occurred through five channels: increased degree of competition, strong demonstration effect in high-end business, expert turnovers from foreign banks to domestic banks, improved corporate governance in collaboration with strategic investors, and financial innovation techniques applied by foreign banking shareholders.

The study suggests that the presence of foreign banks has indeed helped improve the overall profitability of the Chinese banks, and has also effectively constrained the scale of loans. The state shares of domestic banks do not significantly contribute to their efficiency improvement. The results of this study highlight the importance of efficiency spillovers which can be brought about by cautious financial liberalisation of a transition economy.

11 East Asian industry transfer, FDI productivity spillovers and US–China trade imbalance

US–China trade imbalance and its political impact

In recent years, the US–China trade imbalance[1] has become an increasingly sensitive issue attracting the attention of not only the United States and China, but also many other trading giants, such as the European Union and Japan. The issue has become highly politicised, and the two countries have encountered great difficulties in coping with it. Trade disagreements seem to have become a normal part of relations between China and the USA. How the two countries deal with the issue matters not only for themselves, but also for the well-being of the entire international community.

US–China commodity trade has been growing fast since China implemented its "reform and opening-up" policy in the late 1970s. Chinese statistics show that the volume of US–China trade soared from US$2 billion in 1979 to $263 billion in 2006.[2] The 2006 figure is even larger by American calculations – US$343 billion.[3] The difference between the Chinese and US figures is largely due to differences in calculating trade statistics and transshipment trade via Hong Kong, which is treated as a part of China in US statistics (Lardy 1994; Lau and Fung 2001).

From any perspective, the USA and China have become mutually important trading partners. By 2009, with US–China trade accounting for 14.0 per cent of US total trade volume, China had become the USA's second largest trading partner, second only to Canada (164 per cent), while the USA was China's largest trading partner country (135 per cent of the total).

With the rapid increase in US–China trade, the nature of the trade imbalance between the two countries has changed dramatically. According to US statistics, the USA has had a trade deficit with China since 1983. Since 2000, China has replaced Japan and become the country with the largest trade surplus with the USA. In 2009, the US–China trade deficit reached $227 billion, accounting for 44 per cent of the total US deficit and 48 times as much as the US trade deficit with its second largest deficit partner, Mexico. The deficit shows no sign of declining.

In recent years, China's growing trade surplus with the USA has caused Washington to increase its pressure on China to revalue the renminbi (RMB). Washington has long expected that a revaluation of the currency would lead to a fall in Chinese exports to the USA, thus alleviating the pressure of unemployment in traditional industries such as steel and textiles. On 21 July 2005, China announced a new "floating management foreign exchange regime". However, this did not reduce US pressure for further appreciation of the RMB.

The trade imbalance has also triggered US accusations of Chinese protectionism. China has faced increasing pressure to lower its tariff level and remove non-tariff barriers, and to open its domestic market further to US imports.

Moreover, trade disputes between the two giants are often affected by domestic politics. Some industrial interest groups in the USA have evoked the special terms in the World Trade Organization's "Protocol on the Accession of the People's Republic of China" and adopted anti-dumping measures

Despite China having taken measures such as purchasing a large number of planes from Boeing – 120 contracted orders in 2005 and another 112 in 2006, excluding orders from Hong Kong and Macau[4] – the US trade deficit with China continues to grow, and this trend seems unlikely to change in the foreseeable future. With growing globalization and regionalization, the US–China trade deficit is becoming an increasingly complicated issue.

Among many factors that have affected the US–China trade imbalance, such as US export controls, China's poor record of intellectual property rights protection, and non-trade barriers (Lardy 1994). East Asian industry transfer, coupled with its consequent productivity spillovers, is one of the most fundamental, although it is often overlooked as relatively trivial, especially among policy-makers. In dealing with their trade disputes, both governments will have to take this factor into account. Needless to say, it has also made US–China trade issues relevant to other East Asian economies.

East Asian FDI in China

East Asian industrial transfer has historical origins. After World War II, Japan implemented export-oriented strategies in order to revive its shattered economy. It concentrated on labour-intensive industries with the aid of the USA and exported labour-intensive products, e.g. textiles and toys, to that country. However, labour costs rose as exports grew because of the usual production factor price equalization effect (Samuelson 1948).

Consequently, the gap between labour costs in Japan and other East Asian economies became wider. In the 1960s, although hourly wages in the Japanese manufacturing sector were only a quarter of the US level, they were still very high compared to other East Asian economies. If the wage level of Japan was 100, the levels of Taiwan and Korea were only 22 and 25, respectively (Ozawa 1993). Because of this yawning gap, Japanese multinationals began to transfer labour-intensive industries to the four newly industrialised economies (NIEs) of South Korea, Taiwan, Hong Kong and Singapore (the NIE-4). In addition, multinationals in the USA and Europe also gradually transferred their mature manufacturing sectors to the NIEs, which experienced strong growth at that time.

The strength of Japanese domestic manufacturing faded gradually in the post-Plaza Accord (1985) era. From 1985 to 1988, the yen appreciated 46 per cent against the dollar and the average price of Japanese export commodities increased. During the 1990s, Japan finished upgrading its industry and by the end of the century had transferred almost all of its labour-intensive manufacturing to the NIEs, Southeast Asia and China.

This process of industry transfer was copied by the NIEs. In the 1970s, the NIEs industrialised rapidly and witnessed a gradual increase in labour costs, just as Japan had previously. Thus the NIEs transferred the production of their labour-intensive industries and some capital-intensive industries to ASEAN and China.

With its almost unlimited labour supply, stable political and economic environment, and pro-export trade regime and FDI policies, China has become a hot FDI destination. Since the mid-1990s, China has been the largest recipient of FDI among the developing countries, and in 2003 it became the largest FDI recipient in the world. In 2005, China was still the world's third largest destination for FDI, second only to the UK and USA. Since the majority of FDI flows between developed countries (Markusen 2002b), it is amazing that China holds such a strong attraction for foreign capital, despite the fact that more than a quarter of its FDI inflow is speculative "hot money" and "round-tripping" capital.

China's actual (utilised) FDI volume shot up from US$0.9 billion in 1983 to US$69.5 billion in 2006, and the proportion of assembly trade increased from 10 per cent in the late 1970s to 47 per cent in 2006. This rapid development of FDI and assembly trade helped China find its niche in a wide range of manufacturing sectors.

Due to the relatively low purchasing power of Chinese consumers and low labour costs, most of the FDI coming into China falls into the resource-seeking or efficiency-seeking categories rather than the market-seeking category. FDI has transferred industries to China and brought significant technology spillover effects, as discussed previously.

The accumulated FDI flowing into China from the five East Asian economies of Japan, Hong Kong, Taiwan, Singapore, and South Korea, from 1979 to 2006, accounted for 67.4 per cent of the total accumulated FDI in China, implying that most of China's FDI originated from the East Asian region.

In the period 1979–2009 more than 65 per cent of China's accumulated contract FDI inflow went to the manufacturing sector. This shows that multinationals have been, via FDI, transferring their manufacturing industries to China.

The East Asian industry transfer process discussed above can be tentatively explained by two theories, namely the "product life-cycle theory" (Vernon 1966) and the "flying geese model" (Akamatsu 1937; Kojima 2000). According to the former, a product's life cycle can be divided into three stages, as a new product becomes a mature product and then a standard product. There is usually a time gap for various products between different countries, a gap which reflects a country's level of technological development and determines that country's position in international competition. Therefore, this gap also determines the pattern of international investment and trade. The flying geese model is usually understood as the development pattern of the East Asian economy in which Japan was the "leading goose" and completed its industrialization first, with the NIEs forming the second-tier industrialised economies, and ASEAN and China bringing up the rear (Bernard and Ravenhill 1995). There has been some research done on the "shifting comparative advantage" and industry transfer in Asia (Dowling and Cheang 2000; Xu and Song 2000; Cutler *et al.* 2003) within the paradigm of the flying geese model.

The hypothetical industry and trade transfer effects proposed by the flying geese model and the product life-cycle theory have been supported by the "eclectic theory of international production" (Dunning 1977) and the more recently developed "firm heterogeneity model" (Melitz 2003). Both of these theories argue that multinational firms that have a strong advantage in intangible assets (e.g. trademarks, blueprints and know-how) can invest overseas and isolate the production of knowledge capital and final products.

However, to our knowledge, barely any research has been done that explores the detailed economic mechanisms and corresponding policy implications of the impact of East Asian industry transfer on the US–China trade imbalance.[5] The aim of this chapter is to close this gap. We identify two proxy variables for East Asian industry transfer and trade transfer, respectively. They are East Asian FDI in China, and trade similarity between China and the FDI origin economies. To check whether the East Asian industry transfer has caused the large-scale trade transfer effects and the resulting huge US–China trade deficit, we now simply need to check whether FDI in China has pushed up the trade similarity level. By doing this, we can overcome the obstacle of quantifying the obscure term "transfer" and can thus test whether the theoretical hypotheses of industry transfer and trade transfer are valid. Data from various sources have been collected, compiled and subjected to serious statistical analysis. The results are overwhelmingly convincing and therefore substantiate the theoretical hypotheses (see Figure 11.1).

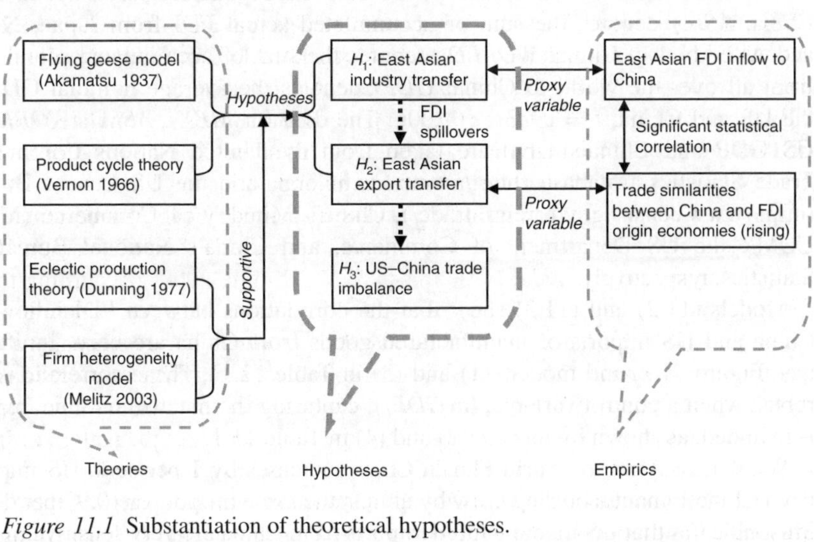

Figure 11.1 Substantiation of theoretical hypotheses.

FDI promotes trade to the USA and increases the trade similarity

The huge inflow of FDI to China has caused Chinese exports to grow dramatically. Although FDI has accounted for a relatively small percentage of total fixed investment (just over 10 per cent after 2000) and the manufacturing output generated by FDI is only about 30 per cent of the total volume, FDI has stimulated both imports and exports on a disproportionate scale due to the characteristics of China assembly trade – namely, large-scale imports and exports with low value added in China. The foreign trade generated by FDI firms accounted for only 4 per cent of total foreign trade in 1986. However, this grew steadily at a rate of 2.5 per cent annually and reached a record 59 per cent in 2006, distributed fairly evenly – imports 60 per cent, exports 58 per cent.

There is a mutually beneficial nexus between FDI and trade in China. Increased exports enhance economies of scale and improve the performance of export-oriented and FDI-related firms. Thus China is able to attract more FDI from other East Asian economies. Interestingly, we find that there is a very significant correlation between East Asian (or world) FDI and US imports from the Chinese manufacturing sector from 1983 to 2006.

We construct econometric analysis models specified as follows:

$$\ln(MEX_t) = C_1 + \alpha_1 \ln(ASIA_t) + \varepsilon_{1,t} \quad (11.1)$$

$$\ln(MEX_t) = C_2 + \alpha_2 \ln(WORLD_t) + \varepsilon_{2,t} \quad (11.2)$$

$$\ln(MEX_t) = C_3 + \alpha_3 \ln(ASIA_t) + \beta_3 \ln(GDP_t) + \varepsilon_{3,t} \quad (11.3)$$

$$\ln(MEX_t) = C_4 + \alpha_4 \ln(WORLD_t) + \beta_4 \ln(GDP_t) + \varepsilon_{4,t} \quad (11.4)$$

where MEX_t denotes the values of US imports of manufactured goods from China; $ASIA_t$ denotes the sum of accumulated actual FDI from Japan, NIE-4 and ASEAN-4 to China; $WORLD_t$ denotes the sum of accumulated actual FDI from all over the world to China; GDP_t denotes the average nominal GDP of the US and China; $t = 1983, \ldots, 2006$. The data for MEX_t, $ASIA_t$ ($WORLD_t$), US GDP and China's GDP are taken from the United Nations Commodity Trade Statistics Database (http://comtrade.un.org/) and the US Census Bureau (http://www.census.gov/foreign-trade/), China's Ministry of Commerce (MOFCOM), the US Department of Commerce, and China's National Bureau of Statistics, respectively.

Models (11.2) and (11.3) show that the correlations between FDI inflows to China and US imports of manufactured goods from China are very significant (see Figure 11.2, and models (1) and (3) in Table 11.1). These correlations are robust when a control variable, $\ln(GDP_t)$, capturing the macroeconomic impact, is included, as shown by models (2) and (4) in Table 11.1.

When East Asian or world FDI in China increases by 1 per cent, US imports from Chinese manufacturing grow by almost the same proportion (0.97 per cent). This indicates that US manufactured imports from China are very sensitive to FDI

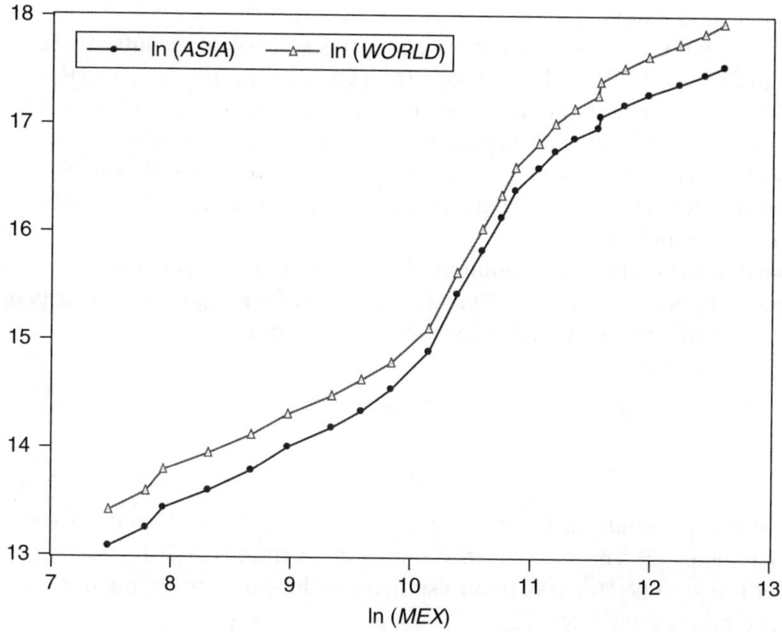

Figure 11.2 Correlation between FDI and US imports of manufactured goods from China, 1983–2006.

Table 11.1 Correlation between FDI and US imports of manufactured goods from China

	Manufacturing imports and Asian FDI		*Manufacturing imports and all FDI*	
	(1)	*(2)*	*(3)*	*(4)*
C	−4.730	−7.751	−4.976	−7.713
	(−7.760)***	(−3.532)***	(−7.810)***	(−2.942)***
$\ln(ASIA_t)$	0.967	0.678		
	(24.855)***	(3.672)**		
$\ln(WORLD_t)$			0.965	0.695
			(24.161)***	(−3.009)***
$\ln(GDP_t)$		0.847		0.790
		(1.526)		(1.140)
R^2	0.97	0.97	0.96	0.96

Notes: The dependent variable is the natural logarithm of the values of US imports of manufactured goods from China, $\ln(MEX_t)$; t-values are given in parentheses; *significant at 10%; **significant at 5%; ***significant at 1%.

inflows to China. Thus, FDI inflow to China is a qualified "barometer" for US manufactured imports.

East Asian economies have transferred export-oriented manufacturing industries to China via FDI, making exports from China on the one hand and those from the FDI origin economies on the other increasingly similar in structure. We used data on the top 100 commodities imported by the USA from China and nine other major FDI origin economies (Japan, South Korea, Hong Kong, Taiwan, Singapore, Malaysia, the Philippines, Thailand, and Indonesia) between 1981 and 2006 to calculate the trade similarity.

We developed the "trade similarity index" from the structural similarity index proposed by Krugman (1991). This index measures the degree of similarity of US imports from two import origin economies. The formula is

$$S = 2 - \sum_i |S_i - S_i^*|$$

where S_i (S_i^*) stands for the share of commodity i in the total imports from country 1 (country 2) The value of this index ranges from 0 to 2. It is clear that the closer it is to 0 (2), the less (more) similar are the structures of the imports from the two origin economies.

We collected US import data from the United Nations Commodity Trade Statistics Database (http://comtrade.un.org/) and the US Census Bureau (http://www.census.gov/foreign-trade/) during 1981–2006 for the calculation of the trade similarity index.

We found that the similarity between US imports from China and those from most of the East Asian FDI origin economies increased gradually over this period (see the upper panels of Figures 11.3 and 11.4). For example, the similarity at Standard International Trade Classification (SITC)[6] three-digit level between US imports from China and from Japan increased from 0.21 in 1981 to 0.68 in 2006.

Taking into account the "flying geese model", we further scrutinised the import-weighted trade similarities between China and the disaggregated East Asian economic blocs – NIE-4 and ASEAN-4 (Malaysia, the Philippines, Thailand, and Indonesia). Data show that the China's trade similarities at SITC three-digit level with NIE-4 and ASEAN-4 increased significantly from 0.62 and 0.21 in 1981 to 0.90 and 1.00 in 2006, respectively

China's trade similarity with the NIE-4 declined temporarily from 1990 to 1996 before gradually increasing from 1997 to 2006. This is partly due to the fact that in the 1990s there was a sharp increase in intra-industry specialisation (Xu and Song 2000). In the post-industrialisation era, the NIEs have specialised in higher-end products and R&D, while China has specialised in lower-end products or assembly. Consequently, China and the NIEs exported different types of goods to the USA, causing trade similarities to decrease temporarily in the 1990s.

This comparison enables us to see that, in general, the trade similarity of China and Japan is not as great as that of China and the ASEAN-4. Prior to 1990, the

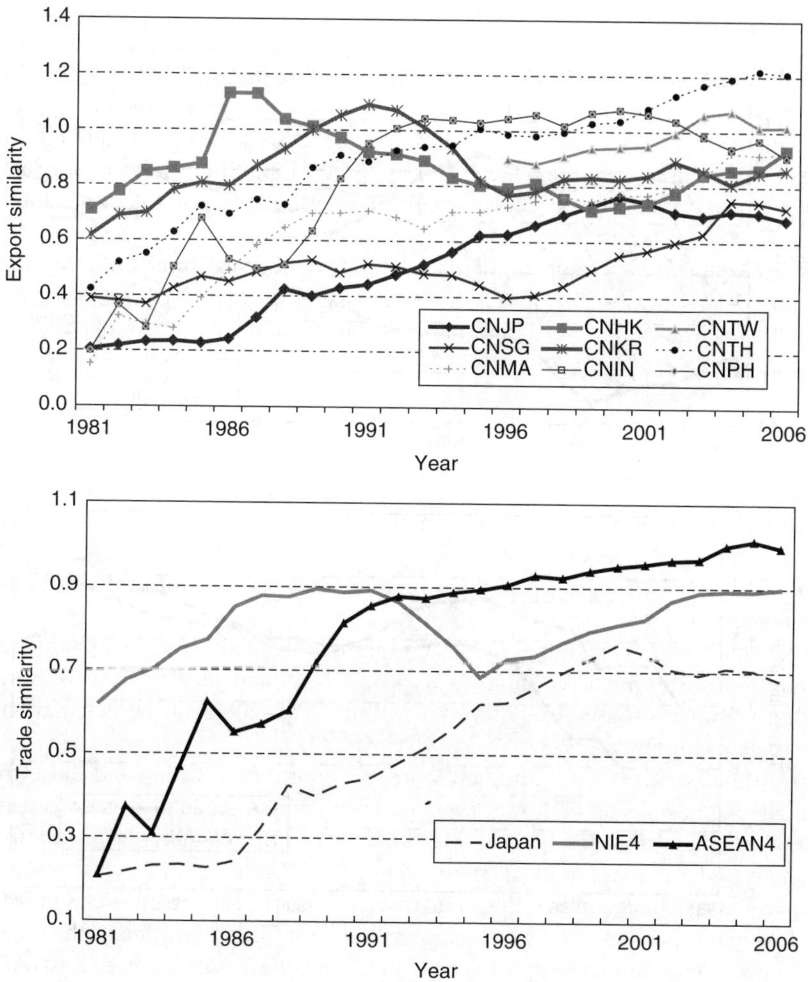

Figure 11.3 Trade similarity (SITC three-digit level).

Source: United Nations Commodity Trade Statistics Database and US Census Bureau.

trade similarity of China with the ASEAN-4 was not as great as that of China with the NIE-4, but it was higher than the latter after 1990.

This dynamic change in the trade similarity between China and the NIE-4 and ASEAN-4 can be explained by the export structure of these economies. In the early 1980s, manufacturing in China was as developed as in the ASEAN-4. However, after the NIEs had poured enormous quantities of export-oriented investment into China and the ASEAN-4, the trade similarity between China and the NIEs and the ASEAN-4 increased rapidly. As the recipient of FDI from the NIEs, the ASEAN-4

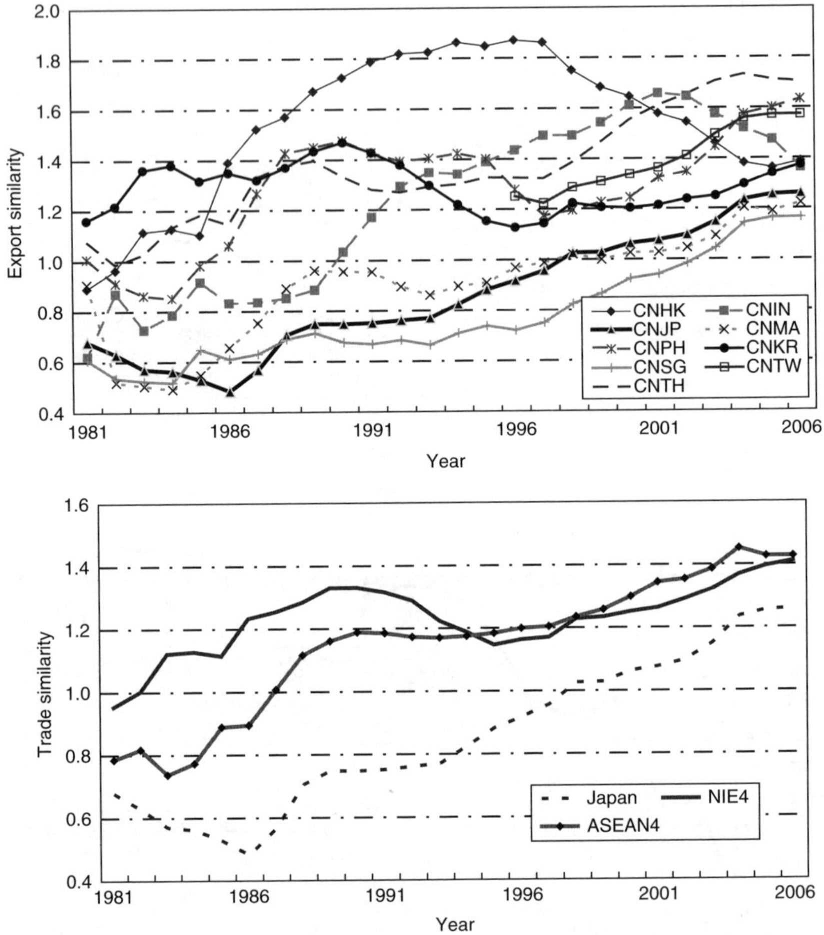

Figure 11.4 Trade similarity (one-digit level).

Source: Same as Figure 11.3.

exported goods to the USA in a similar pattern to China since they were upgrading their trade structure just as China was, and the share of manufactured commodities increased in the exports of both the ASEAN-4 and China.

One interesting question here is why the trade similarity is still rising if Japan and the NIEs are upgrading and specializing in higher-end products, while transferring labour-intensive product manufacturing to the Chinese mainland. There are three factors behind this phenomenon. First, the industry transfer does not completely hollow out the industries concerned. Second, the FDI spillover effects, coupled with Chinese domestic R&D inputs and improved human capital, have been pushing the Chinese industry and export structures to converge with those of Japan and the NIEs. The final factor is a statistical one. In comparing Figures 11.3 and 11.4, we find that trade similarities calculated at SITC one-digit level are higher than those based on SITC three-digit level, *ceteris paribus*. This is because SITC one-digit statistics exhibit a lower degree of commodity heterogeneity. Even among SITC three-digit statistics, some commodities with quite different labour–capital input ratios may be grouped into a single category, and this also causes a slight inflation of the trade similarity index used here.[7]

In comparing the trade similarity of China with economies such as the G8 countries, Latin America (Mexico, Brazil, and Venezuela), Australia, Nigeria, and Russia, we found, as expected, that the trade similarities between China and the developed economies are rising at a considerable speed, while those between China and transitional economies and less developed countries such as Russia and Nigeria are declining. This implies that by accepting FDI and industry transfer, China is catching up with the developed countries in the trade structure hierarchy. Moreover, as FDI recipients, the ASEAN-4 and the Latin American economies have successfully embraced industries transferred from abroad and achieved convergence with the industry structure of developed countries.

There is a very significant correlation between FDI inflows from different origins and the similarities of US imports from China and other FDI origins. When the FDI inflow from an East Asian economy (e.g. South Korea) increases by 1 per cent, the similarity of US imports from China and the East Asian economy will increase by 0.07 per cent (see below for details of the statistical model). This implies that the more East Asian economies invest in China, the more evident the accumulated industry transfer effects and subsequent impact on the trade similarities will become.

We constructed pooled least squares models as follows:

$$\ln(TS_{i,t}) = C_5 + \alpha_5 \ln(FDI_{i,t}) + \varepsilon_{5,i,t} \tag{11.5}$$

$$\ln(TS_{i,t}) = C_6 + \alpha_6 \ln(FDI_{i,t}) + \beta_6 WTO_t + \varepsilon_{6,i,t} \tag{11.6}$$

$$\ln(TS_{i,t}) = C_7 + \alpha_7 \ln(FDI_{i,t}) + \beta_7 WTO_t + \gamma_7 RMB_t + \varepsilon_{7,i,t} \tag{11.7}$$

where $TS_{i,t}$ denotes the trade similarity index, i = Japan, Korea, Taiwan, Hong Kong, Singapore, Malaysia, Indonesia, Thailand, and Philippines, $t = 1983, \ldots, 2006$; $FDI_{i,t}$ denotes the accumulative FDI from the corresponding origin economies; WTO_t is a dummy variable, equal to 1 after 2001, which measures the impact of China's entry into WTO; and RMB_t is another dummy variable, equal to 1 after 1994, which captures the effects of RMB depreciation in that year. $TS_{i,t}$ index values are calculated based on trade data collected from the United Nations Commodity Trade Statistics Database and the US Census Bureau. $FDI_{i,t}$ values are based on data collected from China's Ministry of Commerce.

Model (11.5) shows that the correlations between FDI inflows to China and trade similarity are very significant (see models (5a) and (5b) in Tables 11.2 and 11.3). These correlations are robust when two control variables, WTO_t and

Table 11.2 Correlation between FDI and trade similarity (SITC three-digit level)

	Model (5a)		*Model (6a)*		*Model (7a)*	
	Fixed effect	*Random effect*	*Fixed effect*	*Random effect*	*Fixed effect*	*Random effect*
C	−1.167	−1.135	−1.156	−1.112	−1.247	−1.156
	(−15.163)***	(−9.595)***	(−13.226)***	(−9.152)***	(−9.946)***	(−7.660)***
$\ln(FDI_{i,t})$	0.074	0.072	0.073	0.070	0.084	0.075
	(11.474)***	(11.316)**	(9.277)***	(9.040)***	(6.309)***	(5.885)***
WTO_t			0.010	0.020	0.011	0.020
			(0.267)	(0.511)	(0.279)	(0.502)
RMB_t					−0.060	−0.027
					(−1.014)	(−0.476)
R^2	0.70	0.40	0.70	0.40	0.70	0.40

Notes: The dependent variable is the natural logarithm of the trade similarity index $\ln(TS_{i,t})$; *t*-values are given in parentheses; *significant at 10%; **significant at 5%; ***significant at 1%.

Table 11.3 Correlation between FDI and trade similarity (SITC one-digit level)

	Model (5a)		*Model (6a)*		*Model (7a)*	
	Fixed effect	*Random effect*	*Fixed effect*	*Random effect*	*Fixed effect*	*Random effect*
C	−0.0651	−0.642	−0.560	−0.551	−0.603	−0.586
	(−12.237)***	(−6.016)***	(−9.340)***	(−4.925)***	(−7.303)***	(−4.527)***
$\ln(FDI_{i,t})$	0.067	0.067	0.058	0.057	0.063	0.061
	(14.895)***	(14.851)***	(10.964)***	(10.919)***	(7.450)***	(7.364)***
WTO_t			0.063	0.065	0.065	0.066
			(2.344)**	(2.412)**	(2.399)**	(2.449)**
RMB_t					−0.028	−0.023
					(−0.755)	(−0.609)
R^2	0.82	0.54	0.82	0.53	0.82	0.53

Notes: As Table 11.2.

RMB_t, capturing the macroeconomic impact, are included, as shown in Tables 11.2 and 11.3.

US import structure

Aggregate imports

Since the 1980s, as trade similarities between China and other East Asian economies have increased, the USA has imported more and more from China. In 2002, China surpassed Japan to become the US's largest East Asian trading partner. As the share of imports from the East Asian region (Japan, the NIE-4, the ASEAN-4 and China) fluctuated within a very narrow band of 32 ± 4 per cent from 1983 to 2004, the import share from China skyrocketed from 0.9 per cent in 1983 to 12.9 per cent in 2004. In the same period, the market share of East Asian economies such as Japan and the NIE-4 underwent a dramatic decline in the USA. This decline shows that China has been receiving industry transfers via FDI from other East Asian economies, especially from Japan and the NIE-4. As they upgraded their industries, these economies transferred their export potential to China. Therefore, exports from China have been replacing other East Asian labour-intensive commodities and some capital-intensive commodities in the US market.

Although the structure of imports from the East Asia region has been redistributed among China and other economies due to industry transfers, the value added in China only accounts for a small portion of the total export volume because China is only an assembly centre. According to Li Deshui, the former director of the National Bureau of Statistics of China, China only earns a small profit marginfrom these exports.[8]

US imports of capital-intensive commodities

US imports of capital-intensive commodities[9] from East Asia have remained at a relatively stable level of around 42 per cent. However, China's share has grown rapidly, rising from 0.1 per cent in 1983 to 14.8 per cent in 2004, indicating that by hosting FDI, China received capital- and technology-intensive industries from other East Asian economies, thus taking over part of the share of the FDI origin economies in the US market. The transfer of capital- and technology-intensive industries into China and the change from labour-intensive to capital- and technology-intensive industries are directly related to the fact that FDI-related firms imported high-technology products on a larger scale.

However, there is a tendency for China's manufacturing sector to export a greater proportion of capital- and technology-intensive commodities thanks to the technology spillover effects of the East Asian industry transfer. In 2002, foreign-invested firms were responsible for 66 per cent of high-tech imports. In 2003, this rose to a record 71 per cent. High-tech products imported by foreign-invested enterprises from Japan, Taiwan, South Korea and Malaysia accounted for 56 per cent of total imported high-tech products. The "geographic technology intensity" of the technology imports induced by FDI from the East Asian economies is far higher than the corresponding "geographic intensity" of FDI. Since East Asian FDI is becoming technology-intensive, the consequent industrial transfer is likely to be technology-intensive as well. If technology-intensive industrial transfer continues, the large technology spillover effect will prompt the upgrading of the industry and export structure to a capital- and technology-intensive one.

US imports of labour-intensive commodities

There has been even faster growth in imports of labour-intensive commodities, which reflects the comparative advantage of China's enormous army of cheap labour. While the share of such imports from the Asian economies fluctuated

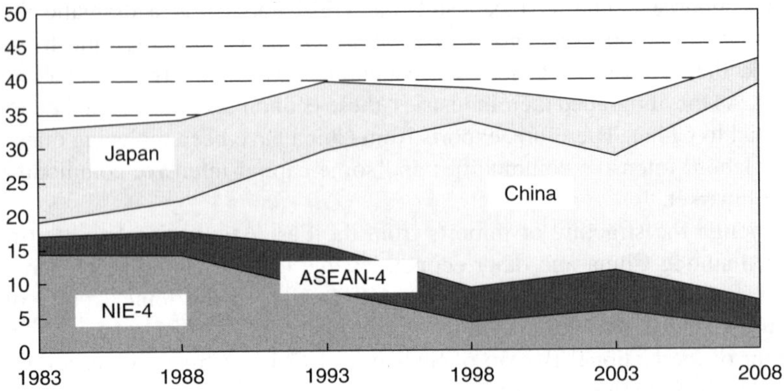

Figure 11.5 Share of labour-intensive commodities in US imports (%).

Sources: United Nations Commodity Trade Statistics Database (http://comtrade.un.org/) and US Census Bureau (http://www.census.gov/foreign-trade/).

within a narrow band of 36 ± 4 per cent from 1983 to 2003, the market share of imports from China leapt from 2.2 per cent in 1983 to 25.1 per cent in 2003 (see Figure 11.5). Labour-intensive products from China "supported" total East Asian export volumes more strongly than capital- and technology-intensive products.

Therefore, the labour-intensive industry transfer effects are more significant than the capital- and technology-intensive industry transfer effects, and this is related to the fact that FDI inflows still focus on labour-intensive industries. Low labour costs, rather than high-tech skills and R&D capacity, are still the major factor attracting FDI inflows. Most of the multinationals investing in China use it as a manufacturing center rather than an R&D centre

"Made in China"[10] commodities have a strong comparative advantage in the US market. Among the top 25 commodities imported from China in 2001 (76.6 per cent of total imports from that country), only one shows a weaker comparative advantage[11] than those imported from other countries. Of these top 25 goods, capital- and technology-intensive commodities account for only 25 per cent of total US imports from China, while the share of labour-intensive commodities is 49 per cent. In 2006, only three commodities dropped out of the top 25 list, which implies that the commodity composition of imports from China is quite stable.

Perspective on US–China trade

History is repeating itself, exhibiting a close analogy to the "product life cycle". The current industrial transfer to China from the East Asian economies is one of the three main industrial structure adjustments and transfers that have occurred since World War II. Japan inherited many labour-intensive industries from the USA in the 1950s and 1960s, during which time Japan-US trade expanded rapidly and triggered the notorious "Japan-US trade wars". In the 1960s and 1970s, both Japan and the USA transferred mature industries to the NIEs. This process was repeated as Japan and the NIEs transferred industries to ASEAN, China, India and Vietnam from the 1980s. From this perspective, it is quite reasonable and natural for China to receive transferred industries from other East Asian economies, causing the subsequent transfer of the trade surplus with the USA.

Due to dynamic changes in labour costs and other factors, the East Asian economies, as important commodity suppliers in the "dollar standard" era, are transferring their labour-intensive industries by relocating their assembly lines to China. Geographically, Japan and the NIEs are the major origins of industrial transfer. In terms of sectoral distribution, industrial transfer has focused on labour-intensive industries. Industrial transfer has a strong trade transfer effect and has exacerbated the growing US–China commodity trade imbalance.

The future of industrial transfer and the subsequent trade transfer is predictable, though slightly mixed. In the first instance, the transfer has been overwhelmingly supported by China's almost unlimited supply of labour and its pro-trade FDI policies. Industrial transfer is inevitable in such an international industrial upgrading and adjustment context and China will no doubt still be the ideal host for East Asian FDI up to 2015. In particular, ethnic Chinese entrepreneurs in Taiwan, Hong Kong, Macau and Singapore are the main driving force for investment in China. Moreover, to preclude disastrous levels of unemployment caused by urbanisation and the radical restructuring of state-owned industries, the Chinese government decided to make best use of China's "comparative advantage" in cheap labour by boosting labour-intensive industries.[12] This policy is very attractive to resource-seeking FDI from East Asia. As long as there is large-volume East Asian FDI coming into China, the trade surplus transfer effects will continue.

However, the effect of FDI in promoting exports to the USA could be affected by rising labour costs in China. As China is pushed to achieve "fair trade", labour costs in some manufacturing industries are growing. Many factories in China's southeastern coastal provinces have been facing a chilling shortage of labour, especially rural workers,[13] in recent years.[14]

Finally, FDI inflows are helping Chinese labour-intensive industries to upgrade and become capital- and technology-intensive. The "export-oriented" FDI from the East Asian economies has been declining gradually since the turn of the present century, giving way to "market-seeking" FDI and capital- and technology-intensive FDI, not only from Asia, but also from North America and Europe.

Policy implications

The US–China trade imbalance is a structural one, reflecting the nature of complementarity between the industry structures of China and the USA and the profound impact of FDI productivity spillovers. Sunset industries in the USA, such as those producing steel, textiles, and TV sets, will gradually shrink as their products lose their cost advantage in international markets. The capacity of these industries to absorb labour is declining and this is causing serious structural unemployment.

This will trigger vigorous lobbying activity and cause economic tension between these two giants on either side of the Pacific. No matter how many high-tech products, such as Boeing aircraft, China buys from the USA, it is still safe to predict that the structural US–China trade imbalance will not be altered fundamentally and there will continue to be many economic disputes between them. Moreover, the politicised voice from Washington urging Beijing to implement reforms on the rule of law, transparency, fairness, open competition and the enforcement of intellectual property rights protection will never be silenced.

EU–China trade is facing a similar problem. China is the EU's second largest trading partner, after the USA; and the EU is one of China's top trade deficit partners.[15] The EU blames this deficit on obstacles to market access in China,[16] while China attributes it to protectionist European policies. Fortunately, the issue of the EU–China trade deficit has not become as politicised as the US–China trade deficit. To avoid getting into "lose–lose" trade disputes such as the so-called "bra wars" of 2005 (Frith 2005), both sides need to negotiate more. However, much like the US–China structural trade imbalance, the EU–China trade imbalance will also be long-lasting and trade disputes between China and the EU are unlikely to be avoided.

The Chinese government has realised that the trade imbalance and the resultant RMB revaluation pressure are the two most important economic concerns in its external relations. Thus, the government is actively considering how to optimise China's trade structure by increasing imports in order to alleviate economic tensions. MOFCOM has strengthened its functional ability to remedy trade disputes and to handle issues such as industrial injury investigations in order to prepare for more intense trade conflict in the future. Also, MOFCOM is taking preventive measures to deal with severe price competition among key Chinese commodities in overseas markets. Such intense price competition frequently triggers anti-dumping retaliation and causes major economic losses for Chinese export firms.[17]

China has also stepped up its lobbying efforts on Capitol Hill since 1997 to achieve more stable US–China political and economic relations, particularly since the failure of the state-controlled petroleum company CNOOC to acquire the American petroleum company Unocal in 2005. The Chinese embassy in Washington, MOFCOM, and its affiliated state-owned companies are hiring the best firms in the USA to lobby on China's behalf.[18] These lobbying activities are expected to counterbalance the great pressure coming from the US sunset sectors and protectionist interest groups.

As for monetary policy, although the RMB had been revalued by only 8.5 per cent by July 2007,[19] it seems pointless for the USA or the EU to urge China to further revalue its currency dramatically. Non-monetary solutions are arguably a better remedy for trade disputes.[20] As discussed in previous sections of this chapter, the East Asian industry transfer over the last three decades has transformed China into an integral assembler in the East Asian production chain. The proportion of value added in China is respectable, but far from extraordinary or dominant. Therefore, a drastic revaluation of the RMB cannot fundamentally alleviate the

US–China trade imbalance, and the impact of RMB appreciation on the US–China trade deficit has so far been insignificant. It is instructive to look back at the Japan–US trade relationship. Although the value of the yen rose from 235 to the dollar in 1985 to 128 in 1988, the US trade deficit with Japan continued to rise, somewhat counter-intuitively, from $46 billion to $51 billion during that period.

Conclusion

With rapid growth in the US–China trade in goods, the bilateral trade imbalance has deteriorated dramatically, becoming an increasingly sensitive issue in US–China relations. Since 2000, China rather than Japan has been the country with which the USA has its largest trade deficit. China's huge surplus with the USA has led to increasingly strong US pressure for a revaluation of the RMB, as well as criticism of Chinese protectionism and the politicisation of trade disputes between the two countries. Among the many important factors that have affected the US–China trade imbalance, the transfer to China of East Asian industry is undoubtedly one of the most fundamental, yet it is usually underestimated.

The accumulated FDI inflow to China from the major East Asian economies between 1979 and 2009 accounted for more than 6 per cent of China's total accumulated FDI. More than 60 per cent of this inflow went to the manufacturing sector. These two figures indicate that FDI from East Asia has caused the transfer of mature labour-intensive industries to China due to continuously rising labour costs in the East Asian industrialised economies.

This large FDI inflow in turn greatly generated significant productivity spillovers to domestic enterprises, as discussed in the previous chapters. This increased Chinese exports to the USA. Fifty-nine per cent of China's foreign trade was accounted for by FDI in 2006, including that from East Asian countries which have transferred export-oriented manufacturing industries to China. Such industrial transfer via FDI has caused the export structures of China and the FDI origin economies to become increasingly similar. The hypothetical positive correlation between industry transfer and export transfer has been subjected to statistical analysis, and the results are overwhelmingly convincing.

Geographically, Japan and the NIEs are the main sources of industrial transfer to China. This transfer has a strong trade transfer effect and exacerbates the growing US–China commodity trade imbalance.

The future of industrial transfers and subsequent trade transfers is slightly mixed due to uncertainties about China's labour costs and the upgrading of the FDI inflow structure, coupled with RMB appreciation. However, much like the US–Japan trade wars of the past, the US–China trade imbalance and the subsequent politicised trade disputes cannot be solved fundamentally until the next industry transfer, when mature industries are relocated out of China. It is safe to predict that until 2015 the trade disputes between China and the USA will continue to be a big headache for both Beijing and Washington due to the perfect complementarity of these two economic giants. Both governments need to be fully prepared, physically and psychologically, to build a better mutual understanding and cooperation through dialogue, negotiations and the removal of trade barriers. This suggestion is equally valid for EU–China trade relations.

The US trade deficit is not a new problem, and there is a clear consensus concerning the ultimate reason for it – the dollar's role as the dominant international currency (Krugman and Baldwin 1987; McKinnon 2001) However, the recent transfer of industry from East Asia to China, attracted by China's huge labour force and stable policy infrastructure, has allowed China to play a significant role in restructuring the East Asian production and exporting system on an unprecedented scale. As the "negotiation representative" for this system in international trade disputes, China undoubtedly has less bargaining power given the fact that its "socialist market economy" is still in its infancy.

As a rising economic power in the sea of mercantilist revitalisation, China is experiencing great pressure to optimise its trade structure and implement institutional reforms of its trade regime. However, China still has a long way to go in that its economic development and stability are still highly dependent on labour-intensive manufacturing and commodity exports.

12 Concluding remarks

Summary

Research questions

One of the most important aspects of foreign direct investment is that it embodies advanced technologies and business practices which can spill over to domestic firms via such channels as labour mobility, backward and forward linkages, export of multinational affiliates and horizontal effects. To pursue the benefit of FDI productivity spillovers, many developing countries adopt preferential FDI policies characterised by swapping domestic market access for advanced foreign technology and productivity.

However, there is debate in the literature on (a) how to quantitatively measure FDI productivity spillovers as an economy-wide and cross-industry phenomenon rather than a region- and sector-specific one; and (b) whether preferential FDI policies can help productivity spillovers. This book, inspired by the above two intriguing questions, has mainly addressed the following research questions: (a) how to quantify the FDI productivity spillovers in a CGE model; (b) how to model the spillovers under three alternative market structure assumptions, namely perfect competition, monopolistic competition with homogeneous firms and heterogeneous firms; (c) how the 2008 corporate income tax reform has impacted the FDI productivity spillover effects; (d) whether FDI spillovers have improved the performance of Chinese domestic banks; (e) whether FDI spillovers have contributed to the phenomenal US–China trade imbalance.

Model construction

This book combines computable general equilibrium modelling and econometric techniques to quantify FDI productivity spillovers. This study is conducted in the context of the Chinese economy, considering the fact that China has been the largest FDI host country among the developing economies since the mid-1980s.

A static 101-sector CGE model was constructed to measure the endogenous productivity spillovers of FDI in China. Spillover effects are analysed under three different market structure assumptions: perfect competition, monopolistic competition, and monopolistic competition with heterogeneous firms.

First, the input–output flows of state-owned, private and foreign-invested enterprises are disaggregated from the original input–output table for China which did not contain ownership information. In the benchmark model four FDI spillover channels (backward linkages, forward linkages, MNE exports and horizontal demonstration) are endogenously incorporated in a perfectly competitive economy. When the model is simulated to counterfactuals, the spillover variables will change endogenously, making productivity spillovers change endogenously as well. Spillover parameters are estimated with Chinese industry-level panel data. Other parameters are taken from GTAP 6 database and the literature.

Second, in the intermediate model, monopolistic competition is modelled to explore how market competition affects the effects of FDI productivity spillovers.

Third, firm heterogeneity has also been incorporated into this model, examining how competition and intra-industry resource reallocation triggered by multinational firms improve industry-level aggregate productivities. The importance of firm heterogeneity, as a newly explored market structure, in modelling trade and FDI has been widely acknowledged.

Fourth, the CGE model is simulated in the above three market structure scenarios with an FDI shock, and the results are compared.

Fifth, experiments of FDI policy reform counterfactuals are also conducted. The experiments simulate a harmonisation of corporate income tax rates over domestic and foreign-invested enterprises. These counterfactuals are of great policy significance not only to China but also to other economies, as countries have increasingly relied on tax incentives to attract FDI.

Finally, stochastic frontier analysis (SFA) is employed to analyse the efficiency of the Chinese banking sector in 2001 and 2007. A panel data model is constructed to examine the causal link between FDI productivity spillovers and the trade imbalance with its largest trade partner, the USA.

This research introduces five novelties. It is the first to endogenise the FDI spillovers by linking spillover effects to spillover channels. Secondly, this research is the first to examine FDI spillovers under the market structures of monopolistic competition and firm heterogeneity. Thirdly, this research has assessed the impact of corporate income tax harmonisation on FDI productivity spillovers. Fourthly, it is the first work to explore the FDI productivity spillover in the banking sector. Finally, the broader impact of FDI spillover effects is examined in terms of its role to the US–China trade imbalance.

Main findings and policy implication

The research results show that the presence of FDI productivity spillovers has generally improved productivity and led to "spillover premium" effects on the total output of domestic enterprises in China. Spillovers make decrease foreign firms' total output. But collectively, spillovers have a positive impact on national aggregate variables – GDP, total output and welfare.

The market structure assumptions of monopolistic competition and firm heterogeneity provide special insights (e.g. in terms of product variety and scale) for this research which the assumption of perfect competition cannot offer. Furthermore, the assumption of firm heterogeneity can provide a more comprehensive measurement of productivity change than perfect and monopolistic competition assumptions do.

We reviewed the literature in Chapter 2 and found few papers studying the effects of FDI productivity spillovers with CGE models. The findings in this research are generally in line with those found in the broad literature. For example, the net productivity spillover effects of FDI can promote GDP, national output and welfare, which is consistent with the findings of Van Meijl and Van Tongeren (1998) and Lejour *et al.* (2008). Another example is the tax reform experiments which imply that the policy of swapping market access for technology was likely to be a success in China. This is also consistent with the stylised facts regarding this policy collected by Long (2005). However, as this research is methodologically novel and involves new research perspectives, many of its findings do not have counterparts in the literature with which to compare.

A higher corporate income tax levied on foreign-invested enterprises alone distorts the economy structure and lowers total output, welfare and GDP. However, an integrated tax reform formula can do a better job by increasing the output level of domestic enterprises and by promoting national welfare. Under firm heterogeneity, the spillover benefit of integrated reform is even more prominent, because the reform can increase the average productivity of all existing enterprises, and raises the possibility of productivity spillovers and the absorptive capacity of domestic enterprises. This is more beneficial to the productivity spillovers from foreign-invested firms to domestic enterprises.

Neither single-sided reform nor integrated reform can increase the proportion of the productivity spilt over from foreign firms to domestic firms in total productivity of domestic enterprises. Taking into consideration the changing pattern of productivity under firm heterogeneity, the tax reform will only temporarily lower the FDI productivity spillover effects; however, it can promote the speed and magnitude of spillovers later.

The results of Chapter 10 highlight the importance of efficiency spillovers which can be introduced by cautious financial liberalisation to a transition economy. Chapter 11 identifies FDI productivity spillovers as one of the most important microeconomic foundations of the US–China trade imbalance.

Directions for future research

- Dynamic modelling. This research is based on a static computable general equilibrium model. However, the accumulation of foreign capital and its subsequent productivity spillovers is a dynamic process. Therefore it would be more appealing to study the FDI productivity spillovers and their economic growth effects in a dynamic CGE model.
- Social accounting matrix (SAM). The CGE model constructed here is based on a transformed Chinese input–output table containing an intermediate input–output block, a value-added block and a final demand block (see Table 5.4).

As the primary concern of this research is with the supply side rather than the demand side of the economy, the input–output table was not extended to a SAM to contain further information on transactions between non-producer agents. But with a SAM the CGE model could provide more detailed measurement of domestic consumption demand and investment demand, and thus making the simulation results more accurate.

- Firm-level data. This CGE model mainly addresses the interaction between foreign enterprises and their domestic counterparts. More accurate spillover parameters ($\boldsymbol{\beta}$ in equation (5.6b)) and Pareto distribution parameters (a and b in equation (5.29)) can be estimated with firm-level data. More importantly, firm-level data can be used to implement more interesting micro-simulation experiments under the assumption of firm heterogeneity. Rutherford and Tarr (2008) have used data from 55,000 Russian households and incorporated them into a CGE model. Their research shows the importance of incorporating the diversity of heterogeneous agents.

Appendix 1

An example of CGE modelling in GAMS/MPSGE

Tables A1.1–A1.5 provide an example of modelling CGE in GAMS/MPSGE syntax (for more details, see Markusen 2002b). Table A1.1 provides a transformed SAM in Part I and initiates two parameters in Part II. Part III is the core model which is written in MPSGE syntax. Part IV implements the benchmark check and counterfactual simulations.

In Part I, positive entries are values of commodity flows into the economy (sales or factor supplies), while negative entries are values of commodity flows out of the economy (factor demands or final demands). A zero row sum implies market clearance while a zero column sum denotes zero profit for production sectors and income balance for consumers.

In Part II, the initial *ad valorem* tax rate (`TY1`) for Y_1 sector inputs is 0. The initial labour endowment level (`LENDOW`) is 1. These parameters will be changed in counterfactual simulations to examine the effects of tax reform and change of country size.

In Part III, the `$SECTOR` statement indicates that the model involves three activities that convert commodity/welfare inputs into commodity/welfare outputs. All the activity levels are unity. For example, activity Y_1 runs at a unitary level, producing 100 units of good Y_1, as displayed in the transformed SAM. Setting unitary initial levels for the activities will make the pairwise comparison between benchmark levels and counterfactual results more straightforward.

`$COMMODITY` states that the model contains two goods, two factors and a special product, welfare. `$CONSUMER` represents the individuals who supply factors and receive transfers from government. The three `$PROD` blocks describe the production for products X and Y, and welfare W.

The production of goods Y_1 and Y_2 follows from a CES production function with unit elasticity of substitution (`s:1`), as Table A1.2 shows. This implies that the CES production technology has a special specification, the Cobb–Douglas form, as discussed in Chapter 5. Assume the production of Y_2 is to solve the problem below:

$$\begin{aligned} \min \quad & P_L L + P_K K \\ \text{s.t.} \quad & Y_2 \leq A_2 L^{\alpha_2} K^{1-\alpha_2} \end{aligned}$$

Table A1.1 A closed economy in GAMS/MPSGE syntax

```
$TITLE A Closed 2 x 2 Economy
* Part I: Transformed SAM
$ONTEXT
Production     Sectors      Consumers
Markets |  Y1    Y2    W    CONS  |SUM
-----------------------------------
  PY1   |  100         -100        | 0
  PY2   |        100   -100        | 0
  PW    |        200   -200        | 0
  PL    | -75   -25          100   | 0
  PK    | -25   -75          100   | 0
-----------------------------------
  SUM   |   0     0     0    0
$OFFTEXT
* Part II: Parameters
PARAMETERS
TY1 ad-valorem tax rate for Y1 sector inputs
LENDOW labour endowment multiplier for counterfactual
  simulations;
TY1=0;
LENDOW=1;
* Part III: Core MPSGE model
$ONTEXT
$MODEL: Markusen
$SECTORS:
  Y1!  Activity level for sector y1
  Y1!  Activity level for sector y2
  W!  Activity level for sector W
     (Hicksian welfare index)
$COMMODITIES:
  PY1!  Price index for commodity y1
  PY2!  Price index for commodity y2
  PL!  Price index for primary factor L
  PK!  Price index for primary factor K
  PW!  Price index for welfare
       (expenditure function)
$CONSUMERS:
  CONS!  Income level for consumer CONS
```

Table A1.2 Production blocks

```
$PROD:Y1 s:1
  O:PY1 Q:100
  I:PL Q:75 A:CONS T:ty1
  I:PK Q:25 A:CONS T:ty1
$PROD:Y2 s:1
  O:PY2 Q:100
  I:PL Q:25
  I:PK Q:75
```

Table A1.3 Welfare block

```
$PROD:W s:1
  O:PW Q:200
  I:PY1 Q:100
  I:PY2 Q:100
```

The cost ratio of the two inputs can be derived:

$$\frac{P_K K}{P_L L} = \frac{1-\alpha_2}{\alpha_2} \Rightarrow \frac{1-\alpha_2}{\alpha_2} = \frac{75}{25} \Rightarrow \alpha_2 = 0.25$$

With $L = 75$ and $K = 25$, the value of A_2 can be obtained:

$$A_2 = \frac{Y_2}{L^{0.25} K^{0.25}} = 3.04$$

Thus the underlying Cobb-Douglas production function is

$$Y_2 = 3.04 L^{0.25} K^{0.75}$$

The above "standard" calibration process, however, can be replaced with "calibrated forms" without calculating the values of parameters of α_2 and A_2. We can get ratio equations for prices and input demands (with lower case letters denoting

Table A1.4 Demand block

```
$DEMAND:CONS
  D:PW Q:200
  E:PL Q:(100*LENDOW)
  E:PK Q:100
```

ratios rather than level variables):

$$py_1 = p_L^{0.25} p_K^{0.75}$$

$$l = y_2 \frac{py_2}{p_L}$$

$$k = y_2 \frac{py_2}{p_K}$$

The parsimony of these "calibrated forms" of the model is fully manifested in Chapter 7 with a benchmark model for the Chinese economy.

Table A1.5 Benchmark check and counterfactual scenarios

```
* Part IV: Benchmark checking and counterfactual
  scenarios
$SYSINCLUDE mpsgeset markusen
PW.FX=1;
$INCLUDE Markusen.gen
SOLVE Markusen using MCP;

* Solve the counterfactuals
TY1=0.5;
LENDOW=1;
$INCLUDE Markusen.gen
SOLVE Markusen using MCP;

TY1=0;
LENDOW=2;
$INCLUDE Markusen.gen
SOLVE Markusen using MCP;
```

As for production taxes on both inputs of labour and capital, the tax (`T:`) revenue is assigned (`A:`) to the agent "`CONS`".

The welfare is "produced" by consuming goods Y_1 and Y_2, with a Cobb–Douglas function as well. The elasticity of substitution here is also one (`s:1`).

In a demand block, the consumer agent demands the utility good `PW` and receives income from his/her endowment, denoted by "`E:`". `LENDOW` is a shift parameter to multiply the endowment amount.

After specifying the core model with parameter values and data imported, the fitness of the model is checked by seeing whether it can replicate the benchmark economy with the price of welfare as the numéraire (`PW.FX=1`), which is shown in Table A1.5. If activity levels of all production sections (`Y1, Y2` and `W`) and consumer (`CONS`) equal 1, and all prices (`PY1, PY2, PL, PK`) are equal to 1 as well, then the benchmark economy is successfully replicated. Then the shift parameters for labour endowment `LENDOW` and production tax `TY1` can be altered to check how the production and welfare levels will be affected in these two counterfactual scenarios.

Appendix 2

The GAMS code and mathematical specification of the benchmark CGE model

This appendix presents the benchmark model in GAMS/MPSGE syntax block by block. In interpreting the benchmark CGE model coded in GAMS/MPSGE syntax, the price ratio equation (5.19a) and input demand ratio equations (5.18a) and (5.18b) discussed in Chapter 5 need to be frequently employed. Equations are categorised into four groups:

(1) Original CES functions.
(2) Ratio equations: prices. These equations are applications of (5.19a). Equation (5.19b) is also applied when the elasticity of substitution (transformation) is equal to one which implies a Cobb–Douglas form.
(3) Ratio equations: input demand or output supply. These ratio equations are applications of (5.18a), or (5.18b) if the production has a CET form.
(4) Level equations. These equations define the level quantities that correspond to output and input demand in the corresponding sector. A level value is a ratio variable multiplied by the base quantity denoted with a bar ($^{-}$) over a variable. The level variables for input demand and output supply will be used in the market clearing equations to be listed in the end of the appendix.

Three groups of market equilibrium equations for factors, Armington goods and traded goods respectively are implicitly contained but "hidden" in the GAMS/MPSGE syntax. In the following discussions, these equations are listed with demands on the left-hand side and supplies on the right-hand side.

Equilibrium of factor markets

The demand for and supply of labour in sector a are given by equation (A2.2.10) and (A2.5.12), respectively. Thus the equilibrium condition for the labour market is:

$$DY\_L(a) = LS(a)$$

Table A2.1 Sectors, commodities and representative agents

```
$SECTORS:
  Y(A)        !SECTORAL PRODUCTION
  YN(A)       !SECTORAL PRODUCTION
  DX(A)       !CET TRANSFORMATION FROM Y(A)
  VA(A)       !VALUE ADDED
  AR1(Z)      !ARMINGTON SUPPLY AT OWNERSHIP LEVEL
  AR(Z)       !ARMINGTON SUPPLY AT INDUSTRY LEVEL
  X(A)        !EXPORT
  M(A)        !IMPORT AT SECTOR LEVEL
  MZ(Z)       !IMPORT AT INDUSTRY LEVEL
  CS          !PRIVATE CONSUMPTION
  G           !PUBLIC CONSUMPTION
  INV         !INVESTMENT
  LZ(Z)       !LABOUR SUPPLY AT INDUSTRY LEVEL
  LTOTAL      !TOTAL LABOUR SUPPLY
  KZ(Z)       !CAPITAL SUPPLY AT INDUSTRY LEVEL
  KTOTAL      !TOTAL CAPITAL SUPPLY
$COMMODITIES:
  PY(A)       !TOTAL OUTPUT
  PYY(A)      !TOTAL OUTPUT
  PAA(Z)      !ARMINGTON PRICE FOR EACH OWNERSHIP
  PA(Z)       !ARMINGTON PRICE FOR INDUSTRY
  PD(A)       !DOMESTIC MARKET PRICE
  PM(Z)       !IMPORT PRICE AT INDUSTRY LEVEL
  PMA(A)      !IMPORT PRICE AT SECTOR-LEVEL
  PX(A)       !EXPORT PRICE
  PC          !CONSUMPTION PRICE
  PINV        !INVESTMENT PRICE
  PFX         !FOREIGN EXCHANGE
  PG          !LUMP-SUM TAX REVENUE
  PVA(A)      !PRICE OF AGGREGATE VALUE ADDED
  WL(A)       !WAGE RATE
  TWL         !NATIONAL-LEVEL WAGE
  ZWL(Z)      !INDUSTRY-LEVEL WAGE
  RK(A)       !RETURN TO CAPITAL
  TRK         !NATIONAL AVERAGE RETURN TO CAPITAL
  ZRK(Z)      !INDUSTRY AVERAGE RETURN TO SCALE
  PF(A)       !FIXED COST
$CONSUMER:
  RA          !REPRESENTATIVE AGENT
  FDI         !MULTINATIONAL(FOREIGN) FIRMS
  ENTRE(A)    !AGENTS TO COLLECT MARKUPS
               AND PAY FIXED COST
  GOV         !GOVERNMENT
```

Table A2.2 Production of value-added composites

MPSGE Declaration

```
$PROD: VA(FNN)     S: 1
  O: PVA(FNN)      Q: (CP(FNN)+DP(FNN)+OP(FNN))
  I: WL(FNN)       Q: CP(FNN)
  I: RK(FNN)       Q: (DP(FNN)+OP(FNN))
$PROD: VA(SNO)     S: 1
  O: PVA(SNO)      Q: ((CP(SNO)+DP(SNO)+OP(SNO))/
                      (1+NTFP0 (SNO)$NTFPFLAG))
  + A:GOV  N: NTFP(SNO)$NTFPFLAG  M:(-1) $NTFPFLAG
  I: WL(SNO)       Q: CP(SNO)
  I: RK(SNO)       Q: (DP(SNO)+OP(SNO))
```

Equations

[1] original CES functions

$$DY\_VA(FNN) = \alpha_{DY\_FNN} \times DY\_L(FNN)^{\bar{\theta}_{FNN\_wl}(FNN)} \times DY\_K(FNN)^{\bar{\theta}_{FNN\_rk}(FNN)} \quad \text{(A2.2.1)}$$

$$DY\_VA(SNO)\frac{1+NTFP(SNO)}{1+\overline{NTFP0}(SNO)} = \alpha_{NY\_SNO} \times DY\_L(SNO)^{\bar{\theta}_{SNO\_wl}(SNO)} \times DY\_K(SNO)^{\bar{\theta}_{SNO\_rk}(SNO)} \quad \text{(A2.2.2)}$$

[2] ratio equations: prices

$$pva(FNN) = wl(FNN)^{\bar{\theta}_{FNN\_wl}(FNN)} \times rk(FNN)^{\bar{\theta}_{FNN\_rk}(FNN)} \quad \text{(A2.2.3)}$$

$$pva(SNO)\frac{1+NTFP(SNO)}{1+\overline{NTFP0}(SNO)} = wl(SNO)^{\bar{\theta}_{SNO\_wl}(SNO)} \times rk(SNO)^{\bar{\theta}_{SNO\_rk}(SNO)} \quad \text{(A2.2.4)}$$

[3] ratio equations: input demand

$$dy\_l(FNN) = d\_va(FNN)\left(\frac{pva(FNN)}{wl(FNN)}\right) \quad \text{(A2.2.5)}$$

$$dy\_k(FNN) = d\_va(FNN)\left(\frac{pva(FNN)}{rk(FNN)}\right) \quad \text{(A2.2.6)}$$

$$dy\_l(SNO) = d\_va(SNO)\left(\frac{pva(SNO)\frac{1+NTFP(SNO)}{1+\overline{NTFP0}(SNO)}}{wl(SNO)}\right) \quad \text{(A2.2.7)}$$

$$dy\_k(SNO) = d\_va(SNO)\left(\frac{pva(SNO)\frac{1+NTFP(SNO)}{1+\overline{NTFP0}(SNO)}}{rk(SNO)}\right) \quad \text{(A2.2.8)}$$

Table A2.2 Continued

[4] level equations		
$DY\_VA(a) = dy\_va(a)(\bar{CP}(a) + \bar{DP}(a) + \bar{OP}(a))$		(A2.2.9)
$DY\_L(a) = dy\_l(a)\bar{CP}(a)$		(A2.2.10)
$DY\_K(a) = dy\_k(a)(\bar{DP}(a) + \bar{OP}(a))$		(A2.2.11)
Variables		
$pva(a)$	Ratio market price for aggregate value added of sector *a*	
$wl(a)$	Ratio wage level of sector *a*	
$rk(a)$	Ratio returns to capital input of sector *a*	
$dy\_va(a)$	Ratio output of aggregate value added of sector *a*	
$dy\_wl(a)$	Ratio input demand for labour of sector *a*	
$dy\_rk(a)$	Ratio input demand for capital of sector *a*	
$DY\_VA(a)$	Output of aggregate value added of sector *a*	
$DY\_L(a)$	Input demand for labour of sector *a*	
$DY\_K(a)$	Input demand for capital of sector *a*	
$NTFP\ (a)$	Endogenous total factor productivity spillovers of sector *a*	
Parameters		
α_{DY_FNN}	Shift parameter of production of value added (*FNN* sectors)	
α_{NY_SNO}	Shift parameter of production of value added (*SNO* sectors)	
$\bar{\theta}_{A\_VA}(a)$	Share of aggregate value added in the total input of sector *a*	
$\bar{\theta}_{A\_wl}(a)$	Share of labour cost in aggregate value-added input of sector *a*	
$\bar{\theta}_{A\_rk}(a)$	Share of capital cost in aggregate value-added input of sector *a*	
$\overline{NTFP0}$(a)	Base total factor productivity spillovers minus 1 in sector *a*	
$\overline{CP}(a)$	Labour input in sector *a*	
$\overline{DP}(a) + \overline{OP}(a)$	Capital input in sector *a*	

Table A2.3 Production

MPSGE Declaration

```
$PROD:Y(A)
    O:PY(A) Q:TOUTPUT(A) A:GOV T:(NTP0(A)+TAXREF(A))
+       P:(1/(1-NTP0(A)))
    I:PA(Z) Q:IOD(Z,A)
    I:PVA(A) Q:(CP(A)+DP(A)+OP(A))

* THIS BLOCK IS FOR THE SCENARIO OF MONOPOLISTIC
  COMPETITION

$PROD:YN(A)
    O:PYY(A) Q:(TOUTPUT(A)*PHI_R(A))
    I:PY(A) Q:(TOUTPUT(A)*[1/(1+MK0(A)$NMKFLAG)])
+       A:ENTRE(A)$NMKFLAG N:NMK(A)$NMKFLAG
```

Equations

[1] original CES functions

$$Y(a) \times \frac{1-\overline{NTFP0}(a)-\overline{TAXREF}(a)}{1-\overline{NTFP0}(a)} = \sum_z DY\_AR(z,a)+DY\_VA(a) \tag{A2.3.1}$$

$$YY(a) \times PHI\_R(a) = Y(a) \times \frac{1+NMK(a)}{1+\overline{MK0}(a)} \tag{A2.3.2}$$

[2] ratio equations: prices

$$py(a) \times \frac{1-\overline{NTFP0}(a)-\overline{TAXREF}(a)}{1-\overline{NTFP0}(a)} = \bar{\theta}_{Y\_AR}(a) \times \sum_z pa(z,a)+\bar{\theta}_{Y\_VA}(a) \times pva(a) \tag{A2.3.3}$$

$$pyy(a) \times PHI\_R(a) = py(a) \times \frac{1+NMK(a)}{1+\overline{MK0}(a)} \tag{A2.3.4}$$

[3] ratio equations: input demand

$$dy\_ar(a) = y(a) \tag{A2.3.5}$$

$$dy\_va(a) = y(a) \tag{A2.3.6}$$

[4] level equations

$$Y(a) = y(a)\overline{TOUTPUT}(a) \tag{A2.3.7}$$

$$DY\_AR(a) = dy\_ar(a) \sum_z \overline{IOD}(z,a) \tag{A2.3.8}$$

Table A2.3 Continued

Variables	
$py(a)$	Ratio market price for gross output of sector *a*
$pyy(a)$	Ratio transformed market price for gross output of sector *a*
$pa(a)$	Ratio market price for Armington aggregate goods of sector *a*
$dy\_ar(a)$	Ratio input demand for Armington aggregate goods of sector *a*
$Y(a)$	Gross output of sector *a*
$YY(a)$	Transformed output of sector *a*
$DY\_AR(a)$	Demand for Armington aggregates
$NMK(a)$	Endogenous mark-up rate (for monopolistic competition scenario)
$PHI\_R(a)$	Productivity ratio (for firm heterogeneity scenario)
Parameters	
$\bar{\theta}_{Y\_AR}(a)$	Share of export value in total output value of sector *a*
$\bar{\theta}_{Y\_VA}(a)$	Share of domestically used value in total output value of sector *a*
$\overline{NTP0}(a)$	Basc value of gross output tax on the production of sector *a*
$\overline{TOUTPUT}(a)$	Total output of sector *a*
$\overline{IODZ}(z,a)$	Intermediate inputs for sector *a*
$\overline{TAXREF}(a)$	Tax differentials (for FDI tax reform simulations in Chapter 7)
$\overline{MK0}(a)$	Initial mark-up rate (for monopolistic competition scenario)

The demand for and supply of capital in sector a are given by equation (A2.2.11) and (A2.6.14), respectively. Thus the equilibrium condition for capital market is:

$$DY\_K(a) = KS(a)$$

Equilibrium of Armington markets

The demand for Armington aggregate goods originates from three blocks, namely production (Table A2.3), public and private consumption (Table A2.9), and investment demand (Table A2.10). So the total demand for Armington aggregate goods is the sum of over these four demands which are represented by equations (A2.3.8), (A2.9.9), (A2.9.10) and (A2.10.5), respectively.

$$DY\_AR = \sum_a DY\_AR(a) + \sum_z G\_A(z) + \sum_z P\_A(z) + \sum_z INV\_A(z)$$

Table A2.4 CET transformation of production

MPSGE Declaration

```
$PROD:DX(A)        T:ESUBAR(A,"EAR")
  O:PX(A)          Q:EX(A)
  O:PD(A)          Q:(TOUTPUT(A)-EX(A))
  I:PYY(A)         Q:TOUTPUT(A)
```

Equations

[1] original CET function

$$Y(a)=\bar{\alpha}_Y\left(\begin{array}{l}\bar{\beta}_{Y\_X}(a)\\ \quad\times DY\_X(a)^{(\overline{ESUBAR}-1)/\overline{ESUBAR}}\\ \quad+(1-\bar{\beta}_{Y\_D}(a))\\ \quad\times DY\_D(a)^{(\overline{ESUBAR}-1)/\overline{ESUBAR}}\end{array}\right)^{\overline{ESUBAR}/(\overline{ESUBAR}-1)} \tag{A2.4.1}$$

[2] ratio equations: prices

$$pyy(a)=\left(\begin{array}{l}\bar{\theta}_{Y\_X}(a)\,px(a)^{1-\overline{ESUBAR}}\\ \quad+\bar{\theta}_{Y\_D}(a)\,pd(a)^{1-\overline{ESUBAR}}\end{array}\right)^{1/1-\overline{ESUBAR}} \tag{A2.4.2}$$

[3] ratio equations: output supply (not "input demand")

$$dy\_x(a)=yy(a)\left(\frac{py(a)}{px(a)}\right)^{\overline{ESUBAR}} \tag{A2.4.3}$$

$$dy\_d(a)=y(a)\left(\frac{py(a)}{pd(a)}\right)^{\overline{ESUBAR}} \tag{A2.4.4}$$

[4] level equations

$$DY\_X(a)=dy\_x(a)*\overline{EX}(A) \tag{A2.4.5}$$

$$DY\_D(a)=dy\_d(a)*(\overline{TOUTPUT}(A)-\overline{EX}(A)) \tag{A2.4.6}$$

Variables

$px(a)$	Ratio market price of export of sector *a*
$pd(a)$	Ratio market price of domestically used goods of sector *a*
$dy\_x(a)$	Ratio export demand for *Y* (with CET specification) of sector *a*
$dy\_d(a)$	Ratio domestic demand for *Y* (with CET specification) of sector *a*
$DY\_X(a)$	Export demand for *Y* of sector *a*
$DY\_D(a)$	Domestic demand for *Y* of sector *a*

Parameters

$\bar{\theta}_{Y\_X}(a)$	Share of Armington aggregate in the total input of sector *a*
$\bar{\theta}_{Y\_D}(a)$	Share of aggregate value added in the total input of sector *a*
$\bar{\alpha}_Y$	Shift parameter of CET transformation function
$\bar{\beta}_{Y\_X}(a)$	CET function parameter
$\overline{ESUBAR}$	Elasticity of transformation in CET function of sector *a*
$\overline{EX}(a)$	Export in sector *a*
$\overline{TOUTPUT}(a)-\overline{EX}(a)$	Output in sector *a* for domestic use

Table A2.5 Labour disaggregation

MPSGE Declaration

```
$PROD:LTOTAL T:1
  O:ZWL(Z) Q:(SUM(A$MAP(Z,A),CP(A)))
  I:TWL Q:(SUM(A, CP(A)))
$PROD:LZ(Z)$(SUM(A$MAP(Z,A),CP(A))) T:TAU_L
  O:WL(A)$MAP(Z,A) Q:CP(A)
  I:ZWL(Z) Q:(SUM(A$MAP(Z,A),CP(A)))
```

Equations

[1] original CES functions

$$LTOTAL = \bar{\alpha}_{LTOTAL} \prod_{z} LZ(z)^{\theta_{zwl}(z)} \tag{A2.5.1}$$

$$LZ(z) = \bar{\alpha}_{LZ} \left(\sum_{z} \bar{\beta}_{LS}(a) LS(a)^{(TAU\_L-1)/TAU\_L} \right)^{TAU\_L/(TAU\_L-1)} \tag{A2.5.2}$$

[2] ratio equations: prices

$$twl = \prod zwl(z)^{\theta_{zwl}(z)} z \tag{A2.5.3}$$

$$zwl(z) = \left(\sum_{z} \bar{\theta}_{wl}(a) wl(a)^{(1-TAU\_L)} \right)^{1/(1-TAU\_L)} \tag{A2.5.4}$$

[3] ratio equations: labour supply

$$lz(z) = ltotal \left(\frac{twl}{zwl(z)} \right)^{1} \tag{A2.5.5}$$

$$ls(a) = lz(z) \left(\frac{zwl(z)}{wl(a)} \right)^{TAU\_L} \tag{A2.5.6}$$

[4] level equations

$$TWL = twl \times \sum_{a} \overline{CP}(a) \tag{A2.5.7}$$

$$ZWL(z) = zwl(z) \times \sum_{\forall map(z,a)} \overline{CP}(a) \tag{A2.5.8}$$

$$WL(a) = wl(a) \times \overline{CP}(a) \tag{A2.5.9}$$

$$LTOTAL = ltotal \times \sum_{a} \overline{CP}(a) \tag{A2.5.10}$$

$$LZ(z) = lz(z) \times \sum_{\forall map(z,a)} \overline{CP}(a) \tag{A2.5.11}$$

$$LS(a) = ls(a) \times \overline{CP}(a) \tag{A2.5.12}$$

Continued

Table A2.5 Continued

Variables	
twl	Ratio total wage level
$zwl(z)$	Ratio aggregate wage level for industry z
$wl(a)$	Ratio wage level for sub-industry sector a
$lzs(z)$	Ratio aggregate labour supply to industry z
$ltotal$	Ratio total supply of labour input
$ls(a)$	Ratio supply of labour for sector a
$LTOTAL$	Total supply of labour input
$LZ(z)$	Aggregate labour supply to industry z
$LS(a)$	Supply of labour for sector a
Parameters	
$\bar{\theta}_{wl}(z)$	Share of labour cost in total labour cost of industry z
$\bar{\theta}_{wl}(a)$	Share of labour cost in total labour cost of sector a
$\bar{\alpha}_{LTOTAL}$	Shift parameter of CET function of total labour
$\bar{\alpha}_{LZ}$	Shift parameter of CET function of labour by industry
TAU_L	Elasticity of labour transformation between ownerships

The total supply of Armington aggregate goods can be obtained by summing equation (A2.7.9) over z:

$$TS\_AR = \sum_{z} AR(z)$$

Therefore the demand–supply equilibrium equation is:

$$\sum_{a} DY\_AR(a) + \sum_{z} G\_A(z) + \sum_{z} P\_A(z) + \sum_{z} INV\_A(z) = \sum_{z} AR(z)$$

Equilibrium of aggregate export and import

The demand for and supply of aggregate export are represented by equations (A2.8.10) and (A2.4.5), respectively. Therefore the equilibrium condition is:

$$DY\_X(a) = X(a)$$

The demand for and supply of aggregate imports are represented by equations (A2.7.12) and (A2.8.14), respectively. Therefore the equilibrium condition is

$$MZ(a) = M(a)$$

Table A2.6 Capital disaggregation

MPSGE Declaration

```
$PROD:KTOTAL T:1
  O:ZRK(Z)  Q:(SUM(A$MAP(Z,A),(DP(A)+OP(A))))
  I:TRK Q:(SUM(A, DP(A)+OP(A)))
$PROD:KZ(Z)$(SUM(A$MAP(Z,A),(DP(A)+OP(A)))) T:TAU_K
  O:RK(A)$MAP(Z,A) Q:(DP(A)+OP(A))
  I:ZRK(Z) Q:(SUM(A$MAP(Z,A),(DP(A)+OP(A))))
```

Equations

[1] original CET functions

$$KTOTAL = \bar{\alpha}_{KTOTAL} \prod_{z} KZ(z)^{\theta_{zrk}(z)} \tag{A2.6.1}$$

$$KZ(z) = \bar{\alpha}_{KZS} \times \left(\sum_{\forall map(z,a)} \bar{\beta}_{KS}(a) KS(a)^{(TAU\_K-1)/TAU\_K} \right)^{TAU\_K/(TAU\_K-1)} \tag{A2.6.2}$$

[2] ratio equations: prices

$$trk = \prod_{z} zrk(z)^{\theta_{zrk}(z)} \tag{A2.6.3}$$

$$zrk(z) = \left(\sum_{\forall map(z,a)} \bar{\theta}_{rk}(a) rk(a)^{(1-TAU\_K)} \right)^{1/(1-TAU\_K)} \tag{A2.6.4}$$

[3] ratio equations: capital supply

$$kz(z) = ktotal \left(\frac{trk}{zrk(z)} \right)^{1} \tag{A2.6.5}$$

$$ks(a) = kz(z) \left(\frac{zrk(z)}{rk(a)} \right)^{TAU\_K} \tag{A2.6.6}$$

[4] level equations

$$TRK = trk \times \sum_{a} (\overline{DP}(a) + \overline{OP}(a)) \tag{A2.6.7}$$

$$ZRK(z) = zrk(z) \times \sum_{\forall map(z,a)} (\overline{DP}(a) + \overline{OP}(a)) \tag{A2.6.8}$$

$$RK(a) = rk(a) \times (\overline{DP}(a) + \overline{OP}(a)) \tag{A2.6.9}$$

$$KTOTAL = ktotal \times \sum_{a} (\overline{DP}(a) + \overline{OP}(a)) \tag{A2.6.10}$$

$$KZ(z) = kz(z) \times \sum_{\forall map(z,a)} (\overline{DP}(a) + \overline{OP}(a)) \tag{A2.6.11}$$

$$KS(a) = ks(a) \times (\overline{DP}(a) + \overline{OP}(a)) \tag{A2.6.12}$$

Continued

Table A2.6 Continued

Variables	
trk	Ratio total return to capital
zrk(*z*)	Ratio aggregate return to capital for industry *z*
rk(*a*)	Ratio return to capital at sector *a*
kzs(*z*)	Ratio aggregate capital supply to industry *z*
ktotal	Ratio total capital supply
ks(*a*)	Ratio capital supply for sector *a*
KTOTAL	Total capital supply
KZ(*z*)	Aggregate capital supply to industry *z*
KS(*a*)	Capital supply to for sector *a*
Parameters	
$\bar{\theta}_{rk}(z)$	Share of capital cost in total labour cost of industry *z*
$\bar{\theta}_{rk}(a)$	Share of capital cost in total labour cost of sector *a*
$\bar{\alpha}_{KTOTAL}$	Shift parameter of CET function of total capital
$\bar{\alpha}_{KZ}$	Shift parameter of CET function of capital by industry
$\bar{\beta}_{KS}(a)$	CET parameter
TAU_K	Elasticity of capital transformation between ownerships

Table A2.7 Armington aggregate

MPSGE Declaration

```
$PROD:AR1(Z) S:10
  O:PAA(Z) Q:(SUM(A$MAP(Z,A),(ARAG(A)-IM(A))))
  I:PD(A)$MAP(Z,A) Q:(ARAG(A)-IM(A))$MAP(Z,A)
$PROD:AR(Z)$ARAGZ(Z) S:ESUBAR(Z,"EAR")
  O:PA(Z) Q:ARAGZ(Z)
  I:PAA(Z) Q:(SUM(A$MAP(Z,A),(ARAG(A)-IM(A))))
  I:PM(Z) Q:(SUM(A$MAP(Z,A), IM(A)))
```

Equations

[1] original CES functions

$$AR1(z) = \bar{\alpha}_{AR1}\left(\sum \bar{\beta}_{AR\_D}(a)AR\_D(a)^{(10-1)/10}\right)^{10/(10-1)} \quad (A2.7.1)$$

$$AR(z) = \bar{\alpha}_{AR} \times \begin{pmatrix} \bar{\beta}_{AR\_A}(z)AR1(z)^{(\overline{ESUBAR}-1)/\overline{ESUBAR}} \\ +\bar{\beta}_{AR\_M}(z)MZ(z)^{(\overline{ESUBAR}-1)/\overline{ESUBAR}} \end{pmatrix}^{\overline{ESUBAR}/(\overline{ESUBAR}-1)} \quad (A2.7.2)$$

Table A2.7 Continued

[2] ratio equations: prices

$$paa(z) = \left(\sum \theta_{AR\_D}(a) pd(a)^{(1-10)}\right)^{1/(1-10)} \quad \text{(A2.7.3)}$$

$$pa(z) = \begin{pmatrix} \bar{\theta}_{AR\_A}(z) paa(z)^{1-\overline{ESUBAR}} \\ +\theta_{AR\_A}(z) pm(z)^{1-\overline{ESUBAR}} \end{pmatrix}^{1/1-\overline{ESUBAR}} \quad \text{(A2.7.4)}$$

[3] ratio equations: input demand

$$ar\_d(a) = ar1(z) \times \left(\frac{paa(z)}{pd(a)}\right)^{\overline{ESUBAR}} \quad \text{(A2.7.5)}$$

$$mz(z) = ar(z) \times \left(\frac{paa(z)}{pm(z)}\right)^{\overline{ESUBAR}} \quad \text{(A2.7.6)}$$

$$ar1(a) = ar(z) \times \left(\frac{pa(z)}{paa(z)}\right)^{10} \quad \text{(A2.7.7)}$$

[4] level equations

$$AR1(a) = ar1(a) \times \overline{ARAG}(a) \quad \text{(A2.7.8)}$$

$$AR(z) = ar(z) \times \overline{ARAG}(z) \quad \text{(A2.7.9)}$$

$$AR\_D(a) = ar\_d(a) \times (\overline{ARAG}(a) - \overline{IM}(a)) \quad \text{(A2.7.11)}$$

$$MZ(z) = mz(z) \times \overline{IM}(z) \quad \text{(A2.7.12)}$$

$$AR1(z) = ar1(z) \times \overline{ARAG}(z) \quad \text{(A2.7.13)}$$

Variables

$paa(a)$	Ratio price level of Armington aggregate of sector a
$pm(a)$	Ratio price level of imported goods of sector a
$pa(z)$	Ratio price level of Armington aggregate of industry z
$ar\_d(a)$	Ratio input demand for domestically produced goods of sector a
$mz(a)$	Ratio input demand for imported goods of sector a
$ar\_a(a)$	Ratio input demand for Armington aggregate of industry z
$ar1(a)$	Ratio Armington output of sector a
$ar(z)$	Ratio Armington output of industry z
$AR\_D(a)$	Input demand for domestically produced goods of sector a
$MZ(z)$	Input demand for imported goods of sector a
$AR\_A(a)$	Input demand for Armington aggregate of industry z
$AR1(z)$	Armington output of sector a
$AR(z)$	Armington output of industry z

Continued

Table A2.7 Continued

Parameters

$\overline{\theta}_{AR\_D}(a)$	Share of domestically produced products in Armington aggregate in sector *a*
$\overline{\theta}_{MZ}(a)$	Share of imported products in Armington aggregate in sector *a*
$\overline{\theta}_{AR\_Z}(a)$	Share of the *a*th Armington goods in upper-level Armington aggregate in industry *z*
$\overline{\alpha}_{AR}$	Shift parameter of aggregation over ownerships
$\overline{\alpha}_{AR1}$	Shift parameter of Armington aggregation
$\overline{\beta}_{AR\_D}(a)$	CES parameter of domestic products in Armington aggregation
$\overline{\beta}_{AR\_M}(a)$	CES parameter of import in Armington aggregation
$\overline{\beta}_{AR\_A}(a)$	CES parameter in ownership aggregation
$\overline{ARAG}(a)$	Armington aggregate in sector *a*
$\overline{IM}(a)$	Import in sector *a*

Table A2.8 Export and import

MPSGE Declaration

```
$PROD: X(A)$EX(A)
  O:PFX Q:EX(A)
  I:PX(A) Q:EX(A)
$PROD: M(A)$IM(A)
  O:PMA(A) Q:IM(A)
  I:PFX Q:IM(A)
$PROD: MZ(Z)$SUM(A$MAP(Z,A), IM(A)) S:2
  O:PM(Z)  Q:(SUM(A$MAP(Z,A), IM(A)))
  I:PMA(A)$MAP(Z,A)  Q:IM(A)$MAP(Z,A)
```

Equations

[1] original Leontief functions

$$FX = \sum_{a} \bar{\theta}_{EX\_A}(a)X(a) \tag{A2.8.1}$$

$$FX = \sum_{z} \bar{\theta}_{IM\_Z}(z)MZ(z) \tag{A2.8.2}$$

$$MZ(z) = \bar{\alpha}_{MZ}\left(\sum_{\forall\, map(z,a)} \bar{\beta}_{MZ}(a)MA(a)^{(2-1)/2}\right)^{2/(2-1)} \tag{A2.8.3}$$

Table A2.8 Continued

[2] ratio equations: prices

$$pfx = \sum_a \bar{\theta}_{EX\_A}(a) px(a) \quad \text{(A2.8.4)}$$

$$\sum_a \bar{\theta}_{IM\_A}(a) pma(a) = pfx \quad \text{(A2.8.5)}$$

$$pm(z)\left(\sum_a \bar{\theta}_{IM\_A} pma(a)^{1-2}\right)^{1/(1-2)} \quad \text{(A2.8.6)}$$

[3] ratio equations: input demand

$$exd(a) = x(a) \quad \text{(A2.8.7)}$$

$$fx = m(a) \quad \text{(A2.8.8)}$$

$$ma(a) = mz(z) \times \left(\frac{pm(z)}{pma(a)}\right)^2 \quad \text{(A2.8.9)}$$

[4] level equations

$$X(a) = x(a) \times \overline{EX}(a) \quad \text{(A2.8.10)}$$

$$MZ(a) = m(a) \times \overline{IM}(a) \quad \text{(A2.8.11)}$$

$$EXD(a) = exd(a) \times \overline{EX}(a) \quad \text{(A2.8.12)}$$

$$FX(a) = fx(a) \times \overline{IM}(a) \quad \text{(A2.8.13)}$$

$$M(a) = m(a) \times \overline{IM}(a) \quad \text{(A2.8.14)}$$

Variables

pfx	Ratio foreign exchange rate
$px(a)$	Ratio price of exported goods in sector a
$pm(z)$	Ratio price of imported goods in industry z
$pma(a)$	Ratio price of imported goods in sector a
$exd(a)$	Ratio demand for export from sector a
$x(a)$	Ratio export activity in sector a
$m(a)$	Ratio import activity in sector a
fx	Ratio demand for foreign currency to import
$mz(z)$	Ratio import activity in industry z

Parameters

$\bar{\theta}_{EX\_A}(a)$	Share of export of sector a in the total export value
$\bar{\theta}_{IM\_Z}(z)$	Share of import of industry z in the total import value
$\bar{\alpha}_{MZ}$	Shift parameter of CES function (A2.8.3)
$\overline{EX}(a)$	Benchmark export value of sector a
$\overline{IM}(a)$	Benchmark import value of sector a
$M(z)$	Import activity in industry z

Table A2.9 Public and private consumption demand

MPSGE Declaration

```
$PROD:G S:1
  O:PG Q:GO
  I:PA(Z) Q:GC1(Z)

$PROD:CS S:1
  O:PC Q:TC
  I:PA(Z) Q:CON(Z)
```

Equations

[1] original CD functions

$$G = \bar{\alpha}_G \prod_z G\_A(z)^{\bar{\theta}_G(z)} \qquad \text{(A2.9.1)}$$

$$CS = \bar{\alpha}_{CS} \prod_z G\_A(z)^{\bar{\theta}_P(z)} \qquad \text{(A2.9.2)}$$

[2] ratio equations: prices

$$pg = \prod_z pa(z)^{\bar{\theta}_G(z)} \qquad \text{(A2.9.3)}$$

$$pc = \prod_z pa(z)^{\bar{\theta}_P(z)} \qquad \text{(A2.9.4)}$$

[3] ratio equations: input demand

$$g\_a(z) = g \times \frac{pg}{pa(z)} \qquad \text{(A2.9.5)}$$

$$p\_a(z) = cs \times \frac{pc}{pa(z)} \qquad \text{(A2.9.6)}$$

[4] level equations

$$G = g \times \overline{GO} \qquad \text{(A2.9.7)}$$

$$CS = cs \times \overline{TC} \qquad \text{(A2.9.8)}$$

$$G\_A(z) = g\_a(z) \times \overline{GC1}(z) \qquad \text{(A2.9.9)}$$

$$P\_A(z) = p\_a(z) \times \overline{CON}(z) \qquad \text{(A2.9.10)}$$

Variables

pg	Ratio government expenditure price index
$pa(z)$	Ratio price level for Armington aggregate of industry z
pc	Ratio private consumption price index
$g\_a(z)$	Ratio government demand for the products from industry z
$p\_a(z)$	Ratio private demand for the products from industry z
g	Ratio government consumption
cs	Ratio private consumption

Table A2.9 Continued

Parameters

$\overline{\theta}_G(z)$	Share of the consumption of goods from industry z in total government expenditure
$\overline{\theta}_P(z)$	Share of the consumption of goods from industry z in total private expenditure
$\overline{\alpha}_G$	Shift parameter of government expenditure function
$\overline{\alpha}_{CS}$	Shift parameter of private expenditure function
$\overline{GO}$	Benchmark total government consumption
$\overline{TC}$	Benchmark total private consumption
$\overline{GC1}(z)$	Government expenditure on industry z
$\overline{CON}(z)$	Private expenditure on industry z

Table A2.10 Investment demand

MPSGE Declaration

```
$PROD:INV S:1
  O:PINV Q:TI
  I:PA(Z) Q:ID1(Z)
```

Equations

[1] original CES functions

$$INV = \bar{\alpha}_{INV} \prod_z INV\_A(z)^{\bar{\theta}_{INV}(z)} \tag{A2.10.1}$$

[2] ratio equations: prices

$$pinv = \prod_z pa(z)^{\bar{\theta}_{INV}(z)} \tag{A2.10.2}$$

[3] ratio equations: input demand

$$inv\_a(z) = inv \times \frac{pinv}{pa(z)} \tag{A2.10.3}$$

[4] level equations

$$INV = inv \times \overline{TI} \tag{A2.10.4}$$

$$INV\_A(z) = inv\_a(z) \times \overline{ID1}(z) \tag{A2.10.5}$$

Variables

$pinv$	Ratio price index for investment
$inv\_a(z)$	Ratio demand for the input from industry z
inv	Ratio investment level

Parameters

$\bar{\theta}_{INV}(z)$	Share of the investment from industry z in total investment
$\overline{\alpha}_{INV}$	Shift parameter of investment demand function
$\overline{TI}$	Total investment value in benchmark economy
$\overline{ID1}(z)$	Investment demand in industry z

Table A2.11 Representative domestic agent

MPSGE Declaration

```
$DEMAND:RA
  D:PC  Q:TC
  E:TWL  Q:(SUM(A,CP(A)))
  E:TRK  Q:(SUM(A,((DP(A)+OP(A))*(1-FOREIGN (A)))))
  E:PFX  Q:(TB)
  E:PINV  Q:(-TI)
```

Equations

[1] agent's activity level

$$ra = twl \times \sum_a \overline{CP}(a) + trk \times \sum_a (\overline{DP}(a) + \overline{OP}(a))(1 - \overline{FOREIGN}(a))$$
$$+ pfx \times \overline{TB} + pinv \times (-\overline{TI}) \qquad \text{(A2.11.1)}$$

[2] consumption and welfare demand

$$dtc = ra/pc = \overline{TC} \qquad \text{(A2.11.2)}$$
$$dwelra = ra/\overline{TC} \qquad \text{(A2.11.3)}$$

Variables

ra	Representative agent
dtc	Demand for total consumption
dwelra	Demand for welfare of representative agent
pc	Price index of final consumption

Parameters

$\overline{TB}$	Trade balance
$\overline{FOREIGN}(a)$	Foreign presence in sector *a*

Table A2.12 Government

MPSGE Declaration

```
$DEMAND:GOV
    D:PG Q:GO
    E:PC Q:(SUM[Z,(GC1(Z)-NT(Z))])
* THIS LINE PROVIDES THE SOURCE OF FDI PRODUCTIVITY
  SPILLOVERS
    E:PVA(SNO)$NTFPFLAG
+   Q:((CP(SNO)+DP(SNO)+OP(SNO))/(1+NTFP0(SNO)))
    $NTFPFLAG
+                R: QNTFP(SNO)$NTFPFLAG
```

Equations

[1] agent's activity level

$$gov = pc \times \sum_z (\overline{GC1}(Z) - \overline{NT}(Z)) + \sum_a py(a) \times \overline{TOUTPUT}(a) \times \overline{NTFP0}(a)$$

Table A2.12 Continued

$$+\sum_{SNO} pva(SNO) \times [\overline{CP}(SNO) + \overline{DP}(SNO) + \overline{OP}(SNO)]$$

$$\times \frac{QNTFP(SNO)}{1+\overline{NTFP0}(SNO)} \qquad (A2.12.1)$$

[2] consumption/ demand

$$tgo = gov/pg = \overline{GO} \qquad (A2.12.2)$$

Variables

gov	Government activity level
tgo	Level of government demand and redistribution

Parameters

No new ones

Table A2.13 Representative multinational firm agent

MPSGE Declaration

```
$DEMAND:FDI
  E:TRK  Q:(SUM(A,((DP(A)+OP(A))*FOREIGN (A))))
  E:RK(A)  Q:DELTAFDI(A)
  E:PFX  Q:2E+5
  D:PFX  Q:2E+5
  D:PC  Q:(SUM(A,((DP(A)+OP(A))*FOREIGN (A))))
```

Equations

[1] agent's activity level

$$fdi = trk \times \sum_{a} [(\overline{DP}(a) + \overline{OP}(a)) \times \overline{FOREIGN}(a)]$$

$$+ \sum_{a} [rk(a) \times \overline{DELTAFDI}(a)] + pfx \times 2 \times 10^5 \qquad (A2.13.1)$$

[2] consumption demand

$$dfdi\_c = \left(pc \times \sum_{a} (\overline{DP}(a) + \overline{OP}(a)) \times \overline{FOREIGN}(a) \right) \bigg/ fdi \qquad (A2.13.2)$$

Variables

fdi	Activity level of multinational firms
dfdi_c	Demand level of multinational firms

Parameters

$\overline{DELTAFDI}(a)$	FDI increment in sector *a*, for subsequent introduction of an FDI shock

Notes

1 Stylised facts on foreign direct investment inflow to China and its spillovers

1 About a quarter of its FDI inflow is speculative "hot money" and "round-tripping" capital. "Round tripping" FDI refers to cross-border investment motivated by the more favourable treatment of foreign as opposed to domestic capital. Domestic investors can transfer their capital out of, and then invest back into, the domestic market. See United Nations Conference on Trade and Development (2003).

2 A review of foreign direct investment and productivity spillovers

1 Author's calculations based on data from United Nations Commodity Trade Statistics (COMTRADE, http://comtrade.un.org/).

4 What do the aggregate data tell us?

1 It has been suggested that export-oriented FIEs may "cherry-pick" the best skilled workers from domestic firms, leading to lower productivity in the latter (Girma and Gong 2008a).

6 Data compilations

1 As introduced in Chapter 1, FIEs are enterprises funded by investment from Hong Kong, Macau Taiwan, and from any country other than the People's Republic of China.

2 SOEs are state-run and state-holding enterprises. They consist of state-owned enterprises, state joint-ownership enterprises, sole state-invested enterprises, and state-holding enterprises. State-holding enterprises are enterprises where the state owns a higher percentage of the assets than does any other single shareholder.

3 Equivalent to approximately US$600,000, at an exchange rate of $\$1 = \text{RMB } 8.27$ in 2002.

7 A benchmark CGE model for the Chinese economy and its extensions

1 As discussed in Chapter 3, the purpose of the numéraire is to normalise all other nominal variables and make simulation results comparable. Theoretically we can choose any nominal variable as the numéraire, which does not affect the quantities in the simulation results at all. Choosing the exchange rate as the numéraire does not imply a fixed exchange rate regime.

8 Magnitude and pattern of productivity spillovers

1 In this model FDI is treated as follow-up investment in the existing FIEs. However, if FDI is treated as greenfield investment which involves starting up new ventures, then the result of simulating "variety" might be different.

9 Swapping market access for productivity spillovers?

1 FIEs include all types of enterprises listed in Table 1.1: solely foreign-owned enterprises, joint ventures, cooperative enterprises, and other types of foreign-invested enterprises.
2 Withholding tax is income tax withheld from employees' wages and paid directly to the government by the employer.
3 "Net taxes on production" are all taxes on production less all subsidies on production. They include various taxes, extra charges and fees levied on production, sales and business activities as well as on the use of factors such as fixed assets, land and labour. In contrast to taxes on production, subsidies on production refer to the government transfer to the production units and are therefore regarded as negative taxes on production.
4 Such endogeneity is similar to the practice adopted in a CGE model (Gooroochurn and Milner 2005), where tourist arrival is endogenously linked to the tax reform.

10 Why was the Chinese banking system able to survive the global financial crisis?

1 Traditionally, there were four "large-sized state-controlled banks", referred to as "Big Four": the Industrial and Commercial Bank of China (ICBC), China Construction Bank (CCB), Bank of China (BOC), and Agricultural Bank of China (ABC). The Big Four became five after 2006, when the China Banking Regulatory Commission added the Bank of Communications to the list.
2 See People's Bank of China, *Report on the International Financial Market* (in Chinese), released on 13 March 2009.
3 According to the data from China's National Bureau of Statistics (http://www.stats.gov.cn, accessed on 22 January 2009), China's GDP growth rates of the four quarters in 2008 were 10.6%, 10.1%, 9.0% and 6.8%, respectively.
4 Data from *The 2008 Annual Report of China Banking Regulatory Commission*, p. 45 (http://www.cbrc.gov.cn/).
5 China Banking Regulatory Commission, http://www.cbrc.gov.cn/, data accessed on 16 January 2009.

11 East Asian industry transfer, FDI productivity spillovers and US–China trade imbalance

1 International trade includes the trade in goods (or interchangeably, commodities) and services. Here, however, the term "trade" refers only to the international trade in goods (commodities).
2 P.R.C. Ministry of Commerce, http://www.mofcom.gov.cn/tongjiziliao/.
3 US Census Bureau, http://www.census.gov/foreign-trade/. All the US trade statistics in this chapter are as reported by the US Census Bureau, unless stated otherwise.
4 The Boeing Company "Boeing in China" (2007), http://www.boeing.com/company-offices/aboutus/boechina.html.
5 Lardy (1994, pp. 71–72, 77–79, 110–114; 2002, pp. 158–161) has identified the industry and trade transfers and has briefly explored the causality between them.
6 The SITC is the international trade statistics standard most widely adopted by member countries of the United Nations. The trade statistics are available from one-digit to six-digit levels. We select one-digit and three-digit levels in the data compilation.
7 For example, both SITC-821.2 (mattress supports) and SITC-821.5 (wooden furniture) are grouped into category SITC-821 (furniture). However, these two types of commodities might vary a great deal in terms of labour–capital input composition.
8 "NBS Press Conference on National Economic Performance in 2005", 25 January 2006, www.gov.cn. Li Deshui's viewpoint is echoed by Yang and Zhengwei (2005), an economist from China's Ministry of Commerce, who estimates that the actual US "trade

deficit" with China is quite trivial considering the tremendous amount of assembly trade and the profits of US multinational affiliates in China.

9 Capital-intensive commodities are machinery and equipment (SITC 7), while labour-intensive commodities are light manufacturing products (SITC 6 and 8).

10 According to the characteristics of the international production networks in East Asia presented in previous discussions, a "made in China" label is misleading, as the products are actually assembled in China rather than being entirely made in China.

11 For a certain commodity (e.g. toys), assume that its share in imports from China is S_1, and its share in total imports from the whole world is S_2. If S_1 is greater than S_2, then we can say that this commodity imported from China exhibits a stronger comparative advantage than the same commodity imported from other countries.

12 Jiang Zemin, keynote speech delivered at the 16th National Congress of the Communist Party of China, 8 November 2002.

13 "Rural workers" are a special group in big cities in China, engaged in low-paid, badly insured, dirty and dangerous work as construction workers, restaurant staff, security guards, manufacturing employees, etc. They are willing to take such jobs because their income would be even lower if they stayed in the countryside.

14 Knowledge@Wharton, "Does a Growing Worker Shortage Threaten China's Low-Cost Advantage?", 15 May 2006; and "Labour Shortage Puzzles Experts", *China Daily*, 25 August 2004.

15 EU–China trade deficit data come from the website of the European Commission (http://ec.europa.eu/trade/issues/bilateral/data.htm).

16 The EU Gateway website lists nine obstacles such as price controls, discriminatory registration requirements, arbitrary sanitary standards, geographical restrictions, joint venture requirements, and discriminatory licensing procedures. (http://europa.eu.int/comm/external_relations/china/intro/).

17 The value of Chinese motorcycle exports was $2.4 billion in 2005, which made China the world's top producer. In 2006, MOFCOM issued a notice requiring motorcycle exporting to be "standardised" which is expected to counter the practice of Chinese motorcycle manufacturers exporting at extremely low prices (MOFCOM 5, January 2006, http://www.mofcom.gov.cn).

18 Marina Walker Guevara and Bob Williams, "China Steps up Its Lobbying Game: The Chinese Government is Hiring the Best of the Best to Advance Its Agenda", Center for Public Integrity September 13, 2005, http://www.publicintegrity.org/lobby/report.aspx?aid=734; and Michael Forsythe, "China Steps up Lobbying Efforts in US Congress (Update 1)" April 19, 2006, http://www.bloomberg.com/apps/news?pid=10000080&sid=atLgA.zbUAYg&refer=asia.

19 Source: People's Bank of China.

20 In testimony delivered before the Committee of Finance of the US Senate on 23 June 2005, Alan Greenspan, the then chairman of the Board of Governors of the US Federal Reserve, said that some observers' policy suggestions on RMB revaluation and a higher tariff on Chinese imports were counterproductive and pointless.

Bibliography

Aitken, B., Hanson, G. H. and Harrison, A. E. (1997) "Spillovers, foreign investment, and export behavior". *Journal of International Economics* 43(1–2): 103–132.

Aitken, B. J. and Harrison, A. E. (1999) "Do domestic firms benefit from direct foreign investment? Evidence from Venezuela". *American Economic Review* 89(3): 605–618.

Akamatsu, K. (1937) 'Waga kuni keizai hatten no sogo benshoho" [Synthetic dialectics of industrial development of Japan]. *Shogyo Keizai Ronso* [*Journal of Nagoya Commercial High School*] 15(1): 179–210.

Alvarez, R. and López, R. (2005) "Exporting and performance: Evidence from Chilean plants". *Canadian Journal of Economics* 38(4): 1384–1400.

Ang, J. B. (2008) "Determinants of foreign direct investment in Malaysia". *Journal of Policy Modeling* 30(1): 185–189.

Antràs, P. and Helpman, E. (2004) "Global sourcing". *Journal of Political Economy* 112(3): 552–580.

Armington, P. S. (1969) "A theory of demand for products distinguished by place of production". *IMF Staff Papers* 16(1): 159–178.

Arrow, K. J. and Debreu, G. (1954) "Existence of equilibrium for a competitive economy". *Econometrica* 22(3): 265–290.

Balistreri, E. J., Hillberry, R. H. and Rutherford, T. F. (2007) "Structural estimation and solution of international trade models with heterogeneous firms". *10th Conference on Global Economic Analysis*, Purdue University.

Balistreri, E. J., Mcdaniel, C. A. and Wong, E. V. (2003) "An estimation of US industry-level capital-labor substitution elasticities: Support for Cobb-Douglas". *North American Journal of Economics and Finance* 14(3): 343–356.

Barboza, D. (2006) "Labour shortage in China may lead to trade shift". *New York Times*, 3 April.

Battese, G. E. and Coelli, T. J. (1995) "A model for technical inefficiency effects in a stochastic frontier production function for panel data". *Empirical Economics* 20(2): 325–332.

Berger, A. N., Hasan, I. and Zhou, M. (2009) "Bank ownership and efficiency in China: What will happen in the world's largest nation?" *Journal of Banking & Finance* 33(1): 113–130.

Bernard, A. B., Eaton, J., Jensen, J. B. and Kortum, S. (2003) "Plants and productivity in international trade". *American Economic Review* 93(4): 1268–1290.

Bernard, M. and Ravenhill, J. (1995) "Beyond product cycles and flying geese: Regionalization, hierarchy, and the industrialization of East Asia". *World Politics* 47(2): 171–209.

Blake, A. (1998) "Computable general equilibrium modelling and the evaluation of agricultural policy". PhD thesis, University of Nottingham.

Blake, A., Deng, Z. and Falvey, R. (2009) "How does the productivity of foreign direct investment spill over to local firms in Chinese manufacturing?" *Journal of Chinese Economic and Business Studies* 7(2): 183–197.

Blake, A., Rayner, A. J. and Reed, G. (1999) "A computable general equilibrium analysis of agricultural liberalisation: The uruguay round and common agricultural policy reform". *Journal of Agricultural Economics* 50(3): 400–424.

Blomström, M. and Kokko, A. (1998) "Multinational corporations and spillovers". *Journal of Economic Surveys* 12(2): 1–31.

Branstetter, L. G., Fisman, R. and Foley, C. F. (2006) "Do stronger intellectual property rights increase international technology transfer? Empirical evidence from U.S. firm-level panel data". *Quarterly Journal of Economics* 121(1): 321–349.

Buckley, P. J., Clegg, J. and Wang, C. (2002) "The impact of inward FDI on the performance of Chinese manufacturing firms". *Journal of International Business Studies* 33(4): 637–655.

Buckley, P. J., Clegg, J. and Wang, C. (2004) "The relationship between inward foreign direct investment and the performance of domestically-owned Chinese manufacturing industry". *Multinational Business Review* 12(3): 23–40.

Buckley, P. J., Clegg, J. and Wang, C. (2007a) "Is the relationship between inward FDI and spillover effects linear? An empirical examination of the case of China". *Journal of International Business Studies* 38(3): 447–459.

Buckley, P. J., Wang, C. and Clegg, J. (2007b) "The impact of foreign ownership, local ownership and industry characteristics on spillover benefits from foreign direct investment in China". *International Business Review* 16(2): 142–158.

Bussolo, M. and Round, J. I. (2003) *Poverty Reduction Strategies in a Budget-Constrained Economy: The Case of Ghana*. OECD Development Centre, Paris.

Cassou, S. P. (1997) "The link between tax rates and foreign direct investment". *Applied Economics* 29(10): 1295–1301.

Ceglowski, J. and Golub, S. (2007) "Just how low are China's labour costs?" *The World Economy* 30(4): 597–617.

Choi, C. (2003) "Does the internet stimulate inward foreign direct investment?" *Journal of Policy Modeling* 25(4): 319–326.

Chow, G. and Lin, A.-L. (2002) "Accounting for economic growth in Taiwan and mainland China: A comparative analysis". *Journal of Comparative Economics* 30(3): 507–530.

Claessens, S., Demirguc-Kunt, A. and Huizinga, H. (2001) "How does foreign entry affect domestic banking markets?" *Journal of Banking & Finance* 25(5): 891–911.

Clerides, S., Lach, S. and Tybout, J. (1998) "Is learning by exporting important? Micro-dynamic evidence from Colombia, Mexico, and Morocco". *Quarterly Journal of Economics* 113(3): 903–947.

Crespo, N. and Fontoura, M. P. (2007) "Determinant factors of FDI spillovers – what do we really know?" *World Development* 35(3): 410–425.

Cutler, H., Berri, D. J. and Ozawa, T. (2003) "Market recycling in labor-intensive goods, flying-geese style: An empirical analysis of East Asian Exports to the U.S." *Journal of Asian Economics* 14(1): 35–50.

Das, G. G. (2007) "Information age to genetic revolution: Embodied technology transfer and assimilation – a tale of two technologies". *Technological Forecasting and Social Change* 74(6): 819–842.

Das, S. (1987) "Externalities, and technology transfer through multinational corporations: A theoretical analysis". *Journal of International Economics* 22(1–2): 171–182.

Deng, Z., Guo, H. and Zheng, Y. (2007) "How East Asian industry transfer affects the US–China trade imbalance: Economic mechanisms and policy implications". *Issues & Studies* 43(3): 165–197.

Dervis, K., Melo, J. D. and Robinson, S. (1982) *General Equilibrium Models for Development Policy*. Cambridge University Press, New York.

Dewatripont, M. and Michel, G. (1987) "On closure rules, homogeneity and dynamics in applied general equilibrium models". *Journal of Development Economics* 26(1): 65–76.

Dixit, A. K. and Stiglitz, J. E. (1977) "Monopolistic competition and optimum product variety". *American Economic Review* 67(3): 297–308.

Dowling, M. and Cheang, C. T. (2000) "Shifting comparative advantage in Asia: New tests of the 'flying geese' model". *Journal of Asian Economics* 11(4): 443–63.

Dunning, J. H. (1977) Trade, location of economic activity, and the multinational enterprises: A Search for an eclectic approach. In B. H. Ohlin and P. Wijkman (eds), *The International Allocation of Economic Activity*. Holmes and Meier, New York.

Dunning, J. H. (1981) *International Production and the Multinational Enterprises*. George Allen & Unwin, London.

Falvey, R., Foster, N. and Greenaway, D. (2004) "Imports, exports, knowledge spillovers and growth". *Economics Letters* 85(2): 209–213.

Falvey, R., Foster, N. and Greenaway, D. (2007a) "Relative backwardness, absorptive capacity and knowledge spillovers". *Economics Letters* 97(3): 230–234.

Falvey, R., Foster, N. and Memedovic, O. (2006) *The Role of Intellectual Property Rights in Technology Transfer and Economic Growth: Theory and Evidence*. United Nations Industrial Development Organization, Vienna.

Falvey, R., Greenaway, D. and Yu, Z. (2007b) "Market size and the survival of foreign-owned firms". *Economic Record* 83(s1): S23–S34.

Falvey, R. and Kreickemeier, U. (2005) "Globalisation and factor returns in competitive markets". *Journal of International Economics* 66(1): 233–48.

Fan, C. S. and Hu, Y. (2007) "Foreign direct investment and indigenous technological efforts: Evidence from China". *Economics Letters* 96(2): 253–258.

Fan, Y., Liao, H. and Wei, Y.-M. (2007) "Can market oriented economic reforms contribute to energy efficiency improvement? Evidence from China". *Energy Policy* 35(4): 2287–2295.

Farrell, D., Gao, P. and Orr, G. R. (2004) *Making Foreign Investment Work for China*. McKinsey Global Institute, McKinsey & Company.

Feenstra, R. and Kee, H. L. (2008) "Export variety and country productivity: Estimating the monopolistic competition model with endogenous productivity". *Journal of International Economics* 74(2): 500–518.

Findlay, R. (1978) "Relative backwardness, direct foreign investment, and the transfer of technology: A simple dynamic model". *Quarterly Journal of Economics* 92(1): 1–16.

Fosfuri, A., Motta, M. and Ronde, T. (2001) "Foreign direct investment and spillovers through workers' mobility". *Journal of International Economics* 53(1): 205–222.

Francois, J. F. and Roland-Holst, D. W. (1997) Scale economies and imperfect competition. In J. F. Francois and K. A. Reinert (eds), *Applied Methods for Trade Policy Analysis: A Handbook*. Cambridge University Press, Cambridge.

Frith, M. (2005) Revealed: How bra wars devastate world's poor. *The Independent* 27, August.

Fu, X. and Balasubramanyam, V. N. (2005) "Exports, foreign direct investment and employment: The case of China". *The World Economy* 28(4): 607–625.

GAMS Development Corporation (2008) *GAMS – A User's Guide*. Washington, GAMS Development Corporation, DC.

Gattai, V. and Molteni, C. (2007) "Dissipation of knowledge and the boundaries of the multinational enterprise". *Review of World Economics* 143(1): 1–26.

Gillespie, G., Mcgregor, P. G., Swales, J. K. and Yin, Y. P. (2001) "A regional CGE analysis of the demand and efficiency spillover effects of foreign direct investment". In N. Pain (ed.), *Inward Investment, Technological Change and Growth: The Impact of Multinational Corporations on the UK Economy*. Palgrave, Basingstoke.

Gillespie, G., Mcgregor, P. G., Swales, J. K. and Yin, Y. P. (2002) "The regional impact of foreign direct investment: Structure and behavior in an ownership-disaggregated computable general equilibrium model". In G. Hewings, M. Sonis, and D. E. Boyce (eds), *Trade, Networks and Hierarchies: Modeling Regional and Interregional Economies*. Springer-Verlag, Berlin.

Ginsburgh, V. and Keyzer, M. (1997) *The Structure of Applied General Equilibrium Models*. MIT Press, Cambridge, MA.

Girma, S. (2005) "Absorptive capacity and productivity spillovers from FDI: A threshold regression analysis". *Oxford Bulletin of Economics and Statistics* 67(3): 281–306.

Girma, S. and Gong, Y. (2008a) "FDI, linkages and the efficiency of state-owned enterprises in China". *Journal of Development Studies* 44(5): 728–749.

Girma, S. and Gong, Y. (2008b) "Putting people first? Chinese state-owned enterprises' adjustment to globalisation". *International Journal of Industrial Organization* 26(2): 573–585.

Girma, S., Görg, H. and Pisu, M. (2008) "Exporting, linkages and productivity spillovers from foreign direct investment". *Canadian Journal of Economics* 41(1): 320–340.

Girma, S., Kneller, R. and Pisu, M. (2005) "Exports versus FDI: An empirical test". *Review of World Economics* 141(2): 193–218.

Glass, A. J. and Saggi, K. (2002) "Multinational firms and technology transfer". *Scandinavian Journal of Economics* 104(4): 495–513.

Gooroochurn, N. and Milner, C. (2005) "Assessing indirect tax reform in a tourism-dependent developing country". *World Development* 33(7): 1183–1200.

Görg, H. and Greenaway, D. (2004) "Much ado about nothing? Do domestic firms really benefit from foreign direct investment?" *World Bank Research Observer* 19(2): 171–197.

Görg, H. and Strobl, E. A. (2001) "Multinational companies and productivity spillovers: A meta-analysis". *Economic Journal* 111(475): 723–739.

Görg, H. and Strobl, E. A. (2005) "Spillovers from foreign firms through worker mobility: An empirical investigation". *Scandinavian Journal of Economics* 107(4): 693–709.

Greenaway, D. and Kneller, R. (2004) "Exporting and productivity in the United Kingdom". *Oxford Review of Economic Policy* 20(3): 358–371.

Greenaway, D. and Kneller, R. (2007) "Firm heterogeneity, exporting and foreign direct investment". *Economic Journal* 117(517): F134–F161.

Greenaway, D. and Kneller, R. (2008) "Exporting, productivity and agglomeration". *European Economic Review* 52(5): 919–939.

Greenaway, D., Sousa, N. and Wakelin, K. (2004) "Do domestic firms learn to export from multinationals?" *European Journal of Political Economy* 20(4): 1027–1043.

Grubert, H. and Mutti, J. (1991) "Taxes, tariffs and transfer pricing in multinational corporate decision making". *Review of Economics and Statistics* 73(2): 285–293.

Halpern, L. and Murakozy, B. (2007) "Does distance matter in spillover?" *Economics of Transition* 15(4): 781–805.

Harrison, G. W., Rutherford, T. F. and Tarr, D. (1994) *Product Standards, Imperfect Competition, and Completion of the Market in the European Union*. World Bank Policy Research Working Paper 1293.

Harrison, G. W., Rutherford, T. F. and Tarr, D. (1995) "Quantifying the Uruguay Round". In W. Martin and L. A. Winters (eds), *The Uruguay Round and Developing Economies* (World Bank Discussion Papers 307). World Bank, Washington, DC.

Harrison, G. W., Rutherford, T. F. and Tarr, D. (1997) "Quantifying the Uruguay Round". *Economic Journal* 107(1405–1430.

Helpman, E. (2006) "Trade, FDI, and the organization of firms". *Journal of Economic Literature* 44(3): 589–630.

Helpman, E., Melitz, M. J. and Yeaple, S. R. (2004) "Export versus FDI with heterogeneous firms". *American Economic Review* 94(1): 300–316.

Hertel, T. W. (ed.) (1997) *Global Trade Analysis: Modeling and Applications*. Cambridge University Press, Cambridge.

Hines, J. R. and Rice, E. M. (1994) "Fiscal paradise: Foreign tax havens and American business". *Quarterly Journal of Economics* 109(1): 149–182.

Hymer, S. H. (1976) *The International Operations of National Firms: A Study of Direct Foreign Investment*. MIT Press, Cambridge, MA.

International Monetary Fund. (2004) *Annual Report on Exchange Arrangements and Exchange Restrictions*. International Monetary Fund, Washington, DC.

Javorcik, B. S. (2004) "Does foreign direct investment increase the productivity of domestic firms? In search of spillovers through backward linkages". *American Economic Review* 94(3): 605–627.

Javorcik, B. S. and Spatareanu, M. (2008) "To share or not to share: Does local participation matter for spillovers from foreign direct investment?" *Journal of Development Economics* 85(1–2): 194–217.

Jehle, G. A. and Reny, P. J. (2001) *Advanced Microeconomic Theory*. Addison-Wesley, Boston.

Jiang, D., Chen, J. J. and Isaac, D. (1998) "The effect of foreign investment on the real estate industry in China". *Urban Studies* 35(11): 2101–2110.

Kamien, M. I. and Schwartz, N. L. (1983) "Conjectural variations". *Canadian Journal of Economics* 16(2): 191–211.

Keller, W. (1996) "Absorptive capacity: On the creation and acquisition of technology in development". *Journal of Development Economics* 49(1): 199–227.

Keller, W. (2004) "International technology diffusion". *Journal of Economic Literature* 42(3): 752–782.

Kimura, F. and Kiyota, K. (2006) "Exports, FDI, and productivity: Dynamic evidence from Japanese firms". *Review of World Economics* 142(4): 695–719.

Kneller, R. and Pisu, M. (2007) "Industrial linkages and export spillovers from FDI". *The World Economy* 30(1): 105–134.

Knight, J. and Yueh, L. (2004) "Job mobility of residents and migrants in urban China". *Journal of Comparative Economics* 32(4): 637–660.

Koizumi, T. and Kopecky, K. J. (1977) "Economic growth, capital movements and the international transfer of technical knowledge". *Journal of International Economics* 7(1): 45–65.

Kojima, K. (2000) "The 'flying geese' model of asian economic development: Origin, theoretical extensions, and regional policy implications". *Journal of Asian Economics* 11(4): 375–401.

Krugman, P. (1980) "Scale economies, product differentiation, and the pattern of trade". *American Economic Review* 70(5): 950–959.

Krugman, P. (1991) *Geography and Trade*. MIT Press, London.

Krugman, P. and Baldwin, R. (1987) "The Persistence of the U.S. trade deficit". *Brookings Papers on Economic Activity* 1987(1): 1–43.

Kugler, M. (2006) "Spillovers from foreign direct investment: Within or between industries?" *Journal of Development Economics* 80(2): 444–477.

Lai, M., Peng, S. and Bao, Q. (2006) "Technology spillovers, absorptive capacity and economic growth". *China Economic Review* 17(3): 300–320.

Lardy, N. R. (1994) *China in the World Economy*. Institute for International Economics, Washington, DC.

Lardy, N. R. (2002) *Integrating China into the Global Economy*. Brookings Institution Press, Washington, DC.

Lau, L. and Fung, K.-C. (2001) "New estimates of the United States-China bilateral trade balances". *Journal of the Japanese and International Economies* 15(1): 102–130.

Lejour, A., Rojas-Romagosa, H. and Verweij, G. (2008) "Opening services markets within Europe: Modelling foreign establishments in a CGE framework". *Economic Modelling* 25(5): 1022–1039.

Lensink, R. and Hermes, N. (2004) "The short-term effects of foreign bank entry on domestic bank behaviour: Does economic development matter?" *Journal of Banking & Finance* 28(3): 553–568.

Lensink, R., Meesters, A. and Naaborg, I. (2008) "Bank efficiency and foreign ownership: Do good institutions matter?" *Journal of Banking & Finance* 32(5): 834–844.

Lin, X. and Zhang, Y. (2009) "Bank ownership reform and bank performance in China". *Journal of Banking & Finance* 33(1): 20–29.

Liu, Z. (2008) "Foreign direct investment and technology spillovers: Theory and evidence". *Journal of Development Economics* 85(1–2): 176–193.

Löfgren, H., Harris, R. L. and Robinson, S. (2002) *A Standard Computable General Equilibrium (CGE) Model in GAMS*. International Food Policy Research Institute, Washington, DC.

López, R. A. (2008) "Foreign technology licensing, productivity, and spillovers". *World Development* 36(4): 560–574.

Long, G. (2005) China's policies on FDI: Review and evaluation. In T. H. Moran, E. M. Graham and M. Blomström (eds), *Does Foreign Direct Investment Promote Development*? Institute for International Economics, Washington, DC.

Madariaga, N. and Poncet, S. (2007) "FDI in Chinese cities: Spillovers and impact on growth". *The World Economy* 30(5): 837–862.

Mansur, A. and Whalley, J. (1984) Numerical specification of applied general equilibrium models: Estimations, calibrations, and data. In H. E. Scarf and J. B. Shoven (eds), *Applied General Equilibrium Analysis*. Cambridge University Press, Cambridge.

Markusen, J. R. (2002a) MPSGE Examples. http://www.mpsge.org/tutorial.pdf.

Markusen, J. R. (2002b) *Multinational Firms and the Theory of International Trade*. MIT Press, Cambridge, MA.

Markusen, J. R. and Trofimenko, N. (2009) "Teaching locals new tricks: Foreign experts as a channel of knowledge transfers". *Journal of Development Economics* 88(1): 120–131.

Markusen, J. R. and Venables, A. J. (1999) "Foreign direct investment as a catalyst for industrial development". *European Economic Review* 43(2): 335–356.

McCarl, B. A., Meeraus, A., Eijk, P. V. D., Bussieck, M., Dirkse, S. and Steacy, P. (2007) Mccarl GAMS User Guide (Version 22.7). Texas A&M University & GAMS Development Corporation.

McKenzie, L. (1954) "On equilibrium in Graham's model of world trade and other competitive systems". *Econometrica* 22(2): 147–161.

McKinnon, R. I. (2001) "The international dollar standard and the sustainability of the U.S. current account deficit". *Brookings Papers on Economic Activity* 2001(1): 227–239.

Melitz, M. J. (2003) "The impact of trade on intra-industry reallocations and aggregate industry productivity". *Econometrica* 71(6): 1695–1725.

National Bureau of Statistics of China (2003a) *China Industrial Economy Statistical Yearbook 2003*. China Statistics Press, Beijing.

National Bureau of Statistics of China (2003b) *China Statistical Yearbook 2003*. China Statistics Press, Beijing.

National Bureau of Statistics of China (2004) *China Industrial Economy Statistical Yearbook 2004*. China Statistics Press, Beijing.

National Bureau of Statistics of China (2006a) *China Economic Census Statistical Yearbook 2004*. China Statistics Press, Beijing.

National Bureau of Statistics of China (2006b) *2002 Input–Output Tables of China*. China Statistics Press, Beijing.

National Bureau of Statistics of China (2007) *China Statistical Yearbook 2007*. China Statistics Press, Beijing.

National Bureau of Statistics of China (2008) *China Statistical Yearbook 2008*. China Statistics Press, Beijing.

Nocke, V. and Yeaple, S. R. (2007) "Cross-border mergers and acquisitions vs. greenfield foreign direct investment: The role of firm heterogeneity". *Journal of International Economics* 72(2): 336–365.

Nocke, V. and Yeaple, S. R. (2008) "An assignment theory of foreign direct investment". *Review of Economic Studies* 75(2): 529–557.

Ozawa, T. (1993) "Foreign direct investment and structural transformation: Japan as a recycler of market and industry". *Business & the Contemporary World* 5(3): 129–150.

Prasad, E. S. and Rajan, R. G. (2006) "Modernizing China's growth paradigm". *American Economic Review* 96(2): 331–336.

Rausch, S. and Rutherford, T. F. (2010) "Computation of equilibria in OLG models with many heterogeneous households". *Computational Economics* 36(2): 171–189.

Reifschneider, D. and Stevenson, R. (1991) "Systematic departures from the frontier: A framework for the analysis of firm inefficiency". *International Economic Review* 32(3): 715–723.

Robinson, S. and Lofgren, H. (2005) "Macro models and poverty analysis: Theoretical tensions and empirical practice". *Development Policy Review* 23(3): 267–283.

Robinson, S., Wang, Z. and Martin, W. (2002) "Capturing the implications of services trade liberalization". *Economic Systems Research* 14(1): 3–33.

Rutherford, T. F. (1995) *Lecture Notes on Constant Elasticity Functions*. University of Colorado.

Rutherford, T. F. (1999) "Applied general equilibrium modeling with MPSGE as a GAMS subsystem: An overview of the modeling framework and syntax". *Computational Economics* 14(1): 1–46.

Rutherford, T. F. and Tarr, D. G. (2008) "Poverty effects of Russia's WTO accession: Modeling 'real' households with endogenous productivity effects". *Journal of International Economics* 75(1): 131–150.

Saggi, K. (2002) "Trade, foreign direct investment, and international technology transfer: A survey". *World Bank Research Observer* 17(2): 191–235.

Samuelson, P. (1948) "International trade and the equalization of factor prices". *Economic Journal* 58(230): 163–84.

Sembenelli, A. and Siotis, G. (2008) "Foreign direct investment and mark-up dynamics: Evidence from Spanish firms". *Journal of International Economics* 76(1): 107–115.

Sen, A. K. (1963) "Neo-classical and neo-Keynesian theories of distribution". *Economic Record* 39(1): 54–64.

Shoven, J. B. and Whalley, J. (1984) "Applied general-equilibrium models of taxation and international trade: An introduction and survey". *Journal of Economic Literature* 22(3): 1007–1051.

Shoven, J. B. and Whalley, J. (1992) *Appling General Equilibrium*. Cambridge University Press, Cambridge.

Springer, K. (1998) *The DART General Equilibrium Model: A Technical Description*. Kiel Working Paper No. 883. Kiel, Kiel Institute for the World Economy, Germany.

Sue Wing, I. (2004) *Computable General Equilibrium Models and Their Use in Economy-Wide Policy Analysis*. MIT Joint Program on the Science and Policy of Global Change, Massachusetts Institute of Technology.

Todo, Y., Zhang, W. and Zhou, L.-A. (2009) "Knowledge spillovers from FDI in China: The role of educated labor in multinational enterprises". *Journal of Asian Economics* 20(6): 626–639.

Tomiura, E. (2007) "Foreign outsourcing, exporting, and FDI: A productivity comparison at the firm level". *Journal of International Economics* 72(1): 113–127.

United Nations Conference on Trade and Development (2000) *Tax Incentives and Foreign Direct Investment: A Global Survey*, United Nations New York and Geneva.

United Nations Conference on Trade and Development (2003) *World Investment Report 2003*. United Nations, New York and Geneva.

United Nations Conference on Trade and Development (2006) *World Investment Report 2006*. United Nations, New York and Geneva.

Van Meijl, H. and Van Tongeren, F. (1998) "Trade, technology spillovers, and food production in China". *Review of World Economics* 134 (3): 423–449.

Vernon, R. (1966) "International investment and international trade in the product cycle". *Quarterly Journal of Economics* 80(2): 190–207.

Walmsley, T. L. and Lakatos, C. (2008) Regional input–output data. In G. B. Narayanan and T. L. Walmsley (eds), *Global Trade, Assistance, and Production: The GTAP 7 Data Base*. West Lafayette, Center for Global Trade Analysis, Purdue University.

Wang, J.-Y. and Blomström, M. (1992) "Foreign investment and technology transfer: A simple model". *European Economic Review* 36(1): 137–155.

Wei, S.-J. (2000a) "How taxing is corruption on international investors?" *Review of Economics and Statistics* 82(1): 1–11.

Wei, S.-J. (2000b) "Local corruption and global capital flows". *Brookings Papers on Economic Activity* 31(2000–2): 303–354.

Wei, Y. and Liu, X. (2006) "Productivity spillovers from R&D, exports and FDI in China's Manufacturing Sector". *Journal of International Business Studies* 37(4): 544–557.

Whalley, J. and Yeung, B. (1984) "External sector 'closing' rules in applied general equilibrium models". *Journal of International Economics* 16(1): 123–138.

World Trade Organization (2008) Secretariat report. *Trade Policy Review: China*. World Trade Organization, New York and Geneva.

Xu, L. and Lin, C.-T. (2007) "Can Chinese banks compete after accession to WTO?" *Journal of Asian Economics* 18(6): 883–903.

Xu, X. and Song, L. (2000) Export similarity and the pattern of East Asia development. In P. Lloyd and X. Zhang (eds), *China in the Global Economy*. Edward Elgar, Cheltenham.

Yang, Z. (2005) "Quanqiuhua shidai de chanye zhuanyi shi Mei dui Hua maoyi nicha de genben yuanyin" [Industry transfer in the age of globalization is the fundamental reason for the US trade deficit with China]. *Guoji maoyi luntan* [*International Trade Forum*] (Beijing), 4: 15–23.

Yao, S., Jiang, C., Feng, G. and Willenbockel, D. (2007) "WTO challenges and efficiency of Chinese banks". *Applied Economics* 39(629–643).

Yasar, M. and Paul, C. J. M. (2007) "International linkages and productivity at the plant level: Foreign direct investment, exports, imports and licensing". *Journal of International Economics* 71(2): 373–388.

Young, A. (2000) "The razor's edge: Distortions and incremental reform in the People's Republic of China". *Quarterly Journal of Economics* 115(4): 1091–1135.

Zhai, F. (2008) "Armington meets Melitz: Introducing firm heterogeneity in a global CGE model of trade". *Journal of Economic Integration* 23(3): 575–604.

Zhang, K. H. (2005) "Why does so much FDI from Hong Kong and Taiwan go to mainland China?" *China Economic Review* 16(3): 293–307.

Zhao, T. (2004) "Comparison between industrial classification in Chinese national accounts and International Standard Industrial Classification for all economic activities". Paper presented to 8th OECD–NBS Workshop on National Accounts, Paris.

Zhao, Y. (2002) "Earnings differentials between state and non-state enterprises in urban China". *Pacific Economic Review* 7(1): 181–197.

Index